THE GARDENER'S LONDON

Buckingham Palace
The Waterloo Vase

The Gardener's London

FOUR CENTURIES OF GARDENING, GARDENERS AND GARDEN USAGE

DAWN MACLEOD

Duckworth

First published in 1972 by Gerald Duckworth & Company Limited, The Old Piano Factory, 43 Gloucester Crescent, London N.W.1.

ISBN 0 7156 0643 3

Printed in Great Britain
by Ebenezer Baylis & Son Limited
The Trinity Press, Worcester, and London

Contents

LIST OF ILLUSTRATIONS ix

FOREWORD xi

ACKNOWLEDGEMENTS xv

SECTION ONE

Royal Gardens

1. Hampton Court 3
2. Nonsuch 30
3. Kensington Palace 38
4. Buckingham Palace 45
5. The Savill and Valley Gardens in Windsor Great Park 54

SECTION TWO

Physic, Botanic and Other Old Gardens

1. The Chelsea Physic Garden 65
2. The Royal Botanic Gardens, Kew 80
3. Fulham Palace 100
4. Lambeth Palace 102
5. The Inns of Court 104

SECTION THREE

Writers and Gardens

1. Francis Bacon 117
2. John Evelyn 120
3. Sir William Temple 126
4. Alexander Pope 129
5. Lancelot ('Capability') Brown 133
6. John and Jane Loudon 134
7. Reginald Farrer 144
8. Theresa Earle 151
9. E. S. Rohde 157
10. E. A. Bowles 165
11. V. Sackville-West 176

SECTION FOUR

Market Gardeners and Nurserymen

1. Market Gardeners and Nurserymen of the 16th, 17th and 18th Centuries 189
2. Alfred Smith 202
3. R. D. Blackmore 205
4. The Rochfords 213
5. Covent Garden Market 217
6. The Gardening Centre, Syon Park 226

SECTION FIVE

Parks and Pleasure Gardens

1. Hyde Park and its Neighbours 237
2. Regent's Park 250
3. Greenwich Park 256
4. Pleasure Gardens of the Eighteenth Century 265

SECTION SIX

Smaller Gardens, and the Horticultural Societies

1. Westminster Abbey, the College Garden 277
2. The Worshipful Company of Gardeners 280
3. Derry and Toms' Roof Garden 285
4. The London Gardens Society 288
5. Some City Gardens 290
6. The Metropolitan Public Gardens Association 297
7. A Town Garden of the Cement and Concrete Association at Wexham Springs 303
8. Elizabeth Coxhead's Garden 306
9. The Royal Horticultural Society 311
10. The Herb Garden at Lullingstone Castle 322
11. The Society of Herbalists 325

SHORT BOOK LIST 327

INDEX 329

TO THE MEMORY OF
MY FATHER
E. N. MOONEY
R.C.N.C.
who during his time at the Royal
Naval College became deeply
attached to the venerable trees and
parklands of Greenwich

List of Illustrations

Buckingham Palace — *Frontispiece*
The Waterloo Vase

between pages

1. Hampton Court. Twelve fountains set in the parterre, *circa* 1720
2. Hampton Court. The Pond Garden
3. Hampton Court. The Maze
4. Hampton Court. The Vine House
5, 6, 7, 8. Nonsuch. Four fountains
9. Kensington Palace. The Dutch Garden — 16–17
10. Kensington Palace. The Orangery
11. Buckingham Palace. The Nash façade (1825) from St James's Park
12. Mr Fred Nutbeam, head gardener at Buckingham Palace, judging a show
13. Sir Eric Savill, KCVO
14. The Savill Gardens in June
15. The Physick Garden at Chelsea, 1795. From the Rev. Daniel Lyson's *The Environs of London*
16. The Chelsea Physic Garden today — 48–49
17. Kew Gardens. Eighteenth-century engraving of George III's Lake with swan boat
18. The Palm House at Kew
19. The Queen's House and seventeenth-century garden, Kew
20. Daffodils at Kew
21. Syon House from Kew Gardens in 1832. Engraved after J. Farrington, RA, for *An History of the River Thames*
22. Lambeth Palace, 1720
23. Jane Loudon, from a miniature — 96–97

		between pages
24.	Theresa Earle	96–97
25.	E. S. Rohde	
26.	E. A. Bowles	144–145
27.	Victoria Sackville-West	
28.	The Tower at Sissinghurst	
29.	Work in a medieval vineyard	
30.	Loading vegetables for market, 1895	
31.	Covent Garden market by Doré	
32.	R. D. Blackmore	
33.	James Lee. From a painting	
34.	Covent Garden market today	192–193
35.	St Paul's Church, Covent Garden	
36.	The Royal Exotic Nursery at South Kensington, nineteenth century	
37.	The Great Conservatory at Syon Park	
38.	Flora's Lawn, Syon Park	
39.	Old Catalpa tree, Syon Park	
40.	St James's Park	240–241
41.	Rotten Row	
42.	Queen Mary's Rose Garden, Regent's Park	
43.	Royal Naval College, Greenwich	
44.	Old Spanish Chestnuts, Greenwich Park	
45.	Title page, catalogue of the Society of Gardeners, 1730	
46.	'The Citizen at Vauxhall', 1755	
47.	Vauxhall on a Gala Night. Early nineteenth-century engraving	272–273
48.	Silver season ticket by Hogarth, Vauxhall	
49.	Westminster Abbey, the Little Cloister Garden	
50.	Roof-top cloister garden, Derry and Toms	
51.	London amateurs showing their garden to Queen Elizabeth The Queen Mother	
52.	Metropolitan Police Station garden near Sloane Square	
53.	All Hallows Wall, London Wall	
54.	Finsbury Circus	304–305
55.	Ellen Willmott	
56.	Gertrude Jekyll, by W. Nicholson	
57, 58.	A town garden by Sylvia Crowe	
59.	The Great Herb Garden at Lullingstone Castle	

Foreword

To show how great has been the contribution made by London to the art and craft of gardening is the avowed aim of this book. Yet it is conceived primarily as an entertainment, being neither a technical treatise nor a comprehensive guide to the subject. The former would have taken greater scientific knowledge than I possess, the latter a larger volume than the publisher would allow. It is concerned with people as much as with plants: with those who have down the ages planned, owned, made and tended gardens; also with the palaces, mansions, legal chambers, castles and humble dwellings connected with them; with orangeries, summerhouses, greenhouses and vineries—with everything built to shelter the owners of gardens and their horticultural treasures. For people, their homes, and their gardens are indivisible.

London, thou art the flour of cities all wrote Dunbar nearly five centuries ago. In the nineteen-sixties the Chairman of the Metropolitan Public Gardens Association recorded in his book *The Flowering City* 'something of the considerable efforts made by the City Corporation to make the City of London one of the most colourful and attractive business centres in the world'. No man can number the gardeners who have toiled in and around London from Dunbar's time to the present day; but the attempt to visualize some of them and to appraise their work is a fascinating enough pastime, with piquancy added by the fact that people tend to regard our modern metropolis as a grimy noise-ridden man-made colossus of stone and cement, rather than as a centre of plant and tree culture.

Most of those who earn their bread in the Capital live far from the sound of Bow Bells; when the day's work ends, London is like an immense seed-pod bursting open to scatter its contents in a wide circle. Without precise adherence to urban boundaries or to a twenty-mile radius from Charing Cross, the area of central London, added to what were in earlier times the villages of Kensington, Islington, Hampstead and the rest, is here combined with that rather vague territory known as 'commuter land'. It is one person's choice, selected from a vast store like an anthology of favourite poetry. Although much had to be left out, I believe that my selected examples are both good and representative. It is not a dutiful book, but one written with enjoyment in the hope that it would give pleasure.

From the vanished Tudor palace and gardens of Nonsuch to that grand conception, the Savill Gardens at Windsor—begun in the reign of King George V, and the splendid modern plantings now being made in the grounds of Buckingham Palace, the monarchy has of right an important place in the story. In our time, many royal palaces and parks are open for all to enjoy; although few of the office strollers, dog runners, child minders and Christmas swimmers in Hyde Park, St James's, Kensington Gardens and Regent's Park realize that but for Henry VIII and his successors (who preserved large tracts of London for royal hunts), these open spaces would not exist for public pleasure now. The Commonwealth did its best to get rid of the lot. Let those who choose to belittle our royal family remember that!

The characters who strut, mince, amble, gambol, stride, plod or creep across the stage of London's gardens are as varied as any sample of humanity could be; yet all are united by the pursuit of horticulture in some form. Bacon 'left the impress of his foot' upon the gravel walks of Gray's Inn; Sir Thomas More in his Chelsea garden loved the rosemary to excess; James I planted a mulberry orchard near the present Buckingham Palace; Queen Anne at her palaces of Kensington and Hampton Court hated and uprooted Dutch William's box; John Loudon early in the nineteenth century persuaded people to plant plane and sycamore in place of yew and fir in London squares; yesterday the Head Gardener at Lincoln's Inn deplored the untidy habits of Loudon's favourites, whose frequent shedding of leaves makes so much work for the sweepers. This constant renewal of foliage makes those trees particularly suitable for life in smoky atmospheres; but smoke itself is gradually being outlawed in the Capital.

In our time, rising wages and shortage of labour cause those in charge to look askance at sweeping, a worry unknown to John Loudon. Weeding women employed by Henry VIII received threepence (old style) for a long day's work. Soon the English gardener's pay will exceed three pounds for an eight-hour day, if it has not already done so by the time this book is in print. The lot of the weeders and sweepers has changed for the better, but the weeds remain much the same. Bindweed plagued Agnes March, Alice and Elizabeth Alen, Kathryn Wite and Jone Abraham at Hampton Court in the sixteenth century as it still vexes Tom, Dick and Harry today. Thistle and dock persist, with charlock, nettle and dandelion, although the quaintly named dodder seems to have moved further out.

Our thriftier forbears cooked young nettles as a green vegetable and ate the *Dent-de-lion* raw in 'sallets', neglected habits which are to some extent being revived; but most of what we eat now in the way of fruit and vegetables has been cultivated by some gardener, and where better could his wealth of produce be admired than in London's great (but doomed) market of Covent Garden?

Let us now praise famous men, says Ecclesiasticus; but this wisdom of the son of Sirach omits to mention such as found out how to cultivate the fruits of the earth. Growers, grafters, hybridizers, seedsmen, nurserymen, plant-hunters—all have flourished and found encouragement in the flowering city, the flower of cities all—London.

DAWN MACLEOD

BERWICKSHIRE 1972

Acknowledgements

Acknowledgements are due:

To HM The Queen for graciously permitting me to explore the garden of Buckingham Palace; to the Assistant Press Secretary; to Mr Fred Nutbeam for a very friendly reception, and for his help with my script; to Valerie Finnis (Lady Scott) for kindly allowing me to use one of her unpublished pictures of the Palace garden as frontispiece; and to Mr David McLintock and the British Entomological and Natural History Society for material from their survey of the Palace grounds.

To Sir Eric Savill, KCVO, CBE, MC, VMH, for a memorable conducted tour of his creations in Windsor Great Park, and for subsequent assistance with my chapter; to Mr E. L. Crowson for his trouble over pictures; to Mrs P. Glanville of The London Museum for help with Nonsuch.

To the Committee of Management, Chelsea Physic Garden, and their Curator; to Mr E. Busby and the Worshipful Society of Apothecaries; to Sir George Taylor, DSc, FRS, FRSE, FLS, VMH, for help with Kew, and to Mr R. W. King, DFC, for vetting the details; to Mr Francis Cowper and Mr Philip Beddingham for hospitality and help in regard to the Inns of Court.

To Bea Howe (Mrs Lubbock) for the portrait of Jane Loudon from her book *Lady With Green Fingers*; to Mr A. E. Villiers and Mrs Odling for some notes on Theresa Earle; to Mr A. Rohde for the rare picture of E. S. Rohde in youth; to Messrs T. Nelson & Sons for extracts from *My Garden in Spring* by E. A. Bowles; to Mr Nigel Nicolson and Messrs M. Joseph for quotations from the work of V. Sackville-West.

To Miss E. J. Willson for the portrait of James Lee and information from her book *James Lee and the Vineyard Nursery*; to Miss J. L. Miller and the Gardening Centre Ltd at Syon Park; to Mrs Gladys Grigg for giving me an interesting time in the *Woman's Realm* garden.

To Mr J. L. Murray, Superintendent, Greenwich Park, for unstinted advice and help in regard to my father's favourite piece of London; to Mr S. M. Gault, MBE, FLS, VMH., formerly Superintendent, Regent's Park, and to the present Superintendent, Mr R. A. Stephenson; to Mr J. M. Fisher,

Superintendent, Hampton Court, for measurements of the herbaceous border; to Eithne Wilkins for the quotation from her book *The Rose-Garden Game*, and to Messrs Gollancz.

To the Dean of Westminster, and to the Head Gardener, Mrs Couchman, for showing me the Abbey garden; to Mr J. G. Fleming and the Worshipful Company of Gardeners; to Messrs Derry and Toms, Miss D. Bowen, and Miss P. Woods, PRO; to Mr Adam Tegetmeier and Mr L. B. Chappell for photographic work. To Mrs J. M. Stimpson and the London Gardens Society; to Mr F. E. Cleary, MBE, FRICS, for pictures and other material from his book *The Flowering City*, and to The City Press; to Mr Michael Upward and the Metropolitan Public Gardens Association; to Mr Miles Hadfield for material from his books and lectures; to Miss N. Franck, MA, and the Information Division of the Cement & Concrete Association; to Elizabeth Coxhead for her hospitality, encouragement, and for details from her book *One Woman's Garden*; to the Royal Horticultural Society and Miss E. Napier for unfailing assistance; to Dr H. R. Fletcher, VMH, for allowing me to use information from his book *The Story of the Royal Horticultural Society*; to Lady Hart Dyke of Lullingstone Castle for her great kindness; to the Hon. Lady Meade-Fetherstonhaugh and the Society of Herbalists.

To the Librarians of the RHS and Guildhall; the Borough Librarians of Greenwich, Hammersmith, Merton and Richmond-upon-Thames; and to Mr J. H. G. Crawford, ALA, FSA (Scot), and his staff at the Berwickshire County Library in Duns, who have obligingly tracked down books for me at short notice. Finally, to the Leverhulme Trust for financial assistance with my researches, and to all who have given of their time, my most grateful thanks.

For remaining illustration copyrights to the following: *Coal News* for 12; Jane Bown for 27; David Brinson for 43, 44; British Museum for 29, 48; Cement & Concrete Association for 57, 58; Department of the Environment for 2, 3, 4, 42; Derry and Toms for 50; J. E. Downward for 13, 14, 28; Hammersmith Public Library for 33; Lady Hart Dyke for 59; HMSO for 9; London Gardens Society for 49, 51, 52; London Museum for 5, 6, 7, 8; National Portrait Gallery for 56; Radio Times Hulton Picture Library for 10, 30, 31, 32, 40, 41; HMSO and the Director, Royal Botanic Gardens, Kew for 18, 19; Royal Horticultural Society for 26, 55; Harry Smith for 16, 20; Syon Park Gardening Centre for 37, 38, 39.

Dawn MacLeod

SECTION ONE

Royal Gardens

Hampton Court

THIS seems to have been one of the first stately homes in Britain to open as a pleasure resort for the people. Soon after her accession Queen Victoria ordered that the State apartments and gardens were to be thrown open to the public. What is more, she decreed that this concession should apply to Sundays—the first place of popular recreation to be so opened. She wished workers and their families to have full opportunity to enjoy the privilege, and persisted in this course despite heavy criticism. It is not easy now to picture Queen Victoria as a desecrator of the Sabbath, but there is evidence that the young monarch was so regarded by many subjects when her views on Sunday opening became known. Although this was not the first occasion on which Hampton Court served as a bone of contention, it may well have been the last. Such deep pools of antique peace now fill the place that even surging Bank Holiday crowds do no more than ripple the surface.

The palace was built by Thomas Wolsey, Archbishop of York, on land leased in 1514 from the Knight Hospitallers of St John of Jerusalem at an annual rent of fifty pounds. The site blended the important advantages of quick access to London by river with rural salubrity. It was a spot both healthy in itself and safely remote from foetid plague spots of the city. The house that Wolsey built was indeed worthy to be called a palace, with its vast quadrangle, a thousand rooms—including accommodation for 280 resident guests—and a series of tapestry-hung chambers of overpowering magnificence. Such display was deemed excessive, even for a man soon to become a cardinal, Papal Legate, and Lord Chancellor of England. The king's richest and most famous subject and his mode of living were satirized by John Skelton:

Why come ye not to Courte?
To whyche Courte?
To the Kynge's Courte,
Or to Hampton Courte?

Unfortunately the king himself was fully sensible of the inordinate display and luxury enjoyed by Wolsey, and although he often walked arm-in-arm with the owner in the pleasure gardens, His Majesty King Henry VIII began to feel disturbing pangs of jealousy. Aware of this submerged but highly dangerous current of feeling, Wolsey sought to restore harmony by 'giving' the palace to his royal master, reserving certain apartments for his own use. Thence he wrote letters to the king, inscribed 'Your Majesty's Manor of Hampton Court'. For a time this ruse appeared to be successful; but when Wolsey failed to obtain the Pope's consent to Henry's divorce from Catherine of Aragon he was stripped of his wealth and power; in October 1529 all his lands and goods were declared forfeit to the king, and he had looked for the last time upon his palace and gardens of Hampton Court. A few months later he was allowed a general pardon and retired to his Province of York, only to be arrested soon afterwards for treason. He died on the way back to London.

Such is the gist of Wolsey's story, to be found in children's history books. On the under side of the medal, seldom displayed, lies the ardent garden-lover who had his grounds alongside the Thames walled and splendidly laid out with fair arbours, alleys, turfed benches and 'knottes', making a haven from affairs of the Church and the realm; a place for rest, fresh air and gentle exercise; an outdoor chapel wherein evensong would be said on fine summer evenings. Worldly the Cardinal Archbishop may have been, but he was never known to neglect his religious duties. The gardens he made were in a sense a link between the old monastic gardens—so soon to be swept away at the Dissolution—and the purely secular pleasure gardens now being planned by land-owning gentry. With Bosworth Field the Wars of the Roses were over; the medieval castle had been rendered obsolete by the new artillery with gunpowder; now grounds could be laid out with no thought of defence, although Wolsey did choose to surround his palace with an old-fashioned moat. The gardens of Hampton Court were, in the main, more typical of the new Tudor Age than was the palace itself.

The 'knotte' or knot garden came into fashion early in the sixteenth century; the close-clipped aromatic herbs used to outline the intricate geometrical designs had hitherto been grown purely for use, in monastic or manorial herb garden. Now they became decorative as well, although the clippings were utilized to strew among rushes upon the floors of the rooms—a version of wall-to-wall carpeting which could be renewed at minimal expense, to provide delicious fragrance underfoot not as yet emulated in the modern product. Wolsey had a liking for saffron-impregnated rushes, and later in the century Queen Elizabeth preferred meadowsweet. Most aromatics were valued, not only for the pleasure given by their perfumes, but for the supposed virtue of protecting people against the pestilence. Spaces in the design were filled with flowers and sifted sand of various colours. Many of these knot gardens had a delicacy of touch and naive charm far superior to the heavy-handed carpet bedding favoured by the Victorians, and, in some municipal parks, still seen today. The gardens founded by Wolsey were perhaps his best gift to posterity, even though they have been greatly enlarged and altered since his time, and the present knot garden is a modern reproduction.

During the sixteenth century the long, straight walks, whether they passed among pleached trees, or were sheltered by climbing plants on trellis-work, or lay in open ground, became known as 'forthrights'. These main arteries of the pleasure-garden corresponded in some measure to the rectangular plan of the building they complemented, while the patterns of mazes and knots echoed the decorative geometric traceries which were fashionable on buildings of the period. These intricate conceits were the 'meanders' to which Shakespeare made reference in *The Tempest*:

> *here's a maze trod indeed*
> *Through forthrights and meanders!*
> (Act III, Scene 3)

Some of Cardinal Wolsey's arbours, or herbers, were doubtless made from rosemary, honeysuckle, musk rose, jasmine and various vines and creepers, and his alleys composed of whitethorn, sycamore, willow and hornbeam trained to arch overhead. In places rosemary was grown up the walls. The covered walks were strewn with clean sea or river sand, carefully sifted upon them so that walkers after rain might not have muddy shoes. But the open walks, not intended for use in bad weather, were turfed or planted with herbs to smell sweet when crushed under foot. Here and there the covered walks had 'windows' cut in the foliage so that strollers might look out on other parts of the garden. This fashion was perpetuated in the type of Dutch garden beloved by William and Mary.

At the time Henry VIII acquired Hampton Court he was a vigorous and not unduly stout man of under forty, addicted to active recreation. He therefore made provision in the grounds for hunting, jousting, tennis, archery and bowls—a game played as far back as the thirteenth century in England. Henry enjoyed two kinds of tennis—the 'close tennys play' and 'open tennys', the latter possibly an early version of lawn tennis. The oblong building he had constructed for close tennis play still stands, and Tennis Court Lane takes it name from this relic. The game is of French origin and, unlike fives, was played with racquets. In Tudor times tennis was reserved for the privileged classes, because it was thought to distract men from keeping up the archery practice useful in war. In 1541 it was prohibited to be played in public, and those who desired to play on private estates had to pay £100 a year for a licence.

The king had three bowling-alleys: two close and one open. The latter bore little resemblance to the velvet sward of our own day, Tudor turf being more like a hayfield and full of bumps. For this reason the close bowling-alley was preferred by those who could afford to have this amenity constructed with level floor of wood or beaten earth. Women played bowls, and before the Dissolution it was permitted to monks in their monasteries. Durham had a bowling-alley for the novices to recreate themselves. It is likely that the beautiful, smooth turf for which Britain is now famous was developed through the centuries because of the demand for level bowling-greens. The smooth green pleasure lawn was not known at Hampton Court until long after the time of Henry VIII.

All that remains of his tiltyard, which occupied a seven-acre site, is one of the five towers in which the spectators sat to watch the pageantry among hangings of gold and silver. (This was turned into a tea-house in 1924, with trees and flower-beds in front, and lawn tennis courts, putting greens and a car park near by.) For gentler exercise, the king had the pleasure gardens extended, and an orchard was planted to the north, where cherries, apples, medlars and melons were cultivated. The King's New Garden, where the Privy Garden now lies, had a mount or mound raised near the river on the south side. It was constructed upon a foundation of bricks, with earth piled on the bricks, the whole planted with quicksets to bind it. When all was firm a summer house, known variously as the Great Round Arbour, the Lantern Arbour or the South Arbour, was built on top. This ambitious structure, three storeys high, had many glazed windows, and a lead cupola surmounted by a heraldic beast carrying a vane.

The artificial mount or mound was a common feature of the old English garden: an idea said to have come down from the Druids. References to the raising of such hillocks are to be found in the sacred books of many religions, and this seems to be allied with the universal veneration felt by mankind for high places; but construction of mounts in Britain continued long after their religious significance had been forgotten. They became garden adornments and look-out towers of purely secular interest. At Hampton Court the king and his courtiers reached the arbour by winding paths likened in a contemporary account to 'the turnings of cockle-shells'. Alongside the walks were placed heraldic lions, greyhounds, harts, unicorns and dragons, carved in stone and holding vanes in their paws or hooves. Sixteen of these 'beestes' stood on the mount and thirty-eight more in the adjacent Pond Garden, all bearing shields painted with the arms of the king and queen in the colours of heraldry, and resting on bases striped in the Tudor colours of green and white. There were also no fewer than sixteen sundials made by Bryce Augustyne, a Westminster clockmaker.

Around the base of the mount one John Hutton planted a ring of three-year-old bushes of rosemary, for which he received payment of two shillings and sixpence. This fragrant shrub, originally brought to Britain by the Romans, died out in these islands and was unknown for centuries, until in the reign of Edward III Queen Philippa of Hainault received a gift of plants from her mother. The legend that rosemary does not grow above the height of Christ when he was on earth bears some resemblance to the usual dimensions of this bush in our time; but accounts of Tudor gardens relate that it entirely covered walls. One is left guessing whether the walls did not exceed about six feet, or whether the plant grew taller then, or whether 'walls' is a misprint for 'walks', and the rosemary sprawled. It is possible that the climate was going through a warmer phase, and that this Mediterranean subject in English soil made extra growth, for on its native terrain it does not usually overtop human beings.

It was prized for its dual-purpose role as protector against both 'venomous worms' (snakes) and evil spirits. The blossom gave nectar to bees which, before the introduction of cane and beet sugars, supplied sweetening used at table.

In addition to the admired rosemary, Henry had his gardens stocked with new plantings of rose (red and white to symbolize the union of York and Lancaster), violet, primrose, gillyflower, sweet william and mint. The choice was restricted, for not until the reign of his daughter Elizabeth and the voyages made by her adventurous subjects to far countries were many of our now common and 'traditional' garden flowers seen in England. The new orchard made to the north of Wolsey's garden was planted with cherries, apples, medlars, pears and damsons, and thirty-four bushels of strawberry roots. These were gathered in the woods, as Thomas Tusser wrote:

Such growing abroad, among thorns in the wood
Wel chosen and picked, proved excellent good.

Young oaks and elms were set among the fruit trees, and it is likely that many trees came from Richard Harris (or Harys), fruiterer and gardener to the king. Early in the sixteenth century he obtained a grant of 105 acres at Teynham in Kent, and fetched from France 'a great store of graftes'. He is said also to have introduced the pippin into this country, so called because it was raised from seed, not grafted. The famous Kent orchards have a long history; but before Harris developed his trade, choice fruit seen on the tables of rich people was mostly imported from France and Holland. Melons were very popular in the sixteenth and seventeenth centuries, and Henry gave a special reward to the gardener who successfuly grew melons and cucumbers for the royal table. Among the evergreen trees and shrubs he chose—juniper, yew, cypress, bay and holly—the latter provided this inconstant monarch with a theme for one of his songs:

As the holly groweth green, and never changeth hue,
So I am—ever have been—unto my lady true.

The most stunning example of artist's licence ever penned.

While his lawful queen, Catherine of Aragon ('beestes' bearing her arms but newly installed around mount and pond), occupied the royal apartments in the palace, Henry was engaged in amorous dalliance with another resident, Anne Boleyn—who came, like his orchard trees, from Kent. The divorce that Wolsey failed to negotiate was procured by the equally ambitious and far less scrupulous Thomas Cromwell, Wolsey's successor, in conjunction with Cranmer, the Archbishop of Canterbury. In 1533 the king's marriage to Catherine was declared null and void, to the horror of all good Catholics. Amid much pomp Henry was married to Anne, and with his latest bride spent the second of his series of honeymoons at Hampton Court, unperturbed by the Pope's thunder. In spite of excommunication and the papal decree that the new marriage was invalid, no sooner had Anne given birth to Elizabeth than Catherine's daughter, Mary, was declared to be illegitimate.

In the year 1535 one John Bereman of Ditton set new pear trees on the mount, whose fruit Anne was never to taste. She enjoyed but three years as queen before the innumerable lover's knots showing her initial 'A' romantically entwined with Henry's 'H', together with her falcon badge, were speedily erased from the walls and ceilings. Only a few on groins below the clock-tower somehow escaped the purge. Jane Seymour, one of the dead queen's ladies-in-waiting, now took her place in the palace. So much for the king's unchanging love for his 'awne darling'. A biennial plant would have served better as his symbol than the long-lived, evergreen holly. Yet each lady in turn believed herself to be the true and lasting spouse, all of them adept at wishful thinking. Jane's life was short, for she died of puerperal fever after giving birth to Prince Edward; but at least she retained the king's favour until the end of her days.

Now began that tremendous upheaval known as the Dissolution of the Monasteries, including Charterhouse, some of whose celebrated bay trees had already been procured to furnish the gardens of Hampton Court. An inventory made when the monastery was surrendered to the king mentions fruit and bay trees, rose-trees, rosemary and other shrubs. Many were taken to the royal gardens at Chelsea. Soon the monarch's desire to have good hunting on his Hampton estate led him to commandeer an enormous tract of land, from the manors of Molesey, Wiseley, Walton, Esher, Weybridge, Ditton and Byfleet, to serve as a chase. This was railed off and stocked with deer, to the great detriment of local inhabitants, who were driven off their holdings without mercy or compensation. That they suffered this tyranny without voicing complaint or organizing rebellion was due, no doubt, to fear of harsh punishment.

The misery caused to humble countryfolk when they are torn up by the roots from familiar soil and banished from the places they know and love is no less terrible today, even though government officials have taken the place of monarchs as dictators and some payments are made to the evicted people. When the report of the Roskill inquiry into siting a third airport for London was issued, smallholders in north Buckinghamshire went on the air to express their bitter feelings about the threat to Stewkley and Cublington. One man, whose family had farmed a piece of this land for about five hundred years, gave a moving account of how much this 'lovely little valley' meant to him; how he had worked it and planned to end his days there as his ancestors had done, and finally to have his ashes scattered on the hill above. This community had pledged itself to resist by all means in its power any move to dispossess it of their land; five hundred Davids from the county that bred John Hampden, now pitting themselves against the Goliath of officialdom and the great whales of the air that would defile their fields. At least they could not lose their heads for such temerity, as the opponents of Henry so often did. Nobody has ever been able to count with certainty the number of citizens who went to the block or stake in the troubled years that led up to and followed the Reformation.

The failure of the king's marriage to Anne of Cleves, a union engineered by Cromwell, cost the Chancellor his high office; while in the gardens of Hampton Court that bun-faced lady spent summer weeks awaiting her divorce. Directly it was promulgated, she was removed to the royal palace of Richmond, whose gardens had for long rivalled those of Hampton. A man named Lovell received a salary of twelve pounds annually for the office of head gardener. In addition to supplying the king's table with fruits and his still-room with herbs and flowers, he had produced evergreen shrubs for the planting of the mount at Hampton Court. Soon Henry appeared in that palace for yet another honeymoon, this time with Catherine Howard. Some stain on the lady's past—which could hardly have matched the blots on her husband's record—was disclosed to the king by Cranmer, resulting in her execution a few months later. It is difficult to picture now, amid the fragrant and placid delights of these gardens, the doomed and wretched victim gazing hopelessly out upon such exquisite surroundings, from which she was dragged to a horrible death. And what were the thoughts of her successor, Catherine Parr, who was so soon to spend her own honeymoon with Henry at Hampton Court? She is credited with wisdom and tact, and became a kind stepmother to the king's children. Did she also pity their mothers, and wonder what her own fate would be?

As the king grew older and stouter he gave up the more active sports, but never lost his fondness for Hampton Court, where he could still walk in the gardens and play at bowls. He sent the young Earl of Surrey to the block, and would have executed Surrey's father, the Duke of Norfolk, had not his own death in January 1547 prevented it. Catherine Parr survived, to become a widow for the second time. (She had formerly been the wife of Lord Latimer.)

The new monarch, Edward VI, reigned under the tutelage of his uncle the 'Lord Protector', Duke of Somerset, who was not popular with the people or with the boy king. When Somerset was executed early in 1552, young Edward's diary laconically recorded: *The Duke of Somerset had his head cut off upon Tower Hill between eight and nine o'clock in the morning*. His next mentor, the Earl of Warwick (who soon became Duke of Northumberland), relaxed the rules, allowing his charge to see the kind ex-queen and Princess Elizabeth; there must have been some happy times during these reunions in the Hampton Court gardens—which Edward greatly preferred to Windsor. But the delicate youth died of consumption at the age of fifteen; a conspiracy to place Lady Jane Grey on the throne came to grief, and Mary occupied the throne of England.

In 1554, with her newly-married husband, Philip of Spain, Queen Mary came to Hampton Court, there to dwell in modest, withdrawn privacy which was the antithesis of the display enjoyed by her royal father. Pageants and jousts were things of the past, and the gates of the palace remained closed. In spite of ruthless oppression suffered at his hands, the people now began to regret 'the good old days of King Harry'; they had persuaded Somerset to remove the palings and deer from Henry's encroaching chase, and so, with their holdings restored, it would have been easier to whitewash the late monarch's reputation. A jovial sinner is usually preferred to a tight-lipped saint. Mary was described by contemporaries as plain, pious, and ill-dressed, while her spouse seemed gloomy and dull; such royalties give small pleasure to their subjects.

Behind the enclosing walls of the palace Mary and Philip may have experienced some quiet pleasure in the gardens. The fruit orchards and ornamental flowers were well maintained, and on his return to Spain King Philip had a garden constructed with towers, moats, alleys and flower-gardens 'after the pattern of the country house in England' where he had lived with Queen Mary. With his flamboyant courtiers, he must have given many a subject for gossip to the weeding-women of Hampton—Agnes March, Alice and Elizabeth Alen, Jone Smeton, Agnes Norton, Kathryn Wite and Jone Abraham, who received threepence a day for their labours. The catholic household ate on Fridays meatless meals consisting of salmon, porpoise, sturgeon, eel, perch, crab, eggs, cheese, oatmeal, and dessert of apples, pears, damsons and nuts. This does not suggest a particularly frugal diet; but the visiting Spaniards are said to have considered the English to be gormandizing heretics with no ideas beyond food and drink. On their next visit to this country Mary proved to be sick with dropsy, and not pregnant as had been hoped. In 1558 she lay ill at Hampton Court; she died that year.

Now the splendour of the old days was renewed, even surpassed, with the accession of Elizabeth and the cultural upsurge of the Renaissance. Explorers in their little wooden vessels set sail for such far distant places as the Cape of Good Hope, Goa, South America and the Magellan Straits, returning to Gloriana with rich spoils which included many strange and rare plants for her gardens. In secluded arbours she would have private meetings with her advisers, receive foreign envoys, and inspect possible suitors—none of whom she was able to accept. Her principal secretary, Sir William Cecil, had a good knowledge of plants and took a keen interest in the gardens of Hampton Court. He obtained many new seeds and bulbs through diplomatic channels, including the Turk's Cap Lily, and no doubt supplied specimens to the royal gardens. His own at Cecil House in London and at Theobalds in Hertfordshire were under the direction of the herbalist John Gerard, whose *Herball* published in 1597 brought him rather more fame than its jumble of contents, largely purloined from other writers, strictly deserved. In Gerard's herb gardens between Ely Place and the Fleet grew all the well-tried herb plants and as many new subjects as the owner could lay hands on. At one time his newly-imported 'Blew Pipe' (Lilac) and Laburnum were a source of wonder to all who saw them in bloom.

Shakespeare, who at the close of the sixteenth century lived near this garden, probably drew from it much of the herbal lore permeating his plays. His knowledge of plants and their uses is unrivalled in the history of authorship, apart from the technical works of botanists and gardeners. From the continent of Europe at this period came other plants new to British gardeners, notably the tulip and the daffodil from Holland, and the carnation known as 'sops-in-wine' which arrived with, and was cultivated by, protestant refugees. They also brought spinach and taught the English to cook it in its own steam—a lesson not always remembered by cooks today.

Although the variety of plants to be seen at Hampton Court greatly increased during the reign of Elizabeth, the lay-out remained much the same as in the time of Wolsey and Henry VIII. Shelter from wind and rain was provided by the carefully pleached trees, and creepers trained over lattice-work, which also gave privacy for confidential interviews. Inside the palace the walls seem to have flowered handsomely too. Thomas Platter wrote a contemporary account of tapestries worked 'in gold and silver and silk, so lifelike that one might take the people and plants for real'. In the cooler seasons Queen Elizabeth liked to enjoy brisk walks—but only when unobserved. To impress her subjects and visitors from abroad, she would take great pains to walk in public with stately grandeur at a slow and dignified pace. Like her father, she enjoyed the hunt, also coursing with greyhounds; she inherited his informed love of music, and presided over sumptuous masques and revels.

In 1590 she had erected in the Clock Court a grand fountain crowned by an imposing figure of Justice. Its solemn looks belied it, for this splendid artefact was designed to play tricks on unsuspecting guests, squirting water at anyone who came within range. Such inventions, which to us seem callow in the extreme, were popular in the late sixteenth and early seventeenth centuries, and perhaps serve to illuminate the many-sided taste of the period. The most refined music and poetry and exquisite craftsmanship in tapestry, needlework and wearing apparel were enjoyed alongside rough practical jokes and horseplay. Presumably the water for Elizabeth's jets came from the Thames. In her father's reign, records show that charges were met for labourers 'ladyng water out of ye Temmes to fill the pondes in the night tymes'.

At the time of the greatest achievement of her glorious reign, the defeat of the Spanish Armada, Queen Elizabeth was mourning the death of her favourite (some say her secret lover), Dudley, Earl of Leicester. The artist who painted the portrait—(now at Corsham Court in Wiltshire)—of her 'haunted by Time and Death' may have had this in mind, and not only her own end. As for Time, she abhorred the thought of old age, and when on leaving Hampton Court in vile weather at the age of sixty-six, she elected to ride although scarcely able to sit a horse, she blazed angrily at Lord Hunsdon for suggesting that it was not meet for one of her years to ride out in such a storm. Elizabeth's reply rings down the centuries: 'My years!—Maids, to your horses quickly' —with which she left Hampton Court for the last time. In March 1603 she died at Richmond.

James VI of Scotland and I of England, who now came to the throne, at first preferred parks to gardens. He liked hunting and other active sports, and had little chance of being familiar with ornamental gardens in his native land. His apparel was dull, even shabby, and with his retinue of Highlanders in weathered garments he must have startled the English. Plain living and high thinking were his habit; he had received a first-class education, perhaps the best enjoyed by any monarch before or since. As a youth he despised the social graces, and disliked music and dancing; but life in England softened his attitude. No doubt his queen, Anne of Denmark, was well pleased to encourage this, for she liked entertainments and had earned dour displeasure in Scotland for her 'night-walking and balling'. At Hampton Court they celebrated their first Christmas with a grand masque, rifling the late queen's wardrobe for costumes. No fewer than five hundred magnificent dresses were found there.

Soon Ben Jonson was enlisted to write masques for the court, with Inigo Jones to design scenery, and in the Great Hall the King's Company of Players (on whose roll the name of William Shakespeare figured) performed plays and interludes which the Queen and Prince of Wales enjoyed more than the King. The Heir to the Throne, Prince Henry, was an athletic and well-favoured youth who excelled at sport and used to the full all the resources for exercise at Hampton Court—tennis, bowls, archery, hunting and the rest. The portrait of him which hangs in the palace shows him at the age of eleven with a slain stag. He has a stronger face than that of his brother Charles, who succeeded as Prince of Wales after Henry's untimely death at the age of nineteen.

The greatest event of King James's reign was the long and solemn conference of clergymen held at Hampton Court in 1604; it brought forth the Authorized

Version of the Bible in English which many of us have been familiar with at Anglican services until very recent years. This king had piety as well as learning, with decided views on the subject of religion, but he showed the minimum of Christian charity towards his humbler subjects. He objected to what he called 'barbarous insolency' of the crowds gathered to watch him hunt, and issued strict regulations to prevent them following the chase. Sunday recreation was tightly controlled—archery (being of likely service to the Crown) was allowed, but playing at bowls and bear-baiting were forbidden. We are not told whether the same rules prevailed within the palace grounds.

James may not have taken much interest in his gardens, but those at Hampton Court were well maintained. In 1614 the under-keeper received £68 3s. 8d. for 'chardges in repaire of His Majesty's Arbours and Walkes in the Gardens at Hampton Courte'. The bill included boat hire for plants and trees brought from London, and horse hire 'of diverse gardeners with their chardges in seeking out and fetchinge of plantes settes and trees' the sum of thirty shillings. By this date the wages of men were one shilling and sixpence daily for gardeners, a shilling for labourers, and fourpence for women. The charges for 'plantes and settes for knottes' show that Henry's knot gardens were not neglected. The Italian fashion of training fruit against sunny walls was adopted here around the start of the seventeenth century, and the 'apricocke, or hasty peche tree' had become fairly common in gardens of great houses. In 1611 William Hogan, Keeper of His Majesty's still-house and garden at Hampton Court, was paid to plant the walls with vines, apricots, plums and peaches. These came from London nurseries by boat, or from the Kentish orchards at Teynham already mentioned. The apricots were helped in their hasty (early) fruiting by liberal applications of cow-dung, horse-dung and the lees of claret at the appropriate time. At the end of the sixteenth century Sir Hugh Platt had written that if goat's milk were given to peach trees as they came into blossom they would produce *pomegranates*; but such wild fancies were derided, with the birth of a more scientific approach to horticulture and much else, as the seventeenth century moved into its second decade.

King James enjoyed a good selection of vegetables from his kitchen garden at Hampton Court, including the skirret—a kind of parsnip—which has since gone out of fashion. Carrot, beet, turnip, peas and beans, lettuce, asparagus, spinach and cucumber were raised, together with chives, mint, tarragon, mustard and other herbs for flavouring. In addition to honey, flowers were used to sweeten dishes. The most useful contribution made to the horticultural world by this monarch was the cultivation in large numbers of the mulberry tree. It had already been grown in England; Queen Elizabeth planted one at Hatfield, and Syon had a specimen dating back to monastic times, but James planted on a large scale and instructed his Lords-Lieutenant that 1,000 mulberry trees were to be sold at three-farthings a plant, and that all who could do so must plant one or more. The largest plantation—of 3,000 trees—was made by the king on land near where Buckingham Palace now stands. King James had planned to start a silk industry in Britain, and the mulberries were intended to supply food for silkworms. But as the Black Mulberry (*Morus nigra*) was cultivated instead of the White Mulberry (*Morus alba*)—whose foliage provides the staple diet for the caterpillar of the moth *Bombyx mori* which spins the silken cocoon filched by man for weaving, the venture was a failure. As a by-product, the Black Mulberry became a valued inhabitant of English gardens, and its succulent fruit forms heavier crops and is more pleasing to human palates than that of the White variety. Several old trees said to date from the time of James are still to be seen in gardens; one so labelled survives in the gardens of Buckingham Palace, but experts doubt the validity of the date ascribed to it.

The tobacco plant, which had been introduced in 1565 by Sir John Hawkins, was severely frowned upon by James I. His criticism of the then new, and growing, habit of smoking this weed in pipes reads sensibly in the light of modern medical research. The custom, he said was 'lothsome to the eye, hatefull to the nose, harmfull to the braine, dangerous to the lungs'. Had the cigarette been invented, perhaps he would have insisted that the makers print his stricture on each packet sold.

The king's most 'lothsome' act was the violent treatment meted out to Sir Walter Raleigh—whose chief introduction, according to legend, was the harmless necessary potato. (This story is not now generally accepted by botanists, who cannot pinpoint exactly how this plant *did* reach our shores.) Raleigh was put to death, to appease the Spaniards, in 1618; Shakespeare had died two years earlier; and so the golden age of Elizabeth was well and truly at an end some fifteen years after her own death.

A happier event of James's reign was the formation of *The Company of Gardiners of London*, which was given its first Royal Charter in 1605, followed by a second conferring some extension of its privileges in 1616, nine years before his death. Anne of Denmark predeceased him, dying in the palace of Hampton Court in 1619. When Charles I brought his child-bride, Henrietta Maria, to the palace the circumspect atmosphere of the gardens gave way to endless bickerings and some violent quarrels. Being French, and a Catholic, the new queen had with her a retinue of French subjects, including no fewer than thirty priests. This brought adverse publicity upon the royal circle; Charles felt obliged to reduce the foreign influx; every time he attempted to do so his bride threw a tantrum—as also did her advisers. When the plague broke out in London the court, hearing that it had reached the neighbourhood of Hampton, hastily removed to Windsor, leaving two of Henrietta's priests who had been in contact with the disease quarantined in one of the towers overlooking the tiltyard.

The herbalist John Parkinson, who had been Apothecary to James I and was appointed *Botanicus Regius Primarius* by Charles, produced in 1629 the first great gardening book in English—precursor of a vast literature which accrued to the subject in the next 343 years. Latin being very much the fashion still, he gave it the cumbrous and weakly punning title of *Paradisi in Sole, Paradisus Terrestris*, the joke being an allusion to his own name—Park in Sun. It was dedicated to Queen Henrietta Maria. So learned a volume deserved a better title; but perhaps, like the rose, it smelt sweet whatever its name. Parkinson's own garden in Long Acre contained many unusual plants, some of them gathered abroad by himself during extensive travels. He was naturally concerned—like all apothecaries of his time—with the medicinal properties of herbs; but unlike the others he was highly sensitive to the beauty and charm of flowers for their own sake. His book is divided into three sections: The Pleasure Garden, The Kitchen Garden, and The Orchard. He gives designs for knots, showing that these are still in fashion, and advocates the planning of generously wide walks and alleys—advice still valid today. The maze, mount, fountain and 'wilderness' were recommended as important garden features, and a wilderness of somewhat formal lay-out was made at Hampton Court. It seems likely that some kind of maze existed in Tudor times, although the one seen today is of seventeenth-century origin. In the kitchen garden 'cole-flower' (cauliflower) was still a novelty, and Parkinson mentions difficulty in obtaining the seed.

In the summer of 1636 a bad epidemic of plague broke out in London. Now Hampton Court was isolated, nobody from the infected area being allowed within ten miles of the gates. This was the year when a doughty Buckinghamshire squire, John Hampden, refused to pay the King's Ship Money, declaring it to be an illegal tax. Charles I chose to make himself unpopular in other ways too. He tried to enclose more land, between Hampton and Richmond, for hunting. Grown bolder, the people voiced loud complaints at the projected enclosure of land, and

1. Hampton Court. Twelve fountains set in the parterre, *circa* 1720

2. Hampton Court. The Pond Garden

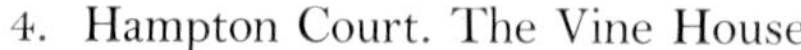

3. Hampton Court. The Maze

4. Hampton Court. The Vine House

5, 6, 7, 8. Nonsuch. Four fountains

9. Kensington Palace. The Dutch Garden

Charles reconsidered the matter. Another of his schemes was carried out. A channel eleven miles long was cut from Longford to the palace to carry water from the River Colne, 'for the better accommodation of the palace, and the recreation and disport of His Majesty'. This canal caused trouble to agriculture by overflowing its banks, and when in 1648 Charles was imprisoned, people lost no time in knocking down the bridges and filling up the channel.

The Italian fashion for placing statues in gardens had been introduced by Charles, but developed in strict moderation at Hampton Court. The pond in the Privy Garden was provided with a large marble fountain topped by a statue of Diana—now removed to the circular pond in Chestnut Avenue. The true Italian architectural garden, based upon what was known of Roman designs, suited better the terrain and climate of Italy; but apart from his lack of hill terraces and flowing water, Charles was short of money. The troubles that led up to the Civil War, and the subsequent Puritan regime, curbed the eruption of grandiose garden schemes in England. After the Battle of Naseby in 1645 Parliament sealed the royal apartments at Hampton Court. Two years later Charles was imprisoned in the palace. It was not a close confinement; the deposed king used the gardens and rode in the park, and was visited by the diarist John Evelyn there. Charles made his escape to the Isle of Wight, being soon recaptured, and in 1649 beheaded. So a rather weak man was turned by events into a martyr, to be remembered in some circles with veneration.

Parliament had a survey of the palace and grounds made with a view to disposing of them. Eventually the parks were sold off to private buyers. When Oliver Cromwell became Lord Protector, he rather surprisingly—and to the benefit of posterity—was instrumental in having them repurchased by the State. He and his family must have been the most homely group ever to inhabit Hampton Court. Although he encouraged the destruction of organs in England's cathedrals, he had one installed in the Great Hall of the palace, for he was musical; Milton is said to have played upon it. As might be expected, the cultivation of fruits and vegetables for the table took precedence during the Commonwealth of ornamental gardening, which sank into the doldrums. But not for long. With the death of Cromwell in 1658 and the inability of his amiable son Richard to assume his father's mantle, the way stood open for the exiled Charles II, who entered London in May 1660 as king amid wild rejoicing.

He had absorbed many French ideas during years spent in France: among them the grand garden designs invented by the architect Le Notre, who had already carried out a scheme devised for Fouquet's château at Vaux-le-Vicomte, and was later to construct the splendours which surround the palace of Versailles The long, imposing avenues, the woodland groves, the terraces, artificial lakes and cascades, statues and fountains, were all planned with amazing skill to magnify man rather than to fit his stature, as earlier gardens had done. Charles II returned to an impoverished kingdom and was therefore unable to emulate the vastly richer (and more securely throned) *Roi Soleil*; but he introduced French ideas on a modified scale, employing a number of gardeners brought over from France.

André Mollet's book *Le Jardin de Plaisir* had an English edition in 1670. In it he writes of alterations to Hampton Court, St. James's and Greenwich—'where this Mighty Prince hath made many notable changes, and added more Royal Decorations since the ten years of his happy Restoration than any of his ancestors ever thought in the Space of a whole Age'. The old, intimate Tudor garden was designed for the peace and privacy of individuals; but, with the emergence of new ideas centred on space and formal display, seclusion disappeared with the outmoded hedge and trellis-work, as larger prospects were opened up. This expansive approach to gardening echoed the era of scientific thought which began with the Reformation. In England the 'new philosophy' of Francis Bacon, which had been veiled during the Civil War and Commonwealth, emerged at the Restoration and led in 1660 to the formation of the Royal Society. The modern scientific outlook may be said to have established itself when this association was launched. Horticulture was one of many studies to be influenced.

At Hampton Court under the supervision of John Rose (a pupil of Le Notre), the great canal ordered by the king was excavated, filled, and planted with avenues of lime trees radiating on either side outwards from the east front of the palace; a semi-circle at the end completed what was known as the *patte d'oie*—'goose foot' design. Rose is often given credit for having grown the first pineapple to be ripened in England; a horticultural feat which for some years no other gardener could match. There is a portrait of him presenting the first pineapple to Charles II.* Later, when communications with the West Indies improved, imported fruit took the place of that which, by now, was being successfully cultivated in gardens of many great houses at enormous trouble and expense. During his work as gardener to the Earl of Essex at Essex House in the Strand, Rose had gained valuable experience in the management of 'cases'

* This is doubtful; there is no record of English-grown pineapples being ripened in the lifetime of Charles II, and Horace Walpole is thought to have invented the title of the picture.

(conservatories) where oranges, lemons and other tender subjects were raised. He wrote a book on vine culture, a craft he had learned in France.

The Frenchified improvements at Hampton Court were nearly complete when in May 1662 this traditional honeymoon palace received Charles II and his bride, Catharine of Braganza. John Evelyn described the grounds as he saw them then: 'The Park, formerly a flat and naked piece of ground, now planted with sweet rows of lime-trees; and the canal for water now near perfected, also the air-park . . . The cradle-work of horn beam in the garden is, for the perplexed twining of trees, very observable'. This last remark suggests that some of the old pleaching remained intact. Evelyn was 'admitted and then sworn one of the Council of the Royal Society' in August that year.

Life at Hampton Court now resumed much of the display and liveliness last seen there in the reign of Elizabeth, with outdoor sports and games, the remodelling of Henry's 'close tennys' court—Charles being addicted to this ball game—and excursions on the Thames in a gondola presented by Venice to the royal couple; together with indoor balls, plays, music and masques. The illicit amours of the king soon caused distress to Catharine and worry to Lord Chancellor Clarendon, who became involved in them as go-between. Pity the man who had the king's orders to persuade his queen that her husband's desire to have his paramour (Lady Castlemaine) installed at court as a Lady of the Queen's Bedchamber had better be granted! It was; and somehow Catharine was dissuaded from carrying out her threat of returning to Portugal. This poor, forbearing lady is said to have been deeply fond of her spouse, and when things had settled down they got on well enough together. After some months the king was criticized for staying so long at Hampton, where he was thought to be neglectful of affairs of State. When he finally took his queen to London by the river, there was such demand for boats that Samuel Pepys went away disappointed, being unable to hire one for love or money.

For nearly two decades the grain harvests in England had failed, or given very low yields, and so corn for bread was fetching an inflated price beyond the reach of humble people. For this reason the potato came into favour as a cheap and easily grown foodstuff. Even Fellows of the Royal Society were pressed into cultivating and spreading knowledge of this strange tuber, which was still almost unknown to the general public in England, although the Irish had already seized on it and proved that it would succeed in the British Isles. In 1664 John Forster issued a book entitled: *England's Happiness Increas'd, or a Sure and Easie Remedy against all succeeding Dear Years; by a Plantation of the Roots called*

Potatoes. Four kinds are mentioned in this treatise: the Sweet, or Spanish Potato; the Jerusalem Artichoke (then often called Canadian Potato); and the Virginian and Irish Potatoes, which were varieties of the tuber we know today.

Now came the best-known (and most severe) epidemic of the Plague in London, followed by the Great Fire. Once again Hampton Court became a refuge from infection for the monarch, although strict quarantine regulations were not this time imposed. Pepys, who stuck manfully to his post in London through fire and pestilence, was allowed to visit the king on 28 January 1666 and be thanked for his good service. Afterwards they walked 'quite out of the Court and into the fields, and then back'. In the gardens there grew the great herb Angelica, whose stem has for generations been candied as a sweetmeat and decoration for cakes. To chew a piece of this plant's root was considered to be a valuable specific against infection by the Plague; no doubt the king and his courtiers tried this simple preventative.

Charles kept up the gardens of Hampton Court throughout his reign, although in later years his visits were short and infrequent, sometimes for a day's hunting, or to show its glories to a visiting potentate. In 1669 the Duke of Tuscany wrote home about the fountains and fanciful water-spouts—surely high praise from an Italian, whose country specialized in such garden adornments. He also liked the 'artificial pastures' of grass—an early reference to the lawn which has since become such a familiar feature of English gardens; and he appreciated the snug places of retirement in the palace precincts.

At Charles's death in 1685 the Duke of York—also a Catholic—succeeded to the throne. He was not popular, and as he had little to do with Hampton Court he falls outside the scope of this chapter. And yet, had he not caused uproar by meddling in the religious observances of his subjects, even to setting aside an Act of Parliament, he need never have gone into exile, and William of Orange would not have been installed in his place. William and his wife Mary, daughter of James, were proclaimed joint sovereigns in 1689, and promised to govern the realm 'according to the Statutes in Parliament agreed on'. Now Hampton Court fairly buzzed with activity, for William found the air so agreeable that he chose to spend the greater part of the year there, and soon after his accession he employed Christopher Wren to build new apartments for himself and the queen.

The Tudor palace was 200 years old, and the first plans involved destruction of all except the Great Hall. In the end the Base Court and Clock Court were left standing; but the third courtyard, round which the State rooms and private royal apartments were ranged, was demolished to make way for the rooms that now enclose the Fountain Court. Because William and Mary reigned jointly, there had to be duplicate rooms with a King's stair and a Queen's stair, still in being. Of brick and Portland stone, Wren's new building was designed in the classic Renaissance style, and the gardens were replanned in the formal French idiom to accompany it, with some Dutch influence added by the Sovereigns. Dutch gardens were divided into small sections by hedges and little canals; large trees were uncommon in Holland; and a revised version of the medieval enclosed garden was made with grilles and thin trelliswork to give a see-through effect of greater spaciousness.

The *clairvoyée* consisting of brick piers with ornamental grilles between them was a device allowing the stroller to obtain distant views. The Tijou screens at Hampton Court, twelve panels originally made for the Fountain Court, were used for that purpose. The grotto was a Dutch introduction of this period, although it was not to become the rage in England until the eighteenth century. Trelliswork, topiary, low shrubs and orange trees, all popular in Holland, multiplied at Hampton Court in the new reign, and bulbs of tulip and hyacinth were freely imported, together with 'urnes and vauzes' (often made of lead) to plant them in.

According to Defoe, William and Mary 'had both so good a judgement in the just proportion of things which are the principal beauties of a garden, that it may be said they both ordered every thing that was done'. The Queen had a sound knowledge of plants, and loved the 'innocent diversion of gardenage'. She was aware that her great fondness for rare plants 'drew an expense after it'; but it was her sole extravagance, and provided employment for many people, so she hoped it would be forgiven her. That great gardener and botanist, Bishop Compton, had been her tutor, and may have inspired her love of plants. She had her collection of 'exoticks' kept in three 'stoves', or hot-houses, each over fifty feet long, heated by means of furnace and flues. Collectors were sent to distant parts of the world to gather plants for this genial and talkative queen—the first in England to play an active part in horticulture.

Soon the western end of the canal cut for Charles II was filled in to make space for the Great Fountain Garden against Wren's new East Front. During the years 1689–1702 many features now familiar to Londoners took shape, including the Broad and Long Walks and the present Maze. The superintendent, George London, a pupil of Rose, who succeeded the latter as Royal Gardener, had worked for Bishop Compton in his famous gardens at Fulham Palace; he was associated with Henry Wise, and during the last reign these men had founded well-known nursery gardens at Brompton. The great semi-circular parterre of the Fountain Garden at Hampton Court was laid out in scroll-work outlined in dwarf box; these curvaceous designs were very much freer in flow than the stiff geometrical intricacies of Tudor 'knottes'. The new scroll-work was mostly filled in with powdered stone in ochre, terra-cotta and grey-blue. Flowers were little used to provide colour in the patterns; but foliage of yew and box was sculpted into formal pyramid and ball shapes to punctuate the scrolls.

Although oranges had been grown in England very much earlier, the orange tree became a more important feature of the Hampton gardens during the Orange reign, as might be expected. They were cultivated in tubs and stored away in winter under the State Apartments on the south front, and in the cloisters of Wren's quadrangle, to be moved out on the terrace when summer came round. After the early death of Queen Mary—she died of small-pox at the age of thirty-three in 1694—the bereaved king suspended work on the improvements at Hampton Court. War with France continued until the Treaty of 1697, and soon afterwards George London went to visit Versailles to see the work of Le Notre.

In 1698 the Palace of Whitehall was destroyed by fire, with the exception of the Banqueting Hall, out of whose window Charles I stepped to go to his execution. King William, who had never cared for Whitehall—London did not suit his asthma—decided, instead of rebuilding the ruins, to go on with the work already begun at Hampton Court. Sir Christopher Wren was instructed to supply estimates for 'fitting the Inside of the Rooms of State', and with this he proceeded at once. The gardens also had additions. The semi-circular Great Fountain Garden was altered to an arc with wings to the north and south, running parallel to the new East Front of the Palace. There are extant interesting contemporary accounts of the removal and replanting of 403 'large Lyme Trees', a feat of transplanting but recently mastered by English gardeners. All the new beds were given borders of box.

The old water gallery in the Privy Garden was destroyed to give a better view of the Thames from the new apartments, and Henry VIII's Mount removed for the same reason. At that time Tudor relics were regarded as so much clutter; they received none of the veneration for ancient structures which has developed in our century. Shrubs and trees from the Privy Garden were transferred to the 'Wilderness' being made on the site of Henry's orchards, and on the cleared space a sunk garden was made in the centre, with raised terracing at the sides and a flight of steps down from the south front of the Palace. The old Pond

Garden was divided into small hedged enclosures in Dutch fashion, where tender plants found shelter.

An elaborate construction in the 'Wilderness'—whose wildness was extremely formal—consisted of ambitious fortifications cut in yew and holly and named 'Troy Town'. A rock garden now occupies the ground. Dutch William had no use for the tiltyard, which was turned into kitchen gardens; the Maze we know was in all probability set by London and Wise at about the same time, together with the Broad and Long Walks. In addition to all this work inside the gardens, the king had a mile-long drive laid out in Bushey Park, lined with chestnut and lime. A large pond was constructed to take the statue of Diana from the Privy Garden, and is still to be seen there.

Had peace lasted longer, this imposing avenue would have been extended through the Wilderness and across the moat to a new entrance, which had been planned for another court, to be built on the old Melon Ground. This must have involved further destruction of the Tudor Palace and its Chapel. Conflict with France broke out again in 1701, and butchery of Hampton Court had to cease: one of the few material and artistic benefits conferred by armed conflict, albeit indirectly. The following year William's horse stumbled at a molehill while he rode in the park at Hampton Court, throwing him, and from the effects of that fall he died two weeks later in Kensington Palace.

His sister-in-law Anne succeeded to the throne, and once more a queen reigned over Britain. She shared Queen Mary's fondness for gardening, but not that lady's liking for box, whose smell she detested so much that orders were given for all the royal gardens to be rid of the shrub. It is known that the new queen did not favour George London, and shifted patronage to his partner, Henry Wise. It is interesting to speculate on whether they might have fallen out over the wholesale destruction of box. This unspectacular plant tends to arouse emotion. People are usually either box-lovers or box-haters; it seldom produces indifference. The wood is so dense and heavy that it will sink in water, and the botanical name, *Buxus*, is derived from the Greek *puknos*, which means dense. Boxes of this wood were called *pyxides*, and from that word the boxwood casket containing the Host became known to the Roman Catholic church as 'pyx', a word retained long after precious metals were used instead of boxwood.

That nostalgic faded smell is compounded of many memories: the whiff of dried rose petals lying forgotten in box or drawer, to provide sudden wealth for the nose of one who unthinkingly opens the receptacle; the comfortable scent of old leather-bound books on a library shelf, drowsing in afternoon sunlight while flies buzz against the window-panes; the mature fruitiness of apples still lying on trays in the loft long after Christmas; the reek of dead bracken trodden underfoot on a damp autumn day. This curious smell of box not only contains within itself a number of such scents, but the compound has power to evoke scenes of childhood and youth—often forgotten for decades—in the minds of all who met it in gardens long ago.

For me it is the essence of an old, walled rectory garden in a village on Salisbury Plain, where a large white-bearded bear of a man dressed up obediently in his canonicals at the behest of a tiny great-niece; of another English country garden where erudite and charming middle-aged cousins, a trio, entertained my adolescent self with croquet, laughter, and conversational brilliance; it recalls, too, a great marble villa in Italy overlooking the Gulf of Spezia, with box-edged walks descending, sun-baked, to the cool blue sea below. To Oliver Wendell Holmes it was 'one of the odours that carry us out of time into the abysses of the unbeginning past; if ever we lived on another ball of stone than this, it must be that there was box growing on it' (*Elsie Verner* (1861)).

Yet Queen Anne hated the smell of box. Poor Queen Anne. She suffered from chronic arthritis, and perhaps the incessant crippling pain caused the desire for a scapegoat, and she vented her spleen on the thousands of harmless box bushes in her gardens at Hampton Court and Kensington Palace. Having disposed of them, she ordered large quantities of turf and gravel instead. The English lawn and the accompanying gravel path came into their own, and are with us yet. Work already in progress at the King's death seems to have been finished, but payments were delayed. A long list of creditors complained bitterly about royal tardiness in settling accounts, among them Jean Tijou who made the ornamental ironwork.

Although Anne took more interest in Windsor and Kensington than in Hampton Court, she enjoyed days of hunting there. She also took the expensive new beverage, tea (pronounced 'tay') in one of the little pavilions, or in the Banqueting House beside the Thames. Alexander Pope wrote:

Here Thou, great Anna! whom three realms obey,
Dost sometimes Counsel take—and sometimes Tea.

As the imported drinks—tea, coffee, chocolate—became better known and cheaper to buy, the old English herbal infusions went out of fashion, except among the poorer countryfolk. Trade with the East reduced the importance of native herb gardens, at least those attached to great houses; but at the same time the supplies of sugar now coming into the country encouraged the consumption of more fruit in pies and puddings, so that as herbs declined orchards increased.

In 1713 Queen Anne had some 'chaise-ridings' made in the park at Hampton. She ordered that holes were to be filled in, drainage channels dug, and grass seed sown to make level, safe ways, down which she careered in a one-horse chaise at considerable speed. During these last months of her life she had the 'great Diana Fountain' repaired under the supervision of Sir Christopher Wren and re-erected in the Bushey Park basin, at a cost of precisely £1,300 14s. 11¼d. She also had a large evergreen hedge made to the north of the Wilderness; there are stone pillars in it bearing her initials A.R., topped by lions, probably erected earlier. The low iron gates belong to the reign of George I and bear his cypher. The planting of a hedge at this point shows that the idea of making a north entrance through the Wilderness had been abandoned. Anne died on 1 August 1714, and the Hanoverian George became king.

George I approved of Hampton Court, where he could live more or less discreetly with his two German mistresses, who seem to have been chosen for their unattractive looks. Madame Schulenberg was soon nicknamed The Maypole for her tall, skinny figure, while the immensely stout Madame Kilmansegg pricked sharp Cockney wits into dubbing her The Elephant and Castle, after a famous London public house. The name Frog Walk for a path running beneath the Tiltyard wall is thought to have been a corruption of Frau Walk, for there the two ugly mistresses used to take the air.

This foreign king who could not speak the language of his subjects was not beloved; yet when James Edward Stuart (the 'Old Pretender') made a bid for the Throne, he gained almost no support—except in Scotland. England preferred to remain safely Protestant under the alien Hanoverian regime. Like his predecessors, George I habitually travelled from London in a state barge on the Thames to Hampton Court, accompanied by a band of musicians. Handel's 'Water Music' was first heard at a river party given for the monarch, who, whatever his failings, appreciated good music.

His son George, Prince of Wales, married the intelligent and ambitious Caroline of Anspach, and the pair made a bid for popularity by trying to become as English as possible, surrounded by a bevy of attractive English maidens and ladies of the Court. In place of his father's pair of German mistresses, the Prince had only one, so far as is recorded, and she the English Mrs Howard—later to become Countess of Suffolk. Pope described her as 'a reasonable woman, handsome, wise and witty, yet a friend', and she kept an honoured place at Court, liked by women as well as by men, for many years. Although there was considerable licence and a great deal of gambling, life at Hampton Court was far more circumspect than in the reign of Charles II. When the king returned from a five-month visit to Germany he was not pleased with the situation, and ill-feeling between father and son, possibly due to jealousy on the part of George I, put a blight on everything. After a time the Courts separated, with the king at Hampton Court and the prince at Richmond. Soon Hampton Court was more or less deserted for some years, and no major changes were made in the palace or gardens.

George II ascended the Throne in 1727, and for the next decade spent part of each summer at Hampton. This monarch frequently joined in stag hunts, but disapproved of hunting the fox; he considered the animal to be better than many of those who pursued it. The use of deer carcases for human food put the stag hunt into a different category, in his view. Once again many affairs of State were conducted at the palace, and the great Sir Robert Walpole was a constant visitor. He practically ruled England at this time, and the now respectably established title of 'Prime Minister' began as a jibe directed at him for taking precedence of other members of the Cabinet.

The astute Queen Caroline made her influence felt, both in the government of the country and in the development of various royal residences and their gardens. At Hampton Court the ferment of new ideas in gardening, coming from the continent and loosely known as the 'back to nature movement', had a weaker impact than elsewhere; it nibbled at the edges of the old formality but did not entirely supersede it. William Kent did not, perhaps could not, turn the place into an English Landscape Park, but contented himself with destroying the scroll work in the Fountain Garden and replacing it with lawns. He also removed all except the central fountain. The meandering curved line, fashionable in the new attempts to echo natural terrain by artificial means in gardens, had no effect on the canal water and walks of Hampton Court, which remain uncompromisingly straight to this day. Because these gardens are fundamentally based on Tudor and Stuart symmetry, it is now considered by many critics that Kent's attempts to impose references, however small, to the 'natural' fashion of his period were far from beneficial. Reinstatement of the animated scroll patterns and the battery of sparkling fountains in the Great Fountain Garden would delight visitors, for this section is decidedly dull at present; even its main lines are obscured by unwieldy evergreens. This, above all others, is a site that cries out for a skilled reproduction of Stuart gardening—which should be well within the scope of today's horticultural experts.

Frederick, Prince of Wales, did not get on with George II any better than the latter had done with *his* father. At the birth of Frederick's daughter there were unseemly scuffles. The king and queen ordered the Princess Augusta to remain at Hampton Court under surveillance, as they suspected imposture. When the time of delivery drew near, Frederick had the princess smuggled out of the palace at night, while his parents were at cards, and took her to London. After the baby's birth a messenger was sent down to Hampton Court in the small hours; the news was received by the king in a violent rage.

After the death of Queen Caroline George II seldom took his court to the palace, although he would spend occasional days there in summer, walking in the gardens with his current mistress, Lady Yarmouth. The legend that on one of these visits he boxed the ears of his grandson, the future George III, is said to have accounted for the latter's aversion to the place. During the late Georgian period, when it was little used by royalty, Hampton Court became more and more of a show place for special visitors—although not open to the general public until the reign of Victoria.

For local residents there was trouble over rights of way in Bushey Park. A path closed by Charles II and reopened by Cromwell became the subject of controversy when the Keeper and Ranger closed it to all except privileged ticket-holders. It fell to a shoemaker named Timothy Bennett—a man in his seventies—to lead a protest movement and finally appeal to the Law, which, in 1752, brought success. The right of way was once again free for all, and has remained open ever since. This happy event occurred shortly after Frederick died, leaving the youthful George as heir to the throne, which he occupied at the death of his ear-bashing grandfather in 1760.

Now England had a truly English monarch again, and there was much rejoicing at the accession of George III. But this domestically decorous monarch never occupied Hampton Court, and little by little the state apartments were cleared of pictures, furniture and other treasures, which were distributed among other royal residences; while the bulk of the palace was divided up into 'grace and favour' suites for people connected with court circles, or eminent individuals who had given signal service to the nation in one way or another. Samuel Johnson in 1776 applied for apartments in the palace, but was refused on the grounds that a long waiting-list already existed.

By then the famous landscape gardener known as 'Capability' Brown had been given oversight of the grounds, in succession to William Kent. Fortunately, he declined to make any significant changes. The only major contribution made in this period was the planting in 1768 of the Great Vine, which is still alive and bearing crops. After more than two centuries of close association with the monarchy and the deliberations, intrigues and scandals which are now history, Hampton Court went into a kind of retirement. The disastrous attempts of George III and Lord North to coerce our colonists in North America were not planned in the royal apartments or gardens, which gradually turned into a placid home for the elderly and the dispossessed.

In the 1780s the King's sister-in-law, Maria, Duchess of Gloucester, lived at the palace with her three lovely daughters, and in 1795, Prince William III of Orange, in flight from republican French troops then invading his own country, was given apartments. It is sometimes said that Frog Walk was not a corruption of 'Frau Walk' but of 'Vrow Walk', derived from the Dutch ladies who frequented it at this time. When the blind and mentally-afflicted king died in 1820, his son George IV had been regent for nearly a decade. He did nothing to revive the former glories of Hampton Court, preferring the mock-oriental garishness of the Pavilion at Brighton.

The gardens of Hampton Court still received many distinguished visitors, notably writers, among them Tom Moore and Sir Walter Scott. Scott's dislike of landscape gardening was succinctly expressed; he described it as 'affectation labouring to be simple'. He would have appreciated the honest formality which had in so large a measure survived at Hampton. Tom Moore wrote of 'gay walks', presumably referring to floral colour; for by now flowers were growing fashionable once more after a decline in popularity during the 'natural' landscape era.

The Duke of Wellington, whose victory at Waterloo in 1815 had made him a national idol, frequently visited Hampton Court, where his mother had occupied a suite since 1795. A seat in the sun, much used by the various old ladies in residence for gossip sessions, he named 'Purr Corner'. Although the next sovereign, the sea-minded William IV, had held office as Ranger of Bushey Park before his accession, he did not inhabit the palace or take much interest in it. One year after the youthful Queen Victoria came to the throne in 1837, she threw Hampton Court open to the public—with which startling innovation this chapter began.

When I visited the gardens of Hampton Court in 1971, they were well-kept and gay with flowers, but some of the plantings seemed a trifle uninspired. The seventeenth-century Sunk Garden had well-clipped yew inside the wall, and patterns neatly defined in box, but within the outlines some large masses of bedding begonias in red and pink gave the visitor a surfeit of monotonous colour and form; while the Pond Garden, although the plants were more varied, combined the rather overbearing gold and bronze tagetes with dahlias in reds and pinks, in a splurge of hot colour uncomfortably reminiscent of cinema carpeting, redeemed in places by charming groups of tobacco plant and cherry pie. The reproduction Knot Garden, with its good outer hedge of box, and smaller box, santolina and dwarf lavender clipped into fine outlines and interlacings, came down in my estimation because of the modern and rather banal annual plants—lobelia, alyssum, bedding begonia—filling in the design.

In the Vine House the great Black Hamburg grape (planted in 1768) had once again produced a good crop. The Maze was attracting the usual crowd of daring explorers; but at the far end of this part of the grounds it seemed a pity that the very fine arched Laburnum Walk should lead only to a dingy 'Ladies' Toilet'. Few people were attracted to pass through it unless in search of that convenience, and then were seldom in the mood to loiter and admire these well-grown and beautifully trained trees. The herbaceous borders at either side of the east front of the palace would, if in one length, far outdo in size any known to me in Britain. Divided as they are by the palace, they still take a high place. The border from the Water Gallery to the south-east corner of the building measures 880 feet, and the length of that part which stretches from the north-east corner to Flower Pot Gate is 1,050 feet. This deserves the championship in regard to length, but as the width is considerably less than that of the Buckingham Palace border, there is not a great deal of difference in area. Only in palace gardens are old-fashioned herbaceous borders of huge size likely to survive into the twenty-first century.

Nonsuch: the lost Tudor Palace

KING HENRY VIII was never short of house-room. The map* shows that he already had no fewer than twenty-one palaces in and around London when, in his arrogant later years, he began the building of Nonsuch with the aim of outshining his rival, Francis I of France. The name 'Nonsuch' means unique, nonpareil, like nothing else on earth; to judge by contemporary accounts the new palace lived up to it. Camden wrote: 'Here Henry VIII, in his magnificence, erected a structure so beautiful, so elegant, and so splendid, that in whatever direction the admirer of florid architecture turns his eyes, he will say that it easily bears off the prize . . . A king who spares no expense, so that the ingenuity of his artists may exhibit such wonders, which ravish the minds and the gaze of mankind by their magnificence . . .'

Allowing for the unctuous flattery which surrounded the monarch (a tax paid by those who wished to gain or retain the king's favour), the superlatives lavished by all comers on this palace suggest that it really did make what today would be called an impact. The adjective 'florid', used admiringly by Camden, would now savour of denigration; but florid it certainly was, and as such suited to the Tudor taste. Its onion-shaped domes, its cupolas and towers rose above a glittering façade of white and gilded stucco, and innumerable statues and bas-reliefs ornamented this fairy-tale castle, to burst with astonishing panache upon the eyes of travellers in the unspectacular Surrey landscape. To one born early in this century amid those over-domesticated slopes, the word 'Nonsuch' savoured of dream or legend. It was hard to believe that such a palace ever existed there. Yet even then the proofs were sound enough, and in recent times excavations have brought more solid evidence in the shape of carvings and other relics from the vanished building. 'A distinctly improbable object to find in Surrey,' as one modern writer has said.

The later Victorians had Lewis Carroll's *Wonderland* for an escape route from humdrum days; in the present century a large part of the civilized world seized on Walt Disney's American film fantasies for the same release; in the

* At the London Museum.

early sixteenth century humble folk dreamed their dreams among the much talked of splendours of court life, which came to a peak in the building of Nonsuch Palace. The analogy with Carroll and Disney extended to the gardens, for there—among bushes, groves of trees, orchards, maze and 'wilderness'—was an ark-load of creatures, all cunningly disposed in their carved poses to trick the unsuspecting visitors into taking them 'for real'. The Disneyland created by Henry VIII lacked only the pixies and gnomes which now, alas, are explosively populating the small gardens of Britain.

The palace, begun in April 1538, was based on the collegiate plan of two-storey buildings ranged round inter-connecting open-air courts. It was not, relatively speaking, very large; being less than 150 yards long, it would have fitted into a modern football field. We do not know the precise circumstances in which Henry chose his site, but it is certain that, once he had decided to build there, nothing was allowed to stand in his way. The Lord of the Manor, Richard Codington, and his wife Elizabeth were obliged to exchange their seat for the Manor of Ixworth in Suffolk—where in the church their memorials may still be seen. In those days of slow travel it must have seemed like banishment to a foreign land, and East Anglia a cold and windy place after the snug corner near Ewell. But they had no choice.

The king at once set to work on clearance of his site, ordering the village church of Cuddington, the manor and village to be razed to the ground. Having dissolved the near-by Priory of Merton, he had the monastic buildings and chapel demolished and the stone carted away to form foundations for the new palace. His inner court was constructed upon ancient graves which had formerly lain beneath the little church of Cuddington, for the monarch was not squeamish. Modern excavation has disclosed details of this plan, showing Henry's sewers driven through the burials and the foundations of the old church. Footings of the west wall of the church tower were incorporated into the palace, and a fountain played where the chancel once stood.

After the village and manor house had been destroyed, nearly 2,000 acres of agricultural land were stocked with deer and turned into a royal chase. The manor and rectory survived only on paper, and in that guise came eventually to the Earl of Arundel's son-in-law, John, Lord Lumley. Cuddington, like its supplanter, must also have been without parallel in its own way, for it had become a manor without a village, a rectory without a church, and a parish (nominally four miles long and a mile wide) of which most lay within the upstart 'parish and manor' of Nonsuch. The sole visible sign now of the great palace is a grassy mound in a park open to the public, and an overgrown chalk pit half a mile away where blocks for the foundations were dug.

Of Henry's 2,000 acres, only 263 survive as an open space, the rest having been built over. Local Authorities in 1937 preserved the remnants of Henry's deer park, together with a nineteenth-century mansion designed by Wyatt, and the site of the palace. The excavations of Nonsuch were carried out in 1959–60, and the diggings afterwards filled in. Of the palace gardens no trace is to be seen. The whole extraordinary concept has to be reconstructed in the mind's eye from contemporary writings: an exercise all the more worth while because we have 'on the ground' nothing like it anywhere in our time.

The rector of the neighbouring parish of Cheam, Dr Anthony Watson, wrote in lush terms of the project at its inception: 'Oh Gods, what Labour, what workmen, what axes, what crowbars, what artists and what sums of money were needed for so great a task . . .' In the midst of all the superlatives it is amusing to come down to earth in a way familiar to most commissioners of new buildings today. In spite of Henry's immense power and prestige, records show that he could not always get workmen to carry out their allotted tasks to schedule. Even when employed by this omnipotent sovereign, builders and craftsmen came and went and occasionally absented themselves for weeks, just as some do now. The king wrote to his Privy Council complaining about the absenteeism of a plasterer named Giles Gering: 'We may, as occasion shall rise, charge both him and others. He is a fellow that glorieth much in himself and his doings.' There is no record of Gering having been charged; probably he could not be dispensed with, and traded upon the knowledge—a principle very much in favour with strikers in our own time. The concourse of more than five hundred workmen camped in tents around the new palace included masons, plasterers, sculptors and artists imported from the Continent. But only the inner court had been fully completed when Henry died in 1547, having spent over £24,000 on his show-piece.

The exterior of the palace was described by Thomas Platter, in his *Travels in England, 1599*, as being built 'entirely of great blocks of white stone on which are represented numerous Roman and other ancient stories . . .' One recalls the chalk-pit, assuming that the stone had been cut there. But Platter was mistaken. The material used was not white stone. The frontage had been decorated with panels of some specially hard plaster, or a type of cement, called *stucco-duro*, two inches thick and moulded into decorative legendary figures and beasts. At least 900 feet of walling were so embellished, the designs being derived from stucco work in the *Galerie Francois Ier* at Fontainebleau. There were also panels of carved slate, similar in style to the French woodcarvings at the same palace, fixed in frames round about the panels of moulded plaster, and hung on the main timbers—probably as a measure of protection against the weather. Fragments of this carved slate which have been taken from the excavations are an inch thick and deeply carved, with edges like the mouldings of picture frames. Many of them were gilded. The great glittering corner towers of the palace were almost certainly of Italian design, for the notebooks of Leonardo da Vinci contain drawings of similar form.

The whole effect must have resembled one of those magnificent wedding-cakes made for great occasions; an edifice in white and gold: fantastic, sparkling, but hardly substantial enough for habitation. There is a story of Queen Elizabeth I, who owned Nonsuch at a later date, and frequently visited it on journeys via Tooting and Beddington to engage in her favourite diversion of the chase. One evening in the last year of her reign, as she returned from a hunt on Banstead Downs, she was completely bemused by the reflection of a fiery sunset in the façade of Nonsuch Palace into thinking that it had caught fire. When this very human mistake was made known to her, it so galled the ageing queen that she left in an ill-humour for Richmond, where she died on 24 March 1603.

Immediately after the death of Henry VIII the work on Nonsuch was halted for a while. His daughter Mary did not care for the place, and at one time she planned to have the edifice destroyed as an economy measure. The Earl of Arundel saved it by persuading her to exchange it for some lands of his in Suffolk, and he then proceeded to complete the palace and laying-out of the gardens. Much of the design appears to have been Italian in style, although the construction and planting was no doubt carried out by the numerous French gardeners who are known to have been employed at Nonsuch by both Henry VIII and Arundel. Precise dates for the various sections are not available; but it is thought that later writers who described them were dealing with the matured results of landscaping and planting done in the king's time with certain additions by Arundel and his heir, Lord Lumley. The gardens, orchard and wilderness must have belonged to the original scheme—intended to connect the palace with the banqueting house, which was sited some 300 yards to the west.

Anthony Watson wrote of the Palace precincts, looking out in one direction on the courtyard and in the other on the maze and the fragrant garden:

> 'Leaving the garden, we enter the Wilderness, which is in fact neither wild nor deserted. The land, which is naturally somewhat hilly and plenti-

> fully watered, is set out with lofty and magnificent tree-lined walks to the South and West. At the end of the path to the South, the trees have been trimmed to form canopies. Through the heart of the Wilderness there are three paths, the middle one worn and sandy, and the others turfed. There are trees for shade and for fruit: almost countless young apple trees, shrubs, evergreens, ferns, vines. To the North is a widespreading circular Plane tree, its branches supported on posts, so that many people can sit beneath it, talking, listening to the calls of animals and birds, or gazing at the wire-fenced aviary. An ancient Oak shows the way straight into the shady grove of Diana, where there are places arched over by the skill of topiary, walls and sandy walks.'

Evidently some of the old Cuddington trees were retained in the new gardens. Watson goes on to mention hidden watercourses in wilderness and groves which 'break out gently in a neighbouring valley. Here there is a pond with shoals of trout'.

In Camden's *Britannia*, issued in 1586 and translated from Latin to English by Holland in 1610, there is a flowery description:

> 'As for the very house it selfe, so environed it is about with Parkes full of Deare, such dainty gardens and delicate orchards it hath, such groves adorned with curious Arbors, so pretty quarters, beds and Alleys, such Walkes so shadowed with trees, that Amenitie or Pleasantnesse it selfe may seem to have chosen no other place but it where she might dwell together with Healthfulnesse.'

Paul Hentzner, a German who visited Nonsuch in 1598, refers to the fountains:

> 'In the pleasure gardens are many columns and pyramids of marble, two fountains that spout water one round the other like a pyramid, upon which are perched small birds that stream water out of their bills. In the Grove of Diana is a very agreeable fountain, with Actaeon turned into a stag, as he was sprinkled by the goddess and her nymphs. There is besides another pyramid of marble full of concealed pipes, which spout upon all who come within their reach.'

Thomas Platter, a Swiss who travelled in England in 1599, described a day at the court of Queen Elizabeth at Nonsuch, with references to the gardens:

> 'We next entered an arbour or pavilion where the Queen sits during the chase in the park. Here she can see the game run past. Then through a wood in the gardens with fine straight long alleys through it. In the very densest part of the wood about here a great many trees are uprooted and cleared, within a breadth of some 18 or 20 feet, along a straight course, so that there is a vista from one end to the other. And here and there they are partitioned off on either side with high boards, so that the balls may be played in the shade of these same alleys very pleasantly, as in an enclosed tennis court, and other amusing pastimes may also be pursued, while the delicious song of the birds in the tall trees, densely planted along the sides in ordered array, afford one great delight. From here we came to a maze or labyrinth surrounded by high shrubberies to prevent one passing over or through them. In the pleasure gardens are charming terraces and all kinds of animals—dogs, hares, all overgrown with plants, most artfully set out so that from a distance one would take them for real ones.'

In all covering about sixteen acres, the gardens of Nonsuch contained a privy garden, kitchen garden, Grove of Diana, orchard, wilderness and plot on which the banqueting house stood. They lay mostly to the west of the palace, towards Ewell; but the kitchen garden was on the east of the kitchens, inside a fourteen foot brick wall, which extended to enclose the privy garden too. Between this and the south front of the palace the ground measured about two hundred feet. There were three mounds: the central was crowned by a fountain with a nymph whose breasts were water-spouts, and the outer pair had falcon perches on them. The knot gardens were described by Watson as having 'plants and shrubs mingled in intricate circles as though by the needle of Semiramis!' He refers to those realistic animals: 'Deer, hares, rabbits, and dogs gave chase with unhindered feet and effortlessly paced over the green!' Unfortunately he does not say how they were made; but rabbits and hares would be very difficult to shape of natural size and realistically in topiary, so it may safely be assumed that they were carvings in stone, marble, or some other permanent material.

When Queen Elizabeth came to the throne the Earl of Arundel made a bid for her hand. Middle-aged, already twice married and with married daughters, unattractive and not of very high rank, he had little chance and was soon rejected; but not before he had entertained the queen lavishly at Nonsuch and won favour for his palace. While he was away recovering from disappointment (and gout) at an Italian spa, she took herself to Nonsuch for another stay, and in 1592 bought it back from the impecunious Lord Lumley, who by that time had inherited it from his father-in-law.

During the last ten years of her reign she spent much time at Nonsuch, enjoying masques, games and private dances with the inner circle of her friends. There is a tradition that she used the Grove of Diana for bathing, and the hedge of 'Lelack' (Lilac) surrounding the pool provided a screen to foil prying eyes. Lilac, then new to British gardens, was described as a 'tree that bears no fruit but only a verie pleasant flower'. A very tough flower too, as I saw in the foot-hills of the Canadian Rocky Mountains. In May, the half-open blossom became coated with frozen rain, so that each spray looked like a Victorian wax posy under a glass dome. Thinking that this would ruin the bloom, we were astonished to find it unharmed and making a fine display less than a week afterwards. Such a phenomenon would not have been observed by Elizabeth in the mild climate of Surrey.

Her successor, King James I of England, called Nonsuch a 'lavish place of nonsense'. His guid Scots commonsense was outraged by such display. This did not prevent him from making use of the park for hunting, together with the short-lived Prince Henry. The palace was assigned to his queen, Anne of Denmark. Charles I, who had extensive repairs done at Nonsuch, also made it over to his queen—Henrietta Maria, as part of her jointure.

In the Civil War, the palace was stripped of its furnishings, and after the king's execution, a Parliamentary Commission made a survey of the building and grounds, valuing the estate at £14,158 12s. 0d. Soon it was purchased by Major-General John Lambert of 'Wimbleton', who had played a leading part in the victories of Dunbar and Worcester. He became a member of the Army Council of officers, but lost favour by opposing Cromwell's bid to assume the title of king. After this episode Lambert retired to his Manor of Wimbledon and to Nonsuch, where he pursued the craft of gardening and became famous for his tulips. The palace reverted to Charles II at his restoration; by chance he returned to this country with a naval escort, which included the frigate named *Nonsuch*. She had been built at Deptford in 1646 by shipbuilders called Pett, one of whom had been Prince Henry's friend.

Although the new monarch liked display and gaiety, he made little use of Nonsuch, which never regained its former splendour. It served, oddly enough, as a repository for the Exchequer monies during the Great Plague, and was visited by both Evelyn and Pepys at that time. On 21 September 1665 Pepys went by coach with £100 to pay fees at the Exchequer at Nonsuch, and 'rode in some fear of robbing'. His diary records how he 'walked up and down the house and park; and a fine place it hath heretofore been, and a fine prospect about the house. A great walk of an elme and a walnutt set one after another in order . . .' He walked also 'in the ruined garden'. Two months later he went again to Nonsuch, and in the November weather, riding horseback, he 'found the ways very bad, and the weather worse, for wind and rain'.

Perhaps the bad roads had something to do with the next owner's lack of interest in the place. Charles II gave Nonsuch to his notorious mistress, Lady Castlemaine, creating her Baroness Nonsuch at the same time. Even that compliment did not attach her to the place, which she left to crumble away, and eventually sold for demolition. The cloud-capp'd towers of this fantastic palace faded like an insubstantial pageant; yet a few remnants were left hidden under the encroaching soil. Fragments of Henry VIII's nonpareil were retrieved during excavations in 1959–60, and put on exhibition at the London Museum in Kensington Palace during 1970.

An inscription dated 1761 in Melrose Abbey fits the picture:

The earth goeth on the earth
glist'ring like gold
The earth goeth to the earth
sooner than it wold
The earth builds on the earth
castles and towers
The earth says to the earth
all shall be ours.

Kensington Palace

UNTIL Dutch William came to London and found the dampness and fogs at St James's Palace unsuited to his chronic asthma, this house in the park at Kensington was known as Nottingham House and belonged to the earl of that name. William and Mary were quite content to remain at Hampton Court, but in response to critical remarks—it was thought to be too far from the capital—they looked round for something closer to Westminster, and purchased Nottingham House for 18,000 guineas. In 1689 Sir Christopher Wren obtained a commission to enlarge and improve the building for royal occupation as speedily as possible. Perhaps the workmen put more speed than skill into the project, for one of the new apartments promptly fell flat, killing some labourers, just after the queen had passed through.

Kensington in those days was described as a pleasant village, far from the fogs besetting Whitehall; but, just because it lay out in the country, the access was unsafe. In the 1680s we read of muddy, unlit lanes molested by highwaymen at night—not at all suited to the comings and goings of royalty and courtiers. When Evelyn wrote on 25 February 1690 of visiting the newly enlarged Nottingham House, which he called a 'very sweet villa, having to it a park, and a straight new way through this park', he had just seen the new road from Hyde Park Corner, which was of a truly regal width, constructed to take three or four coaches abreast, with lanthorns placed at equal distances on either side of it. A contemporary considered the effect when all these lights were lit to be 'inconcevably magnificent'. Apparently the well-known landscape gardener, William Bridgeman, was responsible for this *Route de Roi* (Rotten Row), for his widow, in a petition to the Treasury for monies due after his death, cites a debt for 'making the Lamp Road in Hyde Park'.

Initially, conversion of the old four-square Jacobean house was made by adding pavilions at each of the corners, and putting a courtyard and entrance on the west side. There were no attempts at grandeur, and the building was known as Kensington House, not Palace. Later, improvements proceeded which were outside Wren's original scheme. In 1691 the queen's apartments at the north-west were extended—the Queen's Gallery with its own staircase being added, together with a separate block for the maids of honour. Then fire destroyed part of the southern range of the courtyard, and in the reconstruction a grand new staircase in marble, with an ornate Guard Chamber, was made for the king. Wren's last addition was the King's Gallery, built in 1695–96. In the meantime Evelyn's 'sweet villa' had turned into a palace. It had also been given some up-to-date conveniences, as an account for a 'forcing Engine, water Cisternes, a Stoole for ye Queene, for making a Seate and covering it with velvet' goes to prove.

The gardens, which no longer survive, covered twenty-six acres; in the years of William and Mary's joint reign nearly £11,000 was spent on them. From the start there must have been a pleasant enough garden, for at an earlier date Pepys had voted it 'a mighty fine cool place . . . with a great laver of water in the middle, and the bravest place for musique I ever heard'. Possibly the gardens attracted the royal eyes in the first place, for in between his political and military battles King William enjoyed 'Gardenage'. Stephen Switzer, well known for his horticultural writings at the time, wrote 'in the least interval of Ease, Gard'ning took up a great part of Time, in which he was not only a Delighter, but likewise a great Judge'. He was fortunate in having a queen equally interested and capable, so that in his absence on military campaigns she kept a shrewd eye on the improvements being made by the celebrated horticulturists London and Wise, who had founded their Brompton Nursery some years earlier. These 'Dutch' gardens were characteristically small, and cut up into compartments, with box hedges, clipped trees, topiary work, neat borders, symmetrical pools, fountains, a canal, and two labyrinths.

The delight taken by William and Mary in their gardens was short-lived, for in 1694 Mary died of smallpox at the age of thirty-three. Her end was quietly heroic. When she heard the terrible diagnosis she ordered everyone who had not had the disease to leave the palace, locked herself in her closet, and prepared for death. It was not long in coming. Afterwards William collapsed; he seldom stayed at Kensington in the ensuing years. The once-loved gardens were left to gardeners, and the more tender plants, such as orange-trees, lemon, and myrtle, were removed to the greenhouses of Messrs London and Wise at Brompton.

When Queen Anne, then thirty-seven, succeeded her brother-in-law in 1702, she made very few alterations to the buildings of Kensington Palace, but changed the gardens to a great extent. Her abhorrence of the smell of box—aggravated, perhaps, by dislike of the late king, whom she nicknamed 'Caliban'—led to the uprooting of all his Dutch hedging and topiary work. Henry Wise had the task of remaking the gardens, which were given a more English flavour at the queen's command. His partner, George London, had had much to do with the supply and planting of box 'Greens' to William and Mary; Wise uprooted them; the firm of London and Wise stood to benefit from the changing tastes of its royal customers.

Wise was paid £1,600 a year for 'keeping all her Majesty's gardens and Plantacons at Hampton Court, the Great Plantacons on the north side of the Castle at Windsor, Garden at the lodge in the Great Parke, Gardens and Plantacons at Kensington . . . and to find all things for keeping up the said Plantacons and Gardens'. Among other things he had to 'find dung and earth for hous'd plants, dung for the several gardens, provide houses and rowl the gardens, make good fruit and forest trees, flowering shrubs and hardy ever-greens *that shall at any time happen to dye, by planting others in their places*'. He also supplied wheelbarrows and all implements including 'a sort of engine to sprinkle the severall trees and plants'. Queen Anne desired to economize on the upkeep of her gardens. The Earl of Portland had formerly been receiving £57 an acre for the work annually; Wise was persuaded to undertake it for only £20 an acre. One of the earliest instructions received from the new monarch was to keep the Home Park at Hampton clear of moles, for upon a mole-hill William's horse had stumbled and thrown him, with fatal result. Unfortunately Anne, like some of her forbears, was extremely tardy in the matter of payment for services rendered to her.

In 1705, when Wise had nearly completed his remodelling of the Kensington Palace gardens, a writer named Bowack described them as 'beautified with all the Elegancies of Art . . . There's a noble collection of Forreign Plants, and fine neat Greens which make it pleasant all the year, and the Contrivance, Variety and Disposition of the whole is extream pleasing'. Although the box had been banished, together with an elaborate affair of topiary fortifications dear to William's military mind, there were still plenty of 'neat Greens'. The main difference seems to have lain in a less four-square lay-out; the lines were flowing and sections led from one to another with fewer compartments; but much of it was still highly formalized.

Anne soon reached out beyond the garden proper to enclose a hundred acres of Hyde Park as a deer paddock, and laid out some more ground up to what is now Bayswater Road. Bowack refers to 'near 30 Acres more towards the North, separated from the rest only by a stately Green House not yet Finish'd; upon this spot is near 100 men dayly at work'. The Green House, now called the Orangery, was designed by Hawksmoor and Vanbrugh, and is one of the greatest glories of the place. The queen used to tend her exotic plants within the shelter of this superb gardenhouse, used sometimes a a summer supper-room, and sometimes as a place in which to take tea amid the scented orange, lemon and myrtles. In recent years there has been talk of turning it into a public restaurant, but so far this has not been allowed. The grand and graceful building, now empty of plants, still provides peaceful seating where strollers may rest and shelter from wind and rain. It would be an affront to see it littered with cardboard coffee-cups and sweet wrappings, for which any modern kiosk may serve as well.

The gardens beyond were made in an old gravel-pit, and entered through gates adjoining the Orangery. Addison praised these in 1712:

> 'I shall take notice [in *The Spectator*] of that part in the upper garden, at Kensington, which was at first nothing but a gravel pit. It must have been a fine Genius for gardening, that could have thought of forming such an unsightly hollow into so beautiful an Area, and to have hit the eye with so uncommon and agreeable a scene as that which it is now wrought into . . . To give this particular Spot of Ground the greater Effect, they have made a very pleasing Contrast . . . for as on one Side of the Walk you see this hollow Basin, with its several little Plantations . . . on the other Side of it there appears a seeming Mount, made up of Trees rising one higher than another in Proportion as they approach the Center.'

Queen Anne was much attached to her Palace of Kensington, and spent a great deal of time there in arthritic seclusion—often companioned by her friends Sarah, Duchess of Marlborough and Mrs Abigail Masham. She died at Kensington in 1714. A few years after the accession of George I, vast alterations were planned by Vanbrugh; in the end these were greatly reduced in scale and grandeur. The many-sided genius William Kent was called in to carry out a number of mural paintings, to the satisfaction of the new monarch. Kent became famous for not only designing alterations to people's houses and gardens; he also changed fashions in furniture, silver, and even dress.

Under George II the palace remained much the same; but the gardens, keenly supervised by Queen Caroline, were once again given a new look—this time by Wise and the talented John Bridgeman, a protégé of Vanbrugh's who succeeded Wise as Royal Gardener in 1728. It was at Kensington that he made the first tentative experiments in the art of 'landscaping' which were later brought to fruition in Kensington Gardens and Hyde Park, with their long avenues of trees and curved ornamental water. He also replaced the old formal gardens on the south of the buildings with wide stretches of grass, where rank and fashion could promenade in what were regarded as 'natural' surroundings. This amenity was open to the public on Saturdays, while the court went elsewhere. The innovation was duly recorded in popular verse:

The dames of Britain oft in crowds repair
To gravel walks, and unpolluted air,
Here, while the Town in damp and darkness lies,
They breathe in sun-shine, and see azure skies.

Two hundred and fifty years ago people were already concerned with pollution: Their escape routes were then much shorter.

After Bridgeman had succeeded Wise, the layout of the Kensington Gardens we know today began to take shape. Wide stretches of grass, untrammelled by flower-beds, were very much in favour, and on this tide of acclaim an extensive area of 'landscaped' garden was made to the east of the palace. Here a large octagonal basin—first filled in 1728 and now known as the 'Round Pond'—was placed in the middle of a semicircular lawn edged with trees, from which immense avenues radiated. A series of insignificant pools to the east of this were thrown together to form the 'New River'—now the Serpentine. When these improvements were complete, in 1731, two yachts were kept on the New River for the diversion of royalty.

William Kent also took a hand in the garden adornment under Queen Caroline's eye. He designed the revolving summerhouse which was erected in 1733 on top of a mount in the south-east corner of the gardens, giving a bird's-eye view of the whole complex. Another of his summerhouses, known as the Queen's Temple, is now a park-keeper's lodge. Kent is believed to have laid out some intricate series of winding paths, similar to those he formed at Chiswick House in 1736; at Kensington they were in the space around the Basin and in the North Gardens. Seen from above it must have looked like a giant jig-saw puzzle.

George II was the last reigning monarch to inhabit the Palace, and after the death of Queen Caroline half the apartments were closed. George III preferred Buckingham House, and for the rest of the eighteenth century Kensington was allowed to fall into a state approaching decay, although the gardens were kept up to some extent, and the public admitted to them. The charming Orangery suffered badly, until in 1816 its pitiful state was noticed and some repairs presently effected. In 1902–3 it was again restored. By that time, no trace of Kent's circuitous paths survived, and the formal lay-out to the north had become utilitarian kitchen gardens. Gradually the barriers were taken down, and by 1861 most of the high walls had been replaced by iron railings. Kensington had become largely a public park. Few today realize that it was ever private.

At the beginning of the nineteenth century the palace was altered for use of members of the royal family, the most notable being Edward, Duke of Kent, who fathered Queen Victoria. He was allocated what had earlier been the king's private apartments, and wheedled the state into converting them to his requirements—a project designed by James Wyatt. This work, completed in 1812, survives to a great extent. The duke, driven abroad by importunate creditors, returned for the birth of his daughter, which took place in the north-east ground floor chamber on 24 May 1819. Later in William IV's reign, pictures were removed from the state apartments to Windsor, and the Duchess of Kent, now a widow, was able to extend her premises to the floor above. In 1836 the girlish Princess Victoria wrote with some excitement of the more spacious quarters now to be her own. 'One of these . . . is my sitting-room and it is *very* prettily furnished indeed.'

A year later she was awakened in one of those rooms with news of her accession, and on 20 June 1837 she held her first council in an ante-chamber on the ground floor of the palace. The young queen now owned Buckingham Palace, and on 13 July she took up residence. Her mother, the duchess, retained rooms in Kensington until her death in 1861. The same apartments were later occupied by the Duke and Duchess of Teck, and the future Queen Mary was born there in 1867.

During the later years of the nineteenth century the palace fabric suffered from rapid deterioration and there was talk of demolishing it. Queen Victoria, fired by affection for the home of her girlhood, was largely instrumental in leading Parliament to vote £36,000 for its repair. The advance was made conditional on the throwing open of state apartments to the public—an event which occurred, after completion of the work, on 24 May 1899, the queen's eightieth birthday. In 1912 the new London Museum occupied these apartments for a time and, following a spell at Lancaster House, returned to the Palace of Kensington, where it now is. The private quarters in the building are occupied by members of the royal family; Princess Margaret and her family have had a London home at the palace for a number of years.

Today's visitor will not see much in the way of gardens; but everyone is free to enter and admire the Orangery, still as it was in Queen Anne's day, except for the absence of exotic plants. Outside the doors, the original terrace of Portland stone is extant, and from the bottom of its steps an avenue leads southwards between large pyramids of bay and holly towards an arboured walk of pleached limes enclosing a formal garden. The sunken garden was laid out in the reign of Edward VII on land which used to carry greenhouses and potting sheds. It attempts to reproduce the type of design seen here before the eighteenth-century landscapists laid hands on the grounds. Three imposing lead fountains were originally used as cisterns inside the palace. Could these be some of the 'water Cisternes' installed for the convenience of William and Mary?

As I looked out from an east window on the upper floor of the palace in the autumn of 1970 at the wide stretches of grass in Kensington Gardens, with its avenues of trees centred around the children's boat pond; at the enclosed garden below, with its beds of roses still in bloom, clumps of pampas grass like Prince of Wales's feathers, chestnut trees in bronze leaf and a catalpa in gold; at the back of the crowned and sceptred Queen Victoria, sculpted by her daughter Princess Louise in white marble; at crooning pigeons and cheeping sparrows, the placid scene seemed to have very little to do with the twentieth century. High-rise buildings, dimly discerned through mist, looked as evanescent as clouds or pillars of smoke; and of traffic there was no sound.

The whole place reeked so strongly of past owners and events that the stream of people visiting the royal apartments and the London Museum appeared unreal as ghosts. Only those powerful invisible spirits were truly alive. Seen from the rear, the palace looks like a rambling country manor-house—an effect which served to impress upon my mind the difference between knowledge and belief. For, although many accounts of Kensington's rustic simplicity before the Industrial Revolution had been studied, this was the first occasion on which I had felt a personal belief in them. Here we may catch an authentic whiff of the very last fragment of rural atmosphere left in London.

Buckingham Palace

DURING the unsuccessful attempt of James I to develop the silk industry in England, he installed a large orchard of mulberries at the end of St James's Park, which afterwards became a tea-garden. It has already been mentioned that the king planted the wrong variety of *Morus—M. nigra* instead of the silk-worm's favourite diet, *M. alba.* The silkworms did not thrive. According to Eleanour Sinclair Rohde, there is evidence that the scholarly James knew all about white mulberries, and in fact ordered these, but for some reason the black mulberry was planted. Whether this was a genuine mistake on the part of suppliers in France, or a deep-laid plot to foil the making of silk in this country, nobody knows. It would be a good exercise for a budding Sherlock Holmes to track down and assemble such shreds of documentary evidence as remain extant.

Originally part of the old manor of Eia (recorded in Domesday Book), the forty-eight acres of land occupied by the present palace and its grounds include part of the unlucky mulberry orchard, and it has belonged at different times to the Abbots of Westminster and to Eton College, coming into possession of the Crown in 1531. Much of the ground was swampy when in 1640 Lord Goring leased twenty-seven acres of this 'King's Park' and built thereon his Goring House. His mansion did not survive for long; it was burnt down, and another mansion built on the site by the Earl of Arlington came to a similar end. John Sheffield, who in youth had been an ardent admirer of Queen Anne, was created Duke of Buckingham when she ascended the throne. He then obtained the land and built Buckingham House. Only the present royal family has omitted to name this phoenix after itself. Yet, had the suit of John Sheffield proved acceptable to Anne, Buckingham would have been a name allied to our monarchy. As it was, he progressed no further than being named 'King John' by the irreverent public. He consoled himself by building what was said to be the finest private palace near London, and wrote most poetically of his library in the garden-house, with 'a little wilderness of black birds and nightingales under the windows'.

George III bought Buckingham House in 1761 as a retreat for himself and the retiring Queen Charlotte from the oppressive ceremonial of St James's, calling it (by 1775) 'The Queen's House'. Here the monarch built up a large family of fifteen children, and a superb library. The latter, much used and applauded by the great Dr Johnson, went to the British Museum after the King's death. It is hard now to picture The Queen's House as a rural oasis surrounded by quiet meadows, with the gentle lowing of cows in place of traffic din; yet so it was described two centuries ago. At Christmas time the queen introduced her German custom of having a decorated tree indoors—the first Christmas tree ever seen in England. The many building operations carried out for this comfortably prolific royal family were rudely handled by critics. 'So many additions have been made on each side,' wrote one waspish pen, 'as to inspire the spectator with the idea of a country parsonage house to which every incumbent has added—one a wash-house, another a stable, another a hen-roost, etc., until the whole is made a mere jumble of patchwork.'

George IV, having already spent vast sums on the oriental splendours of Brighton Pavilion, managed to squeeze from Parliament a grant of £200,000 for the repair and improvement of Buckingham House. In fact he had it rebuilt within the shell by John Nash, and at the king's death in 1830 more than £600,000 had been spent on the project, still incomplete. In the end it was finished by another architect at a total cost of £719,000. A candid visitor from Germany considered all this a waste of money, saying that for his part he would not live in it rent free. William IV was not attracted by the place, and when Westminster Palace was destroyed by fire he went so far as to offer it to Parliament as a permanent substitute—a suggestion the government declined. The king then proposed that it should be used as a barracks for the Guards. When this came to nothing he moved in himself, after some delay caused by installation of the new gas lighting. Thomas Creevey, one of the many critics who have sharpened their wits on this unfortunate building (now dubbed 'Palace'), said that it should rather be called 'The Brunswick Hotel'. He wrote: 'The costly ornaments of the State rooms excell all belief in their bad taste . . . raspberry coloured pillars without end, that quite turn you sick to look at'.

Queen Victoria did not share in the general distaste, in spite of an atrocious plumbing system which discharged sewage on to the leads near her dressing room and occasionally spewed it up into the kitchens. Within three weeks of her accession she had moved in, to write appreciatively of the 'pleasant and cheerful rooms', while her spaniel enjoyed exercise in the gardens. In sprightly mood the young queen chose furniture and ordered a new throne, which was 'not to cost above £1,000'. She also had a hot water pipe installed for filling her moveable bath. Before long she decided to marry Prince Albert. Nobody knows what he thought of his new home.

As the royal family increased with the incessant births of children, accommodation proved inadequate and the queen wrote an urgent appeal to her Prime Minister about it. Peel procrastinated, and *Punch* published a cartoon of her begging for money to house husband and children. Finally Parliament voted funds for extension of the palace, with a proviso that Brighton Pavilion must be sold to raise part of the sum required. It was sold to the town of Brighton for £50,000, and Queen Victoria purchased Osborne House in the Isle of Wight instead, to serve as a summer retreat. Certain chimney-pieces from the Pavilion were taken for use at the palace. In the course of rebuilding a new east front appeared, and the Marble Arch which had been erected at the gates to commemorate the victories of Trafalgar and Waterloo was demoted to its present site at the junction of Park Lane and Oxford Street. The new wing incorporated in its façade the famous balcony where royalty has shown itself to the public ever since, on great occasions. The house used by George III and Charlotte as a rural refuge from the pomp of St James's had become a focal point of ceremonial, and still is: even such privacy as it possessed in the earlier years of the century now menaced by high-rise building in the vicinity.

The garden covers about thirty-nine acres, with the palace at its eastern end. It has always been of the 'natural' type, with some faint lingering flavour of the rural pastures from which it was made—land named on seventeenth-century maps as 'Mulberry Garden Field', 'Adam's Pasture', 'Upper and Lower Fields', 'Goring Great Garden', with smaller parcels between them. A large part of this fairly level area is now mown turf, with fine groups of trees, shrubberies, a winding artificial lake, a high shrub-covered mound, and the famous herbaceous border known to thousands of guests at summer garden-parties. Some writers have assumed it to be the largest border in the kingdom. It measures just over 520 feet; but the rocky border alongside the lawns of Holyrood Palace in Edinburgh is said to be 300 yards in length—900 feet. At all events the Queen appears to head the list, whether in England or Scotland, as seems only right and proper. The grand Evelyn terraces at the Duke of Northumberland's Albury Park in Surrey are half a mile in length; but the ducal flower-borders are not wholly continuous.*

George IV initiated the 'landscaping' of Buckingham Palace grounds, commissioning W. T. Aiton, then Superintendent of Kew and Kensington Gardens,

* The border at Holyrood is also divided.

to carry out the work. It continued during the reign of William IV and was still incomplete when Victoria became queen. At that period Belgravia was being fast developed for housing, and so the palace lost its rural surroundings for ever. The lake had previously been excavated and the mound raised—this last designed to screen the stables from the palace windows. Soil taken out from the site of the lake (nowhere more than six feet in depth) was insufficient to make a mound of adequate height for the purpose, and in a parliamentary debate of March 1832 there is a lurid account of this construction 'going up by contract in the garden of Buckingham Palace from the rubbish and filth brought in from all parts of the town'. As the young queen happily survived sewage seeping into the building, she may have felt little concern at having a fairly new rubbish tip outside.

By 1840 Prince Albert was busy designing gravel walks along the top of the mound and across it, paths long since overgrown. At this time the gardens were thought to be deficient in flowers, so provision was made for a handsome flower garden to the north of the palace. Most of the present walling was in place by the 1830s, but it was heightened at various times later in the century, and the *chevaux de frise* put up to protect the queen from intrusion. Prince Albert had a smaller mound by the Queen's Gallery raised to screen her from prying eyes, which even in demure Victorian days were all too common. Although the details have been changed from time to time, the basic plan of this garden has not altered in a hundred and fifty years.

Provision of water for the lake caused trouble. The nearest natural flow is the Tyburn, which ran originally from where the Marble Arch now stands, to the east of the palace and so into the Thames. Lord Goring (who built the seventeenth-century Goring House here) put the water into a conduit. At first the lake was supplied from a reservoir built on the site of the arch at the top of Constitution Hill, fed by a main from the Serpentine. This was in 1827–8, and the lake in those early days is referred to as the 'fish pond'. By 1840 it needed repair, for the water-fowl had grubbed off the gravel edging. A more permanent bank, constructed of Kent flints, defeated their ravages. In 1854 the water was found to be in a foul state, polluted by bird droppings, London soot and other offensive matter. The Managers of the Chelsea Waterworks were asked to estimate for a supply. Although they said that by 1856 an abundant supply of pure water could be made available, there seems to be no evidence that the plan was ever carried out. Lord Palmerston's idea for draining the lake and using the site for flower-beds was not pursued.

In 1857 some wells were sunk. Nobody knows what happened to them. Ten

10. Kensington Palace. The Orangery

11. Buckingham Palace. The Nash façade (1825) from St James's Park

12. Mr Fred Nutbeam, Head Gardener at Buckingham Palace, judging a show

13. Sir Eric Savill, KCVO

14. The Savill Gardens in June

15. The Physick Garden at Chelsea, 1795
From the Rev. Daniel Lyson's *The Environs of London*

16. The Chelsea Physic Garden today

years later, the water being in shocking condition, the lake was drained, cleaned out, and provided with a 12-inch pipe from the well on Duck Island in St James's Park—a supply still in use. No more do the gardeners complain, as they did in 1883, that the water is so foul-smelling as make work near it impossible in hot weather. Waterfowl were there from the beginning, and as long ago as 1840 special arrangements were made for their comfort: 'inclined boards for wading fowl were placed at intervals along the margin of the lake where the banks are deficient, and a few troughs for feeding the birds'. The flamingos, comparative newcomers, arrived from the Zoo in 1959. So far as can be ascertained, the 3½ acres of water forming this ornamental lake contain gudgeon, dace, roach and perch. At the north-western end an artificial cascade was formed in 1960 from flattish slabs of Banbury sandstone found elsewhere in the grounds. This soft, crumbly material gives a pleasant air of age and informality to the very well arranged construction. Water is allowed to flow down it only when the royal family is in residence. Some interesting new plantings are to be seen in the vicinity, including golden elder, golden robinia, *Cornus kousa*, varieties of *Sorbus* and a group of *Metasequoia glyptostroboides*, the Chinese 'Dawn Redwood'. Mr Fred Nutbeam, the Queen's Superintendent Gardener, showed me some more rocks, encrusting Queen Victoria's mound not far from his house. These natural-looking boulders were in fact man-made, but the secret of their composition has been lost.

The largest area of the garden consists of mown lawns, which are carefully tended, fertilized and kept almost weed-free; many guests from abroad may be glad to see a few English daisies poking up their heads in places, while the intrusion of a single-flowered Chamomile (the ancestor of our modern grass for lawns) pleases those with a feeling for historical associations. It must not be assumed that the plant dominates one patch of lawn. The sward is formed of grass and Chamomile in association, and Mr Nutbeam explained that this partnership worked because the plants were at their best in different seasons, one supplying lush green when the other had faded. Chamomile alone would look shabby in its off-season, and would prove unsuitable without grass intermingled. As far back as 1666 the Chamomile is known to have flourished in Tothill Fields, not far from the present palace grounds.

Of garden ornaments, the great Waterloo vase (see frontispiece) was brought here from Osborne in 1903, and the pair of bronze Indian cranes, now standing in immobile but life-like poses beside the lake, were presented to Edward VII at the Delhi Durbar. The white and graceful 'Mariner's' summerhouse came from the Admiralty—Spring Gardens, Whitehall—in 1901, and the tea-house was constructed in 1938. John Nash designed two greenhouses for the garden front; one remains, and the other was removed to Kew by order of William IV in 1836. It now stands near the Orangery and is known as the Aroid House.

Many wild plants have become naturalized in the palace grounds, including a Giant Hogweed, the South European Chervil (*Chaerophyllum aureum*), Winter Heliotrope, Golden Garlic, Dog's Mercury and the wild Bluebell, which hybridizes freely with the garden species (*Endymion hispanicus*), producing blue, pink and white colour forms. Bulbous spring plants have been introduced in quantity—including 100,000 crocuses, 8,000 *Iris reticulata*, 8,000 snowdrops, 7,000 scillas, 3,000 chionodoxas, 1,000 winter aconites, 1,000 fritillaries, 100,000 narcissi. Various hawthorns have seeded, and the common laburnum; also sycamore, plane, horse chestnut and Turkey oak. Plants of ling, cross-leaved and Dorset heaths and the broad buckler fern came into the garden in peat blocks which were used to prop up the rhododendron beds.

There are upwards of a hundred different named varieties of rhododendron and thirty of azalea; seventy-five kinds of camellia, the same of rose, and over fifty sorts of delphinium, mainly planted in the northern part of the garden, where such popular roses as 'Peace' and 'Queen Elizabeth' flourish in large groups, together with thousands of lilies. Trees are grown for shelter and privacy; some fast-growing poplars put in parallel to Grosvenor Place, and ten-year-old Indian chestnuts planted in 1961 along the Conservatory Walk, are now helping to screen off high-rise blocks.

Of specimen trees, the Swamp Cypress near the Waterloo Vase, the Pagoda Tree (*Sophora japonica*) to the west of the lake, and a Silver Maple are perhaps the finest. Several plane trees are at least seventy feet high, and may be one hundred and fifty years old. An aged mulberry near the back gate is said to have been planted in 1609, when James I formed his mulberry orchard; but there are serious doubts about this. Mulberries acquire a venerable look at a comparatively early age, like the Cedar of Lebanon, and the original orchard did not extend to the site of this tree. Another mulberry, growing near the sundial, is about seventy years old, and stems from a scion of Shakespeare's mulberry at Stratford-upon-Avon.

In 1960 the South London Natural History Society* made a detailed study of the natural history of the garden at Buckingham Palace, by gracious permission of Her Majesty Queen Elizabeth II. The section on birds lists a greater variety

* Now the British Entomological and Natural History Society.

of breeding pairs than some of us would expect to find in the middle of a vast metropolis like London. No doubt the large surrounding area of parkland with its fine trees—for which we have to thank the monarchy—has contributed to the wealth of bird life found in the precincts of the palace. Of water birds, the mallard and tufted duck numbered seventy or eighty residents, with a few pochard and Canada goose, ten moorhen and eight coot. In the trees some fifty wood-pigeons crooned, a pair of carrion crows were believed to breed, and the jay was sometimes seen. On the banks of the lake several pied wagtails were commonly observed. Great tits, blue tits, song and missel thrushes, blackbirds and robins made the garden resound with their song in season, and greenfinches, chaffinches, dunnocks, house-sparrows and starlings, with some spotted flycatchers, make up the list published a decade ago.

Mr David McLintock, in the summing-up which forms the closing pages of the report, comments on the ever-changing details of natural history in this place. The algae known as 'Blanketweed', which used unpleasantly to shroud the lake water, has largely gone from the surface since the advent of the flamingos. They brought in with them from the Zoo a new inhabitant in the shape of a scarce water flea. Spiked water milfoil disappeared at about the same time, leaving only the white water lily floating and flowering. The wide stretches of lawn grass show numerous worm casts in the winter months, and flocks of birds may then be seen at work probing the turf.

The privacy of this garden, which is of paramount importance to the Queen and her family, is also greatly appreciated by the birds. No cats are allowed, and squirrels are absent. The effect of encircling walls—accompanied by fairly dense shrubberies and many trees—in reducing noise is remarkable. A photograph has been published showing a duck's nest containing a clutch of six eggs, placed right up against the boundary wall by Grosvenor Place. In fact, nesting conditions for those privileged birds which reside in the Queen's garden must be among the very best in London.

The name of Buckingham Palace holds a certain magic for all but the most hardened cynics among us. My generation was not brought up on Christopher Robin and his visits to see the Changing of the Guard—a story in which his nurse's Christian name rhymed so usefully with 'palace'—but at an impressionable age I was told by a family friend, the late Sir Stanley Goodall, that had my father not been sacrificed in the First World War, he would have become Director of Naval Construction and received a knighthood in place of the speaker. Then my mother and I might well have gone down to Buckingham Palace, and right inside the doors, too. Later on, after his work in the Second World War, my surviving brother did go down to the palace, to receive his CBE. I had never been there, or expected to see more than the façade. Then came the contract for this book, and sudden realization that the garden of Buckingham Palace must on no account be left out. As it is my rule never to write of gardens which I have not visited (apart from those no longer in existence, when recourse must be made to documents and pictures), a request went to the Press Secretary, and, by gracious permission of the Queen, I was allowed to see the palace garden.

How appropriate it seemed for me, a gardener since childhood, to enter the royal domain by a small door which had been passed many a time without thought of where it led; and how pleasant to ring the bell of the gardener's house and be welcomed by Mr Nutbeam with simple unceremonious courtesy. That June afternoon in Ascot week, 1971, when I was privileged to explore the royal garden under his guidance, was dismally, hopelessly *wet*. Yet the visit was anything but a wash-out. For two hours he took me round the partially submerged walks, exhibiting with genial vivacity the improvements already carried out, and describing plans for the future. His knowledge and enthusiasm proved so engrossing that the cold water running down my neck and seeping into my shoes passed unnoticed. Had there been beds of burning coals, these might have been crossed with impunity, so absorbed were we in 'gardenage'. I felt very much at home, for had we not shown people round the gardens of Inverewe in similar conditions? With a rainfall of over sixty inches in Wester Ross, one could not wait for fine days. In his recent autobiography, *As I Remember*, the Master of the Queen's Musick, Sir Arthur Bliss, CH, gives an amusing account of how the late Mairi Sawyer of Inverewe insisted on showing him her fifty acres of woodland garden in drenching rain. He has remembered that experience for twenty years. I shall not forget the gardens of Buckingham Palace as long as I live.

The dingy shrubberies known to Queen Victoria and her children, and which I had expected to see, are being replaced by imaginative and splendid modern plantings. It is not a simple task, for it would not do for any part of this royal garden to be cleared and left thinly sprinkled with young shrubs and trees. While we are at liberty to tell a guest that in two or three years' time our latest project will be worth seeing, the Monarch in her London home would not care to do so. The whole place must appear fully clothed all the time, and essential changes have to be carried out more or less by stealth. The transformation is being achieved in the most ingenious way, by working outwards from the unseen rear or centre of each large group. The hidden part is first cleared of old laurel, blackened conifers and other unwanted growths, the tired soil removed and replaced by good loam, compost and peat. Then a host of new plants—rhododendron, azalea, eucryphia, magnolia, pernettya and many other attractive flowering shrubs and trees—are very carefully arranged and left to grow. When this 'core' has become established, the adjoining screen of shrubs is given similar treatment. Finally the outer defences are removed and replaced by heaths and other low subjects. Only then is it apparent to those using the walks that an entire section of shrubbery has been remade, from the inside outwards.

The choice of plants and their grouping is being carried out with great skill and taste, and it is good to know that the palace will soon have one of the finest gardens of 'natural' style to be seen anywhere in Britain. It should be mentioned that this work is being developed by Mr Nutbeam, as he proudly said, 'in direct contact with the Queen'. There are no go-betweens. Another asset, which earlier gardeners lacked, is the increasing purity of the atmosphere in London. The policy of enforcing smokeless zones has achieved a silent revolution, something for which modern science can be unreservedly praised, for the benefits are untold, and affect both plants and people. Many a bush which would look bedraggled and sick in London's sooty soil in my childhood will now appear clean and shining with health. The Queen and her Superintendent Gardener have been quick to grasp the opportunity. The best gardeners are usually too busy to describe their work on paper, and Fred Nutbeam is no exception; but when the sad day of his retirement comes, as come it must to everyone, I hope the Royal Horticultural Society will obtain from him for its *Journal* an account of how, in the nineteen-sixties and seventies, the garden of Buckingham Palace was transformed. It is not generally known that the gardens are classified as a 'Royal Park', and so Mr Nutbeam's full rank is that of Assistant Superintendent, Royal Parks, Central Division. But I expect he is more than content to be described as the Queen's Gardener-in-Chief, London.

The Savill and Valley Gardens in Windsor Great Park

WHAT nation other than the British would have clung tenaciously to the creation of a magnificent new garden throughout a major war and its chilly aftermath? This is what happened between 1939 and 1951 in the woods of the Crown Estate at Windsor. In 1931 Eric Savill—a young man, not then knighted—was appointed Deputy Surveyor of Windsor Parks and Woods, an estate of 15,000 acres; later, in 1937, he became Deputy Ranger. At the time of his arrival in Windsor there were no gardens in the whole of his area. The East Terrace at Windsor Castle had a well-established garden, laid out by Sir Geoffrey Wyatville for George IV, with a central pool, lawns, sculpture and vases, together with parterre beds filled in season with brightly coloured flowers; a charming old-world garden existed on the site of the former moat to the south-west of the Norman Tower, and there was a garden at Frogmore in the Home Park; but nowhere in this royal estate were to be found plants brought home by great collectors of the nineteenth and early twentieth centuries. Now, forty years afterwards, the whole nation—and its many visitors from abroad—are able to enjoy the magnificent Savill Gardens, Valley Gardens, Heather Garden and Rhododendron Species Collection (removed from Tower Court at Ascot), which lie in the Great Park, between three and four miles from the town of Windsor.

At the time of Mr Savill's appointment, the Duke and Duchess of York, who later became King George VI and Queen Elizabeth, both enthusiastic garden-lovers, were making their own garden at Royal Lodge; while the late Duke of Windsor (then Prince of Wales, later to reign briefly as King Edward VIII), was developing at his home, Fort Belvedere, an outstanding collection of rhododendrons, many of which were later given to the Savill Gardens. King George V and Queen Mary were on the throne, both interested in gardens, and the queen especially knowledgeable on this subject. The time for inauguration of a new royal garden was clearly propitious, and when the young Savill suggested in 1932 that a site on the east side of the Great Park near Englefield Green would make an attractive small woodland garden, his proposal received every encouragement from the monarchy. Nobody then foresaw—least of all its originator—how the modest project would succeed and expand.

Much of the land selected for the making of this 'natural' garden was a thicket of laurel, elder, and *Rhododendron ponticum*. The latter plant is often thought of as a 'native', although it was not introduced into the United Kingdom from the Near East until 1763. Its homeland to the south of the Black Sea, the ancient kingdom of Pontus, supplied the shrub with its botanical name. Our forefathers in Jane Austen's day used to force it, strange as that may seem to us now. As a pot-plant it was greatly esteemed in London. At a later date enormous quantities were propagated and set out by the great landowners, until it became little more than an invasive weed—a sad case of the mighty falling into disrepute. According to Alice M. Coats, the groves of arbutus that feature in the landscape of Killarney in Eire are menaced by this prolific rhododendron, which is smothering the arbutus seedlings and may ultimately cause the extinction of that lovely tree. At Windsor it grows enormous, and seeds so prolifically that its clearance posed a tricky problem for the gardeners; but in time the task was completed and planting of finer species could begin. As many trees as possible were retained, and a ditch (needed to drain the land) was used to form an ornamental stream and two good-sized ponds.

At first there were no flowers beside the water, but a great character named Harry Wye, the park foreman, soon went off on his bicycle to barter a hamper of rabbits—valued food in those pre-myxomatosis days—for a stock of kingcups from a neighbour's water garden. As bracken and scrub were cleared off the land, bluebells and primroses appeared, and with the addition of imported daffodils and hamamelis the spring scene soon became a gay one. A rabbit-proof fence had to be run round the perimeter, and as the rabbit harvest declined and then ceased, there was a change in the barter system. Before long plants were being propagated in such numbers that some were available for exchange with gardeners for other species. The mauve and purple *Primula denticulata* arrived in an unexpected way. Seeing the large masses used for bedding in St James's Park in springtime, Eric Savill asked the superintendent what became of them after the display finished. When he discovered that the plants were discarded, he asked for the entire collection, and a lorry-load came for naturalization in the Windsor woods. Some, planted on the site of an old bonfire, flourished, while others flagged. The acid soil did not suit them unless mixed with wood ash, so a circle planted on the remains of the wood fire was left as a reminder to primula-lovers.

By 1934 many trees and shrubs were becoming established, with underplantings of bulbs, primulas and pond-side subjects. A great day came in the spring when King George and Queen Mary arrived to see the new garden. All concerned realized that much would depend on the impression it made on Their Majesties. This visit was not without an element of drama. As the Royal party approached it passed beneath a large old holm oak, one of whose sweeping boughs actually grazed Queen Mary's toque. She turned, gave it a severe glance, and passed on, while those in charge of the garden held their breath. Before leaving, the queen turned to Eric Savill and said with a brilliant smile, 'It is very nice, Mr Savill, but isn't it rather *small*?'—a sign that approval had been given, and expansion could follow.

Then came the Second World War, and new developments had to cease while available resources were centred on maintenance of what had already been planted. Little by little the skilled men were called up, until only a few older men and some women on the estate remained to battle with weed control and the watering of valuable subjects during periods of drought. Now the production of food took first place on the land, and in 1941 the Crown Estate Commissioners, encouraged by the king, revived a farm created in 1791 by George III and abandoned for over seventy years. In order to use this area for agriculture, something had to be done about the large herds of deer, both red and fallow, which roamed the park, where they had been for centuries. Of the thousand head, 300 were segregated in 300 acres of unserviceable land, in order to keep up the old tradition; the rest were slaughtered for food. By the end of the war a good farm of 2,000 acres had been brought into being, and the farms at Windsor now exhibit prize-winning stock at many shows.

The Windsor estates were not immune from air-raids; two hundred high explosive bombs fell in the park, and in 1942 two cottages were destroyed. Children evacuated from London were housed in Cumberland Lodge and elsewhere, and altogether the rhododendrons, eucryphias, magnolias and other choice plantings had a rough time. Lawns turned into hayfields, and clear sheets of water became clogged with lilies and pond weeds, while paths disappeared from sight. In spite of active pursuit for their food value during this time of stringent rationing, rabbits multiplied and did considerable damage.

Nobody was more surprised than Eric Savill when, released from more urgent duties at the war's end, he and the returning staff found that casualties were minimal, and many plants had seeded themselves, becoming naturalized in large drifts among the trees: notably azalea, stranvaesia, enkianthus and *Styrax japonica.* Shrubs originally planted a few feet apart had spread to form solid clumps, while stripling magnolias had developed into trees eighteen or more feet in height. This first exploration of his perforce neglected creation must have brought intense delight to its originator. Clearing and pruning went on apace, woodland walks were freed from encroachment, and grassy paths restored. Some visitors who had enjoyed wartime visits missed the wilderness and thought that, with too much trimming and smoothing, the gardens had lost charm—a view with which it is easy to sympathize.

My own one-time home at Inverewe in Wester Ross looked, when I first knew it, like a natural woodland gorgeously flowering at nearly all seasons, with little sign of man's intervention. This effect was entirely artificial; but so cleverly contrived that even those of us who knew that Osgood Mackenzie had created the miracle upon a barren rocky peninsula beside Loch Ewe found its 'naturalness' compelling. Directly the National Trust for Scotland took over these lovely gardens from Osgood's daughter and successor Mairi Sawyer in 1953, work was begun to widen and straighten the winding peaty paths and give them harder surfaces; to clip and prune and neaten the shrubs, and bed out little circles or squares of smaller plants in front of the species rhododendrons. Trimming up and precision took the place of artistic casualness, until in a decade nearly all the 'wild' and 'natural' beauty of effect had been gardened out. It is extremely difficult to strike a balance between nature and art, particularly in woodland gardens; many visiting parties apparently wish to walk in such places dry-shod at all seasons, and to emerge without mud on their town-bred shoes. There may be a case in these circumstances for *not* giving the customer all he wants.

After the war a great wall was built along part of the Savill garden's northern boundary. This measures seventy yards long and eighteen feet in height and is constructed of bricks salvaged from the bombed debris of London. Buttresses at twenty-foot intervals provide shelter for tender plants, and carry many climbers—including the violet-scented yellow Banksian rose from China and some fine specimens of ceanothus, the 'Californian Lilac'. In protected beds at the wall's foot are many unusual and exotic plants. The whole scheme provides a mute but lovely memorial to the many Londoners who perished under the ruins of their homes.

In 1946, although the conflict had ended, food remained scarce. The king decided that the deer still remaining at Windsor would have to go. A hundred head were taken to Richmond, to preserve the strain, and the rest were slaughtered. For the first time in recorded history man had taken over the whole of Windsor Great Park for his farming and forestry schemes, and no deer grazed there. At this time a programme of horticultural expansion went ahead also, and the now famous Valley Gardens came into being with a nucleus of magnolias, eucryphias, Japanese maples, azaleas and rhododendrons—many of them the gift of Messrs Aspro, the firm that took over Wexham Place near Slough for industrial use. The late Eustace Wilding had made a notable garden there which the directors of Aspro did not require, and the transfer of its treasures was easily made to near-by Windsor.

The appointment of Mr T. H. Findlay as head gardener placed his unusually wide knowledge and skill, particularly as a grower of rhododendrons and camellias, at the disposal of what in 1951 became known as 'The Savill Garden' by command of the king. These gardens have been steadily enlarged and developed from that day, and they are well worth a visit at any season of the year. There is even a Winter Garden, in flower on Christmas Day. In spring there is a riot of blossom; later on the various hydrangeas and eucryphias 'blow', as our ancestors would have said; the camellia-like stewartia is one of the less common delights, and *Koelreuteria paniculata*, the 'Golden Rain Tree'. Autumn brings a blaze of berry, fruit and glowing foliage. Anyone who looks critically at what has been achieved will appreciate Sir Eric's wisdom in making straight lines taboo here. To ensure natural contours, he sent his men to walk from one point to another, and marked their courses. They took the easiest and most convenient routes without studying the matter, and on these tracks the paths were laid out. He also frowned upon the arrangement of small plants in rings round the boles of trees, a practice which is horribly destructive of natural effect. Instead, he had all planting based on the great Gertrude Jekyll's precept of 'drifts'.

From the start these gardens have enjoyed the personal interest and assistance of the royal family: first of all King George V and Queen Mary, then King George VI and Queen Elizabeth, and now Queen Elizabeth II and the Duke of Edinburgh. Queen Elizabeth The Queen Mother, a child of that great garden St Paul's, Walden Bury, and sister of David Bowes-Lyon who did so much for the Royal Horticultural Society, is herself a keen and well-informed gardener with a particular love of the genus Magnolia. Under her influence the Savill Garden has acquired a complete collection of species and hybrids grown in this country, including the great *M. campbelli, M. mollicomata* and *M. sargentiana var. robusta,* all of which may end up as large as forest trees.

During the lifetime of King George VI, he and Queen Elizabeth visited the gardens assiduously, deriving immense pleasure from them. The king lived long enough to see the Valley Garden well established, also the making of the Kurume Punch Bowl. This saucer-like depression houses a quantity of evergreen azaleas in fifty varieties, collected in Japan by E. H. Wilson, and familiarly known as the 'Wilson fifty'. They were placed in irregular groups containing from fifty to two hundred plants in each, and it has been estimated that at least fifty thousand azaleas were used in this project. Japanese maples accompany them, together with enkianthus, stranvaesia and the fascinating *Styrax japonica,* which bears 'snowdrop' flowers in the month of May. The Valley Garden and Rhododendron Species Collection lie about a mile to the south of the Savill Garden; together they form an important part of Windsor Great Park—about one-tenth of the total 4,500 acres. They have separate entrances, and the stranger must be ready to take a little trouble to locate these; but the effort is well rewarded.

The excellent illustrated guide-book to the Savill Gardens contains a large map with numbered squares. References in the text make it a simple matter to locate most plants and trees. My visit with two habituées from Sunningdale in June 1971 took place after a period of heavy rainstorms, followed by a perfect day of sunshine and quick-moving cloud shadows, and the first sight of those great beeches near the entrance, with a magnificent carpet of newly-washed moss beneath them, will never be forgotten. The moss was soft and silky, and lay upon gentle folds of ground with light and shade playing over it, seeming as though some hand must have laid it a few moments earlier, so elegantly smooth and shining it appeared, so free from weeds or the least speck of rubbish. Nowhere else have I seen such moss. It is named *Leocobryum argenteum,* and has been given a special mention in the rules for visitors, wherein people are asked to keep to paths and lawns to avoid damaging ground plants, such as daffodils, lilies and dog's-tooth violets, and the 'brilliant green moss under the beech-trees'. Those who make use of the terrace outside the restaurant may look across to the beech wood and its silky carpet.

As the booklet so wisely says, it is better for morning visitors to explore the garden in a clock-wise direction, turning left beyond the stream at the head of the upper pond; while in the afternoon an anti-clockwise tour gives a more pleasing light, with the sun more or less behind one's back. This photographer's trick is valuable for garden viewing, and particularly so in a woodland garden. In June it was too late to see the 'Alpine Meadow' lit up with narcissus, crocus and fritillary; but primula, meconopsis and a battalion of the erect and powerful Himalayan lily (*Cardiocrinum giganteum*) were very near their peak in an adjacent sector. Overhead shade, and a high water-table suit these plants. On the occasion of this June visit pools of rain water all over the walks soaked our shoes, but the glorious picture made by many forms of the 'Blue Poppy of Tibet', companioned by primulas, hostas, bog iris and rodgersias, caused forgetfulness of discomfort.

For my latest visit to the Valley Gardens the weather was warmer and drier, although October had come. How difficult is the task of the descriptive writer when faced with such a grand conception as this! To begin with, it changes—as all gardens must—from month to month, and, like all woodland places, it derives much of its enchantment from effects of light and shadow. One needs to live close at hand for at least twelve months to understand and appreciate all its moods. As I had already learned at Inverewe, first impressions bear only a fleeting resemblance to the deep, enduring mental pictures developed after a year's close study. People have different ideas about the best time to visit the Valley Gardens. One will tell you that spring is undoubtedly the finest period; another chooses the blossoming time of rhododendrons; some local residents never fail to admire that part called the 'Winter Garden' at Christmas, when *Rhododendron jacksonii*, *Hamamelis mollis* and the Winter Cherry can often be found in full flower.

In a lecture to the Royal Horticultural Society in 1968 Lanning Roper said that, although lovely in winter, the Valley Gardens came into their own in spring. But I think he was right when he concluded:

> 'The Valley Gardens are always satisfying, thanks to the lie of the land, the openness of the site, the remarkable variety yet restraint of the planting, and the fact that you can see the gardens from so many vantage points—the bottom of the valley, paths curving along slopes, and from high ridges with fine views in different directions. There are fine views down long, wooded glades to Virginia Water, and the mossy slopes are covered with bold plantings of forsythias, cherries, early magnolias, rhododendrons in soft pinks, pale yellows and mauves, with fascinating foliage ranging from huge-leaved species such as *R. falconeri* and *R. sino-grande* to smaller glaucous-leaved ones, including *R. cinnabarinum*, *R. concatenans* and *R. glaucophyllum*.'

To list all the interesting trees would be to form a catalogue of names. Two species of great value, not as yet very commonly known, may be dwelt upon. The North American River Birch, *Betula nigra,* does an arboreal strip-tease, shedding rolls of loose bark to disclose a smooth pinkish-cream trunk; when mature, the bole of this birch is bear-brown in colour and almost hairy as well. The other species—which I am sorry to say carries the dreadful name of *Metasequoia glyptostroboides* (let us adopt the vernacular 'Dawn Redwood')—has a remarkable history. It was first described in modern times from fossil material obtained in 1941, and had been considered extinct until, a few years later, specimens were discovered alive and well, growing beside streams in North-east Szechuan in China. Seeds were harvested by collectors from the American Arnold Arboretum, and distributed to a number of institutions on both sides of the Atlantic. From these seeds sprang many plants now thriving in American and European collections. At the RHS Gardens at Wisley, a seedling of February 1948 has grown to a height of nearly fifty feet in the Wild Garden, and in the Savill Garden one is over sixty feet.

The Dawn Redwood resembles to some extent the Swamp Cypress (*Taxodium distichum*). Both species are deciduous, and provide good autumn colour. The delicate pale green feathery foliage of the Redwood develops yellow, russet and pinkish tones in the Fall, more tender and subtle than the deeper rusty hues of the Cypress, which turns colour later and often retains its leaves until the end of November. At Corbridge in Northumberland an example of the newly-found Dawn Redwood was received from the Royal Botanic Garden in Edinburgh in 1949, and kept under cover for three years because it was not thought to be fully hardy. At the end of this period of coddling it was planted out, and is now growing nicely, undisturbed by spring frosts in that bleak country—so distasteful to the Roman Legions who manned the Wall.

Sir Frederick Stern reported to the Royal Horticultural Society in 1967 that, of the specimens tried out at Highdown, some were put in the dampest spots, and others up above on the Down. The latter made the best progress, and the tallest had reached a height of twenty-six feet. At Grasse in the South of France the Vicomte de Noailles has a Dawn Redwood, planted in 1953, which grew to thirty-eight feet in thirteen years. This tree is growing in a 'dampish prairie' of good ordinary soil, and is kept well watered in dry summer seasons. In Rhode Island, USA, a tree raised in 1948 from seed brought from China by the Arnold Arboretum expedition had reached forty-eight feet. In sandy soil, with hot, dry summers, very cold winters, and winds of hurricane force, it has survived and seems at home. So far no viable seeds have occurred, but this tree (according to Wisley) may be propagated successfully from cuttings. All these trials* of a hitherto unknown tree suggest that the Dawn Redwood is sufficiently hardy and tolerant to be worth considering as a specimen and woodland subject in its own right, and not merely as a curiosity.

Sir Eric Savill evidently thought so when he installed a large group of these trees on a gentle slope in the Valley Gardens, overlooking Virginia Water but not alongside the lake. To my mind this unusual tree looks even better in association with its own kind than it does as a single specimen, and that ferny grove is a highlight of the Valley Gardens which should on no account be missed. Not every great gardener in retirement is as fortunate as Sir Eric. In his lovely Garden House he looks out at Smith's Lawn and the splendid forest trees of Windsor, while the garden which bears his name, together with the Valley Gardens, is accessible to him at all times. No longer bearing the burden of responsibility for these, he is close at hand to watch over his plantings and to observe the pleasure they bring to countless visitors. That collection of Dawn Redwoods must be at or near the top of their list and his own.

I enjoyed his hospitality on a perfect day in early autumn, when the sun retained much of summer's warmth and the woodlands, lightly burnished by the approaching Fall, were interleaved with shadows bold and deep. The welcoming house, in its bright but secluded setting; the quiet confidence with which the maker of these gardens showed some of his favourite plantings; the exhilaration of viewing a grand conception, finely achieved and well maintained, in company with its designer and architect, all combined to produce one of those rare occasions—short in duration on the clock-face—which in memory has a quality of life capable of enhancing ordinary existence in after years when one is far removed from the source.

Every season brings an increase in the number of visitors to these unique gardens. Following Sir Eric's retirement at the age of seventy-five, the Savill Garden is now supervised by Mr T. H. Findlay, and the Valley Gardens and the Nurseries by Mr John Bond, a young man of great knowledge and experience. These gardens grow in beauty as each planting matures. The Crown Estate Commissioners have been obliged to prohibit dogs in the Savill Garden, and no picnics may be held inside the gates. A small admission charge is made. There is ample parking for cars. No visitor to Britain should fail to see these great modern 'Royal' gardens in Windsor Great Park.

* See *RHS Journal*, 1967.

SECTION TWO
Physic, Botanic
and Other
Old Gardens

The Chelsea Physic Garden

ONE of the charms of this old garden lies in its elusive character. Because it is not open to the public, few trouble to inquire its whereabouts, and even some local residents are unaware of its existence. Two aged Chelsea Pensioners gave me blank stares when I inquired the way. Only the Ranelagh Gardens, where they sat in the sun, and their Royal Hospital grounds were familiar to them; clearly they assumed that I had mistaken either the name or the locality of my goal. The Physic Garden is in fact situated a short distance from the pensioners' stately home in Chelsea, with an entrance gate in the Royal Hospital Road and another in Swan Walk. A third, more imposing, entrance—one that appears in early engravings of the place—faces the Embankment and the Thames on the south side of the walled enclosure. These handsome gates, embellished with the arms of the Apothecaries' Society, are seldom in use; but, being of wrought-iron with plenty of peep-holes, they allow a good view from outside of the main walk and the building at the far end. They may be found by the diligent walker going east for a few minutes from the Albert Bridge.

Unfortunately the four Cedars of Lebanon, planted in about 1683, which used to form a conspicuous landmark, have all disappeared. A pair sited in the middle of the three and a half acres were felled in 1771 because they took too much sunlight from surrounding plants; but those near the pillars of the south gates, the last of which survived until 1903, died natural deaths—perhaps hastened a little by the increasing smoke of London, as the city crept close to the Physic Garden. It is said that these were the first cedars in England to produce cones; from all the evidence it seems fairly certain that they were among the first Lebanon Cedars to be planted in this country.

Dr Dartrey Drewitt, in a preface to his book *The Romance of the Apothecaries' Garden at Chelsea*, writes of an invitation given to him early in the nineteen-twenties to represent the Royal College of Physicians on the Managing Committee of the Chelsea Physic Garden (now controlled by Trustees of the London Parochial Charities), and of the pleasure he found in learning the long history of the Garden: a story he describes as 'a minute fraction of the great human past'.

For him this study contained 'all the novelty of a journey in an unknown country'.

This apothecaries' garden in Chelsea was not the earliest example of its kind in Europe. Padua in Italy possessed one in 1545, and that at Oxford preceded London's by fifty-two years. But John Gerard's famous herb garden in Holborn* and the Tradescant enterprise in Lambeth, both of them plant collections of high repute and great interest to botanists, may be regarded as worthy forerunners of this, the official garden of the Apothecaries' Company of London. In the seventeenth century the word 'physic' was a more comprehensive term than it is now, being used to embrace all natural science. A physic garden was then instituted for scientific purposes, and not solely for the cultivation and study of plants used in medicine, although those formed a high proportion of the stock. It is interesting today, when even more drugs are manufactured in laboratories than was the case in Dr Drewitt's time, to discover that most of the medicinal plants still named in the British Pharmacopeia are poisonous ones. Foxglove (Digitalis), Henbane (Hyoscine), Monkshood (Aconite), Hemlock (Coniine), Thornapple (Stramonium), and Autumn Crocus (Colchicine) together with the romantically-named Belladonna obtained from Deadly Nightshade, would have been familiar to him, although so many of the harmless herbs of healing used by out forefathers had already become part of the great human past.

In that past lie all the painful experiments by which mankind learned such differences as those between the wholesome fruit of the bramble and the sinister black berries of the Nightshade; between astringent roots of Bistort (which nourished him with their starch and, by shrinking the intestine, reduced the amount of food required) and the deadly growths of Monkshood. Knowledge gained by practical experience gradually accumulated, and those who mastered and made use of it to advise others became medicine-men, no doubt with a spice of hocus-pocus thrown in to impress the patients. These specialized users of plants were in fact the first botanists, long before the word had been coined, or herbals printed, or the Linnean classification of plants invented.

The London Society of Apothecaries, which came into being in the reign of James I, was initially part of the Grocers' Company. In 1617 it broke away, seeking independent status; an attempt unpopular with the Grocers. With the king's support, the Apothecaries stood firm, and were granted their charter. This carried with it responsibility for improving the quality of drugs sold to

* Records of the College of Physicians show that Gerard agreed in 1587 to superintend the first botanic garden of that college.

His Majesty's subjects, and of controlling the qualifications of the vendors. The civic authorities were at first reluctant to recognize the new society, and seven years passed before the Lord Mayor sent an invitation to the Apothecaries to be present, along with the other City Companies, to hear the Christmas Day sermon in St Paul's Cathedral. After that ceremony the Lord Mayor and Aldermen exchanged civilities with the Apothecaries, who presented the Lord Mayor with a tun of wine. In the following year they took part in the Lord Mayor's annual procession on the Thames, using a barge hired for the occasion, under their own banners.

One of the members, Thomas Johnson, is still remembered for the enlarged edition of Gerard's *Herball*, which he issued in 1633. The title-page shows, among other plants, a branch bearing a large number of bananas. This, the first ever seen in Britain, was given to Johnson by 'Dr Argent, President of the Colledge of Physicians', who had it from someone aboard a vessel home from Bermuda. The long greenish-yellow fingers of this strange fruit, hung up to ripen in the window of Johnson's shop in Snow Hill, must have attracted a great deal of attention from passers-by. Johnson cut open the bananas when he judged them to be ready, and reported favourably on their pleasant flavour and absence of seeds. He little thought that in years to come barrow-boys would be selling loads of this exotic fruit on the streets of London. Practically nothing had been known of the Bermudas until Sir George Summers, shipwrecked there in 1609, provided Shakespeare with ideas for *The Tempest*. According to a manuscript of the seventeenth century found among the papers left by Sir Hans Sloane, the fig, orange, vine and plantain (banana) were not indigenous in the 'Bermudaes', but had been introduced into the islands. Apparently the great western banana industry, with its fleet of ships carrying the fruit to Europe, must be numbered among the many enterprises started by experimental botanists and gardeners to the ultimate benefit of mankind. Towards the close of his life Johnson was awarded the degree of MD at Oxford, and became a Freeman of the Apothecaries' Company.

Through financial troubles, civil war and plague the Apothecaries somehow managed to endure. In the Great Fire of London their hall and library—together with many of the members' houses—were lost, and salvaged Company plate had to be sold to help pay for rebuilding. Next they required a garden, wherein to cultivate and study rare plants and to raise seeds now being brought to the capital in quantity from overseas. In 1673 a plot of land some 3½ acres in extent, situated along the river at Chelsea, was leased from Lord Cheyne for a rent of

£5 a year; here the Physic Garden began, and here it still is. Chelsea was then a country manor, having cornfields, pasture land, a common, and a pleasant village set beside the Thames. Wren's great military hospital had not yet been designed. The King's Road, well made and gravelled at royal expense, had just been completed for Charles II to drive from Whitehall direct to the old Fulham ferry (mentioned in Domesday Book) *en route* for Putney and his palace at Hampton Court, whose gardens were being remade in the fashionable French style.

The new garden of the Apothecaries, sufficiently far from the smoke of London to be suitable for the culture of rare and delicate plants, had the sweet water of the Thames alongside. At that happy period the water ran clear and unpolluted, and good hauls of salmon were obtained from it in the springtime. There was a creek at hand to float the Company's new barge, and a boat-house was built in the south-east corner of the ground. Part of this building disappeared in fairly recent times; the site may still be seen; now that the Embankment (engineered in 1874) has encroached on the Thames mud-banks, the water seems a long way off, and it is hard to picture the Apothecaries landing conveniently at the gates of their garden. Their barge was a four-oared boat, with a room in the stern not unlike a gondola's cabin, the whole decorated with flags and banners. This modest craft could not compare with those of the larger and wealthier City Companies, which had eight or more oars apiece.

At the Accession of George I, the watermen who rowed the many barges then using London's river as a highway were given a handsome coat and badge by the Irish actor Thomas Doggett, to be competed for each year. The race for Doggett's coat and badge is still rowed in July on the Thames, although motorized craft now predominate there, and the use of the river as a natural highway for travellers has, unfortunately, been largely given up. The course used to terminate at the Old Swan Tavern beside the Physic Garden, but now continues farther upstream. Swan Walk was formerly a mere footpath; at its tavern Samuel Pepys received a severe shock. His diary for April 1666 records that he drove in a party with some ladies and children, thinking to have a merry time at the inn; but on arrival they found it closed for the plague. They turned back 'with great affright, I for my part in great disorder'.

In the current bedlam of traffic noise, the old name for that section of the Royal Hospital Road which runs along the northern boundary of the Physic Garden—Paradise Row—seems highly incongruous, and is now almost forgotten. Paradise, meaning an enclosed garden or park, denoted the great garden of Sir

Thomas More in Chelsea, which existed long before the Apothecaries made their little paradise. More's garden, visited by Erasmus and Holbein, was described as being 'wonderfully charming, both from advantages of its site and also for its own beauty. It was crowned with almost perpetual verdure; it had flowering shrubs, and the branches of fruit trees interwoven in so elegant a manner as to appear like a tapestry woven by Nature herself.' Here More's favourite, the Rosemary, grew luxuriantly. In the sixteenth century all the land bounded by the present Church Street, Beaufort Street, Fulham Road and the Thames belonged to More. At the north-east corner stood a big tree known as the 'Queen's Elm', where Queen Elizabeth I, walking with Lord Burleigh, took shelter from a rainstorm. By 1625 this part of the ground had been incorporated in Chelsea Park, which had iron gates opening upon the Fulham Road. It was graced by fine cedars, mulberries, elms and thorns, all set, country-style, in long grass. In 1875 Dr Dartrey Drewitt, by means of a letter to the London *Times*, did his best to preserve this open space for the benefit of posterity. He was not successful, and within a year it had been completely built over by the Elm Park Estate.

The Apothecaries' Garden suffered from a number of teething troubles. Being so far from it at the headquarters of the Company in Blackfriars, the Master and Wardens were unable to keep a close watch, with the result that theft, neglect and discontent were rife, and the gardener soon demanded more than the house and wages of £30 per annum agreed upon when he was appointed. Some members thought that the Garden was proving too great an expense to be practicable. The majority decided to keep it going somehow, and subscriptions were invited for this purpose. A high wall was erected to foil thieves—a defence against knavery which also served to protect the plants from inclement weather. Many more fruits were grown—nectarines, peaches, apricots, cherries and plums—and the water-gate installed on the south side of the garden. The Cedars of Lebanon were planted in 1683. The first greenhouse and stove in England was erected in the Garden in 1681.

An apothecary named John Watts now had charge of the Garden, a keen botanist with a European reputation, who made exchanges with the Dutch University of Leyden. In 1684 a young medical student, Hans Sloane, came upon the scene for the first time. One of his letters describes a visit he paid to Mr Watts:

> 'I was the other day at Chelsea, and find that the artifices us'd by Mr Watts have been very effectual for the Preservation of his Plants, insomuch

> that this severe winter has scarce kill'd any of his fine Plants. One thing I much wonder to see, the *Cedrus Montis Libani*, the Inhabitant of a very different climate, should thrive here so well, as without Pot or Green House to be able to propagate itself by Layers this Spring. Seeds sown last Autumn have as yet thriven very well, and are like to hold out.'

In the following year Evelyn visited the Garden, writing in his diary for 7 August 1685:

> 'I went to see Mr Watts, keeper of the Apothecaries' Garden of simples at Chelsea, where there is a collection of innumerable rarities of that sort; particularly, besides many rare annuals, the tree bearing Jesuit's bark, which had done such wonders in Quartan Agues. What was very ingenious was the subterranean heate, conveyed by a stove under the conservatory, all vaulted with brick, so as he [John Watts] has the doors and windows open in the hardest frosts, secluding only the snow.'

The story of the spread of Cinchona, 'the tree bearing Jesuit's bark' is one that bears repetition. The wife of a seventeenth-century Spanish Viceroy had brought the Peruvian bark to Spain, for the relief of ague; Jesuit missionaries took it back to Rome for similar purpose; an apothecary named Talbot cured Charles II of an ague with the powdered bark; it was justly famed far from the country of origin; but many explorers tried without success to procure living specimens for transfer to their own lands. The secret was jealously guarded by the natives of Peru. One of the exploring botanists was murdered; another managed to smuggle some plants of Cinchona as far as the mouth of the Amazon, but lost the precious cargo in a violent storm, after the long and hazardous journey by boat. It was not until 1860 that C. R. Markham, who had succeeded in bringing live specimens to Britain for cultivation at Kew, was able to establish the invaluable tree, source of what we know as quinine, in India.

The Apothecaries' Garden, after weathering a number of financial and other troubles, during which it could not even manage to keep its barge on the river, came at last into a secure haven as a result of the purchase of the Manor of Chelsea by the distinguished physician, Sir Hans Sloane. In February 1722 he offered to lease the Physic Garden to the Apothecaries in perpetuity for a fixed annual payment of £5—no more than was paid at the start. The document stated that this was designed to enable them 'to support the charges thereof, for the manifestation of the power, wisdom and glory of God in the works of

Creation', and to show how plants useful to man may be distinguished from 'those that are hurtful'. It was stipulated that fifty specimens from the Garden, all different, should be dried, mounted and labelled for the Royal Society each year for the next forty years. This requirement meant that no fewer than 2,000 different plants must be grown during that period. In fact, more than 3,000 specimens were supplied to the Royal Society; these were later housed in the Natural History section of the British Museum, at South Kensington.

The life story of Hans Sloane is one of triumph over early disability. Born in Ireland in 1660 of mixed Scottish-English parentage, he was the youngest of seven brothers. His schooldays ended at sixteen, when tuberculosis of the lungs laid him low for several years. Disciplined to a carefully ordered physical regime, he also managed to pursue his studies, including those in botany, and qualified in medicine. At one stage in his career he joined an expedition to Jamaica, where he collected 800 plant specimens, and later wrote a history of the island and prepared a catalogue of its flora.

He became physician to Christ's Hospital, and generously gave free service to the poor of his district. In 1716 George I gave him a baronetcy—the first such honour to be awarded to a member of his profession. In 1719 he was elected President of the Royal College of Physicians, and in 1727 he succeeded Sir Isaac Newton as President of the Royal Society. In 1742 he moved from Bloomsbury to his Manor House in Chelsea, together with his library and a vast collection of treasures valued at £80,000. Here he lived until his death in 1753 at the age of nearly ninety-three. His collection was offered to the nation under the terms of Sloane's Will for the nominal sum of £20,000; it comprised 50,000 books and manuscripts, 23,000 coins and medals, 3,000 gems and 'antiquities' and 16,000 natural history specimens. These were bought to form the nucleus of the British Museum at Montague House, and were added to by the Royal Library given by George II. Few who use the facilities under the great dome in Bloomsbury today give a thought to the Hanoverian monarch and his honoured physician, who were responsible for the inception of that vast library.

It was on Sloane's advice that Philip Miller in 1722 was put in charge of the Apothecaries' Garden, where he remained until his death in 1771. He is chiefly remembered for his *Dictionary of Gardening*, which went through many editions, bringing international fame to the author and praise from the great Swedish botanist Linnaeus. During his time in Chelsea two hot-houses and a greenhouse were built, with Sir Hans Sloane to lay the foundation stones. Miller was the first gardener in Britain to effect the germination of exotic seeds by subjecting them to the heat of a tan pit. Among the useful services performed by the Apothecaries at this stage, the provision of cotton seed for Georgia—a British colony named after George II—initiated the great cotton industry there. In the Garden, a fine statue of Sloane was installed, sculpted by Rysbrack, who also carried out Sir Isaac Newton's monument in Westminster Abbey. At first it stood under cover in a greenhouse, but in 1748 it was removed to the present site, where it stands in full view of those who look through the iron gates in Swan Walk.

Accounts of the first visit paid by the Swedish botanist Linnaeus to Britain in 1736 have some interesting sidelights on his character. A letter of introduction to Sir Hans Sloane, from the well-known Swedish physician and botanist, Dr Boerhaave, was couched in flowery terms, saying that Linnaeus and Sloane were 'two men whose like cannot be found in the world'. Not impressed, Sloane found Linnaeus dull, and was thoroughly bored by his company. At the Chelsea Physic Garden, Philip Miller thought him conceited and ignorant. The version given to a correspondent by Linnaeus puts a slightly different complexion on things:

> 'When I paid Philip Miller a visit, the principal object of my journey, he shewed me the garden at Chelsea, and named me the plants in the nomenclature then in use . . . I held my tongue, which made him declare next day, "That botanist of Clifford's does not know a single plant". I heard this.* I said to him, as he was going to use the same names, "Do not call these plants thus; we have shorter and surer names."
>
> 'Then he was angry and looked cross. I wished to have some plants for Clifford's garden, but when I came back to Miller's he was in London. He returned in the evening. His ill-humour had passed off. He promised to give me all I asked for. He kept his word, and I left for Oxford having sent a fine parcel to Clifford.'

In the end Linnaeus described the English as 'the most generous people on earth.' Clifford was a rich banker in Haarlem, a director of the Dutch East India Company and owner of a magnificent garden which Linnaeus was arranging. Apparently the latter habitually bestowed praises on himself: a foible not appreciated in England. As Dr Dartrey Drewitt slyly comments, Linnaeus had not been at an English public school. On better acquaintance, the true quality of his genius shone out, and his brash manner was forgiven. Perhaps his existence at

* Probably said in English to a bystander.

home, with a shrewish and domineering wife—described by a pupil of his as having often driven pleasure from the society of their house—may have caused him to be tiresomely self-assertive when away from her.

In 1748 another Swede, Peter Kalm, a pupil of Linnaeus, arrived at the Physic Garden. He noted that the land around it in Chelsea was almost entirely devoted to nursery and vegetable gardens. The same was true of the land on all sides around London. 'The vast London, and the frightful number of people which there crawl in the streets, pay the market-gardeners many-fold for their outlay', he wrote. He was struck by the amount of broken bottle-glass fixed to walls to deter intruders, and by the quantity of drink that must have been consumed from those bottles.

He observed with amazement that everyone in England, even labouring folk, wore a wig. 'The boy is hardly in his breeches before he comes out with a perruque, sometimes not smaller than himself.' He discussed with Philip Miller the vitality of long-buried seeds, and admired the largest orangery, 'where smoke makes six bends in one of the walls before it escapes'. Orangery was then a common name for a house into which the 'tender greens' were taken for the winter: the 'greenhouse', a term still in use.

Kalm also visited the ageing Sir Hans Sloane, who was deaf and bed-ridden, but mentally alert. He approved of Kalm's projected journey to America in search of plants. There is no record of the Swede's opinion of the American house at that period, but he complained of cold English cottages, with no moss packed in the roof for insulation, and grates that allowed all the heat from the fire to escape up the chimney. They managed these things better in his native country. One of the many plants he brought back from America was the ericaceous Kalmia, named after himself and known as the 'Calico Bush' by countryfolk in its native land.

Before Philip Miller died in 1777, he made use of the Linnean system of plant classification for the last edition of his *Gardener's Dictionary*. Later on, the Linnean and Horticultural Societies erected in Chelsea Old Church a monument to his memory. During Miller's time at the Physic Garden, the Lord Mayor of London had issued an appeal for disabled soldiers who were returning to England after having 'put down the rising in Scotland'. The Apothecaries raised £200 for this fund. North of the Border one is apt to forget that *both* sides suffered in time of war; the 'Forty-five' is a great landmark in Scottish history—the last attempt of the Stuarts to regain the Throne—and its failure was regarded by most Scots as a grievous blow.

In 1771 a different kind of landmark disappeared for ever from the Physic Garden, where the two central Cedars of Lebanon were felled to allow more light into the plantations. A merchant paid £23 for the timber. This is not the wood from which the cedar pencil was made, although the purchaser may have assumed it to be valuable for that purpose. The pencil 'cedar' wood came in fact from a juniper (*Juniperus virginiana*). Originally, the great juniper of Bermuda (*Juniperus bermudiana*) was used for pencil-making; but this species died out and the Virginian tree was utilized in its place. Of the other two Cedars of Lebanon at Chelsea, one died in 1878 and the last survived until 1903.

Through an extraordinary chain of circumstances, the great herbarium and collection of books and papers made by Linnaeus was acquired after the Swedish botanist's death by a young English medical student, James Smith, whose acumen and keen interest in botany were financed in this undertaking by his father. These precious purchases were housed by Smith in Paradise Row, close to the Chelsea Physic Garden. Too late the government of Sweden woke up to realize the folly of allowing the life-work of Linnaeus to be removed from his own country. The deal had been perfectly legitimate, and there was nothing they could do to retrieve the treasures. But good care has always been taken of them in England, and in 1788 they served as a nucleus for the foundation of the Linnean Society. James Smith was the first President of this learned body, which has now been in existence for nearly two centuries.

Over twenty years earlier, young Joseph Banks was living with his widowed mother in a large house near the south-east corner of the garden; as a budding naturalist, he must have been familiar with the original quartet of Lebanon Cedars. A literary bookseller of Paradise Row, one Thomas Faulkner, who published many anecdotes of Chelsea, described how young Banks and his friend Lord Sandwich (a member of the notorious Medmenham group) used to engage in all-night fishing expeditions on the Thames. The river banks in those days were host to numerous wild plants and other forms of life, and Joseph became intensely interested in natural history. It is said that he borrowed his mother's copy of Gerard's *Herball* to study for pleasure in his free time at Eton. As the heir to a considerable fortune, Banks was equipped to indulge his predilection for botany in various ways. While a student he endowed a lectureship in the University of Oxford, and in 1768 he sailed with Captain Cook for the 'great Southern continent'.* There he amassed a huge collection of plant specimens, drying them on the shores of what was appropriately named Botany Bay.

* Australia.

The ship returned to Deal in 1771, and in the following year Banks visited Iceland, where he collected a large quantity of volcanic rock, for transfer from the grim slopes of Hecla to the sheltered haven of the Apothecaries' Garden in Chelsea. The blocks of lava may still be seen on the rockery, together with some forty tons of stone rescued from the old Tower of London by Stanley Alchorne, an apothecary who became Demonstrator of Plants to the Society. Two years before the making of the rockery, William Forsyth, a pupil of Philip Miller, had been appointed Gardener to the Physic Garden. He is chiefly remembered for the cheerful spring shrub named after him—Forsythia. During his term of office (long before the Embankment was constructed), a series of exceptionally high tides on the Thames flooded the garden to a depth of fifteen inches. Forsyth later became Superintendent of the royal gardens at Kensington Palace; in 1773 he introduced William Curtis, and he was responsible for having the latter made Demonstrator in succession to Alchorne. Curtis is well known for his *Flora Londoniensis* and for the *Botanical Magazine*, which is still flourishing.

Seeds and bulbs were constantly arriving at the Physic Garden, sent by Sir Joseph Banks, Sir James Smith—the founder of the Linnean Society—and many other botanists. Students and apprentices of the Society of Apothecaries went on long botanical expeditions; sometimes through the fields of Islington to Hampstead Heath; sometimes south of the river to Battersea fields, where the Fritillary grew, as it still does nearer the source of the Thames; sometimes to Wandsworth, Putney or Hammersmith. All these forays were led by the Demonstrator. Each student carried a tin box, called a vasculum, for specimens; but protocol forbade the carrying of greatcoat or umbrella. The medicinal values of plants found on these rambles were discussed and expounded in the evenings after the field work was done.

In 1829 came the innovation of throwing open the Physic Garden to all students of medicine and botany; hitherto it had been used only by the Society of Apothecaries. This decision had greatly expanded the teaching duties by the time John Lindley was appointed Professor of Botany in 1835. The son of a Norfolk nurseryman, Lindley came to London as librarian to Sir Joseph Banks, where he was well placed for improving his knowledge of botany. He progressed to the post of Secretary to the Royal Horticultural Society, and later accepted the Chair of Botany at University College. For a while Robert Fortune, on Lindley's recommendation, held office as Curator at the Physic Garden, but he soon found himself transferred to the John Company as adviser on the cultivation of tea in India. In 1851 he took 2,000 tea plants and 1,700 sprouting seeds in Wardian cases to North-west India.

The Wardian case played a large part in the successful movement of living plants from one country to another. Nathaniel Ward was a physician practising in London's East End; a city doctor with an overpowering interest in natural history. Before his professional work began, he would set out at first light in summertime, going as far afield as Wimbledon Common and Shooter's Hill in search of wild flowers and other living things. One day he buried a chrysalis in a wide-mouthed bottle full of moist earth and placed it in a window. While watching for the chrysalis to hatch, he observed that some little plants had begun to sprout in the soil. So he tried a larger, enclosed glass case for growing plants, with great success. Faraday lectured on this invention at the Royal Institution, and Ward published a book: *The Growth of Plants in Closely-glazed Cases.*

With this type of case, it now became possible to transmit growing plants from one country to another with very little trouble and almost a hundred per cent success. They were protected from wind, salt spray and other pollution, and remained permanently moist without watering. By this means Robert Fortune was able to move tea plants from China to the Himalayas as if by magic; the Cinchona went in safety from South America to the East; Chinese bananas travelled in comfort to Samoa and Fiji. A large, fixed Wardian case may still be seen at work in the Chelsea Physic Garden, full of filmy ferns which thrive in their damp and draught-free glass case, untouched by soot or snow. It is awe-inspiring to imagine how much the world we know has been altered by means of this unspectacular contrivance, whose inventor is scarcely remembered by the tea-drinkers, quinine-takers, or banana-eaters of the present century. The plant bottles which have of late become fashionable as house adornments are, of course, direct descendants of the Wardian case which the learned Dr Nathaniel created in 1829.

The eventful year 1874, when the Embankment was constructed, might—had the developers got their way—have swept the Physic Garden from Chelsea. When the scheme was first mooted, the Society was offered a section of Kew Gardens in return for its land; but the terms of Sir Hans Sloane's Will made it impossible for the Apothecaries to agree, even if they had not considered Kew too far away to suit their purposes. Away went many picturesque river-stairs, gardens, wharves and barges, to the disgust of artists and others interested in the preservation of such features. Carlyle, severely practical, preferred the new promenade for his walks abroad, and Ruskin accepted the change for his sake;

its solid bastion against Thames mud and the attendant smells must have made life more salubrious.

Trees in the Physic Garden did not benefit from the change, for the high tides no longer sent rich supplies of river water percolating through the mud banks to their roots, and many of them died in consequence. A veteran which did survive, the Maidenhair or Ginkgo tree, was one of the first specimens to be grown in England in modern times. It had been brought here from China, where it had been deemed sacred, and tended in the precincts of temples. Long before man appeared on this planet, the Ginkgo flourished in great forests peopled by megalosaurus, iguanodon, and pterodactyl. Known as the 'fossil tree', it had been considered extinct by European geologists and botanists, before its discovery in China. Sir David Prain, who became Director of the Royal Botanic Garden at Kew in 1905, believed the Gingko to be the tree of the 'willow-pattern' plate. When an old Ginkgo is examined, the side branches, covered all the way down with small leaves, and turning up at the end of a downward swoop, do resemble the so-called 'willow' hanging over the bridge. The old specimen tree at Chelsea came to a sad end when the local authority took a strip of land from the north side of the garden for road widening.

A venerable English Yew still stands, reputedly the largest of its kind in London; for company it has an old Cork Oak, a Catalpa, two good Tulip trees (*Liriodendron tulipifera*), an aged Persimmon from the southern United States, a Gleditschia, Koelreuteria, and a Chinese 'Dawn Redwood' (*Metasequoia glyptostroboides*), which, like the Ginkgo, had been considered extinct. It was found in 1945 in Szechuan. There is also a young oriental plane of distinguished pedigree. It is a seedling from the tree in Cos under which Hippocrates is said to have taught.

After the building of the Embankment, the Chelsea Physic Garden fell into something resembling a decline. Botany grew much less important in medical training, as plant medicines were superseded by chemicals manufactured in laboratories. Expenditure had to be curtailed, and the Curator (Thomas Moore) spent most of his time studying ferns. After his death in 1893, as neither the Royal Society nor the College of Physicians would accept responsbility for the Gardens, the Society of Apothecaries requested the Charity Commissioners to formulate a scheme which would legally allow the Trust to be relinquished. As there was still a demand for the Garden for use by students of the Royal College of Science, the London polytechnics, and certain schools, the Trustees of the London Parochial Charities agreed to provide funds for its maintenance, supplemented by a Treasury grant each year. A strip of land was sold to the Chelsea

Vestry for £1,950, to allow widening of the Royal Hospital Road, and with £4,050 borrowed by the Trustees, the present Curator's house, lecture room and laboratory were built. These were opened in 1902, together with new glasshouses.

The objects of the Charity, as defined by the scheme of 1899, are: 'The Charity and its endowments shall be administered exclusively for the promotion of the study of Botany, with special reference to the requirements of

(*a*) General education;

(*b*) Scientific instruction and research in Botany, including Vegetable physiology, and

(*c*) Instruction in Technical Pharmacology as far as the culture of medicinal plants is concerned.'

The Garden and its accompanying library and lecture rooms provides today for research and teaching over a wide field, reaching students in twelve university colleges, six medical schools, twelve training colleges, eight polytechnics, and various GLC schools; to these some 35,000 examination specimens are supplied annually. The living plant collection in the Garden contains about 5,000 species. A large section is devoted to Natural Order beds, wherein close on 100 families are represented. As befits a Physic Garden, early medicinal plants are a feature, together with culinary herbs in modern use. The exchange of seeds with other botanic gardens is going on all the time; thousands of packets pass from one institution to another every year. Research facilities are currently in use by the Agricultural Research Council, the British Museum (Natural History), Chelsea College of Science and Technology, the Medical Research Council, and the Imperial College of Science and Technology. As Lord Morton writes in the official booklet: 'It will be seen that nearly 300 years since its foundation the Chelsea Physic Garden is more active than at any period in its history and plays no unimportant part in the scientific life of the second half of the twentieth century.'

Unlike some scientific institutions, it is also a very attractive garden in which to wander purely for pleasure. Nearly all the plants look cared for and healthy; only the rosemary seemed a little dejected. Despite the growth of smokeless zones, this plant does not appear to flourish in London as it used to do in the time of Sir Thomas More. My last glimpse of the Garden took in a fine bunch of mistletoe growing on a *Crataegus oxycantha*, which set me wondering if today's young descendants of the old apothecaries have fun with it at Christmas time.

Mention must be made of the fine library of botanical books. These were acquired mainly in the seventeenth and eighteenth centuries by the Society of Apothecaries, and are held by the present Committee of Management on permanent loan. The valuable old books have been carefully restored in recent years. Two heavy oak presses, said to be the original library cupboards ordered in 1739, now stand in the lecture-room adjoining the library. The last surviving Cedar of Lebanon, felled in 1903, provided wood for a library table.

The Worshipful Society of Apothecaries of London, founded by James I in 1617, is a Craft Guild whose early members, as I have mentioned, seceded from the Grocers' Company because they felt that they had sufficient technical knowledge to compound medicines, which were formerly imported from abroad. In the first century of their existence as a separate body, the apothecaries began to give advice and to supply medicines without the intervention of a physician. The College of Physicians exercised its legal powers in an attempt to suppress this form of medical practice; but in 1703 the Society carried a test case to the House of Lords and gained a decision in its favour.

The Apothecaries' Act of 1815 gave the Society the legal right to grant licences to practise medicine throughout England and Wales and entrusted to it the duty of controlling that practice. The General Medical Council was established in 1858, and following the passing of a new Medical Act in 1886 the Society's Licence became a fully registrable qualification in medicine, surgery and midwifery. The Society holds examinations for this diploma in eleven months of every year, and numbers of young doctors embark upon their careers with this qualification. In 1946 the Society founded the first postgraduate diploma in Industrial Health; and in 1962 the first in Medical Jurisprudence.

The Society's home has been on the present site—that of the Black Friars Monastery—since 1632. The entire premises were burned down in the Great Fire of 1666, being completely rebuilt by the end of 1668, substantially as they are now. The staircase was erected in 1671; the panelling of the Great Hall and Court Room was installed between 1670 and 1695. The ormulu 24-branch candelabrum was given to the Society in 1736 by Benjamin Rawling—whose full-length portrait, in a red robe, hangs in the hall. In the Court Room there is a portrait of Gideon de Laune, who first agitated for the separation of the Apothecaries from the Grocers. This picture was dragged away to a place of safety during the Great Fire by one of the Society's apprentices.

The Chelsea Physic Garden owes its existence to the Society; but in our time the majority of students who work there are engaged in botanical rather than medical study of the plants.

The Royal Botanic Gardens, Kew

Go down to Kew in lilac-time,
In lilac-time, in lilac-time:
Go down to Kew in Lilac-time,
(It isn't far from London!)

THOSE lines from a poem by Alfred Noyes, popular between the two world wars, are seldom remembered now. Yet they serve to illustrate what Kew still means to that amorphous entity known as 'the general public'—a place to visit at pleasant seasons of the year, to stroll on grass, to admire and sniff quantities of scented blossom, without the slightest regard for botany and plant history, or knowledge of whether the species in bloom happen to be rarities.

During my London-based youth I was sometimes taken to Kew to see cherry or lilac in flower, or the giant water-lily named after Queen Victoria, but for years remained in ignorance of the fact that this 'public park' was really something much more. Kew is indeed all things to all men, and those who wish to enjoy it as an open-air spectacle are as welcome as the most erudite plant specialists at work in the herbarium; yet the primary object is to act (as the official guide states), as a scientific institution.

Although here grouped with another physic and botanic garden, Kew would also have been eligible for a place in the first section, having been 'Royal' from its inception over a century ago. It was formed in the main from two estates bought by the royal family during the eighteenth century. George II and Queen Caroline lived on the Ormonde Lodge estate, which ran beside the Thames from Richmond Green to Kew, while their son Frederick, Prince of Wales, inhabited the Kew estate stretching from the present southern boundary of the gardens, by the Pagoda, to Kew Green. It was Frederick's widow, the Dowager Princess Augusta, who in 1759 started a botanic garden on nine acres of land south of the present Orangery: the modest beginning of what is now a world-famous collection and second to none.

On the orders of Princess Augusta, the architect Sir William Chambers embellished her garden with Orangery, Pagoda, and 'ruined arch'. The Orangery served as a greenhouse for the best part of a hundred years; the original herb garden lay in front of it. Some of the trees planted in 1762 have survived, including the huge Maidenhair Tree (*Ginkgo biloba*), False Acacia (*Robinia pseudoacacia*), Pagoda Tree (*Sophora japonica*), and a Turkey Oak.

When George III succeeded his grandfather in 1760 the Kew and Richmond estates were joined, and an observatory was set up on the site of Ormonde Lodge. With the assistance of Sir Joseph Banks as unofficial Director, the Royal Head Gardener, William Aiton, carried out a certain amount of development in the Botanic Garden; but Sir Joseph's vision, his dream of making Kew into a great plant exchange, spreading knowledge of those valuable to mankind throughout the civilized world, did not come to fruition in his lifetime. In the end this vast project was to materialize under the guidance of Banks's protégé, William Hooker, and under the latter's brilliant son Joseph, who became his father's assistant and later the Director. (He had been named after Banks.)

It was not to be a smooth progression. Following the death of the famous Sir Joseph Banks in 1820, things began to go very much awry, and William Townsend Aiton, son of William, was not able to maintain the course that his wise and learned mentor had charted. Money made available for the Botanic Garden was cut down, and he was made Director-General of all the royal gardens, so becoming too busy to devote much attention to Kew. John Smith, the foreman, deserves credit for keeping up a good standard in difficult circumstances. Ill-informed government officials sought to make economies by breaking up the priceless collection so laboriously acquired down the years of Kew's existence, offering plants in lots to other organizations, including the Botanic Society's gardens in Regent's Park and the Horticultural Society's at Chiswick. It is to their credit that they refused. Short-sighted officials planned to convert the Botany Bay House—crammed with valuable specimens from New Holland (Australia) into a vinery, and the Cape House also.

When news of this vandalism leaked out, there was a public outcry. In the Upper House Lord Aberdeen inquired whether the Government intended to abolish the Royal Botanic Gardens at Kew, which he considered to form a 'part of the state and dignity of the Crown'. Under mounting pressure the Government gave in, and proposals for demolishing the gardens were abandoned. Responsibility was transferred to the Commissioners of Woods and Forests from the oddly-named Board of Green Cloth. It was commonly thought that

Aiton would soon retire, and Sir William Hooker, then holding the Chair of Botany at Glasgow University, longed to become Director of Kew. For a while it seemed as though his interest in, and manifest fitness for, this important post were not going to bring the coveted reward. He knew all the right people; he had had the patronage of Sir Joseph Banks; but there were influences hostile to spending money on the Botanic Gardens, and these had first to be overcome. Hooker, who wanted above all to follow where Banks had led, nearly gave up hope. Then, in 1841, he was suddenly offered the Directorship. He was so amazed that he could scarcely believe it. Of course he recovered his wits, and accepted the appointment.

William Townsend Aiton was less pleased. He had been blamed for deficiencies, but responsibility lay with his employers, and this made him bitter. Retaining his post as Royal Gardener until 1846, and now shedding the load of the Botanic Garden only, he claimed that all the printed books and drawings were his own property, together with journals, account books and correspondence. Some records were retrieved for Kew after Aiton died; but William Hooker was obliged to begin his great task without any of these important documents. He agreed to run the garden for the sum previously expended—a mere £3,700 per annum—and to accept the modest salary of £300, so keen was he to undertake the work. In order to accommodate his own fine library, and the enormous herbarium to which his life had been dedicated, he needed a large house. Thirteen rooms were initially occupied by his collection, and to help with the expense a rent allowance of £200 was granted. The botanical world of London thus acquired (at minimum cost) not only the services of a great botanist, but the finest herbarium in the world, to draw scholars and raise the international reputation of Kew beyond anything yet imagined.

In May 1841 William Hooker wrote to his beloved son Joseph, who was then in South Africa:

> 'This is probably the last letter I shall ever write to you from Glasgow. All my books are gone—about 60 great packages, all my plants arranged and unarranged—much of my furniture: the rest I hope will go on Saturday . . . henceforth "Kew" is my residence and your residence: or rather a very pretty place within ten minutes walk of Kew called *Brick-farm* . . . we are within 400 yards of the Thames and opposite Chiswick, the Duke of Devonshire's place.'

On reaching London, his goods (in five different vessels) were transferred into lighters and taken to the banks of the Thames at Brick-farm. Hooker's wife and three daughters were in Jersey for health reasons; so, as he said in Joseph's letter, he arrived 'all alone and no one to meet me'. After the somewhat austere climate of Glasgow he was enchanted by the luxuriant growth in his new home: 'The trees so noble and full of leaf, the Laburnum so full of blossom.' No doubt this helped to assuage his loneliness.

The eleven acres which William Hooker took over consisted chiefly of Princess Augusta's botanic garden of 1759, with some three acres of arboretum. By the end of 1841 another four acres had been added. The new director's first innovation was the opening of Kew to the public from early morning until dusk, including the glasshouses. In Aiton's time visiting hours had been very restricted and the public rigidly shepherded. Everyone predicted dire catastrophe when these rules were suddenly relaxed. By the end of a year over 9,000 people had passed through the gardens, and the Director's optimism was fully justified. No damage worth mentioning had been done. Soon the nobility and gentry rolled up in their carriages to admire all the improvements, dismounting to walk among the crowds accompanied by the charming and enthusiastic Hooker. An excellent diplomat and showman, he astutely put the needs of Kew to those who could fill them, and thus obtained many a coveted plant or cutting from owners of notable gardens. The Royal Horticultural Society passed a resolution that henceforth plants and seeds received from its collectors were to be divided with the Royal Botanic Gardens. No wonder this collection grew apace.

In 1842 Queen Victoria sanctioned a major extension, which brought another forty acres to the area already managed by Hooker. The greater Kew drew more people, and in 1844 the annual count rose to 15,000 visitors. In his report on the gardens after four years as Director, William Hooker showed how the policy of distribution had been useful to countries all over the world; many had reciprocated by sending gifts to Kew of plants hitherto unknown to horticulture in the United Kingdom. Two plant collectors (Purdie and Burke) had been sent overseas by an arrangement between the Duke of Northumberland, the Earl of Derby and himself, expenses being shared. Everything went well; when Queen Victoria and Prince Albert paid Kew a visit in 1843, the Director was able to present his son Joseph, newly returned from a long Antarctic voyage with a wealth of unique botanical specimens.

The year 1844 is remembered for the large greenhouse then built at Kew. Decimus Burton's Palm House is still one of the most beautiful glasshouses ever constructed. The dimensions—362 feet in length, 100 feet wide, 66 feet high, made it among the largest of its day. The estimated cost of £5,000 seemed very extravagant to most people; few discovered that the real outlay amounted to over £8,000. A hundred workmen were employed on the project, all at the same time. This magnificent building served as a focal point for the landscaping that Hooker had for long wished to carry out in the Royal Botanic Gardens, and he took full advantage of it. Today one's first glimpse of it across the water suggests some bizarre type of submarine which has just surfaced from the pond. The small area of water is all that remains of a lake created here by George III and largely filled up in 1812. Of the Palm House it was said that 'palms now grow where painted Britons were wont to snare water-fowl'.

Expansion at Kew continued apace. In 1845, at the age of seventy-nine, William Aiton retired from charge of the Pleasure Grounds, and these 200 acres, hitherto separated from the Botanic Gardens by stout fences and ha-has, were thrown into a greatly enlarged 'Kew Gardens' under Hooker. The making of a national arboretum and landscaping of the whole area now became practicable. By 1847 the number of visitors had risen to 64,000. The queen in 1842 had given part of her land adjacent to Kew Green so that some dignified entrance gates, also designed by Decimus Burton, might be erected there: work completed in 1848. The Broad Walk was laid out from these gates for a distance of about 200 yards, with a turn at that point before it continued for another 500 yards to the Palm House. Three ways radiating from the main entrance and opening up some lovely vistas, were finished in 1851. The director was indefatigable. He lived for Kew. Even so, he himself was amazed at the success of all his plans. As many as 4,000 to 5,000 plants were sent in one year to countries all over the world; with the coming of the steamship, plants and cuttings travelled faster and arrived in better condition. Soon the land under Hooker's control amounted to 650 acres, including the Old Deer Park at Richmond. His reputation grew and spread as rapidly as the area under his supervision. The University of Oxford bestowed on him the honorary degree of DCL. His son Joseph was acquiring many laurels, too, and laying the foundation of a scientific career even more distinguished than that of his father.

In between many journeys to far distant countries, Joseph was able to give valuable help to Sir William. He also provided Charles Darwin with much data, which the latter fully acknowledged as being of the greatest assistance to him during the period when his theory of the origin of species was being worked out. Botany served endless purposes. A physic garden for the use of medical students became one of the educational departments at Kew. This was reported in 1854 as being 'very serviceable to students of medicine and others'.

Then there was William Hooker's embryo museum of useful plants, made in the Glasgow days to demonstrate the economic value of many plants in different parts of the world. He used his collection, set out in an old fruit store, to impress the Commissioners of Woods and Forests with the need for a display of this nature at Kew. They were sufficiently convinced to sponsor the building of quarters to house exhibits, and in 1847 the first Museum of Economic Botany was opened for public inspection and use. It engendered nationwide interest and approval, and contributions poured in. Soon there were three such buildings at Kew, all full of valuable material.

Meanwhile Joseph Hooker had steadily enhanced his reputation as an intrepid traveller and plant-collector, and was engaged upon a trilogy of books dealing with the Ross Antarctic Expedition in the ships *Erebus* and *Terror*, of which he had been a member. Sir William had for some time been hoping to obtain his son's services for Kew, and now offered to present his famous herbarium to the nation on condition that Joseph was appointed as Director's assistant. This manœuvre did not at first succeed, and Joseph, who hated wire-pulling, seized an opportunity to go plant-hunting in India. During an absence of over three years he climbed in the Himalaya to 19,000 feet, the highest altitude known to have been reached by man. This constituted a record until 1856, when two German brothers reached 22,230 feet. Joseph sent home quantities of herbarium specimens, exhibits for his father's botanical museum, and magnificent rhododendrons from Sikkim. They included *R. argenteum* with silver lined leaves; the red flowered *R. arboreum* and *R. barbatum*; *R. falconeri* with golden plushy undersides to its foliage, and the purple *R. nivale*, found at 18,000 feet. These were soon propagated in Britain, and spread to gardens as far apart as Inverewe in Wester Ross and Cornwall and the Scilly Isles. Queen Victoria had some sent to Osborne, and at Kew the old Hollow Walk was transformed into the Rhododendron Dell.

It is difficult now to recapture the horticultural excitement of mid-Victorian times, when plant collectors were continually bringing new plants and seeds home for growers to raise; owners of great houses vied with one another to flower the new acquisitions first, and the climate of opinion might justly be compared with the enthusiasm of gold prospectors taking nuggets from their pans. Botany was a fashionable study among the leisured classes, and innumerable talented ladies produced exquisitely detailed water-colours of flowers. In fact, plants at that time caused as many thrills as specimens of moon-rock have created in our own day. Who shall say which novelty has conferred the greater pleasure and benefit on the human race?

It must not be forgotten that Kew, during the Directorship of Sir William Hooker, regularly sent out plant collectors all over the world. In his book about the Royal Botanic Gardens issued in 1908, W. J. Bean wrote:

> 'In 1843 W. Purdie was sent to the West Indies and New Granada, and J. Burke to Western North America. From 1847 to 1850, Berthold Seeman was attached as botanical collector to H.M.S. *Herald* during her voyage in the Pacific. He was succeeded in the same post by W. G. Milne from 1852 to 1859. Seeman subsequently went to Fiji (1860–1), and Milne afterwards collected on the West Coast of Africa (1862–6). Charles Barter joined Baikie's expedition to the Niger in 1859, but died at Rabba in the following year. His position as botanist to the expedition was filled by Gustav Mann, who returned safely to England in 1863. Charles Wilford was sent out to collect seeds and herbarium material in Korea, Formosa, etc. He was employed from 1857 to 1860. On his recall, his place was filled by Richard Oldham, who collected in Japan, Korea and Formosa. Oldham died from dysentery in 1864, and with his death came to an end the long succession of Kew collectors which had begun with Francis Masson when he went to South Africa ninety years before.
>
> 'Owing to the establishment of numerous foreign and colonial botanic gardens, with which Kew kept up a regular correspondence, the employment of specially appointed collectors became no longer so necessary. And when the leading nurserymen took up the practice and generously let Kew share in their collectors' consignments, still less was an official collector required. It should always be remembered, however, that Kew was the pioneer in this work. Before Masson went out to the Cape in 1772, the introduction of extra-European plants was a haphazard affair. But from that date until the death of Oldham in Amoy, an almost continuous stream of new plants was pouring into England from Kew collectors or from *alumni* living abroad.'

In 1850 the Department of Woods and Forests split up, part of its work being taken over by the new Board of Works and Public Buildings. The Richmond Old Deer Park stayed with Woods and Forests, while the Royal Botanic Gardens and Pleasure Grounds of Kew were transferred to the Board of Works. So it came about that Sir William Hooker was relieved of responsibility for the

Deer Park. Fortunately for Kew, some dividing walls had been removed in 1846, giving splendid vistas of parkland and the Thames banks, with Syon Park in the distance. These arrangements lasted until 1903, when Kew was again transferred—this time to the Board of Agriculture and Fisheries. Such changes made little or no difference to the running of the Gardens; the Director's authority was unchallenged.

One of the many valuable experiments conducted from Kew was the afforestation of Ascension Island in the South Atlantic, which followed Joseph Hooker's exploration of this bare and sterile spot. In 1843 he described it as having but one tree and no shrub growth whatever. Sir William Hooker arranged for Kew to send out plants and seeds year by year, with gardeners to look after their installation and care, a project so well handled that in 1865 an Admiralty report described the results in glowing terms. The island was then under naval control, and the official description of its vegetation ran as follows:

> 'The island now possesses thickets of upwards of 40 kinds of trees, besides numerous shrubs and fruit trees—of which, however, only the guava ripens. These afford excellent timber for fencing cattle-yards . . .'

The spread of all this plant life improved the water supply, a benefit which visiting ships enjoyed, together with a good range of fresh vegetables. Thus the entire aspect and economy of the island were changed for the better, owing to wise advice and practical help given by the Royal Botanic Gardens.

In June 1850 the great aquatic lily, *Victoria regia*, was first flowered at Kew. In that year nearly 180,000 people passed through the gates. The small tank in which the lily originally grew soon proved to be inadequate for its gigantic spread, and a new house with a circular tank 36 feet in diameter was erected for it in 1852. At the same period the Queen's Cottage at Kew had its grounds freshly laid out for the pleasure of Queen Victoria and the Prince Consort. In 1853 the new and somewhat revolutionary step of opening the gardens, hot-houses and museums on Sundays created a stir. The queen had long since decreed that Hampton Court should be accessible to her subjects on the sabbath; but Kew was the first, and for long the only, scientific institution to adopt this policy. That it was appreciated by the public is obvious from the attendance figures, which increased by 100,000 in the ensuing year.

At this time Sir William Hooker, now aged sixty-seven, began to find the distance between his dwelling, 'Brick-farm' (subsequently renamed West Park) and the Botanical Gardens irksome. In addition, the housing and care of an ever-growing herbarium cost him a great deal, and the gift by his father-in-law, Dawson Turner, of his own fine collection made the problem of space even worse. With his usual aplomb he set wheels in motion which resulted in the acquisition of Hunter House as the official herbarium for Kew. This meant that the Director no longer needed the accommodation provided by West Park; soon a convenient house on the Green was made available to him, and that has been the official residence ever since.

With his son Joseph safely back from the East, settling down to matrimony at 350 Kew Road, and preparing his *Himalayan Journals* for publication, Sir William's happiness was nearly complete. The finishing touch was put when in 1855 Dr Joseph Dalton Hooker was appointed Assistant Director of the Royal Botanic Gardens.

The *Himalayan Journals* were dedicated to Charles Darwin, with whom Joseph had kept up a long and affectionate correspondence since 1843. In these letters many ideas were discussed in detail, ideas which Darwin gradually built up into his theory of the origin of species. A book with that title was published—to evoke a storm of protest—in 1859. It is worth recording here that in 1862 Darwin wrote to Joseph Hooker saying: 'For years I have looked to you as the man whose opinion I have valued more on any scientific subject, than anyone else in the world.' It seems likely that, but for the influence of Joseph and of the eminent geologist Charles Lyell, Darwin's famous book might never have been published. By coincidence the naturalist Alfred Russel Wallace had, all unknown to Darwin, been thinking along similar lines far away in Malaya. In the very month of June 1858 when the *Origin of Species* neared completion in manuscript, Wallace sent home a brief account of his original theory that only the fittest survived. Darwin was stunned. The similarity of Wallace's ideas to his own was so great that a synopsis of the new book might have been accepted by Wallace as his own. Being a man of finely honourable character, Darwin felt unable to push forward publication of his book before Wallace could make his theory known. In the end Hooker and Lyell persuaded him to proceed, after an abstract, together with the paper written by Wallace, had been read before the Linnean Society. Fortunately Wallace did not doubt that Darwin had conceived his idea some twenty years earlier than he, and became a great admirer of his rival's work.

That work had been very greatly assisted by Joseph Hooker's unrivalled knowledge of plant distribution; and, as complete and accurate classification was essential to pin-point geographical distribution, Joseph became stimulated by Darwin to greater and more accurate examination of world flora. For very good economic reasons (improvement of crop plants, control of disease, etc.) developing countries are vitally interested in their native plants. In the 1850s Sir William persuaded the Treasury to allow him to spend money on the compilation of floras of the Commonwealth, and thus initiated the work which has been the principal preoccupation of the bulk of Kew scientists ever since. While Joseph toiled at his desk, dealing with wagon-loads of fresh acquisitions for the herbarium, his father was active in the gardens outside. A new nursery, formed in 1855, raised quantities of trees for London parks, notably English elm and plane; the latter having been first raised by that great gardener John Tradescant at Lambeth under the Stuarts. This decorative tree, with its patterned bole and dangling tassels of seeds, has become the best-known tree of our metropolitan parks. Its constant renewal of bark makes it unusually tolerant of sooty atmospheres. In 1858 1,000 planes and 500 elms were supplied to Hyde Park by Kew, and 500 planes went to Battersea Park, while in the 30 acres surrounding the Queen's Cottage at Kew nearly 1,800 trees were installed.

Sir William now began to press for another glasshouse to take plants from temperate regions. 'I feel it to be my imperative duty as Conservator of this property to say that, unless we can commence the needful structure during the year 1859, I cannot answer for the preservation of the remains of this noble collection.' Even by 1841 some of the shrubs had reached the top of existing greenhouses, and had had to be mutilated to keep them down; seven years later one of the oldest of these houses became too dilapidated to repair, and was in consequence demolished. The Director's *cri-de-coeur* brought swift response. The House of Commons sanctioned a grant, and Decimus Burton was called in to design a worthy companion for his great Palm House. By 1862 Sir William saw the central block and two octagons completed; but the wings for some reason were not finished until many years later, after his death. Although eminently suited to its purpose, the Temperate House is stolid and earth-bound in character, unlike the floating ethereal 'ship' which houses the palms. Possibly it is aesthetically valuable to have this marked contrast between the two glasshouses.

Meanwhile Edward Stamp had presented Kew with a grand flagstaff, 118 feet high. This suffered a sad fate while being towed up the Thames from the docks, being cut in halves by a tug-boat. It was spliced and made ready for hoisting, but a gale sprang up and upset the derrick, breaking the pole into three sections. Stamp, who traded in Canadian timber, promptly sent over an even larger tree, measuring 159 feet. In 1860 Princess Mary Adelaide recorded in her diary the ceremony of erecting this latest addition to the scene at Kew:

> 'Immediately after breakfast we hurried to the Pleasure-grounds to see the flagstaff set up by sailors and shipwrights before the delighted eyes of the frantically excited Hookey, the astonished eyes of Kewites of all classes, and the disapproving eyes of our party who considered it highly tea-gardeny!'

This flagstaff had to be replaced in 1919, and again in 1959, when a Douglas Fir nearly 400 years old and 225 feet long was presented by the Government of British Columbia in commemoration of the first centenary of the Province (1958) and Kew's own bicentenary (1959). The Royal Engineers were brought in to erect the pole, and it still stands today upon Victory Hill.

Among many projects of benefit to mankind which have been initiated at Kew, the spread of the Cinchona plant, whence quinine is extracted, has given immeasurable relief to sufferers from malaria and other tropical diseases. C. R. Markham brought live specimens from Peru for cultivation by Kew, and later established the plant in the Nilghiri Hills in South India. Seeds of other species were obtained from Ecuador and Bolivia, and in 1860 large plantations of Cinchona were made in both Ceylon and India. By 1893 quinine was being produced in such amounts as to make it possible for the people of Bengal to buy five grains for a farthing. This precious 'Red Bark' had been jealously guarded by the Indians of South America, and those plant collectors who managed to spread its cultivation for the benefit of mankind in other countries did so at risk of their lives. Other plant exchanges of great economic value included the transfer of cork oak from Spain and Portugal to South Australia, tea from China to Assam ('China' tea), and coffee, tobacco and tropical fruits to Queensland.

The most dramatic story is that of the great rubber hunt. As far back as the days of Columbus this strange elastic substance had been seen and marvelled at. The explorer noticed people in Haiti playing with balls which would 'rebound incredibly in the aire'; but mankind was slow to grasp the useful possibilities of this gum. Charles de la Condamine, the Frenchman who led an expedition to Brazil in 1735, brought back articles made by the Indians from the 'caoutchouc', and in 1770 Joseph Priestley coined the name 'rubber' for this substance when he saw a draughtsman erasing pencil marks with it. America began to manufacture waterproof coats and boots early in the nineteenth century, and guttapercha was imported into Britain early in the eighteen-fifties. Although useful for some purposes, this gum was not truly elastic. Sir William Hooker exhibited guttapercha in his Museum of Economic Botany, and in his Handbook for 1861 asked for live plants of the allied species of *Sapotaceae* growing in the East Indian islands, Madagascar and Guiana.

It so happened that a young man named Wickham had gone off by himself to explore unvisited sectors of Central and South America, where he used his artistic ability to sketch the many strange plants seen along the way. He issued a journal of these travels, in which Joseph Hooker noticed a drawing of *Hevea brasiliensis*, the best of all rubber trees. The Hookers had already obtained seeds of that tree with the idea of starting rubber plantations in India and the East Indies, but after a long sea voyage in over-hot conditions none were viable. When young Wickham received a letter from Kew asking him to do his utmost to procure a second consignment, he was in a dilemma. It was now illegal to take the rubber tree or its seeds out of the country, and he could not think how to circumvent this restriction.

By great good luck he found a British ship without a cargo at the very time when the rubber fruit was ripe. He boldly chartered the whole ship, in the name of the Government of India, and together with the British Consul paid a call on the port authorities. The explorer expatiated upon the beauties and wonders of Brazil, and said how much he would like to take a collection of plants home for Queen Victoria's Botanic Gardens at Kew. The highly flattered officials, delighted by this enthusiasm, at once agreed to sanction the apparently harmless project. With essential clearance papers in his pocket, Wickham had the ship taken out of Pará harbour, and in a short time the precious baskets of rubber seed were lifted from the hold and slung up on deck to keep cool. As soon as the ship docked in the Port of London, the smuggled cargo was rushed to Kew in a special train. Before long thousands of rubber seedlings were growing merrily, and in a matter of months Ceylon received about 2,000 young trees to start its plantations. Others went to Malaya, and the whole rubber industry of Asia eventually sprang from those parent seeds brought out of Brazil by Henry Wickham. Like so many pioneers, he seems to have gone without the honours his resourcefulness merited.*

As to the ethics of the business—well, it may not have been ethical of Brazil to wish to retain plants of value to people all over the world! The steady help rendered by Kew in the development of British possessions overseas was praised

* He received a knighthood, but fifty years after the exploit.

by Joseph Chamberlain in the House of Commons in 1898: 'I do not think it is too much to say that at the present time there are several of our important Colonies which owe whatever prosperity they possess to the knowledge and experience of, and the assistance given by, the authorities at Kew Gardens. Thousands of letters pass every year between the authorities at Kew and the Colonies, and they are able to place at the service of those Colonies not only the best advice and experience, but seeds and samples of economic plants capable of cultivation in the Colonies.'

In addition to all their work at Kew, the Hookers were constantly engaged in writing books of immense worth to botanists. In 1864 Sir William finished his *Species Filicum*, a work in five volumes which had taken him eighteen years to produce. It is still a standard work of reference for pteridologists, as the students of ferns are known. He promptly began his final study of the same subject, *Synopsis Filicum*, which he continued until a few days before his death in August 1865. He was just eighty years old. A memorial plaque in Wedgwood jasper ware was placed in Kew Parish Church on the Green. It shows a profile head of the great botanist, surrounded by a delicate design of his favourite plants, the ferns.

It was a foregone conclusion that Joseph Hooker would be appointed Director in succession to his father. He took up the office in November of the same year, modestly saying that he would endeavour to conduct the affairs of Kew as zealously (though he feared never as efficiently) as his father had done. Like his father, he continued to publish important books on botanical subjects. His *New Zealand Flora* (Part 1) had come out in 1864. The gigantic *Genera Plantarum*, written in collaboration with George Bentham, took twenty-six years. The first part was issued in 1862 and the last in 1883. Then there was a weird African plant—the *Welwitschia*—to occupy him for hours every day. His monograph on this curious vegetable, which makes only one pair of leaves to last for a lifetime of a hundred years, was considered to be a masterpiece.

The great Hooker herbarium, containing a million specimens, and the four thousand volumes left in the library of Sir William, together with no fewer than seventy-six bound volumes of letters from botanists all over the world, were purchased by the nation for £7,000 in 1866. All these valuable records now belong to Kew. The new Director soon had to plan a massive scheme of replanting in the Gardens. The great freeze, with heavy snowfalls, of January 1867 destroyed a large number of the older trees and quantities of shrubs, leaving a trail of ruin which would have daunted a lesser man. Joseph preferred to treat it as a great opportunity, and set to work having impoverished soil renewed. When this was ready to receive the new plantings, he indulged his passion for landscape gardening.

Before long the Cedar and Hawthorn Avenues were in being, and creation of Pinetum, Holly Walk, Azalea Garden and Berberis Dell developed well, together with grassy avenues radiating from the Pagoda, and a long walk parallel with the Thames. When not outdoors at Kew superintending all such operations, the Director made speeches as President of the British Association, received degrees of LLD at Cambridge and DCL at Oxford, and represented British Botanists in Paris and St Petersburg. In 1871 he went plant-hunting in the Atlas Mountains, a tour described in the published *Journal* of 1878.

He came home to face trouble. It was another instance of meddling by government officials, such as had nearly wrecked the Royal Botanic Gardens after the death of Sir Joseph Banks. Endless niggling attempts were made to undermine the Director's authority and impede the work of Kew. In 1872 Joseph Hooker wrote to his friend Bentham that he longed to throw up his appointment, as his life had 'become detestable'. The scientific world rallied to his support and would not allow him to suffer defeat at the hands of ignorant and bumptious individuals. A group of eminent men sent a memorandum to the Prime Minister, couched in the most trenchant terms. Mr Gladstone parried the thrust, and for a time the situation was balanced on a knife-edge; but under pressure of public opinion, which held Kew and its Director in high esteem, he shifted the official responsible for Hooker's persecution, and all trouble ceased. The eminence of Hooker in the scientific world was marked by his election as President of the Royal Society in 1873.

The honour was closely followed by the shock of personal bereavement, when his wife Frances died suddenly in the following year. For a while the Hooker family was looked after by some cousins, who came to live in the house on Kew Green. After some two years Joseph married again, giving the children a much-loved stepmother. Only his eldest daughter, Harriet, failed to accept the situation happily; before long this problem was resolved by her own wedding. She married the botanist William Thistleton-Dyer, who became Assistant Director at Kew and later succeeded his father-in-law as Director. All was now well again in the Hooker ménage.

An event of major importance in the story of the Botanic Gardens occurred in 1876, when the Jodrell Laboratory opened. Its object, the furthering of scientific research into the physiology and structure of plants, had not received much attention for a number of years in Britain. Students had been obliged to go to France or Germany to pursue their interests, in establishments which catered for such objectives and provided equipment for the latest techniques. William Thistleton-Dyer was put in charge of the new laboratory, a post for which his work with Huxley had fitted him. He belonged to the new school of plant physiologists, a field of research outside the Director's experience, but one he believed to be essential to the future development of botany. He had every confidence in Dyer, and left him in charge at Kew while he went to America on a plant-hunting tour. The queen had just made him Knight Commander of the Star of India, so he was now Sir Joseph Hooker.

In 1879 Kew faced another bout of severe storm damage. This time it was violent hail, which broke nearly 4,000 panes in the glasshouses. Fortunately these were soon repaired, and the contents do not seem to have suffered much harm. In 1880 Sir Joseph planted more trees, and next year the Rock Garden was constructed to take a large bequest of alpine plants. That was the great era of rock gardening, when everybody who owned any sort of garden went crazy about 'rock work'. It took over half a century to eradicate the worst follies and hideosities perpetrated during this period. At Kew it was possible to do the job on a suitable site and on a large scale, with rocks of boulder-size imported from such terrain as the Cheddar Gorge in Somerset. People who poked little pieces of tufa rock into poor soil at the end of a lawn did not seem to realize that their kind of 'copy' was not worth making.

An innovation in the form of an art gallery came to maturity at Kew with the opening of the Marianne North Gallery in 1882. Miss North, one of those dauntless Victorian spinsters with an insatiable appetite for travel, had painted flowers under trying and often perilous conditions in every corner of the globe, all with the utmost fidelity to both the plants themselves and to their natural surroundings. The results, 848 paintings of scenes and plants (many of them even, at that date, threatened by 'development' in their native terrain) were presented to Kew, together with the handsome building that housed them, by the artist herself. Unfortunately they were hung *en masse* without space between the frames, and the artistic—as distinct from botanical—merit of so many highly decorative studies is greatly reduced by overcrowding. I wish some body like the Arts Council would provide an enlarged gallery, so that the exhibits might be more tastefully shown; the terms of the gift require all Miss North's paintings to be hung together.

Sir Joseph Hooker's last great work, supervision of the *Index Kewensis*, took ten years. It was financed by Charles Darwin, and serves as a memorial to the friendship of many years between these two great nineteenth-century scientists. In 1885 Hooker was able to relinquish his duties at Kew and devote himself solely to botanical studies, while his son-in-law reigned over the Royal Botanic Gardens. It was thought at the time that Hooker was obliged to resign on medical grounds—doctors were said to have given him only two more years to live. If this was the case, they were very much mistaken, for he enjoyed another twenty-six years in retirement, very active years at that. He gave up using spectacles at ninety and died in 1911 at the age of ninety-four. The suggestion of a Westminster Abbey interment beside his friends Lyell and Darwin was not acceptable, for he had expressed a wish to be buried in the family grave at Kew. A plaque in jasper Wedgwood ware commemorates his abiding interest in botany.

The forty years following Sir Joseph's death included two world wars, but these did not prevent Kew from making some scientific advances. Foundation work leading to the establishment of the rayon industry was carried out in the Jodrell Laboratory, where much useful research had been undertaken since its foundation in 1876. The need for solution of urgent problems in plant pathology led to the formation in 1919 of what eventually became the Plant Pathology Laboratory of the Ministry of Agriculture at Harpenden, which has played an essential part in the immense improvement in agricultural and horticultural production since 1939. During the Second World War research at Kew was of great service to the nation, notably from the suggestion of Dr R. Melville that rose-hips should be used as a source of Vitamin C.

In general, the need for Kew to play a major role in Commonwealth matters, so far as plants and their products were concerned, declined rapidly as countries began to manage their own affairs. Other organizations, such as the Tropical Products Research Institute, came to the fore in specialized fields. When Sir George Taylor became Director of Kew in 1956, he found an institution which had lost part of its role and was coasting along on the rest of its work as it had done since the Hookers' time. Institutions which do not move, where research is concerned, must inevitably get left behind, and this was beginning to happen at Kew. Sir George called in expert advice from a number of senior scientists, and their recommendations were followed. As a result, the Jodrell Laboratory was rebuilt and its work extended, a large new wing was added to the Herbarium, and the horticultural education scheme was revised, together with a number of other improvements.

In 1965 the new two-storied Jodrell Laboratory provided accommodation and facilities for Research Fellows, Post-graduate students and research workers from Britain and overseas; it is affiliated with the University of Reading. Plant anatomy, cytology, physiology and biochemistry sections are now in being, and by 1970 the new laboratory had issued a long list of publications, with titles as various as 'Flower colour and pigment composition in Rhododendrons', 'Germination of the seeds of natural species', 'The history of the strawberry', and 'Chromosome numbers of Pelargonium species and cultivars'.

It is always difficult to explain scientific work in non-technical terms, and a highly dangerous task for any but the trained scientist to attempt. It therefore seems prudent to quote from a booklet issued by the Royal Botanic Gardens on the work of the Jodrell Laboratory, rather than to essay an original description.

> 'Anatomy Section. The staff of this department devote themselves primarily to research. Participation in advisory work is a subsidiary function, implementing the methods and results of original investigation . . . The department has developed microscopical methods for the identification of a wide range of plant material, whole or fragmentary. Powdered material is hydrated by simple chemical treatment and stained. Fragmented material is graded according to particle size under the stereozoom microscope. Surface strips and sections are prepared from larger pieces and stained or subjected to other histochemical tests.
>
> 'Preparations are submitted to light microscopy revealing their composition and any structural features of diagnostic value. Comparison with preparations from named reference material confirms the identification.
>
> 'Specimens commonly determined include commercial timbers, charcoals and other archaeological samples, seeds, roots, crude drugs of vegetable origin, foodstuffs and herbs. Samples submitted may require checking for purity as well as naming. Any adulterants are estimated by numerical proportion or percentage weight and identified. This service is used frequently by members of the public, commercial firms, research institutions and other government laboratories.
>
> 'Members of the staff are required occasionally to act as professional consultants and may have to display their expertise during litigation. Technical advice is given to plant anatomists from all over the world, and many visit the anatomical laboratories for periods of study and discussion.
>
> 'These twin aspects of the anatomical work are mutually sustaining, and the knowledge gained from each has reciprocal implications. Arising from these investigations, there has accumulated a reference collection of 40,000

17. Kew Gardens. 18th-century engraving of George III's Lake with swan boat

18. The Palm House at Kew

19. The Queen's House and 17th-century garden, Kew

20. Daffodils at Kew

21. Syon House from Kew Gardens in 1832
Engraved after J. Farrington, RA, for *An History of the River Thames*

22. Lambeth Palace, 1720

23. Jane Loudon, from a miniature

24. Theresa Earle

25. E. S. Rohde

microscopic slides of the vegetative parts of flowering plants. This is available for consultation.

'Anatomy has proved itself to be a useful taxonomic tool, corroborating evidence from other methods, underlining resemblances and differences and sometimes indicating fresh alignments and phylogenetic trends. It will continue to evolve its role in classification and can also provide valuable contributions in the fields of morphogenesis, variation, adaptation and population studies. It is intended to initiate joint projects with other departments at Kew and elsewhere, to integrate the investigation of selected problems which might be expected to yield to concerted attack from different directions and disciplines. Reversing the recent fashion of over-specialization, the Jodrell can exert a unifying influence advancing our science on a broader botanical spectrum.'

The Cytology Section has this to say:

'During the last ten years this section has made studies of chromosome constitution and breeding systems of a wide range of plants mainly of tropical and subtropical origin. The precise nature of the investigation has largely been dictated by the character of the large living collection at Kew. As is the case with all other Botanic Gardens, there are many taxa but rarely if ever is any one represented by adequate samples from a number of natural populations. Studies of chromosomes based on such material must then be broad and comprehensive rather than intensive. Population cytology cannot often be practised, with the consequence that the dynamics of chromosome evolution cannot adequately be observed. New collections made with this point in mind will ultimately correct this deficiency, and meanwhile some population analyses are being made on species which are readily accessible.'

The work of the Physiology section is

'concerned mainly with investigations into ways in which plant growth and development are controlled in relation to environment. The aspects being studied include germination and dormancy mechanisms in seeds and fruits; responses to photoperiod and temperature as factors regulating vegetative development and flowering; the mineral and organic nutrition of young orchid seedlings growing asymbiotically *in vitro*, and the occurrence and distribution of natural growth-promoting and inhibiting substances in plant tissue.

'Seed germination studies aim to provide information as a guide to storage procedures and testing methods used in the running of the recently established Seed Bank . . .'

'Germination under natural conditions may be a vital character determining the geographical distribution and spread of species. Attempts are being made to find ways of expressing the germination character of a large number of species . . . in a way that allows correlations to be made between their germination responses and the geographical range of a particular species.'

'The work of the Physiology Section is likely to extend in the future to embrace research on scientific methods (e.g. tissue culture) of rapid plant multiplication, which will have great practical significance for the farmer and horticulturist.'

'The aims of research undertaken in the Biochemistry Laboratory are twofold: "One, to investigate the distribution of a wide variety of chemical substances in plants for use in classification *per se*, and two, to study variation in biochemical processes in plants with a view to uncovering underlying operations in plant speciation." '

Sir George Taylor's efforts in the scientific field to swing Kew back into the main stream were more than equalled by his attention to the horticultural side of the Gardens. To him we owe the splendid Heath Garden, and the unique and lovely Queen's Garden behind Kew Palace. This is a careful replica of a seventeenth-century example. Gardens of this period were highly formalized, with pleached alleys, parterres, and a mount or vantage point for viewing the concept as a whole. Here at Kew there is now to be seen something all too rare in Britain: a seventeenth-century garden in which *only* plants available at the time have been used. Too often the so-called 'Tudor' garden, the 'parterre' and 'herb garden' contain such anachronisms as the bedding begonias in the reproduction knot garden at Hampton Court, zonal pelargoniums, gaudy petunias, and—at Scotland's most lovely Adam mansion, modern floribunda roses to upset the period atmosphere on the terrace outside. Such mass-produced plants are cheap, easy to maintain, flower over a long period, and seem to please most of the visitors. It is easy to understand the owners and gardeners who take the line of least resistance in these difficult days. But what a pity it is that our sense of period in gardening is so far below that displayed in furnishing and interior decoration. Perhaps the Garden History Society under the active Presidency of Mr Miles Hadfield will bring about a revolution in this matter.

Another imaginative project initiated by Sir George Taylor was the leasing in 1965 from the National Trust of Wakehurst Place near Ardingly in Sussex, for use as a satellite to the Royal Botanic Gardens. The magnificent collection of trees and shrubs which has been built up there in the last sixty years, coupled with the kinder climate, unpolluted atmosphere and better soil, make it ideal for the purpose. It is hoped to assemble such botanical collections that the reputation of Kew will be enhanced thereby. Over the years this estate should become, like Kew itself, a national possession of which we may well be proud, and, like its parent, a bringer of prestige in the estimation of other nations.

Sir George Taylor, VMH, retired from the Directorship of Kew in 1970. He was succeeded by Professor J. Heslop-Harrison. It is too early yet to evaluate the effect of the change, but the scientific impetus given by Sir George will not be lost, and may be pursued with even greater force under the new Director. The scientific future of the Royal Botanic Gardens looks, according to those who should know, rosy. Directors have many duties, one being the reception of royal visitors. So many royal visits have been paid to Kew that it would be impossible to list them all; but the first of Professor Heslop-Harrison's term of office was out of the ordinary and caused some surprise in Britain. The Emperor of Japan and his Empress, on a state visit to the Queen, went down to Kew in October 1971 and there planted a *Cryptomeria japonica.* We must not let that tree remind us of the horrors of the war when Japan was our enemy. Rather shall it whisper of a time when wars shall cease. The Royal Botanic Gardens at Kew will always be a haven of peace and serenity, both for Londoners in their thousands and for visitors from all over the world.

Fulham Palace

THE name 'Fulham' is said to derive from *Volucrum domus*, meaning 'habitat of birds', and when the Danes dug a moat to keep off the Saxons from the site of the present palace, the surrounding country was mostly marshland, occupied by herons and spoonbills. The latter bird is recorded as having nested there in 1521. The Bishops of London have had a roost here even longer, since before the Norman Conquest, continuously used except for the short period of the Commonwealth. Before Fulham became a built-up area, this was the 'country residence' of the Bishops, who had also a town house in London.

The garden has a long history—for a garden, that is. Two Bishops of London have been notable as gardeners: the Elizabethan Bishop Grindal, and Bishop Compton (1632–1713), who occupied the palace for close upon forty years and was thus able to watch his plantings mature. Grindal introduced the tamarisk, and cultivated choice grapes and other fruits, of which he often sent a selection to the queen. His successor, Aylmer, is said to have destroyed much of his work and cut down some good trees. This is an occupational hazard suffered to an unusually serious extent by ecclesiastical gardens, which have to endure frequent changes of master. Lack of continuity can menace the larger trees, which take forty or fifty years to reach their full stature, but may live for centuries if properly treated.

Bishop Aylmer, who is accused of having cut down 'a noble crowd of trees at Fulham' (among them some fine elms), is believed to have earned the queen's displeasure and a ban on any further destruction. When sold by Parliament in 1647, the palace grounds—'thirtie-six acres and a half by admeasurement' consisted of 'courts, courtyards, orchards, gardens, walkes, fish-ponds, and 3 closes of pasture, all encompassed by a moat'. There were some 700 trees, osier-beds, and salmon fishing in the Thames. There is no mention of those trees being cut down and sold for timber by the purchaser, Colonel Harvey, although this was common enough practice at the time.

Bishop Compton did more than any other incumbent for the gardens. He had a wide knowledge of botany, and, according to Stephen Switzer in his *Iconographia*

Rustica had '1,000 species of exotick plants in his stoves and gardens, in which last place he had endenizoned a great many that have been formerly thought too tender for this cold climate'. One of those was the passion flower, which the Bishop's gardener described as an inhabitant of swampy places, to be planted in very cool and moist conditions and continually 'fed with Water'. The good Bishop admitted students of botany and horticulture and gave generously of his learning to all interested visitors. Tutor to Princess Mary (afterwards Queen to William of Orange) and to Princess Anne, he played a major role in bringing William to England. To him Queen Mary probably owed her great love of 'gardenage', which she confessed 'drew an expense after it'; both she and the king consulted the bishop frequently about their many schemes for the gardens of Hampton Court and Kensington.

John Evelyn used to visit Fulham Palace. In his *Diary* for October 1681 he mentions that in the bishop's garden he first saw the 'exceedingly beautiful *Sedum arborescens* in flower'. J. C. Loudon described Compton as 'the greatest introducer of foreign trees in his century'. Many of them came from North America, where the Reverend John Banister, a missionary botanist, collected for the Bishop and lost his life while plant-hunting towards the close of the seventeenth century. There grew at Fulham the black Virginian walnut, the flowering ash, honey locust, various oaks, cedars, hollies, junipers, maples, magnolias, dogwoods, hawthorns; the 'false acacia'—or robinia, and liquidambar.

Compton died in 1713 and his successor took no interest whatever in his rare plants, choosing to remove many to make room for more vegetables and fruit. Two nurserymen, Christopher Gray of Fulham and Robert Furber of Kensington,* are known to have bought a number of Bishop Compton's plants. At the beginning of this century Alicia Amherst reported that the great black walnut, or hickory, had survived until the latter years of the Victorian age, as did the tulip tree. The honey locust planted by the bishop survived until 1905, and the flowering ash until 1907. One or two other bishops planted trees—cedars were fancied by Bishop Porteous in the late seventeenth century, and deciduous cypress and ailanthus by the nineteenth-century Bishop Blomfield. In more recent times the garden has been curtailed, to make a long, narrow 'Bishop's Park' and riverside walk for public enjoyment.

* The first illustrated plant catalogue was issued by Furber.

Lambeth Palace

THE manor of Lambeth or Lambehith was given by the Countess Goda, sister of Edward the Confessor, to the See of Rochester. Finding it to be conveniently situated for Westminster, the Archbishops of Canterbury at first rented it and eventually acquired the manor for use as an episcopal palace, where they lived in great state. It is on record that Charles I ordered Archbishop Laud to maintain three separate tables for the entertainment of different ranks of men, as his predecessors had done. This palace saw much feasting and many royal visits, particularly in Tudor times. Centuries before the Embankment that we know was constructed the Archbishops had their own landing-stage on the Thames, preferring river travel by barge to the seas of mud which in bad weather made coach roads hazardous if not impassable.

'Clarendon's Walk', now under the Embankment, was the site of a famous dialogue between Laud and the Earl of Clarendon. The latter strongly advised the prelate to moderate his exceedingly haughty behaviour, which was causing men to be 'universally discontented'. This advice went unheeded, and before the Civil War began Laud paid the price of his intransigence; he was sent to the Tower and beheaded. During his episcopate, the Thames caused havoc with an abnormally high tide in November 1635, 'the greatest tide that hath been seen'; water burst through the gates of Lambeth Palace and flooded the walks, cloisters and stables. This must have occurred before the advent of the archbishop's tortoise, which long outlived him, to expire 'through the carelessness of a gardener' in 1757. Its age is sometimes given as 110; but if it belonged to Laud it will have been a little older than that.

In Cranmer's time the garden boasted a summerhouse of unique and exquisite workmanship, of which no trace remains. Even the site upon which it stood is no more remembered. For centuries fig-trees clothed the library walls, reaching up to a height of fifty feet, if contemporary descriptions are to be believed. Of the white Marseilles variety, very sweet, fragrant and juicy, these were said to have been planted by Cranmer's successor, Cardinal Pole. They have long since disappeared. In 1691 there was erected a greenhouse, 'one of the finest and costliest about the town, of three rooms, the middle having a stove under it'. Apparently the builders carelessly placed it so near the church that the sun did not reach it in winter until nearly noon, 'a fault owned by the gardener but not thought of by the contrivers': the kind of muddle still made on occasion by our vaunted 'planners' today. In accordance with the fashion set by William and Mary, the reigning archbishop housed orange and lemon trees and other tender 'greens' here in winter.

The original garden of about sixteen acres is now severely curtailed, for in this democratic era ten acres have been released for use as a public park; but there is still a peaceful enclosure surrounding the palace of the archbishop.

The Inns of Court

THERE are now four surviving Inns of Court, in which are vested the exclusive discretion of call to the Bar—Gray's Inn, Lincoln's Inn, and the Inner and Middle Temple. In addition there were formerly Inns of Chancery, whose function was said by the late Sir Dunbar Plunket Barton to be analogous to that of the Public School preparing candidates for university education.* Those attached to Gray's Inn were Staple Inn and Barnard's Inn, both on the south side of Holborn. The timbered, gabled façade of Staple Inn, preserved by the Prudential Assurance Company, is familiar to frequenters of Holborn, and seekers who walk in under the archway find a quiet little courtyard with paved walks, seats, and a well in the centre. On the porter's lodge is a notice: HORSES AND RUDE CHILDREN NOT ALLOWED. Presumably at the time when this was put up the porters were permitted to chastise any rude children who dared to thumb noses at it. Dickens wrote of the Staple Inn garden that it was 'one of those nooks the turning into which out of the clashing streets imparts to the relieved pedestrian the sensation of having put cotton in his ears and velvet soles on his boots'. Barnard's Inn, which also possessed a small courtyard with trees and paved walks, was turned into a school by the Mercer's Company.

Gray's Inn became an Inn of Court in the fourteenth century and was thereafter the abode of barristers. The site was in earlier days the manor of Portpool or Purpool, the London residence of the Lords de Grey of Wilton. There is still a Portpool Lane leading out of Gray's Inn Road. In 1308 this manor comprised a messuage or dwelling-house, a chauntry, gardens, dove-house and windmill, as was common to manors of the time. Until the late sixteenth century the arms of Gray's Inn were similar to the 'barry of 8 argent and azure' of the de Grey family, with a slight heraldic difference in the border. After that the present gold griffin on a black ground was adopted; records of this change are incomplete and the reason not clear. There is some additional confusion because over the great gateway to the Inner Temple gardens there is a griffin, while the crest over a gate in Gray's Inn is a winged horse, Pegasus, which belongs to the

* *Country Life*, 6 November 1937.

Inner Temple. These exchanges were made to commemorate the long friendship existing between the two societies, a sociable benefit fostered by their mutual interest in masques and revels.

The present chapel is thought to have been built on the site of the former chauntry, which was served by a chaplain from the convent of St Bartholomew in Smithfield. Among the residents of Gray's Inn were Samuel Butler, Dr Johnson —who removed there from Staple Inn in 1758, Goldsmith, Southey and Cobbett. The Inn's most famous author, Francis Bacon, became a Bencher in 1586; the fields long in use for archery and other sports were laid out as gardens after his advent. The legend that Bacon planted one of the catalpa trees 'from a seedling introduced by Sir Walter Raleigh' is now discounted, for all the most learned plantsmen declare that the catalpa did not arrive from North America until 1726, a century after Bacon's death. Legends are fascinating, and often turn out to have a factual basis. It may be that the growing of a catalpa by a nurseryman named Bacon in Hoxton early in the eighteenth century caused this one to arise. There are now three specimens in the garden. The oldest is on the west side of the path; its echo on the east is said to have come from a cutting of the first. Another was planted in 1949, to carry on the tradition. The enormous reclining veteran looks ancient enough to have seen Bacon, but the catalpa has a way of posing as senile sooner than people imagine.

In 1591 the Benchers of Gray's Inn planned to enclose parts of their back field within a brick wall, the work to be supervised by 'Mr Angel and Mr Bacon'. The back field eventually became the pleasure garden and walks, which were further enlarged in 1608 by the pulling down of stables and cottages. Bacon's ideas of gardening were grandiose in scale, for he remarked that a garden should consist of thirty acres. I have not been able to discover the acreage of Gray's Inn when he made the pleasure garden from fields, but it seems to have been larger than it is now. For some reason the famous essay 'Of Gardens' is often said to have been based upon Theobalds Park and not to derive from Bacon's personal knowledge of horticulture. The truth is that, after inheriting Gorhambury in 1601, he began in 1608 to regenerate his neglected gardens, gaining 17 years of practical experience before the essay appeared in 1625. It was said that even when Lord Chancellor he would descend from the Woolsack 'to investigate the economy of manure beds'.

In 1597 it is on record that the sum of £7 15s. 4d. was due to 'Mr Bacon for planting of trees in the Walkes'. In the following year orders were given for 'more yonge elme trees in place of such as are decayed'; also a new 'rayle and quick-sett hedge to bee set uppon the upper long walks at the good discretion of Mr Bacon and Mr Wilbraham, soe that the charges thereof doe not exceed the sum of seventy pounds'. That there were many good trees here before Bacon's time can be verified from the records of Gray's Inn. In 1583 there were 'in the grene Court XI Elmes and III Walnut Trees', and so on, to a total of eighty-seven mature elms, with four young ones and an ash.

Of plants, Bacon wrote: 'I do hold it in the royal ordering of gardens there ought to be gardens for all the months in the year; in which severally things of beauty may be seen then in season'. Although few today can have a separate garden for each season, the idea of planning plants within a small compass which give beauty of flower or foliage all the year round is given the greatest importance in modern books and articles. Bacon liked daffodils and tulips, monkshood, columbine, 'lilies of all natures', French marigolds, 'hollyoaks', gilliflowers, musk roses, sweet-briar, wallflower and honeysuckle. He loved 'green grass kept finely shorn' as much as he disliked knot gardens, topiary, vases and statues. Nevertheless the Benchers erected one of him in South Square. His description of scented blossoms is poetic: 'The breath of flowers is far sweeter in the air (where it comes and goes like the warblings of music) than in the hand.' A splendid way of telling people that one prefers not to have a picked bunch. In 1609 Bacon had a mound or mount raised in the north-west corner of the garden, and on it a pavilion in memory of Jeremy Bettenham, formerly Reader of Gray's Inn. This garden house was a pretty little octagon with open sides and a roof supported on slender pillars. From it a magnificent view could be enjoyed, stretching over open country to the wooded hills of Hampstead and Highgate. The pavilion and mount were both removed in 1755, but the elegant flight of shallow steps still in being at the north end of the garden is associated with Bacon.

Six years after Bacon's death Samuel Pepys was born, and when he reached manhood he greatly enjoyed promenading in Gray's Inn gardens with Mrs Pepys after church on Sunday mornings. Access to the gardens of all the Inns of Court was easily obtained by those who could claim acquaintance with one of the Benchers. Addison described Sir Roger de Coverley marching up and down the terrace, 'hemming to himself with great vigour, for he loves to clear his pipes in good air'. *The Tatler* used to record such gossip as 'I was last week taking a solitary walk in the gardens of Lincoln's Inn, a favour that is indulged me by several of the Benchers who are my intimate friends'. This favour seems to have been given to a wide circle, but the public in general were not admitted. Seeing the fashionable world let loose in these places, visitors from abroad quite naturally took them for public parks. One such mistake appeared in print in 1765:

> 'Besides St James's Park, the Green Park and Hyde Park, the two last of which are continuations of the first, London has several public walks, which are much more agreeable to the English, as they are less frequented and much more solitary than the Park. Such are the gardens contained within the compass of the Temple, Gray's Inn and Lincoln's Inn. They consist of grass plots which are kept in excellent order, and planted with trees, either cut regularly or with high stocks: some of them have been laid out for culinary uses. The grass plots of the gardens at Lincoln's Inn are adorned with statues, which, taken all together, form a scene very pleasing to the eye.'

Gardens must have existed on the Temple site from a very early date. When the Templars built their church in the twelfth century (a lovely building which suffered badly from bombing in the Second World War), it was surrounded by open country and by a few great houses and conventual premises standing in gardens and orchards. After the Templars were suppressed the property came into the hands of the Knights of St John, in 1324, and as that Order had its own establishment in Clerkenwell it granted possession to students of the Common Laws of England. The area known as 'Temple Gardens' today, used to be the 'Great Garden' of the Inner and Middle Temple, while the 'Outer Temple' lay beyond the City limits.

In the reign of James I, when Bacon was busy making gardens at Gray's Inn, the Temple also received attention; it is on record that a mulberry was set in Fairfield's Court and nuts and figs in Fig Tree Court. The accounts show that money was expended on posts and rails, and the painting thereof. In all probability such entries refer to small painted posts, rails and trellis-work placed in Tudor fashion round about the flower beds. During the Commonwealth payments were made to the poor of Greenwich to cut turves on Blackheath and transfer them in lighters to Temple Stairs. No fewer than 5,000 turves, each measuring 3 feet long by a foot broad, were supplied for the Temple Garden, besides 392 loads of gravel at 2s. 6d. the load for the walks. In the time of William and Mary a small garden was set apart for the Benchers, laid out in the fashionable Dutch style. This was known as the 'little' or 'privy' garden. A sundial was fixed to the wall, and a central fountain set about with orange trees in tubs. The fountain seems to have been one of the practical joke 'waterworks' which suddenly squirted water over the unsuspecting visitor. There was also a paved summer house, and an alcove with seats.

The 'masques' which were considered to be of great consequence in the sixteenth and seventeenth centuries were designed, not as mere entertainments, but rather as means of educating the students, who were to be trained in manners, deportment, and all civilized arts. There is extant a description of a 'Maske of Flowers' by the 'Gentlemen of Gray's Inn' on Twelfth Night 1613. The scene was

> 'a garden of glorious and strange beauty, cast into foure quarters, with a crosse walke and allies compassing each quarter. In the middle of the crosse walke stood a goodly fountaine, raised on foure columnes of silver. The garden walls were of brick artificially painted in perspective, all along which were placed fruite trees with artificiall leaves and fruite. The garden within the wall was rayled about with rayles of three foote high, adorned with ballesters of silver, between which were placed pedestalls beautified with transparent lights of variable colours. Upon the pedestalls stood silver columns, upon the toppes whereof were personages of gold, lions of gold and unicornes of silver. Every personage and beast did hold a torchet burning that gave light and lustre to the whole fabrique.
>
> 'Every quarter of the garden was finely hedged about with a lowe hedge of Cipresse and Juniper; the knottes within set with artificial flowers. In the two first quarters were two piramides, garnished with golde and silver, and glistering with transparent lights, resembling carbuncles, saphires and rubies. In every corner of each quarter were great pottes of gilliflowers, which shadowed certain lights placed behind them, and made resplendent and admirable lustre. The two further quarters were beautified with Tulipaes of divers colours, and in the middle, and in the corners of the said quarters, were set great tufts of several kinds of flowers receiving lustre from secret lights placed behind them.
>
> 'At the farther end of the garden was a mount raised by degrees, resembling bankes of earth, covered with grass; on the top of the mount stood a goodly arbour, substantially made, and covered with artificiall trees and with arbour flowers, as eglantine, honnysuckles, and the like. The arbour was in length three and thirtie foot, in height one and twenty, supported with termes of gold and silver. It was divided into sixe double arches and three doores answerable to the three walks of the garden. In the middle part of the arbour rose a goodly large turret, and at either end a smaller. Upon the toppe of the mount, on the front thereof, was a banke

> of flowers, curiously painted behind, while within the arches the maskers sate unseene.
>
> 'Behind the garden, over the toppe of the arbour, were set artificiall trees, appearing like an orchard joyning to the garden, and over all was drawne in perspective a fermament like the skies in a cleere night. Upon a grassy seat under the arbour sate the garden gods, in number twelve, apparrelled in long robes of greene, with rich taffata cappes on their heads, and chaplets of flowers. In the midst of them sate Primavera, at whose intreaty they descended to the stage, and marching up to the king sung to lutes and theorboes.'

This elaborate stage scenery appears to have been a very faithful replica of the typical garden design of the period. According to Sir Dunbar Plunket Barton, Bacon may have borne the expenses of this great masque himself—a total of £2,000.

The 'Walkes' of Gray's Inn were, for some two hundred years after their creation, the most fashionable promenade in all London. James Howell in 1621 wrote of them as 'the pleasantest place about London, and you have there the choicest society', and John Stowe the historian describes them as 'open to the air and the enjoyment of a delightful prospect—for many years much resorted unto by the gentry of both sexes'. Pepys and his wife liked going there 'to observe the fashions of the ladies', and Dryden mentioned the 'Walks' as a favoured rendezvous in 1668. Addison is said to have planted a tree there. The place had its unhappy incidents also. In 1701 a Captain Greenwood killed a Mr Otway in a duel in the garden of Gray's Inn, and was found guilty of manslaughter.

Ten years later the gardener was instructed to admit 'no ordinary men, women or children into the Walkes, nor noe lewd or confident women nor any in vizor maskes'. He was also bidden to suffer no person to break any boughs from young trees. In spite of these precautions great damage was reported in 1718, and the gardener was thereupon authorized to turn out disorderly persons and lock up the Walkes, particularly on Sunday afternoons, the worst time for trouble, provided that he had the consent of any three Benchers.

In 1755 the mount was taken away, by order of the Bench, without any reason being assigned. The summerhouse may have been in a ruinous state, or the buildings to the north may have destroyed the outlook and rendered it unpopular. Various other alterations were carried out in the Walks at this period. Twenty years later Charles Lamb was born in a back room at 2, Crown Office Row, near the terrace where paced the lawyers described in his Elian essay *The Old Benchers of the Inner Temple*. After living elsewhere, Lamb and his sister returned in 1800 to the Temple, spending eight years at 16, Mitre Court Buildings and nine at 4, Inner Temple Lane, overlooking Hare Court and its pump.

'Do you know it?' Lamb wrote to Manning. 'I was born near it, and used to drink at that pump when I was a Rechabite of 6 years old. Here I hope to set up my rest, and not to quit till Mr Powell, the undertaker, gives me notice that I may have possession of my last lodging.' Poor Lamb, he did not have his wish, but left the Temple for good and died at Edmonton in 1834. He confessed to a great love of Gray's Inn: 'I think it is now better than 25 years ago, that walking in the gardens of Gray's Inn—they were finer than they are now—the accursed Verulam Buildings had not encroached upon all the east side of them, cutting out delicate green crankles and shouldering away one of two of the stately alcoves of the terrace. The survivor stands, gaping and relationless, as if it remembered its brother. They are still the best gardens of any of the Inns of Court—my beloved Temple not forgotten,—have the gravest character, their aspect being altogether reverend and law breathing. Bacon has left the impress of his foot upon their gravel walks.'

In a book written about the Inner and Middle Temple by H. H. L. Bellot in 1902 I came upon a letter from Charles Lamb to his physician which, while it has nothing to do with the gardens, has everything to do with the personality of the writer, who still seems to haunt the precincts of the Inns of Court. The usually abstemious Lamb explained a rare lapse in these words:

> 'Dear Sir, It is an observation of a wise man that "moderation is best in all things". I cannot agree with him "in liquor". There is a smoothness and oiliness in wine that makes it go down by a natural channel which I am positive was made for that descending. Else, why does not wine choke us? Could Nature have made that sloping lane, not to facilitate the down going? She does nothing in vain. You know that better than I. You know how often she has helped you at a dead lift, and how much better entitled she is to a fee than yourself sometimes when you carry off the credit. Still, there is something due to manners and customs, and I shd. apologise to you and Mrs A. for being absolutely carried home upon a man's shoulders thro' Silver Street, up Parson's Lane by the Chapels (which might have taught me better), and then to be deposited like a dead log at Gaffar Westwood's, who, it seems, does not "insure" against intoxication. Not that the mode of conveyance is objectionable. On the contrary, it is more

easy than a one-horse chaise . . . I protest I thought myself in a palanquin, and never felt myself so grandly carried. It was a slave under me. There was I, all but my reason. And what is reason? And what is the loss of it? And how often in a day do we do without it just as well? Reason is only counting 2 and 2 makes 4. And if on my passage home I thought it made 5, what matter? 2 and 2 will just make 4, as it always did before I took the finishing glass that did my business. My sister has begged me to write an apology to Mrs A. and you for disgracing your party.

'Now, it does seem to me that I rather honoured your party, for everyone that was not drunk (and one or two of the ladies, I am sure, were not) must have been set off greatly in contrast to me. I was the scapegoat. The soberer they seemed. By the way, is magnesia good on these occasions? Three ounces of *pol med sum ante noct in rub can.* I am no licentiate, but know enough of simples to beg you to send me a draught after this model. But still, you will say (or the men and maids at your house will say) that it is not seemly for an old gentleman to go home pick-a-back. Well, maybe it is not. But I never studied grace. I take it to be a mere superficial accomplishment. I regard more the internal acquisitions. The great object after supper is to get home, and whether that is attained in a horizontal posture or perpendicular (as foolish men and apes affect for dignity) I think little to the purpose. The end is always greater than the means. Here I am, able to compose a sensible and rational apology, and what signifies how I got here? I have just sense enough to remember I was very happy last night, and to thank our kind host and hostess, and that is sense enough, I hope.'

Charles Lamb.

This epistle was given to Mr Bellot by a daughter of Mr A., whose house during the years 1829–32 was frequently visited by Lamb.

At the beginning of the eighteenth century the Temple Gardens seem to have been well supplied with flowering plants, and as Sir Thomas Hanmer was a member it is not surprising that his speciality, the tulip, was extensively grown. He raised a new variety, the 'Agate Hanmer', which became popular. There are entries in the accounts for 'Junquiles', Dutch Crocus, and the 'Armathagalum or Starre of Bethlehem'. (No doubt Ornithogalum was the botanical name the scribe attempted to set down.) In pots in the Great Garden there were fifteen yew trees, twelve variegated phillyreas—'striped fillerayes'—and twenty-eight standard laurels, besides box, holly and juniper bushes. For the Benchers' Garden *Daphne mezereum* was ordered, and laurustinus. The walls were clothed with climbing roses and jessamine, or jasmine; in connection with the training of these, there are entries covering expenditure on 'nails, list and hatt parings for the jessamy wall'.

Benchers of the Middle Temple had their own sanctuary, later known as Fountain Court. Christopher Hatton, whose Ely Place was not far off, greatly admired this fountain, which, he noticed, always forced its stream to 'a vast and almost incredible height'. It then stood within a rectangular palisade of wood, together with some trees, and was surrounded by Purbeck stone paving. At a later date the fence was replaced by iron railings. It was in this Court that Ruth Pinch in *Martin Chuzzlewit* waited for her brother, 'with the best little laugh upon her face that ever played in opposition to a fountain'. Dickens described the latter splashing in the sun; 'laughingly its liquid music played, and merrily the idle drops of water danced and danced, and peeping out in sport among the trees, plunged lightly down to hide themselves . . .'

Tougher scenes than those are enacted in the Temple Garden in Shakespeare's *Henry VI*, when the Earl of Somerset says 'Let him that is no coward nor no flatterer, But dare maintain the party of the truth, Pluck a red rose from off this thorn with me.' To which challenge the Earl of Warwick responds, 'I love no colours, and without all colour Of base insinuating flattery I pluck this white rose with Plantagenet.' Presently Richard Plantagenet utters the taunt: 'Now, Somerset, where is your argument?' And the Earl replies, 'Here in my scabbard, meditating that Shall dye your white rose a bloody red.' Warwick gloomily prophesies: 'this brawl to-day, Grown to this faction in the Temple-garden, Shall send between the red rose and the white A thousand souls to death and deadly night.'* And so it did; but to us in the twentieth century a thousand casualties in the Wars of the Roses seems infinitesimal compared with the ghastly toll of modern warfare, such as hit the Temple, and all London, in the Second World War. But enough of wars.

It is a strange sequel that, in the early days of the Royal Horticultural Society, its shows were held in these same Temple gardens, and of course, then as now, the rose was queen of flowers. Shakespeare's martial characters would have had greater choice among the varieties produced by breeders, as long ago as May 1888, when the embryo of the modern Chelsea Flower Show was held in two tents. Even by the time of Elizabeth I the briars red and white of the Plantagenet garden would have been increased to a fair show, with damask, musk, Provence and cinnamon roses, and *Rosa mundi*, the 'York and Lancaster' rose. 'Shadows

* *Henry VI*, Part I, Act II, Scene IV.

we are and like shadows depart' said the old sundial in Pump Court; but although men and women depart, the Inns of Court continue, and so do their gardens.

In July 1970 I was entertained to luncheon in the Great Hall of Gray's Inn—a magnificent edifice, reconstructed from the 'Olde Hall' in 1556–9, the cost being shared by all Fellows of the Society in residence. This hall measures 70 feet long and 35 feet wide, with a height to the apex of the hammer-beam roof of 47 feet. Severely damaged in the Second World War, it was one of the first London buildings of note to be rebuilt when hostilities ended. This highly-skilled replica was carried out by first-class craftsmen with the utmost fidelity. Fortunately the armorial glass and the richly-carved oak screen, reputedly the gift of Elizabeth I, were stored in a safe place and are undamaged. Also saved were many portraits, including those of the Virgin Queen, Burghley, Francis Bacon and his father (Sir Nicholas Bacon), Sir Philip Sidney, Lord Howard of Effingham. This significant experience impressed upon my mind the marriage of history and humanity which has, over many centuries, produced the evolving laws of England.

Outside in the Walks, the aged Catalpa a-sprawl on the smooth grass carpet, unscathed by fire and high explosives, keeps its secret inviolate. Nobody can be certain of its real age until it expires and the number of its rings is counted. Not far away is a refugee, a tree found growing amid the rubble after the war, and transferred to its present site in 1950. Probably the seed was dropped into the ruins of the Library by a bird. It is an ailanthus, or 'Tree of Heaven'. My host took me through into the gardens of Lincoln's Inn, where we saw the undercroft by Inigo Jones, scene of the duel in the film of *Tom Jones*. The Great Garden of this Inn is open to the public during the luncheon interval, as is the garden of Gray's Inn during the summer, from noon for two hours.

We met the head gardener of Lincoln's Inn, where some of his men were sweeping piles of leaves from the wide walks. Reference was made to J. C. Loudon, whose advocacy of the tree here seen in numbers, the London plane, is described elsewhere in this book. The great pollution of the atmosphere in Loudon's time was endured by the plane far better than by the conifers which were fashionable before he set about changing the appearance of so many Squares. By its constant shedding and renewal of bark and foliage, the plane rids itself of soot deposits. Now things are changing, for with the Smoke Abatement Act pollution has declined significantly, and the renewals are no longer so necessary. As labour is now scarce and expensive, heavy leaf fall puts a serious burden on resources, and the plane is becoming less popular as a result. Nevertheless, these fine old trees are of great value in the scene, and surely worth their keep. We were told about the various uses to which the legal profession still puts its gardens, among them garden parties, wedding receptions, and fetes. A merry-go-round was imported on one such occasion not long ago into the sober precincts of Gray's Inn to entertain child visitors. In sheltered corners of Lincoln's Inn the vine, wistaria and fig still flourish, and the old blue Tradescantia, a typical London flower.

SECTION THREE

Writers and Gardens

Francis Bacon

John Evelyn's *Kalendarium Hortense* of 1664 is often described as the earliest gardener's calendar; but Bacon's famous essay *Of Gardens* to some extent anticipated the work of Evelyn. Having written that he held it 'in the royal ordering of gardens' that there ought to be gardens for all months of the year, in which severally things of beauty might then be in season, he proceeded to take readers through the garden year, month by month, describing the flowers in great detail. He deals with grounds of thirty acres in extent, divided up into a four-acre 'green', or lawn, six acres of heath or 'desert', and twelve acres of garden proper, with alleys in between. He liked a garden to be square and enclosed by hedges, with arched openings in it some ten feet high and six feet wide; these to be constructed upon pillars of carpenter's work.

Bacon looked with disfavour on the fashion, current in his time, for the knot garden. 'As for the making of knots or figures, with divers-coloured earths, that they may lie under the windows of the house on that side the garden stands, they be but toys; you may see as good sights many times in tarts.' He admitted fountains, but deplored aviaries. His heath, or 'desert' as he called it, he desired to be 'framed as much as may be to a natural wilderness'. This was not a woody place, but a low jungle of bushes and undergrowth, with sweetbriar, honeysuckle and wild vine rioting. The ground was 'set with violets, primroses and strawberries; for these are sweet and prosper in the shade'. Perhaps he meant the wild strawberry. 'I like also,' he continues, 'little heaps, in the nature of molehills (such as are in wild heaths) to be set, some with wild thyme, some with pinks, some with germander, that gives a good flower to the eye.'

Bacon's interest in manure has already been mentioned. He tried an experiment with strawberries—this time of the cultivated variety—which foreshadows the use of liquid manure long before the idea was commonly used. 'Strawberries watered now and then (as once in three dayes) with Water, wherein hath been steeped Sheepes-dung, or pigeon-dung, will prevent and come early. And it is like the same Effect would follow in other Berries, Herbes, Flowers, Graines, and Trees. And therefore it is an Experiment, though vulgar in Strawberries, yet not brought into use generally: For it is usuall to helpe the Ground with Mucke; and likewise to recomfort it sometimes with Mucke put to the Roots; But to water it with Muckwater, which is like to be more forcible, is not practised.'

He does not stop there.

> 'Besides the two Means of accelerating Germination formerly described, the Mending of the Nourishment and Comforting of the Spirit of the Plant, there is a third; which is the Making way for the Easie Comming to the Nourishment, and drawing it. And therefore gentle Digging and Loosening of the Earth about the Roots of Trees, and the Removing Herbes and Flowers into new Earth, once in two yeares, (which is the same thing; For the new Earth is ever looser,) do the greatly further the Prospering and Earlinesse of Plants.
>
> 'But the most admirable Acceleration by Facilitating the Nourishment, is that of Water. For a Standard of a Damaske Rose with the Root on, was set in a chamber where no fire was, upright in an Earthen Pan, full of faire water, without any Mixture, half a foot under the Water, the Standard being more than two foot high above the Water: Within the Space of ten dayes the Standard did put forth a faire Greene leafe and some other little buds, which stood more than seven Daies . . .'

Bacon took a deep interest in trees. This next piece of advice is perhaps designed to 'comfort the spirit' of the tree. 'A Tree, at first Rooting, should not bee shaken, until it hath taken Root fully: And therefore some have put two little Forkes about the Bottome of their Trees, to keepe them upright; but after a yeares Rooting, then shaking doth the Tree good, by Loosening of the Earth, and (perhaps) by exercising (as it were) and stirring the Sap of the Tree.' This extract from his posthumous publication, *Sylva Sylvarum*, shows that no point was too small to engage his attention. All his life he laboured to master universal knowledge in philosophy and science, coupled with important legal appointments that culminated in his becoming Lord Chancellor.

He discarded most of the vulgar fallacies of his time, using trenchant language to discredit them. 'There are many Ancient and Received Traditions and Observations, touching the *Sympathy* and *Antipathy* of Plants; For that some will thrive best growing neare others; which they impute to *Sympathy*: And some worse; which they impute to *Antipathy*. But these are Idle and Ignorant Conceits; And forsake the true *Indication* of the *Causes* . . . For it is thus;

Wheresoever one *Plant* draweth such a particular Juyce out of the Earth, as it qualifieth the Earth; So as that Juyce which remaineth is fit for the other Plant, there the Neighbourhood doth good; Because the Nourishments are contrarie, or severall: But where two *Plants* draw (much) the same Juyce, there the Neighbourhood hurteth; For the one deceiveth the other.'

It is easy to be amused by the 'quaint' wording of such thoughts as these; but when one considers the slender encouragement given to experimenters at the time, and the limited means at Bacon's disposal, one may well end by humbly admiring the greatness of his mind and character. Whatever the modern horticulturist may think of his theories in general, this famous quotation holds good for us all; it is too seldom given in full:

> 'God Almighty first planted a garden; and, indeed, it is the purest of human pleasures; it is the greatest refreshment to the spirits of man; without which buildings and palaces are but gross handy-works; and a man shall ever see that, when ages grow to civility and elegance, man comes to build stately sooner than to garden finely: as if gardening were the greater perfection.'

John Evelyn

Born in 1620 and living in four reigns and the interlude of the Commonwealth, Evelyn became extremely adaptable and managed, without being a 'Vicar of Bray', to steer clear of trouble; during the Cromwellian era he escaped for much of the time to the Continent of Europe, where he travelled extensively and wrote with well-informed and perceptive taste of the architecture and arts. With hidden royalist sympathies, he appeared (when in England) to conform outwardly to the Parliamentarian regime, but after the Restoration he had strong links with the Court of Charles II and held a number of minor offices. His celebrated *Diary*—kept from about 1631, when he 'began to observe matters more punctually, which I did use to set down in a blank almanac', includes in the published version a retrospective view of his existence from birth; clearly he did not keep a diary from that moment. It was not set up in print until 1818; the publisher, with great lack of imagination, then considered it to be of purely antiquarian interest.

Horace Walpole pictured him, in the rather stilted language common to the period—a style not adopted by Evelyn in his *Diary*:

> 'If Mr Evelyn had not been an artist himself, as I think I can prove he was, I should yet have found it difficult to deny myself the pleasure of allotting him a place among the arts he loved, promoted, patronised; and it would be but justice to inscribe his name with due panegyric in these records, as I have once or twice taken the liberty to criticise him. But they are trifling blemishes compared with his amiable virtues and beneficence; and it may be remarked that the worst I have said of him is, that he knew more than he always communicated. It is no unwelcome satire to say, that a man's intelligence and philosophy is inexhaustible. I meant not to write his life, which may be found detailed in the new edition of his 'Sculptura', . . . but I must observe, that his life, which has extended to eighty-six years, was a course of inquiry, study, curiosity, instruction, and benevolence. The works of the Creator, and the minute labours of the creature, were all objects of his pursuit . . . He was one of the first promoters of the Royal

> Society; a patron of the ingenious and the indigent; and peculiarly serviceable to the lettered world; for, besides his writings and discoveries, he obtained the Arundelian Marbles for the University of Oxford, and the Arundelian Library for the Royal Society.'

As befitted a Fellow of the Royal Society, which he helped to found, Evelyn's many-sided interests included a scientific approach to a problem that is still with us in places; in 1661 his book *Fumifugium* made proposals for ridding London of its smoke-pall. In 1664 he published his *Sylva: or a Discourse of Forest Trees.* That same year his *Diary* for 24 October records: 'I went to visit Mr Boyle, whom I found with Dr Wallis and Dr Christopher Wren, in the tower of the schools, with an inverted tube, or telescope, observing the discus of the sun for the passing of Mercury that day before it.' Intellectual society was far less regimented in the seventeenth century than it is apt to be now, and a gentleman of many interests was not scorned by professional scientists of the calibre of Boyle and Newton. Academic boundaries and qualifications were as yet in embryo, or in some cases not even conceived.

Evelyn was a deeply religious man, an Anglican. Much of his *Kalendarium Hortense* is taken up with notes on the sermons he has listened to in church. That he was not in the least dull has been certified by the volatile Samuel Pepys, who wrote: 'He and I walked together in the garden with mighty pleasure, he being a very ingenious man; and the more I know him, the more I love him.' Pepys also describes a merry evening spent in Evelyn's company: 'Mr Evelyn such a spirit of mirth that in all of my life I never met with so merry a two hours as our company this night was. Among other humours, Mr Evelyn's repeating of some verses made up of nothing but the various acceptations of *may* and *can*, and doing it so aptly upon occasion of something of that nature, and so fast, did make us all almost die with laughing, and did so stop the mouth of Sir J. Minnes in the middle of all his mirth (and in a thing agreeing with his own manner of genius), that I never saw any man so out-done in all my life . . .'

Although his father had a considerable fortune, John Evelyn's early education was received from the village schoolmaster at Wotton in Surrey. On the whole he seems to have shown little aptitude for the kind of study offered him at school or university, nor did he care for life in the Middle Temple. During the Commonwealth he acquired Sayes Court at Deptford, where he began in 1653 to plan and plant the garden, as he records on 17 January. 'I began to set out the oval garden at Sayes Court, which was before a rude orchard, and all the rest one entire field of 100 acres, without any hedge, except the hither holly-hedge joining to the bank of the mount walk. This was the beginning of all the succeeding gardens, walks, groves, enclosures and plantations there.'

Holly-hedges figure in a shocking incident many years later, when Sayes Court was let to 'the Czar of Muscovy', who visited England with a view to studying methods of ship-building at the dockyard in near-by Deptford. Evelyn's servant wrote to his master of this influx: 'There is a house full of people and right nasty.' The particular nastiness which upset Evelyn was the Czar's destructive way of amusing himself in the garden. One peculiarly dotty recreation consisted in having someone wheel him in a barrow *through* the great hedges—treatment from which they never fully recovered. Evelyn recorded on 9 June 1698:

> 'To Deptford, to see how miserably the Czar has left my house, after three months making it his Court. I got Sir Christopher Wren, the King's surveyor, and Mr London his gardener to go and estimate the repairs, for which they allowed £150 in their report to the Lords of the Treasury.'

In May 1700 Evelyn succeeded to his father's estate at Wotton, where he took up residence. Here he was also to experience destruction of a garden—this time from natural causes, for a great storm in 1703 felled more than 1,000 trees in sight of his house. He died in London in his eighty-sixth year.

He was never tired of urging people to plant trees, even when, as Miles Hadfield says 'what we now call amenity value could only on the slightest pretext be linked with utility. Of walnuts, for example, "they render most graceful avenues to our country dwellings"; of the perfections of the lime "Its unparalleled beauty for walks"; the only excuse that he makes for urging the planting of the strawberry tree, "too much neglected by us", is that Bauhin commends the charcoal for goldsmith's work.'* Holly drew raptures from Evelyn:

> 'Is there under Heaven a more glorious and refreshing object of the kind, than an impregnable hedge of about four hundred foot in length, nine foot high, and five in diameter; which I can show in my now ruined gardens at Sayes Court (thanks to the Czar of Muscovy) at any time of the year, glittering with its armed and varnished leaves? The taller standards at

* *Gardening in Britain* (1960).

> orderly distances, blushing with their natural coral: it mocks the rudest assaults of the weather, beasts, or hedgebreakers.'

The quick-growing Mediterranean cypress came into fashion in his time, raised—as he tells us—from British seed. It was reputedly tender; Evelyn admits that our cruel east winds 'do sometimes mortally invade them that have been late clipped'. How true this was is borne out by the fact that nearly every cypress in England was killed in the severe winter 1683–4. Evelyn praised the yew, which had no such flaw of weakness:

> 'Being three years old you may transplant them, and form them into standards, knobs, walks, hedges, etc., in all of which works they succeed marvellous well, and are worth our patience for their perennial verdure and durableness. I do again name them for hedges, preferable for beauty, and a stiff defence to any plant I have ever seen, and may upon that account (without vanity) be said to have been the first to have brought them into fashion, as well for defence, as for a succedaneum for cypress, whether in hedges or pyramids, conic spires, bowls, or what other shapes, adorning the parks or larger avenues with their lofty tops thirty foot high, and braving all the efforts of the most rigid winter, which cypress cannot weather.'

The later editions of *Sylva* conclude with 'some encouragements and proposals for the planting and improvement of His Majesty's Forests, and other amenities for shade and ornaments'.

Evelyn was a great encourager of talent wherever he found it. He 'discovered' Grinling Gibbons, and brought his skill in woodcarving to the notice of Charles II and of Wren; he also became the sponsor of two gardeners, London and Wise, whose nursery at Brompton roused him to compose a long panegyric on 'that vast and ample collection which I have lately seen and well considered at Brompton Park near Kensington'. George London, who had been gardener to Bishop Compton at Fulham Palace, gained there useful knowledge as to what was hardy and what was not. (At one time cauliflowers were actually given the protection of greenhouses!) The Brompton nursery was founded in 1681, and Henry Wise went into partnership with London in about 1687. London was gardener to William and Mary, Wise to Queen Anne. A labourer in their nursery is supposed to have penned the following lines:

If He who the first garden made
Had put in Wise to keep it,
Made Adam but a labourer there
And Eve to weed and sweep it;
Then men and plants had never died,
Nor the first fruits been rotten;
Brompton had never then been known
Nor Eden e'er forgotten.

That jingle is more akin to a modern advertisement than is Evelyn's 'Advertisement' of London and Wise, if only because of its brevity. Anyone who advertised a nursery today in over a thousand words, many of them long ones, would hardly attract the favourable attention he hoped for. No doubt Evelyn knew his public. He wrote with the greatest confidence:

> 'I cannot conceive but it must needs be a very acceptable Advertisement, and of Universal concern to all Noblemen, and Persons of Quality, Lovers of Gardens, and Improvers of Plantations (of all Diversions and Employments the most Natural, Usefull, Innocent and Agreeable) at what Distance soever from a Place of so easy and Speedy Correspondence and which is so nere this great City, to give this Notice.'

A few pages further on he says that he has

> 'long observed (from the daily practice, and effects of the laudable Industry of these two Partners) that they have not made Gain the only mark of their pains; but with Extraordinary and rare Industry endeavour'd to improve themselves in the Mysteries of their Profession, from the great Advantages, and now long Experience, they have had, in being Employ'd in most of the celebrated Gardens and Plantations which this Nation abounds in; besides what they have learn'd Abroad, where Horticulture is in the highest Reputation.' [This was the rub: Abroad had for long been the place where Britons went for the furnishing of their orchards and plantations. Now London and Wise had provided a 'Magazine' such as had never before been seen in this country. Evelyn goes further, calling it] 'Such an Assembly, I believe, as is nowhere else to be met with in this Kingdom, nor in any other that I know of . . .'

Evelyn's great horticultural work, often referred to simply as his *Sylva*, was in reality a three-part compilation, of which *Discourse of Forest Trees* is the first. Then comes *Pomona*, or *An Appendix concerning Fruit-Trees*, followed by the *Kalendarium Hortense*, or *Gardener's Almanac*. The last part proved the most popular, and was reprinted a number of times. To the ninth edition Evelyn added *Acetaria, a Discourse of Sallets*. Herein are many plants not now looked upon as salad vegetables, such as spinach, asparagus, dandelion, hop and melon. It was to some later impressions of the *Almanac* that Cowley attached his poem of *The Garden*, with a preface that sums up the aspirations of many people in the late twentieth century also:

> 'I never had any other desire so strong, and so like to Covetousness, as that one which I have had always, that I might be master at last of a small house and large garden, with very moderate conveniences joined to them and there dedicate the remainder of my life to the Culture of them and study of Nature.'

In his introduction to Evelyn's *Sylva*, Cowley wrote of the author:

> 'I know nobody that possesses more private Happiness than you do in your Garden; and yet no man who makes his Happiness more publick, by a free communication of the Art and Knowledge of it to others.'

Evelyn's words about trees never fail to move me:

> 'Men seldom plant trees till they begin to be Wise, that is, till they grow Old and find by Experience the Prudence and Necessity of it. When Ulysses, after a ten years' Absence, was return'd from Troy, and coming home, found his aged Father in the field planting Trees, he asked him, why (being now so far advanc'd in years) he would put himself to the Fatigue and Labour of Planting that which he was never likely to enjoy the Fruits of? The good old man (taking him for a Stranger) gently reply'd: I plant (says he) against my Son Ulysses comes home.'

Sir William Temple

Sir William Temple (1628–99) was a politician—he engineered the marriage of Mary and William of Orange—a writer, and a very keen horticulturist. In 1655 he married Dorothy Osborne, whose well-known letters to him were published in 1888. He lived, and gardened, first of all at Sheen and later on at Moore Park near Farnham. His grounds at Sheen were among the most highly praised gardens in the vicinity of London, famous in their own right as well as for the prestige of their owner and his association with William III and with Jonathan Swift, who became Temple's secretary at Sheen in 1689. (Swift went home to Ireland, was ordained, and returned to Temple at Moore Park, where he first met Esther Johnson, 'Stella'.)

Sir William's famous horticultural essay, *Upon the Gardens of Epicurus*; *or, Of Gardening in the Year 1685*, is too prolix and stilted to be found digestible by most modern readers, and the early pages, which contain an account of the gardens of the Ancients, is a curiosity of doubtful value. The essay gains significance when it deals with gardening in 1685, and the best parts are, as might be expected, those dealing with the garden he knew best—his own, at Sheen.

> 'But after so much ramble into ancient times and remote places, to return home and consider the present way and humour of our gardening in *England*, which seem to have grown into such vogue, and to have been so mightily improved in three or four and twenty years of His Majesty's reign, that perhaps few countries are before us; either in the elegance of our gardens, or in the number of our plants; and I believe none equals us in the variety of fruits, which may be justly called good; and from the earliest cherry and strawberry, to the last apples and pears, may furnish every day of the circling year. For the taste and perfection of what we esteem the best, I may truly say, that the French, who have eaten my peaches and grapes at *Shene*, in no very ill year, have generally concluded, that the best are as good as any they have eaten in France, on this side *Fontainebleau*; and the first as good as any they have eaten in *Gascony*; I

mean those which came from the stone, and are properly called peaches, not those which are hard, and are termed pavies; *Italians* have agreed, my white figs to be as good as any of that sort in *Italy*, which is the earlier kind of white fig there; for in the latter [later] kind, and the blue, we cannot come near the warm climates, no more than in the *Frontignac* or *Muscat* grape.

'My orange-trees are as large as any I saw when I was young in France, except those of *Fontainebleau*, or what I have seen since in the *Low Countries* . . . When I was at *Cosewelt* with the Bishop of Munster, that made so much noise in his time, I observed no other trees but cherries in a great garden he had made. He told me the reason was, because he found no other fruit would ripen well in that climate or upon that soil; and therefore instead of being curious in others, he had only been so in sorts of that, whereof he had so many, as never to be without them from *May* to the end of *September*.'

It appears from Temple's letters that he tried, in the year 1667, to emulate the Bishop's success with cherries to bear crops from May to Michaelmas. At Sheen, the site of an ancient priory, he filled all his leisure time with experiments in horticulture, in which he took great delight, as Macaulay mentions in his *Essays*.

Lysons provides a picture of Temple's amanuensis, Swift, acting as escort to the king:

'King William, who had known Sir William Temple on the Continent, and had a great esteem for his talents and character, frequently visited him at Sheen and pressed him to become his Secretary of State. When his patron was lame with the gout, Swift usually attended his Majesty in his walks round the garden. The king is said on one of these occasions to have offered to make him a captain of horse, and to have taught him to cut asparagus in the Dutch manner.'

What, one wonders, did Swift do with this royal offer and the horticultural hint?

In 1691, after Temple's removal to Moore Park, a gardener named Gibson made a survey of several gardens near London. It is sad to read once again that familiar story of a garden going downhill after the owner's departure.

'Sir William Temple, being lately gone to live at his house in Farnham, his garden and greenhouse at *West Sheene*, where he has lived of late years are not so well kept as they have been, many of his orange trees, and other greens, being given to Sir John Temple, his brother, at *East Sheene*, and other gentlemen; but his greens that are remaining (being as good a stock as most greenhouses have) are very fresh and thriving, the room they stand in suiting well with them and being well contrived, if it be no defect in it that the floor is a foot at least within the ground, as is also the floor of the dwelling-house. He had attempted to have orange trees to grow in the ground (as at Beddington), and for that purpose had enclosed a square of ten feet wide, with a low brick wall, and sheltered them with wood, but they would not do. His orange trees in summer stand not in any particular square or enclosure, under some shelter, as most others do, but are disposed on pedestals of Portland stone, at equal distance, on a board over against a South wall, where is his best fruit, and fairest walk.'

Temple summed up his attitude to horticulture thus:

> 'The use of gardens . . . as it has been the inclination of Kings and the choice of Philosophers, so it has been the common favourite of public and private men; a pleasure of the greatest and the care of the meanest; and indeed an employment and a possession for which no man is too high or too low.'

Alexander Pope

Pope, born in London in 1688, was the son of a Roman Catholic draper. His health was never restored after a serious (unspecified) illness in boyhood. As his body was subsequently distorted, this may have been the disease now known as poliomyelitis. He was largely self-educated, and his first published verse, he afterwards asserted, was written at the age of sixteen. Seven years later, as a member of Addison's circle, he began to write articles for *The Spectator*. Before long he was associating with Swift and John Gay, collaborating with the latter in an unsuccessful comedy in 1717. Much of his later writing was pungently satirical, including the *Dunciad*—a satire on dullness.

He was thirty when he leased the villa overlooking the Thames at Twickenham where, for the next twenty-five years, he was to become absorbed in the laying out and planting of a garden. This original creation had many traces of old-style formality, yet in spite of that managed to develop the idea of a garden designed to be a picture, based on an amalgam of natural landscape and the easel pictures produced by painters. He is said to have considered his creation to be the last word in naturalism; but drawings show it to have been planted with regiments of trees in straight lines, with twin mounds to right and left of the central vista, which culminated in an obelisk—bearing scant resemblance to any landscape thrown up by nature in the wild.

In his famous *Epistle to Lord Burleigh* he formulated his theory of garden lay-out:

To build, to plant, whatever you intend,
To rear the column, or the arch to bend,
To swell the terrase, or to sink the grot;
In all let NATURE *never be forgot . . .*
Consult the genius of the place in all;
That tells the waters or to rise, or fall,
Or helps th' ambitious hill the heav'n to scale,
Or scoops the circling theatres in the vale,
Calls in the country, catches opening glades,

Joins willing woods, and varies shades with shades,
Now breaks, or now directs, th' intending lines,
Paints as you plant, and as you work, designs.

His garden was free from the excess of topiary work commonly found in his time, and satirized by Steele:

Adam and Eve in yew; Adam a little shattered
by the fall of the tree of knowledge in the great
Storm: Eve and the serpent very flourishing.
St. George in box; his arms scarce long enough,
but will be in a condition to stick the dragon by next April.
A green dragon of the same, with a tail of ground ivy for the present.
An old maid of honour in wormwood.
A quickset hog, shot up into a porcupine.
A lavender pig, with sage growing in his belly.

It was at other, greater, gardens—those of Hampton Court—that a curious little drama took place which was afterwards immortalized by Pope's poem *The Rape of the Lock.*

Close by those meads, for ever crown'd with flowers,
Where Thames with pride surveys his rising towers,
There stands a structure of majestic frame,
Which from the neighb'ring Hampton takes its name . . .

One summer's day in the time of Queen Anne, a party of people came down the river for some hours of pleasure at the palace. After they had dined, they began to play at the popular card game of *Ombre*, and during an interval a servant brought in apparatus for making coffee. A Miss Arabella Fermor ('Belinda' of the poem) had bent her head over this when young Lord Petre snicked off a curl dangling down her neck. Arabella flew into a rage, the thief refused to return his trophy, and the meeting broke up in disorder. Pope wrote *The Rape of the Lock* in mock-heroic vein in the hope of reconciling the disputants with a jesting account of the affair.

Pope's garden is described as having retiring and assembling shades, well managed surprise and contrast, concealed boundaries, picturesque clumps, narrowing vistas and contrived gloom—all of which greatly excited his contemporaries. Directly he had leased the villa, he employed men to work on his garden, and by 1720 was able to write of his trees 'like new Acquaintances brought happily together, are stretching their arms to meet each other and are growing nearer and nearer every hour'.

Apparently he received advice from Bridgeman, for he wrote in 1725 about the turfing of a 'little Bridgmannick theatre'; while Kent designed for him an elegant temple with dome or cupola supported on rustic pillars, and faced entirely with shells. Between the front of the house and the Thames lay a sloping lawn, with woody thickets on either hand forming wings to the villa, and terminating in small pavilions fitted with seats and inscribed urns. There was a landing-stage by the water, and busts of Homer, Virgil, Cicero and Marcus Aurelius to greet the visitors on arrival.

The principal garden, or wilderness, lay on the far side of the road behind the villa. Pope had a subterranean passage made to connect the two parts of his domain. This feature started as a utilitarian crossing place, but was gradually extended to provide a series of caves, or grottoes, which became a kind of museum. From the exit of this tunnel into the garden one had a first view of the shell temple, and in the reverse direction the underground passage framed a glimpse of the river: 'a beautiful remote appearance, where vessels suddenly glance on the eye and again vanish from it in a moment'. Close to the temple stood a large mound designed by William Kent; this feature earned criticism for its 'stiff and bad rise', although the view from the summit was excellent. Pope delighted in taking his guests up to the shaded seat to survey his domain while he pointed out its glories.

The stone obelisk in memory of his mother, which closed the main axis or vista, also made a focal point at the end of two secondary vistas alongside walks reached from naturalistic glades on the verges of the ground. The planting of trees and shrubs bordering the main axis was cunningly contrived by means of false perspective to give an increased appearance of size. Evergreens were placed near the obelisk because, as Pope wrote, 'You may distance things by darkening them and by narrowing them more and more toward the end, in the same manner as they do in painting.' He frequently told his visitors that he had so contrived the lay-out as to make 'the garden look like a landscape hung up'.

There were no fences or walls to enclose the wilderness, for Pope made shrubberies and woodland so dense that the lanes bounding his site were invisible. 'He gains all, who pleasingly confounds, surprises, varies and conceals the Bounds.' A later owner hacked down the groves to such an extent that he 'desired the three lanes to walk in again, and is now forced to shut them out by a wall, for there was not a muse could walk there but she was spied on by every country fellow who went by with a pipe in his mouth'. Pope had a long path to the north of his garden, with a seat at one end and a statue at the other; a wide glade here was probably the site of his little Bridgmannick theatre. The path connected his vegetable garden, vineyard and greenhouses, whose produce gave him great satisfaction.

The quantity of statues and urns seems excessive to modern tastes: 'A Venus with stone pedestall, a Mercury with a wood pedestall, 4 bustos antike with stone termes, a stone statue with a wood pedestall, 4 lead urns, 16 stone urns and pedestalls.' Some of the vases were designed by Kent for this garden. I have not been able to discover what Pope spent on his kingdom, but it must have been a large sum. He used to admit that he neglected writing to devote more time to the garden, and said that he preferred to win fame as a gardener. In 1736 he extended his plantings, and at the end of the year, after many excursions to advise others about their gardens, he was able to write to Ralph Allen that he was now busy planting for himself. 'I thank God for every wet day and for every fog that gives me the headacke but prospers my works.'

By 1740 his attention was fixed upon the grotto, at whose entrance he erected a rustic arch 'composed of various stones, thrown promiscuously together, in imitation of an old ruin', with an inscription from Horace inset on a marble slab. Lord Pembroke was taken in by this fake, and wanted to know where the devil Pope had procured the antique. Friends were pressed to send him stones of all kinds; Ralph Allen sent many loads of Bath stone from his quarries; 'fine sparry marble' came from Lord Edgecumbe's quarry; Cornish amethysts, Bristol diamonds, Plymouth marbles, Brazil pebbles, tin, copper and silver ores; brain stones from Mr Miller of Chelsea; even humming-birds, are listed in the materials Pope gathered for this obsessive creation underground. All these furnishings, together with the statuary and urns, were left to Martha Blount in his will; sad to say, the landlord claimed the contents of the grotto as fixtures and fittings.* Most of the garden has long since been built on; only vestiges of the grotto remain. It is now the property of St Catherine's Convent, Pope's Villa, and may be seen by appointment on Saturday and Sunday afternoons. Pope died in 1744 and was buried in Twickenham Church.

* James Boutwood, 'Pope's Essay in the Picturesque', *Country Life*, March 1968.

Lancelot ('Capability') Brown

'CAPABILITY' BROWN (1716–83) can hardly be classed as a writer, for only one instance of his having put his ideas on paper can be traced. The scarcity value of this letter makes it worthy of inclusion here. It was written in June 1775 to a certain Thomas Dyer whose friend (unnamed) in France desired to lay out his grounds in the English manner.

Brown wrote:

> 'I have made a Plan according to your desire, as well as I could, from the survey and description you sent me, which I wish may be of use to the owner. In France they do not exactly comprehend our ideas on Gardening and Place-making which, when rightly understood, will supply all the elegance and all the comforts which Mankind wants in the Country and (I will add) if right, be exactly fit for the Owner, the Poet and the Painter. To produce these effects there wants a good plan, good execution, a perfect knowledge of the country, the objects in it, whether natural or artificial, and infinite delicacy in the planting, etc.; so much Beauty depending on the size of the trees and the colour of their leaves to produce the effect of light and shade so very essential to the perfecting of a good plan: as also the hideing what is disagreeable and shewing what is beautifull, getting shade from the large trees and sweets from the smaller sorts of shrubbs etc. I hope they will in time find out in France that Place-making, and a good English Garden, depend intirely upon Principle and have very little to do with Fashion; for it is a word that in my opinion disgraces Science wherever it is found. I dare say you will think I have said enough, and therfor will only add that I am with very Sincere respect Your obliged and obedt. sert.
>
> Lancelot Brown.'*

* Dorothy Stroud, 'Capability Brown', *Country Life*, 1950.

John and Jane Loudon

A London house—3, Porchester Terrace, Bayswater—bears a blue-and-white plaque affixed to it by the London County Council, now re-named the Greater London Council.

HERE LIVED
JOHN AND JANE
LOUDON
1783–1843 and 1807–1858

Their
Horticultural Work
Gave New Beauty to
LONDON SQUARES

When Mr Loudon first arrived in London, he was very much struck with the gloomy appearance of gardens in the centre of public squares, which were then planted almost entirely with evergreens, particularly with Scots pines, yews and spruces. Before the close of the year 1803 he published an article in *The Literary Journal*, entitled 'Observations on laying out the Public Squares of London', in which he criticized freely the taste (or lack of it) displayed in the trees commonly seen. In his opinion yews and firs should be banished, for the effect of smoke on their foliage was extremely drab, and the admixture of deciduous trees with the remaining evergreens would improve the London scene out of all knowledge. He named the oriental and occidental planes, sycamore and almond as ornamental species able to withstand the city smoke. It is interesting to see how precisely his ideas were adopted, for such trees may now be found in most of the squares. He also selected many of the fine trees in Kensington Gardens, designed little lodges near the gates, and suggested the bandstand near the Round Pond.

This brilliant and hard-working young man, who had begun his horticultural training at Dickson's Nursery in Edinburgh, was the son of a Scottish farmer.

Like many a Scots gardener, he decided that London should bring him opportunity, and set about making his dreams come true. He had always had a flair for writing since schooldays, and was also a very accomplished draughtsman. He published his illustrated *Encyclopedia of Gardening* in 1822, and launched *The Gardener's Magazine* in 1826. Herein he reviewed an extraordinary novel, an early example of 'science fiction' long before that term had been minted. It was called *The Mummy*, and dealt with the resurrection of an Egyptian Pharaoh, who returned, not to the world of the early nineteenth century, but to the twenty-second century A.D. The prophecies of what the world would be like seemed wildly fantastic at the time, but many of them have already proved to be surprisingly accurate. Space-travel, the Welfare State, milking-machines and interior-spring mattresses were a few of the innovations described. John Loudon imagined the author to be some scientifically-minded young man, and was astounded to discover the small, ringleted Miss Jane Webb. In 1830 she became his wife, and the couple settled down in Porchester Terrace.

Between 1835 and 1838 John Loudon's great work, *Arboretum et Fruticetum Britannicum*, appeared in eight parts, four of text and four of illustrations. The year 1838 also saw his book *Suburban Gardener and Villa Companion*, which appealed to the large number of professional people now inhabiting prosperous suburbs a little way out from the City. Some years earlier he had suffered badly at the hands of incompetent doctors who, in attempts to alleviate pain in his right arm, caused damage which led eventually to amputation. Although for some years he managed to carry on his work of writing and illustrating horticultural books and articles, together with the supervision of his garden, he was glad to have his wife's assistance instead of depending on hired secretaries and gardeners. It became their habit to work together in their library far into the night, and, while engaged in this arduous service to her husband, Jane rapidly increased her own knowledge. But her training in horticulture was not confined to theory.

When she married, her ignorance was profound; she 'could not imagine anyone more ignorant of plants and gardening than herself'. But John was quite as anxious to teach as she was to learn, although his highbrow approach daunted her a little at first. Before long, clad in gauntlets of her own design, with clogs on her little feet, she learned to dig with a specially light spade. She described this initiation in her book *Gardening for Ladies*, issued in 1840.

'The first point to be attended to, in order to render the operation of digging less laborious, is to provide a suitable spade; that is, one which shall be as light as is consistent with strength, and which will penetrate the ground with the least possible trouble. For this purpose the blade of what is called a lady's spade is made not more than half the usual breadth, say five or six inches and of smooth polished iron. It is surmounted, at the part where it joins the handle, by a piece of iron rather broader than itself, which is called the tread, to serve as a rest for the foot of the operator.

'The handle is about the usual length, but quite smooth and sufficiently slender for a lady's hand to grasp, and made of willow, which is tough and tolerably strong though much lighter than the ash generally used for gardeners' spades. The lady should also be provided with clogs, the soles of which are not jointed, put over her shoes; or if she should dislike these and prefer stronger shoes, she should be provided with what gardeners call a *tramp*; that is, a small plate of iron to go under the sole of the shoe and which is fastened round the foot with a leathern strap and buckle. She should also own a pair of stiff thick leathern gloves, or gauntlets, to protect her hands, not only from the handle of the spade, but from the stones, weeds etc. which she may turn over with the earth, and which ought to be picked out and thrown into a small, light wheelbarrow, which may easily be moved from place to place.

'It must be confessed that digging appears at first sight to be a very laborious employment, and one peculiarly unfitted to small and delicately formed hands and feet; but by a little attention to the principles of mechanics and the laws of motion, the labour may be very much simplified and rendered comparatively easy. The operation of digging, as performed by the gardener, consists in thrusting the iron part of the spade, which acts as a wedge, perpendicularly into the ground by the application of the foot, and then using the long handle as a lever to raise up the loosened earth and turn it over.

'It must be remembered that all operations that are effected rapidly by the exertion of great power, may be effected slowly by the exertion of very little power if that comparatively feeble power be applied for greater lengths of time. A lady, with a small light spade, may, by repeatedly digging over the same line, and taking out only a little earth at a time, succeed in doing with her own hands all the digging that can be required in a small garden . . . and she will not only have the satisfaction of seeing the garden created, as it were, by her own hands, but she will find her health and spirits wonderfully improved by the exercise, and by the reviving smell of fresh earth.

'The necessary implements for digging being provided, the next thing to be considered is the easiest way of performing the operation. . . . By inserting the spade in a slanting direction and throwing the body slightly forward at the same time, the mass of earth to be raised will not only be much less [than if the spade had been inserted perpendicularly] but the body of the operator will be in a much more convenient position for raising and turning it, which may thus be done with perfect ease. The time for digging should always be chosen if possible when the ground is tolerably dry; not only on account of the danger of taking cold by standing on the damp earth, but because the soil, when damp, adheres to the spade and it is much more difficult to "work" (as the gardeners call it) than when it is dry.

'Every lady should be careful, when she has finished digging, to have her spade dipped in water and then wiped dry; after which it should be hung up in some warm, dry shed or harness room to keep it free from rust; as nothing lessens the labour of digging more than having a perfectly smooth and polished spade. Should the earth adhere to the spade while digging, dipping the blade in water occasionally will be found to facilitate the operation.'

All that carefully worded advice is still sound, except that women are able to use a larger spade now, and with stainless steel it is less trouble to maintain tools in good condition. Recent pioneer work in the use of compost, a field in which Mrs Theresa Earle's great-niece, Lady Eve Balfour, has played a large part, also the Soil Association and Dr Shewell-Cooper's Good Gardeners' Association, has led many people to dispense with digging altogether, once the ground has been cleared of perennial weeds. No good will be done by putting a rich layer of compost and straw on top of thistles and docks—except to the thistles and docks. Membership of the Soil Association and the Good Gardeners' Association is well worth the few pounds in annual subscription; the latter will analyse your soil and tell you precisely how to nourish it and grow sound, healthy plants without using chemical fertilizers or pesticides. Nothing like Dr Shewell-Cooper's library of books, the ABCs of *Roses*; *Pruning; Soils, Humus and Health; Flowering Shrubs; Fruit Growing*, etc., each one obtainable for less than £1, was available in Jane Loudon's day.

Her training was by no means confined to theory. In addition to being taught to dig, she watched her husband as he directed the planning and planting of an arboretum in their London garden—a miniature containing about sixty trees and shrubs which he hoped to control by means of root-pruning. He also made a collection of roses and peonies. He used his garden for experimental purposes, and as an exhibit to show clients what he proposed to plant in his schemes for their own gardens. He was a stickler for order, and everything in the place had to be neatly and indelibly labelled. Jane spent a lot of time in removing decayed blooms, withered leaves and seed-pods from his plants, and when bad weather prevented this she took refuge in a garden shed. Here she inscribed botanical names on porcelain labels in Indian ink, varnishing them afterwards to preserve and waterproof the lettering. She also weeded the beds—John loathed the sight of a weed—and learned how to plant bulbs and pot up rare and delicate plants sent to her husband by friends abroad.

The potting-shed at Porchester Terrace must have been a dream of neatness and efficiency. It housed all kinds of potting material—loam, peat, sand, leaf-mould, chalk, soot and lime, together with pots of every size. There were cupboards for the storage of bulbs, corms and tubers, and a whole shelf of tins for seed. As Jane became more deeply involved in these matters she developed a craving for knowledge which was not easily satisfied. Existing books were either too advanced for a novice, or too highly specialized, and her husband was too preoccupied with his professional work to attend to incessant queries. These experiences during her early years in a garden made her understand the needs of others, and inspired her to write the down-to-earth books which brought her so much acclamation.

In *Gardening for Ladies,* she defines her purpose clearly:

> 'I do this because I think books intended for professional gardeners are seldom suitable for the wants of amateurs. It is so very difficult for a person who has been acquainted with a subject all his life to imagine the state of ignorance in which a person who knows nothing of it finds himself, that adepts often find it impossible to communicate the knowledge they possess. Thus, though it may at first sight appear presumptuous in me to attempt the teaching of an art of which for three-quarters of my life I was ignorant, it is that very circumstance which is one of my chief qualifications for the task. Having been a full-grown pupil myself, I know the wants of others in a similar situation; and having never been satisfied without knowing the reason for everything I was told to do, I am able to impart these reasons to others.'

Her education as a gardener was comprehensive and thorough. John Loudon was fond of saying that to be a good gardener one must be a good botanist.

Wishing to attract more women into its folds, the Horticultural Society announced, at an opportune moment for Jane, that Mr Lindley would deliver a set of six botanical lectures. She attended the course, took careful notes, and became a prize pupil. By that time her husband had formed a plan for turning her into the best lady gardener in Europe. His theory, that 'the most artistical flower-gardens may be laid out by ladies' was developed in his *Suburban Gardener and Villa Companion* of 1838, in which he compares the skill required to design a garden with that of the dressmaker who is able to cut out and assemble the different parts of a dress. His success in making every lady her own garden designer may have been minimal, but he certainly saw his wife blossom out as a good practical flower gardener herself, and one whose influence helped to create many more through the medium of books and articles.

Pruning was not considered suitable work for women, but Jane set herself to overcome that prejudice. She managed to deal with 'quite large branches, having procured from the Kensington Nursery a pair of small and elegant pruning shears'. She had a tender heart for plants. One task which she could not bring herself to perform was carried out by her husband, who poured nearly boiling water over a box of hyacinths to forward them. Jane was particularly fond of hyacinths. At that time nobody visited the Dutch bulbfields, and 'Springfields'—the Lincolnshire show garden now open to the British people—lay more than a century off; but a Dutch florist in Shepherd's Bush had several thousand bulbs growing and flowering under canvas. This was a great attraction to Londoners in the season, among them Jane Loudon, who described the scene as a 'blaze of beauty'.

A daughter, Agnes, was born to the Loudons in October 1832. John was hard at work on his major work, *Arboretum Britannicum*, a vast undertaking requiring heavy expenditure of both energy and cash, and the devoted Jane was soon up and helping him as before. She wrote at this time:

> 'Having realised that all the drawings of trees should be made from nature, John had seven artists constantly employed, and he was frequently in the open air with them from his breakfast at seven in the morning till he came home to dinner at eight in the evening, having remained the whole of that time without taking the slightest refreshment and generally without even sitting down.'

In his introduction Mr Loudon expresses something of his great love for trees:

> 'Trees are not only, in appearance, the most striking and grand objects of the vegetable creation; but, in reality, they are those which contribute the most to human comfort and improvement . . . Man may live and be clothed in a savage, and even in a pastoral, state by herbaceous plants alone; but he cannot advance further; he cannot till the ground, or build houses or ships, he cannot become an agriculturist or a merchant, without the use of trees.'

Unhappily much of this is less true now than it was then, and the agriculturist is given to depleting the land of trees in order to make more room for quick crops and for huge machines to manœuvre in his service.

By the time Queen Victoria was crowned in 1838 John Loudon had completed his mammoth work on trees, and, according to Jane, exhausted himself in the process. 'His constitution was naturally very strong, but it was impossible for any human powers to bear for any length of time the fatigue he underwent.' Many of his draughtsmen worked in the Duke of Northumberland's Syon Park, now the home of the great Gardening Centre and Exhibition; some were employed drawing plants at Loddige's Hackney nursery; for the supervision of others, John had to travel even farther afield. Not only physical strength was depleted: he was worried over debts to printer and wood-engraver amounting to £10,000, and in constant pain from a swollen knee.

Nothing stopped him from working. Books, articles and pamphlets were produced at such a rate that today nobody seems able to list them completely. *The Gardener's Magazine* had been kept going, but success waned as other periodicals caught the public fancy. Now Jane began to think that perhaps she might take a hand in the restoration of their fortunes. She had already contributed occasional articles to the magazine, but she now launched out as the author of a book—her *Ladies' Flower Garden*, issued in monthly parts. Writing a review of this, her husband said, 'We think it but justice to state that this is an elegant work and one which will be found no less beautiful than it is useful'. Jane's first garden book to appear as one volume was the now famous *Gardening for Ladies*; it was the first to be published on that subject since Charles Evelyn wrote *The Lady's Recreation* in 1707, and had an immediate success when it came out in 1840 under the colophon of John Murray.

In 1841 the parts of her *Ladies' Flower Garden* which dealt with bulbs were collected under the title of *Ornamental Bulbous Plants*. It has charming coloured plates of lilies, gladioli and irises, many of them kinds now lost to horticulture. Jane became almost rapturous when describing gladioli; one variety had 'petals which at sunset take a curiously shifting hue like shot silk'. This was deliciously scented—particularly at dusk—and she therefore recommends it for use in window boxes or for tubs on a veranda. Another, called 'The Viper' was introduced into England in 1794, then lost, reintroduced in 1825, and lost again. It had green and brown petals, striped, and was supposed to resemble the head of a snake. It was also fragrant. Where did it come from, and where has it gone? Both varieties sound more interesting than the showy, scentless modern 'Glad', or 'Gaudyola' as a child called it.

The year 1841 also brought publication of *The Ladies' Companion to the Flower Garden*, by John and Jane Loudon—the only work bearing the names of husband and wife as co-authors. It is a dictionary of botanic and vernacular names of flowers commonly grown in gardens at the time, with articles on the making of shrubberies, borders, gravel walks and parterres. The dedication to Mrs Lawrence of Ealing Park, Middlesex, describes her in these terms: *A Zealous Patron of Floriculture, an Excellent Botanist, and one of the First Lady Gardeners of the Present Day*. This lady was the wife of William Lawrence, a friend of the Loudons who, in his capacity as surgeon (eminent in his time) had treated John Loudon with some success. His wife, whom he married in 1828, first laid out a two-acre garden at Drayton Green, which Loudon considered to be the most remarkable of its size in the London neighbourhood. She was one of the first women to be admitted to membership of the RHS, an event which took place in 1830. In 1840 the Lawrences moved to Ealing Park, where Queen Victoria and the Prince Consort went at 9 p.m. to see a night-flowering cactus. Louisa Lawrence gained fifty-three medals, including the Knightian Medal, in exhibitions, and succeeded in flowering the remarkable *Amherstia nobilis* before any of her rivals, out-doing the Duke of Devonshire at Chatsworth. She died before the institution of the Victoria Medal of Honour, otherwise she would undoubtedly have joined Gertrude Jekyll and Ellen Willmott in that august circle.

The Loudons had many friends who were well-known in different spheres, beginning with Charles Dickens and Thackeray, and including Mark Lemon and John Leech of *Punch*. Mrs Gaskell, author of *Cranford*, was a friend of Jane's. John, who had drawn and painted as a young man, and exhibited at the Royal Academy, knew the Landseer brothers, Daniel Maclise, Frith and other artists. After the debts had been paid, the money so hard-earned was allowed to flow out on entertaining—dinner-parties for twelve being of common occurrence at Porchester Terrace—and the company of this clever couple was much sought after in London's social life. Travels to the north of England and up into Scotland were undertaken by all three Loudons; John developed a serious illness and took to his bed. By the autumn of 1841 he seemed better; his *Hortus Lignosus Londinensis* appeared in ten parts, while Jane worked on her *Botany for Ladies*. In the spring of 1842 John was again seriously ill, this time with inflammation of the lungs. Later that year the family went to the Isle of Wight for a holiday, which proved to be the sick man's last jaunt. He reached London in a bad state, and William Lawrence diagnosed incurable disease of the lungs. During the autumn and winter he grew steadily weaker, while continuing to write without ceasing.

In 1843, on the last night of his life, he dictated to Jane some material for a book to be called *Self-Instruction for Young Gardeners*. This went on until midnight, when he consented to go to bed. Unable to sleep, he was up again at dawn, looking so ill that Jane hastily dressed herself. He told her that he would be unable to complete the book, and asked her to arrange for a friend to do so. An hour or two later John Claudius Loudon died in his wife's arms, aged sixty. He is buried in Kensal Green Cemetery.

Left a widow at thirty-six, Jane Loudon was not only the breadwinner, but had her husband's cherished garden to care for. There were debts to be paid off, money was scarce, the staff had to be reduced. Agnes, the dear little daughter, had been spoilt (as she herself said in later life), and had some absurdly grandiose ideas. Luckily John Loudon had been far ahead of his time in the belief that women should develop their gifts to the full and work as professionals in any sphere they chose. As his wife, Jane had already acquired knowledge and confidence, which were now of vital importance to her as the mainstay of the home.

The award of a small Civil List pension to the widow of 'the eminent horticulturist John C. Loudon' lightened her financial load a little; and, when asked to see her late husband's last book through the press, she resumed her work at the desk where labours had so long been shared happily with him. The first piece of work she carried out was the short memoir of him in the introduction to his *Self-Instruction for Young Gardeners*. Her next task, the writing of *The Lady's Country Companion*, which came out in 1845, took the form of a series of letters to a young girl who had recently married and gone to live in a country manor house. Two more books followed quickly—*British Wild Flowers* and *The Amateur Gardener's Calendar*, both issued in 1846. After this effort, Jane felt herself to be 'written out'—her creative life over.

Then came bad news. In 1849 she was invited to visit the publishers, Longman, at their city offices, where she was told that her husband's writing was already being neglected by the reading public. Royalties had dropped sharply, and instead of an income of £800 the total receipts from his books and her own would not exceed £400. She went back in a dazed state, wondering how to keep the home going and provide for Agnes, now growing up and needing more clothes and a maid to care for them.

Suddenly a fresh career opened before her astonished eyes. She received an invitation to serve as Editor of a new journal for women, to be called *The Ladies' Companion at Home and Abroad*, a periodical intended for serious-minded women who required something better than trash of the *Forget-me-Not* type (hitherto thought suitable for their sex). Jane accepted, and took up her new task with enthusiasm. For seven months the paper flourished, and Jane enjoyed the work, which was carried out in her own comfortable study with all her husband's reference books at hand. Then sales began to drop, and soon the publishers called for Jane's resignation. They had decided to appoint a man in her place.

Jane sat alone in the library, thinking of her late husband and wondering what to do. His spirit seemed near, giving her courage. She must compose something first-class for her last appearance in print as Editor of *The Ladies' Companion*. Her column ended like this:

> 'Real and vital happiness depends only on *ourselves*. If once the mind can grasp this truth, and with firmness and courage resolve to draw happiness from sources whence alone it springs, no storms from without will permanently shake us, no fears depress, no trials overcome us.'

There is very little else worth recording about her life. Money worries and the emotional entanglements of Agnes bore heavily on her last years. She did little more creative work, and died on 13 July 1858, to be buried beside her husband in Kensal Green Cemetery.

Reginald Farrer

REGINALD FARRER (1880–1920) a 'forceful, bizarre person' according to Miles Hadfield,* was a plant-collector from the Ingleborough limestone country of Yorkshire, where he gardened and later had a nursery. He was a better writer, on travels in search of plants, than other collectors who may have reached a higher rung of the ladder among the *élite* of the Royal Horticultural Society. His father was High Sheriff of Yorkshire, his ancestry gentle; but, because of the handicap of a cleft palate, Farrer was not sent to a Public School—which in England means a privately exclusive, fee-paying establishment. Perhaps this helped him to retain his marked individuality, his uninhibited enthusiasms and disregard of what was considered to be 'good form'. He was not averse from showing off, and his manners were not always polite; but he was undoubtedly a great character and a fine plantsman.

Here is a quotation from his book *The Rainbow Bridge* (1960), describing life among Tibetans in Tien Tang:

> 'The service proceeds with ringing of bells, and chimes and chanting, litanies, antiphons and psalms: and a stout ecclesiastic, flat-faced and whiskered like a butler, is predicating from the pulpit, to the occasional obbligato of a bell. On he goes and on, sitting cross-legged and hieratic in his place: but as soon as attention seems likely to flag, devotion is opportunely sustained—and in a manner that Christian Churches might very profitably copy. For now, out of the depths of blackness far away in the left-hand distance of the dark, there arises a bustle; a door is thrown open, and on a shaft of light there pours in a procession of novices and acolytes from the adjacent cookhouse, each bearing one of those sumptuous buckets full of tea. A new liveliness perks up in the congregation: everybody produces a wooden bowl: the shaven-headed Ganymedes go round, administering sustenance to each from their buckets. Contentment shines, and the sound of sipping takes the place of sacred song: after which the bucket-bearers retire again to replenish their store against another later

* *Gardening in Britain* (1960).

26. E. A. Bowles

27. Victoria
Sackville-West

28. The Tower at Sissinghurst

29. Work in a medieval vineyard

30. Loading vegetables for market, 1895

31. Covent Garden market by Doré

32. R. D. Blackmore

33. James Lee. From a painting

interval in the service, and the holy offices are resumed with revivified attention.

'There could be no doubt that we were liked in Tien Tang. Day by day the stream of Lamas and Lama-lings never ceased, and our stock of marvels never seemed to stale. They loved looking at picture-books and sketches too. Murray's *Japan*, with its reproductions of Buddhas and temples, aroused the enthusiasm of the old schoolmaster-monk and his flock of pupils: he wrote me their Tibetan names, and his own, with my stylo, as a thrilling change from his own clever pen of wood, cloven like our nibs at the end. They had a very sharp eye for flowers, and looked at the sketches long and carefully, with one eye telescoped through the hand as their habit is. Gurgles and snores of satisfaction followed, and an astonishing aptness of recognition. Not only had they their own names, in fact, for the wild flowers, but also a smart instinct for relationships and differences between them. "Nig-munk, nig-munk", they nodded approvingly at *Primula stenocalyx*; and when they saw *Androsace tibetica* pictured, they knew that this was also "Nig-munk", and said so—thus making my heart clap with delight, after so many years of worthy people who can never be got to see that all pansies and violets are Viola, and all jonquils and daffodils, Narcissus, to say nothing of such further flights of perspicacity as detecting at a glance the essential identity of Primula and Androsace.'

Farrer and his travelling companion, Bill Purdom, one night 'embarked after dinner on a hair-raising adventure. In the inebriating balmy light of a moon three-fifths to the full, we sauntered artlessly out, as if without any aim in particular, and in a careless-seeming leisure made our way deviously over the scented sea of iris in the plain. We were, in fact, bent on securing clumps of two special forms, and were anxious to avoid any suspicion or enmity that we might incur from the monks, by openly putting spade into their sacred soil. Personally I believe that by this time we might have carried off the whole plainful by cart-loads without comment, if we had liked: however, it was huge fun, feeling so surreptitious and conspiratorial. One might have been going secretly by night to disentomb some hallowed corpse. On the bank, just above a particular albino, I remember two monks were sitting, in fact drumming and chiming and chaunting in the starry stillness: but we crept past them severally, unobserved. I discovered my plant pale as a phantom under the moon. Trepidating, and in a breathless hush, for fear any rash noise should distract those two devout blurs on the bank to noticing our sinister attitudes and activities, we successfully got up the clump unnoticed, and made off through the scented surf to the other. This, too, without suspicion, we achieved, and so triumphantly returned across the grassy plain, toward the sleeping white smear of the monastery, cold and dead in the moonlight, under the cold ghostly pallor of the enveloping cliffs behind.'

In 1914 Farrer and Purdom set out to explore 'in the interests of horticulture and forestry, the whole of the Kansu-Tibet Border, from south to north'. In *On the Eaves of the World* (1960) Farrer describes this tremendous journey in detail. In the second volume there is an amusing account of a severe ducking he experienced when his pony fell into a mountain stream while it was in spate, with Farrer in the saddle.

> 'A little higher up we came to a bridge by which it was necessary to cross. It was a typical Tibetan bridge of poor class, arching high over the stream at the narrow point of a combe, and in no very good repair, with the rails all gone and half the planks also. Purdom's pony disliked the look of it, so he got off and led the beast across. I meanwhile, no attendant being immediately at hand to do the same for mine, sat philosophically quiet on "Spotted Fat", waiting on his mood. If he decided that the bridge was feasible, I would let him proceed; otherwise I would not urge him, but would wait till the Go-go came up. On no account would I be bothered to get off and tug him across, then undergo all the miseries of mounting on a soaked saddle. However, all went well. "Spotted Fat" sniffed at the bridge for a moment, and then began solemnly to advance step by step, picking his way delicately from rickety pole to pole. Beneath me, far down between the gaps of the planks, I could see the boiling ice-grey water of the churned torrent, and in my ear there was a general roar. And suddenly I became aware that "Spotted Fat" was sidling out towards the unprotected edge, in evident disapproval of the vacancies between his feet. A paralysis possessed me as I felt his hindquarters swinging out more and more perilously. Purdom's frozen face of horror advancing to meet me remains photographed on my mind as the last thing I remember ere, incredulous to the last, I was conscious of a stumbling subsidence behind me, a splintering crash, and there was barely time to release my feet from the stirrups in a spasm of prudence before "Spotted Fat" and I, no longer one but two, were falling, falling through twenty feet of emptiness, and down into the glacial abysses of the river.
>
> 'Down and down into the icy water we sank, and as I slowly mounted through the depths of grey glare it seemed as if I should never emerge

again to the light of day. When I did so I was already below the bridge, being rapidly borne down stream towards that engaging gorge, whose charms I now envisaged from quite a different standpoint. There was no swimming possible, and no struggling. Heavy mountain boots held me so deep and upright in the water that only at interval could I get my mouth above the current, and a heavy macintosh encumbered all my movements. From this, in a spasm of rage, however, I immediately released myself, and away ahead it sailed towards the ghyll, precursor of my own doom; while I myself impotently floundered and bubbled in the tide, being smoothly and quite passionlessly swept onwards at the pace of a rapid train. Desperately I struck out at each rocky headland as it raced into sight, and raced away behind me again out of reach. They came and passed with the uncanny quick elusiveness of nightmares, seeming to be held out only to be withdrawn again at once, like things slid in and out on the wings of a theatre. I could study the primulas in their crannies as they fled blandly by.

'My latter end was already plainly in sight, but no high and holy thoughts possessed me, as would have been proper, nor any panoramic vistas of memory. Instead, I was consumed with rage over so ignominious a conclusion, a rage that even extended to Purdom, who meanwhile was hopping along from promontory to promontory with cheerful smiles and shouts of encouragement. The least he could have done, I felt, was to jump in and perish also, as the dramatic exigencies of the moment demanded. Yet there he was, still on terra firma, grinning like a grig, if grigs do grin. Spuming and burbling I drove onwards to my solitary death, each instant lower and lower in the water, each instant lower and lower in spirits, as each of Purdom's futile attempts to stretch me out a hand from the flying promontories fell short. Spluttering my indignation to the high gods, I was whirled straight towards the race, and abandoned hope; when suddenly I felt the point of a rock beneath my toe. Frantically I sought lodgment on it, but could not stand against the flood, and in an instant was torn onwards, only immediately after to come to rest as ignominiously as any dead Tepo, on a long wide shallow where not so much as a kitten could easily have drowned. Purdom, in fact, had all along seen this quite inevitable rescue, and the whole drama was dissipated. There was nothing for it but to wade tamely ashore like a duck, in fits of laughter, with my breeches bellying out in tight balloons of water. Only the Go-go a little rose to the heights of the situation, for he now came running up with his face gone pale to the colour of bad mud, and his eyes standing out as if on stalks with terror. As for "Spotted Fat", that prudent animal had swum straight ashore without the slightest effort. Had I clung to his tail, instead of thinking myself so clever for dissociating myself from him in time, I should not have had a moment of trouble or suspense as to my ultimate destiny.'

Farrer discovered many new species, and a number of plants now in cultivation bear the name *Farreri*; but the finding of that glorious gentian, *Gentiana farreri*, was perhaps the most thrilling moment of his career, and a find which nearly failed to reach cultivation. He tells the story in *The Rainbow Bridge*:

'Hardly had I started when, in the fine turf that crowned the top of a sloping boulder, there stared at me a new gentian, a gentian that instantly obliterates all others of its race, and sinks even *G. verna* and *G. gentianella* into a common depth of dullness. When the first awe was over, I gave tongue for Bill, and together in reverent silence we contemplated that marvel of luminous loveliness . . .

'The collector's dream is to have some illustrious plant to bear his name immortal through the gardens of future generations, long after he himself shall have become dust of their paths. Mere beauty will not do it; for the plant may fail and fade in cultivation, and his name be no more known, except to the learned, as attached to a dead dry sliver on the sheets of a herbarium. To become vividly immortal in the Valhalla of gardeners, one must own a species as vigorous as it is glorious, a thing capable of becoming, and remaining, a household word among English enthusiasts . . .

'*Gentiana farreri* bids fair to be as solid a permanency as *G. gentianella* itself. It is perfectly hardy, and—what is very remarkable in any gentian, but miraculously so in a gentian so miraculously beautiful—it is perfectly vigorous and easy to deal with in any reasonable conditions of culture in a cool place not parched or waterlogged. Shall I add that, in addition to growing so freely, and flowering so lavishly in so late and dull a moment of the year, this preposterously good-tempered exception to the rule of its race keeps its glory open, rain or shine, can be struck from cuttings as copiously as a viola, and layered along its shoots as complacently as any carnation.

'And its beauty! Nothing could I foretell of its temper and future history that day, as I stood rapt in contemplation before the actual plant, the last and greatest event of my second season, and well worth the whole two years' expedition, anyhow, merely to have seen it. A fine frail tuft like grass radiating some half dozen fine flapping stems—that is *G. farreri*, quite inconspicuous in all the high lawns of the Da-Tung . . . [in Kansu]. Until it flowers: and every day in early September brings a fresh crashing explosion of colour in the fold of the lawns. For each of those weakly stems concludes in an enormous upturned trumpet, more gorgeous than anything attained by *G. gentianella*, but in the same general style and form. But the outline is different, with a more subtle swell to the chalice, and that is freaked outside in heavy lines of black-purple that divide long vandykes of dim periwinkle blue with panels of Nankeen buff between; inside the tube and throat are white, but the mouth and the wide bold flanges are of so luminous and intense a light azure that one blossom of it will blaze out at you among the grass on the other side of the valley. It literally burns in the alpine turf like an electric jewel, an incandescent turquoise.

'Do you wonder if I stood spell-bound? Do you wonder if my heart also sank to my boots in despair? For how was I to get this glory home? A plant that only blooms in the beginning of September—when will it seed? The only possible chance that I could see lay in transporting living clumps; for we clearly could not go on waiting for the seed to ripen. Nor was there anyone we could trust to collect it after we had gone. And yet to miss this would be to miss the apex of my whole expedition. So I did transport the living clumps; with what awe and attendance you may judge. And the Trans-Siberian journey killed them all. My disappointment cut so deep that I put it behind me, and resolutely banished the memory of that gentian from my heart. Months passed, and the war submerged me in work, and London engulfed me, and the garden ceased to exist, except as a remote memory. But in the August of 1916 a little package reached me from the Botanic Garden in Edinburgh. Would I give the history of the enclosed gentian? I tore open the box, and there, large and lovely and luminous as ever, was the lost Da-Tung gentian, which I had dismissed all hope of ever seeing again.'

Seemingly, when collecting seed of *Gentiana hexaphylla* in 1914, Farrer had noticed some larger and thicker and darker in the pod than usual, and had given them a separate number. And those seeds, raised at the Botanic Garden in Edinburgh, had produced the plant which Farrer found later in bloom and lost in transit:

'On so frail a thread, and across so complete an intervening gulf of gloom, was accomplished the introduction to our gardens of so pre-eminent a plant. In any calendar that reckons only the really important things for human happiness (rather than the mere deaths of Sovereigns, and conclusions of peaces made of pie-crust), large and red will be the letters that mark the August day which first revealed my Gentiana to cultivation.'

Farrer died in October 1920 at the early age of forty, far away in the wilds of Upper Burma, alone with native servants. 'A man whose indomitable enthusiasm for plants drove on a body classed as unfit for soldiering to a lonely death in the mountains, defeated in the end by exhaustion, rain and mist.' (Miles Hadfield.) In one of his books he wrote words well suited to be his own epitaph.

> 'All the wars of the world, all the Caesars, have not the staying power of a lily in a cottage border . . . The immortality of marbles and of miseries is a vain, small thing compared to the immortality of a flower that blooms and is dead by dusk.'

Although he was not a Londoner, his work has influenced gardens, particularly rock gardens, in and around the capital to an immeasurable extent. His first book, *My Rock Garden,* issued in 1907, was followed by *The English Rock Garden* in two volumes, written in 1913 and delayed by the First World War until its appearance in 1919. This authoritative work has been reprinted many times. It was largely due to Farrer's influence that the Alpine Garden Society was founded in 1929. He derided the 'almond pudding schemes' and the 'style of the Dog's Grave' on which so many rockeries were based, and set an entirely new standard of taste in the design of rock gardens: 'A few large stones, lying on their broadest face, firmly set, deeply buried'—novel ideas then, but now taken for granted by every garden designer of repute.

Farrer introduced a number of plants which have become extremely popular, notably the 'Threepenny-bit' rose and that scented shrub which used to be segregated in Chinese Imperial Palace gardens, the *Viburnum fragrans.* This shrub was first brought to England by Farrer's friend Purdom, but little notice was taken of it, it was lost, and Farrer reintroduced it and made it known through his writings. In 1959 the Royal Horticultural Society instituted the Farrer Trophy in his memory. It is awarded annually to the best exhibit of plants for rock garden or alpine house at one of the fortnightly shows.

Theresa Earle

'Mrs Earle of the Pot-Pourri books', our grandmothers (or great-grandmothers) called her. Edward Marsh, in *A Book of Reminiscences* (London, 1939) describes her volumes as having been much loved at the time, but 'lacking that quality which keeps the head of a book above the waters of oblivion'. Yet he goes on to describe her as being memorable 'as an English Worthy, if not as a writer'. She was undoubtedly a 'character', and as such people become more and more scarce in the modern world, she merits a few pages here. A good gardener she must have been, with a wide range of knowledge and considerable artistry in the planning of her effects made with plants, both indoors and out. She called her first book 'pot-pourri' because she did not wish to emulate the many works concerned with the ABC of horticulture, and she had the original idea of mixing in the cooking of produce with its cultivation, a device which, as her output of writing grew, she extended to include many extraneous matters.

The opening chapter of her first book *Pot-pourri From a Surrey Garden*, published in 1897, contains a description of the garden she loved in childhood.

> 'I was brought up for the most part in the country, in a beautiful, wild, old-fashioned garden. This garden had remained in the hands of an old gardener for more than thirty years, which carries us back nearly a century. Almost all that has remained in my mind of my young days in this garden is how wonderfully the old man kept the place. He succeeded in flowering many things year after year with no one to help him, and with the frost in the valley to contend with in spring. It was difficult, too, for him to get seeds or plants, since the place was held by joint owners, whom he did not like to ask for them. The spot was very sheltered, and that is one of the greatest of all secrets for plant cultivation. An ever-flowing mill stream ran all round the garden; and the hedges of China-roses, Sweetbriar, Honeysuckle and white Hawthorn tucked their toes into the soft mud, and throve year after year. The old man was a philosopher in his way, and when on a cold March morning my sisters and I used to rush out after

lessons and ask him what the weather was going to be, he would stop his digging, look up at the sky, and say: "Well, Miss, it may be fine and it may be wet; and if the sun comes out, it will be warmer." After this solemn announcement he would wipe his brow and resume his work, and we went off, quite satisfied, to our well-known haunts in the Hertfordshire woods, to gather violets and primroses for our mother, who loved them. All this, you will see, laid a very small foundation for any knowledge of gardening; yet, owing to the vivid character of the impressions of youth, it left a memory that was very useful to me when I took up gardening later in life. To this day I can smell the tall white double Rockets that throve so well in the damp garden, and scented the evening air. They grew by the side of glorious bunches of Oriental Poppies and the on-coming spikes of the feathery *Spiraea aruncus*. This garden had peculiar charms for us, because, although we hardly realised it, such gardens were already beginning to grow out of fashion, sacrificed to the new bedding-out system, which altered the whole gardening of Europe.'

Her father, the Hon. Edward Villiers, a great-grandson of the second Earl of Jersey, died in 1843 at the age of thirty, from undiscovered tuberculosis. The widowed Mrs Villiers brought up Theresa (born in 1836), Ernest (1838) and the twin girls Edith and Elizabeth (1841) on a fairly small income, helped by relatives with the loan of houses, including the Hertfordshire mill whose garden Theresa later described in print. She had a generous nature, and never tired of praising the beauty of her younger sisters, the twins Edith and Elizabeth. The former became the wife of E. R. Bulwer-Lytton, better known as the first Earl of Lytton, sometime Viceroy of India. At the age of twenty Theresa was given the opportunity of serving as Maid of Honour to Queen Victoria—a grandeur which she declined. Henceforth she was known in royal circles as 'radical Theresa', or 'T'. She had none of the grace of her lovely mother and sisters, being decidedly podgy in figure, short, and of somewhat homely features; but what she lacked in looks she made up in wit, vivacity and what Edward Marsh calls 'that perfecting dash of tartness which saves benevolence from insipidity'. She had a great understanding of young people, and acquired a large collection of spurious 'nephews' and 'nieces', all of whom called her 'Aunt T'—among them the author just quoted, 'Eddie' Marsh.

She and her husband, Captain Charles Earle, at first brought up their three sons on small means in a house at Watford. They were both agnostics, and puzzled about the best way to teach the boys in matters of religion. They moved in a circle which included Oscar Wilde, the Gladstones, John Morley and T. H. Huxley, so the latter's advice was sought by Theresa, who had a very warm admiration for the great scientist. 'My dear Mrs Earle,' he replied, 'you should bring the boys up in the mythology of their age and country.' In 1878 legacies allowed the family to live in a far more lavish style in London, and to keep their own carriage. The 'radical T' wrote that the first time they drove out in this equipage she felt 'horribly ashamed'. Captain Earle, who had been delicate in his younger days, grew healthier and wealthier, thus, as she said, taking from her her true vocation—that of 'nursing an invalid and being a good poor man's wife'.

Possibly this change of circumstances, together with their acquisition of a Surrey house—'Woodlands' at Cobham—turned her energies in the direction of gardening and, later, of writing. Aided and abetted by a devoted niece (a genuine one), she produced the hotch-potch entitled *Pot-pourri From a Surrey Garden*. Never has an unknown author had so great and instantaneous a success at the ripe age of sixty. An army of friends and relations in London acted as 'promoters', causing a bookseller at Hatchard's shop to exclaim that he didn't call it a literary success but a *social* success—a story which Theresa loved to tell against herself. The book appeared at Whitsuntide in 1897. Captain Earle read it, and seemed gratified by his wife's talent. Later that week he went out bicycling with one of his sons, and, losing control of the machine on a steep hill, was thrown on his head and died without regaining consciousness. His widow lived on at 'Woodlands' for another thirty years, and died peacefully in 1925 at the age of eighty-nine.

She busied herself with gardening and writing, for readers demanded a sequel to the first pot-pourri, and that was followed by a third. Next came her volume of *Letters to Young and Old*, followed by *Memoirs and Memories*. This last is full of interesting material; but the haphazard pot-pourri manner of arranging her ideas never left her, and, in the absence of an index, makes these difficult to digest. Having suffered in childhood from rather vague illnesses, she was subjected to a series of treatments by orthodox physicians, most of which made her feel worse. Finally she was put into the hands of a homoeopath. 'All strong medicines were stopped, and I believe the benefit of homoeopathy, like the water cure, was from allowing nature to have full play, and to do the best for herself—rest, fresh air, and a healthy life, and above all no tonic or alcohol or stimulant of any kind.' For the rest of her long life she abjured tea and alcohol, and eventually became a vegetarian and an advocate of unadulterated foodstuffs. Her favourite niece, Lady Betty Balfour, had a daughter, Lady Eve Balfour, whose pioneering work in the organic method of soil cultivation would have delighted Great-aunt 'T'. Her book, *The Living Soil*, has already become a classic.

It is interesting to find Mrs Earle enjoying the pleasures provided for gardeners by the Royal Horticultural Society seventy-five years ago just as much as Elizabeth Coxhead does now.* Under 'February' in the original *Pot-pourri* we find:

> 'One of my great pleasures in London in the early spring is going to the exhibition of the Royal Horticultural Society, at the Drill Hall, Westminster. I think all amateurs who are keen gardeners ought to belong to this society—partly as an encouragement to it, and also because the subscriber of even one guinea a year gets a great many advantages. He can go to these fortnightly exhibitions, as well as to the great show at the Temple Gardens in May, free, before the public is admitted. He has the run of the society's library in Victoria Street; he receives free the yearly publications, which are a series of most interesting lectures; and he is annually presented with a certain number of plants. These fortnightly meetings at the Drill Hall are instructive and varied; an amateur cannot go to them without learning something, and I am surprised to find how few people take advantage of them.'

In May of the same year she writes:

> 'This is the first day of one of the great gardening interests and treats of the year—the Royal Horticultural Show in the Temple Gardens. I go every year now, and should be sorry to miss it. How odd it seems, that for years and years I never went to a flower show, or knew anything about them, and now they have become one of the interests of my life! The great attraction this year is the revival of what are called old-fashioned late single tulips—Breeders, Flames, etc. Those who like to buy the bulbs, ordering them carefully by the catalogue, may have their gardens gay with tulips for over two months, certainly the whole of April and May. The quantity of apples, for so late in the season, was what struck me as almost the most remarkable thing at the show. One of the great growers told me that he had tried every conceivable plan for keeping apples, but that nothing answered so well as laying them simply on open, well-aired shelves in a fruit-house that was kept free from frost.'

* See *Elizabeth Coxhead's Garden*, (p. 309).

She had her favourite plants, and described their habits and needs well; as in the paragraphs about early Dutch Honeysuckle and Lemon Verbena.

> 'One of the most precious of May flowers, and one not nearly enough grown, is the early Dutch Honeysuckle. It is nearly white, though it dies off yellow. It deserves, if only for picking, a place in every garden. Being an early bloomer, it requires a warm spot, and would do admirably against the low wall of any greenhouse. Those precious frontages to greenhouses, in what I call "gardeners' gardens", are so often left unused, neat, empty and bare. On these wasted places many lovely things would grow, and none better than this beautiful Dutch Honeysuckle, with its double circles of blooms, its excellent travelling qualities, and its powerful sweet scent, unsurpassed by anything. It is, I suppose, like many things, better for good feeding. It wants nothing but cutting back hard as soon as it has made its summer growth after flowering, to keep it well in its place. It flowers profusely year after year, and it is easily increased by summer layering.
>
> '*Aloysia citriodora** (Sweet Verbena) is a plant that is a universal favourite. I have never known anyone, not even those who dislike strongly scented flowers, not be delighted with the delicious refreshing smell of its leaves, which they retain long after they are dried. Yet you go to house after house, and find no plants growing out of doors. Their cultivation is simple, and they require but little care to make them quite hardy; out of five or six plants which I have out of doors, only one died in the hard winter two years ago. If you have any small plants in your greenhouse, put them out at the end of May, after hardening off, in a warm sunny place, either close to a wall or under the shelter of a house wall. Water them, if the weather is dry; and do not pick them much the first year, as their roots correspond to top growth. Cut off the flowers as they appear. When injured by frost, never cut the branches down till quite late the following year. It is this cutting-back that causes the death of so many plants; the larger stems are hollow, and the water in them either rots or freezes the roots. In November cover the roots of the Verbena with a heap of dry ashes; this is all the care they require, and they will break up stronger and finer each year.'

I have tried this in the south of England, and proved it to be true. It is important to wait until the weather is really warm before expecting to see the dry-looking plant show signs of life. Suddenly it will be covered in green knobs, and summer is on the way.

* Now *Lippia citriodora.*

Theresa Earle was always interested in fragrant herbs, for cookery and for scenting her house; she influenced her large public in the cultivation of herbs many years before Eleanour Sinclair Rohde took up this branch of horticulture and spread her immense erudition and practical knowledge of herb growing far and wide.

Here is Mrs Earle's recipe for 'Sweet-bags for Armchairs':

> 'On the backs of my armchairs are thin Liberty silk oblong bags, like miniature saddle-bags, filled with dried Lavender, Sweet Verbena, and Sweet Geranium leaves. The visitor who leans back in his chair wonders from where the sweet scent comes.'

She recommends an aromatic seasoning, for use with vegetables or meat.

> 'Take of nutmegs, mace and bay leaves, one ounce each; of cloves and winter savory, two ounces each; of basil and thyme, three ounces each; of cayenne pepper and grated lemon peel half an ounce each; two cloves of garlic. All to be well pulverized in a mortar, sifted through a fine sieve, and stored in a corked jar.'

E. S. Rohde

Eleanour Sinclair Rohde (1881–1950) was born in India, the only daughter of John Rohde of the Travancore Civil Service. Her brother was a war casualty. At fifteen she was sent to the Ladies' College at Cheltenham, where she did well in English and French; later she read history at St Hilda's Hall, Oxford. Degrees were not bestowed on women at that time, and there is no record of her having returned to take such an award. In the year 1906 her parents went to live at Reigate in Surrey, and Eleanour spent most of her life there at Cranham Lodge. The Rohde family, of Danish origin, came to England early in the eighteenth century.

Personal details of this very reserved lady are scarce, but thanks to Mr Arthur Rohde I am able to use a little-known photograph of her in youth. Eleanour Rohde never married. She made a name for herself by writing erudite books about gardens and their histories, and in particular herb gardens. She also contributed regularly to many papers and magazines, including *Country Life*, *The Sphere*, *The Field*, *The Countryman* and *The Times*. She held office as President of the Society of Women Journalists. In *Who's Who* for 1943 she gave as her recreations 'a herb farm and cottage gardening'. It seems possible that this concentrated and abiding interest in herbs developed in childhood, although Mr Rohde could not trace the 'Great-aunt Lancilla' mentioned in *Herbs and Herb Gardening*, published by the Medici Society in 1936. The following extract is taken from that book:

> 'My own first recollections of sweet-leaved geraniums go back to the days when as a child I used to stay with my Great-aunt Lancilla. And whenever I smell those leaves I am instantly transported to her house, and in particular to the broad, sunny passage which led to the kitchen. The sun came pouring through the sloping glass roof, and there was a whole bank of the sweet-leaved geraniums, reaching well above my head. Pinching the leaves was always a joy, for the scents were so rich and so varied. And those scents now never fail to remind me of a gracious old lady who looked well to the ways of her placid, well-ordered household and was loved by

everyone who served her, and every man, woman and child in the village.

'When I think of scented gardens I remember hers first and foremost, for although since those days I have seen many gardens, I do not think I have ever seen a pleasanter, homelier one. The house was Georgian, and the short drive to it was flanked on both sides by pollarded lime trees. I have only to shut my eyes to hear the hum of the bees now. The drive was never used by the household nor indeed by anyone who came on foot, for the shortest way from the village was through a gate leading from the road to a side door. The path was perfectly straight, and bordered on either side by very broad beds, and except in winter they were full of scent and colour. I can see the big bushes of pale pink China roses and smell their delicate perfume; I can see the tall old-fashioned delphiniums and the big red peonies and clumps of borage, the sweet-williams, the Madonna and tiger lilies and the well-clipped bushes of lads-love. Before the time of roses I remember chiefly the Canterbury bells and pyrethrums, and earlier still the edge nearest the path was thick with wallflowers and daffodils. I have never seen hollyhocks grow as they grew at the back of these borders, and they were all single ones, ranging from pale yellow to the deepest claret.

'Beyond this path, on one side was the big lawn with four large and very old mulberry trees. As a child it frequently struck me that considering how small mulberries were compared to apples, plums and so forth, it was really little short of a miracle what a glorious mess one could get into with them in next to no time. Amongst the flowers Great-aunt Lancilla loved most were evening primroses. I have never since then seen a large border, as she had, given entirely to them. She used to pick the flowers to float in finger-bowls at dinner.

'I can see the kitchen garden, too, with its long paths and espalier fruit trees and the sweet-peas grown in clumps, and they *were* sweet peas then, deliciously scented. And big clumps of gypsophila and mignonette, which everyone in those days grew to mix with the sweet peas. There were great rows of clove carnations for picking, and never have I smelt any like them. Nor have I since tasted the like of the greengages which grew against the old wall. Is there anything quite so good as the smell and taste of a ripe greengage, picked hot in the sun? I can see the orderly rows of broad beans, lettuces, peas and scarlet runners and stout cabbages. The onions and "sparrer grass" were the special pride of the old gardener's heart. I can see the well and hear the pleasant clinking sound of the bucket as it was let down.

'I can see old Gregory attending to the bee-hives with the calm, gentle movements which characterize all experienced bee-keepers. He invariably talked to the bees when he was attending them, and one day when, as a small child, I was watching him I asked "Do the bees understand what you are saying to them, Gregory?" "Understand, Missie?" he replied. "Just as much as horses and dogs and cattle; it stands to sense an' reason they do! An' sometimes I thinks they understan' more nor we do."

'And the raspberries and gooseberries! My Great-aunt had a favourite Aberdeen terrier, who, incredible though it may seem, loved ripe gooseberries. He used to sit up, as though he were begging, and eat them off the bush and wail aloud every few minutes whenever his nose was pricked.

'I love to think of the huge beds of lily-of-the-valley, where one could gather and gather to one's heart's content for friends in the village. But my chief recollection of that kitchen garden is of roses. Cabbage roses and *La France* and *Gloire de Dijon* and "Maiden's Blush", and if one gathered armfuls it seemed to make no difference. Those were the days when people filled their rooms with innumerable small vases of flowers, but my Great-aunt, who always went her own way entirely, loved to have big bowls of flowers everywhere, even in the passages of her house.

'And how well I remember the sweet, subdued scent of pot-pourri; for as well as flowers there were in every room big open bowls of the pot-pourri she loved to have about her. In many of the bowls there were oranges stuck with cloves. Everyone loves picking these up and sniffing them, yet few people make them now-a-days.'

The writer of those words certainly did her best to encourage a revival of the old pleasures, by publishing many recipes for sweet-bags, pot-pourri and the like.

Her first book, *A Garden of Herbs*, was issued by the Medici Society in 1920, followed by *The Old English Herbals* in 1922. So far as I am able to ascertain, she had not yet started her nursery garden for the propagation and sale of 'Aromatic Plants, Bee Plants, Herbs and Uncommon Vegetables', which she catalogued in later years at Cranham Lodge. Kathleen Hunter, who took over the stock and removed it to Cornwall after Miss Rohde's death in 1950, could not supply the precise date at which the nursery was begun. It seems likely that this was at first a private garden, to be developed commercially during the nineteen-twenties. During the two decades immediately preceding the Second World War, Eleanour Rohde published an amazing collection of books about herbs and gardening. Research for her longest work, *The Story of the Garden*, must have absorbed much of her time for years. *The Scented Garden* (1931) has a comprehensive collection of recipes for pomanders, pot-pourri, perfumed snuffs, candles, toilet waters and oils; material from this book appeared again in a third herb book, of greater horticultural interest, *Herbs and Herb Gardening* (1936), in which she used the practical experience gained in her own nursery.

The Story of the Garden attempts to recapture the atmosphere of an old convent garden.

> 'Gardens on the sites of old monastic lands have a charm peculiarly their own, and those on the sites of old nunnery gardens preserve I think even more of their character. At Carrow Abbey, for instance, the atmosphere still seems dominated by the generations of quiet nuns who from Stephen's reign to the Dissolution must have loved this secluded place. Above all, one is conscious there of the personality of that radiant laughter-loving saint, The Lady Julian of Norwich, who must often have frequented this garden. It was only a few hundred yards away (at the anchorage in the churchyard of St. Julian's church at Conisford) that the "Sixteen Revelations" were made known to her, the inspiration of her *XVI Revelations of Divine Love*, which is by many held to be the most beautiful of all English mystical writings. The peace of centuries haunts gardens such as these, and it will be a sad day indeed if they should ever be destroyed.'

It is impossible in a small space to do justice to the large amount of information which is packed into *The Story of the Garden*. It ends with gardens of the Victorian and Edwardian eras; has a chapter on the gardens of America; takes readers through the splendours of ancient Egypt and Babylon, of Chinese and early Mexican gardens, to Druidic 'mounts' in Britain: London with its Llandin, or sacred eminence, the Tor at Glastonbury, St Katherine's Hill at Winchester and the Round Table Mound at Windsor; and so to the formal Tudor and Stuart pleasances, with their ornamental mounds or mounts derived from the holy hills of earlier centuries. A Druid prayer which this author quotes might easily be of early Christian origin:

> *Let God be praised in the beginning and the end.*
> *Who supplicates him he will neither despise nor refuse.*
> *God above us, God before us, God possessing all things;*
> *May the Father of Heaven grant us a portion of mercy.*

Miss Rohde examines the medievel mystical poem, *Romance of the Rose*; flowered tapestries, such as the fifteenth-century French *Lady of the Unicorn* in the Cluny Museum in Paris; *Books of Hours* with their pictures of 'Mary Gardens'; and depicts the patron saints of gardening.

'Two were venerated throughout the Middle Ages—Saint Phocas and Saint Fiacre, and it is pleasant to think we can claim the latter, for in spite of his name he was either a Scottish or an Irish prince. Saint Phocas is, however, the earliest patron saint of gardening. He lived in the third century outside the city of Sinope in Pontus. His life was divided between prayer and work in his little plot, where he grew vegetables for the poor, and flowers. In a time of persecution two strangers came and craved his hospitality, and the saint bade them welcome and gave them of his best, as he did all poor travellers. That night they told him they were searching for Phocas, a Christian, and had orders to slay him. The saint did not reply, but after his devotions he went into his little garden and dug a grave. Next morning, when the strangers were about to depart, he told them he was Phocas. They were overcome with horror, but the saint led them into the garden and bade them fulfil their orders. They cut off his head and he was buried among the flowers he had tended. Saint Phocas is represented outside the cathedral of Palermo, and among mosaics in St. Mark's, Venice.

'Saint Fiacre, who lived in the seventh century, left his home to preach to the heathen Gauls near Meaux. He was welcomed by Saint Faro and lived as an anchorite in the forest there, where he made a garden and lived unharmed by wolves and wild boars. According to one tradition his garden was miraculously enclosed with the help of the Evil One, and a woman told the Bishop. The Bishop wisely went himself to see the saint, and finding the woman's tale untrue he put a curse of blindness on any woman who went near Saint Fiacre's cell, or so they believed. Even in the seventeenth century no woman would enter his chapel in the cathedral of Meaux; it is on record that in 1648 Anne of Austria refused to enter it. There is a miniature of Saint Fiacre in a *Book of Hours* in the *Bibliotheque Nationale*, showing the saint with a spade in his hand in the garden, and in the background the Cathedral of Meaux. The page has a border of flowers and leaves and butterflies. Beneath it is written part of the office for his day, which in translation runs thus:

> "This Saint according to the law of his God struggled even unto death and was not terrified by the words of the wicked, for he was founded upon the firm rock of Christ.
>
> The just man will grow like a lily.
> *Response:* And he will flourish in the sight of God."

> Most of us today are more familiar with Saint Fiacre as the patron saint of cab drivers in Paris, who used to hold meetings near a chapel dedicated to him. From this custom sprang the name by which the French cab came to be known, *fiacre*.'

In her later article, 'The Patron Saints of Gardening', written for *The Garden* in January 1948, Miss Rohde added Saint Maurilius to her list. This saint spent a large part of his life in Britain, so we may reasonably claim his patronage for British gardeners. He is depicted in an Angers tapestry of about 1460, with a halo and a violet coloured robe, digging with a long-handled spade. The surrounding garden contains fruit trees, gooseberry bushes and flower beds. In another section of the same tapestry he is shown offering a dish of fruits to a British princess, who is seated with her husband at a table spread for a banquet. 'He is still venerated in Angers', writes Miss Rohde, 'although here we seem to have forgotten him.' Although she does not mention Saint Sylvanus, some authorities classify him as a patron of gardeners.

Her published books number nearly a score, without counting those in which she collaborated with other writers. *Oxford College Gardens* (1932) describes the gardens as she saw them, with the addition of much historical matter. This was followed in 1934 by *Gardens of Delight* and *Shakespeare's Wild Flowers*, both full of small fragments of history. On the horticultural side she contributed several articles to *The Encyclopedia of Gardening*, and during the Second World War issued some very practical books: *Vegetable Cultivation and Cookery, The War-Time Vegetable Garden, Culinary and Salad Herbs*. She collaborated with Eric Parker, one-time Editor of *The Field*, in *The Gardener's Week-end Book*. Her last work, reprinted after her death, was called *Uncommon Vegetables and Fruits, How to Grow and How to Cook*.

Herb farms were considered to be of value to the community during the Second World War, and therefore had the right to employ labour. By a curious chance I met a friend of far-off schooldays who had for a while gardened for Eleanour Rohde at Cranham Lodge, and soon afterwards I found an article by the employer describing some of her war-time staff: 'I don't engage my war-time staff. They engage me. During the last two years we have asked each other at intervals "Who next will join the circus?" ' Her first amateur gardener was a brilliant woman who liked roughing it and slept in a shed. The next, a racing motorist of Czech nationality, could cope with any task from bringing a child into the world to laying out a corpse. He also played the violin. Another Czech, a young lad, ate wild rose hips and scolded his employer for wasting this most valuable foodstuff. A 'society beauty' in a luxury caravan used to entertain the other workers, sometimes in Miss Rohde's time; an airman's wife brought a dog as large as herself; and, finally, there was my old friend, described as 'an ex-schoolteacher who never uttered an unnecessary word, but whose silences expressed whole books'.

The silent one was more expansive with me. She had arrived on the scene in March 1941 to find Miss Rohde ill in bed. At this time of her life she was the breadwinner for the family. Her old mother was still alive, and a fairly large house with the herb gardens and staff had to be kept going. An elderly cousin, a graduate, helped with chores, while the maid, Ethel, said she preferred working in the garden and regarded her normal duties as waste of time. She was apt to take violent dislikes to people, but apparently considered my friend to be a congenial member of the household, and they packed plants for postal delivery together.

> 'The place was at its lowest ebb. There was no working gardener, so for a time I weeded jungles, dug up plants, and made myself generally useful. I saw rather more of Miss Rohde than most of my fellow gardeners, because I came and went to her house in the mornings, collecting orders and then cycling to one or other of the gardens to dig up plants. An extra acre of ground (rented, I assume) called *The Farm* was situated about half a mile from Cranham Lodge. It had heavy clay soil, but the compensation for working it lay in a lovely view of Reigate Hill. Another piece of land, the big garden of an empty house, lay in the opposite direction and had sandy soil. Here there were some beautiful trees, which provided welcome shade, and we had glorious weather in those war years. It was a pity that Miss Rohde did not trust any of us to do more than the most monotonous work of weeding or hoeing. A local greengrocer, who bought her produce, used to come along and sow the seeds and be really responsible. This was partly why several of us left after a time. I think she was forced to be "on the make", and this made her appear a little stingy to us. I was not personally drawn to her, which made me uncomfortable in her presence, and I suppose she sensed that.'

Kathleen Hunter, who took over the herb garden and business when the author relinquished it, moving the stock first to Cornwall and later to Argyll, sent me a different aspect of the author.

> 'She had a charming presence, gentle and kind and rather "mystic". In others it could have been termed "vague", but somehow not in her. She was a very strict vegetarian. She was ill when I knew her, and forced by ill-health to give up. I never worked with her at Cranham Lodge.'

Miss Hunter's partner, the late Mr T. T. Melross, had at some period worked with Miss Rohde and found her 'prickly at times'; her responsibilities, added to about ten years of failing health, would surely account for that, and must be regarded charitably.

A next-door neighbour, Mrs Mary Goodchild, sent me a last memory of Eleanour Rohde.

> 'I went in every morning to do her typing, letters and articles, proof-reading—and, in those last weeks before her death, rendered her some personal services. She was a tall, regal figure, very lovely to look at, with great old-world charm. A remote person and dignified, but in spite of her remoteness she had friends all over the world. These she had made during a six-month tour before the war, when she lectured in many countries, including the United States. An invitation to lecture in South Africa after the war had to be declined for health reasons. We met her only one year before the end, but we all loved her very much.
>
> 'She had been keen on gardening from an early age, and her father bought additional land behind the Lodge for her to cultivate. In later years she developed a successful nursery there, supplying plants to customers by post. She designed a scented garden at Lullingstone Castle in Kent, which may be seen when the Castle is open to the public. She gave many broadcasts for the BBC, and her last one, a contribution to the Schools Programme, was actually recorded in her sick-room. She died in a nursing-home in Reigate on 23 June 1950, just before her sixty-ninth birthday. *The Times* printed half a column of obituary on 24 June.'

E. A. Bowles

THE name of E. A. Bowles, 'greatest amateur gardener of this century, and the most distinguished botanist and horticulturist serving the Royal Horticultural Society'* is still fresh in the minds of many garden-lovers, although he died nearly twenty years ago, in his eighty-ninth year. Not long before his death, this wise and gallant old man attended the Annual General Meeting of the Society and presented the Victoria Medal of Honour to its new President, the Hon. David Bowes-Lyon, in words that moved everyone—some to tears, as Dr Fletcher observed. Mr Bowles said:

> 'I feel very unworthy to present this, our highest honour, to one so eminent and so kind as he has always been. Perhaps I might be likened to the skull or the mummy at the feast which the ancients placed beside their good food to remind them that they were getting on in years. I need no such reminder. You have only to look at me. I am almost ashamed to come and hobble about among you as I do, and if it were not for the kindness of all that I meet here at the RHS, who are always ready to give me a hand and keep my feet from stumbling, I do not know that I should be able to carry on. But if I give up the RHS and the pleasure I get from it, what will become of me? I do not think that life would be worth living.
>
> 'Now that I know that we have such an able President to look after our affairs it does not much matter if I get even a little older and am no longer able to come here. Mr President, I have great pleasure in presenting to you the Victoria Medal of Honour. In making this presentation I doubt whether my technique is correct. For instance, ought I to place it in the President's left hand and ask *him* to transfer it to his right hand for presentation to himself? Anyway, I thank you all for conferring upon me the great honour of presenting this Medal to one of the kindest and best friends that I have.'

Bowles himself had received the VMH in 1916; the Veitch Memorial Medal in gold in 1923; the Peter Barr Memorial Cup for his work on Narcissus in 1934,

* H. R. Fletcher, *The Story of the RHS* (1969).

and many other awards. He had been a member of the RHS Council since 1908, a vice-president since 1926, and chairman of several committees. As he had forgotten more than most members of his committees were ever to know, he would at times be impatient, and if provoked he could be devastating. Of a particular daffodil proposed for an award he took a dim view and strenuously denied its merit. On a vote, the daffodil won, and as the meeting dispersed someone said, 'Well, Mr Bowles, I think that was a popular decision, don't you?' 'Yes,' Bowles answered, *'and so was the release of Barabbas!'*

The President wrote of him after his death:

> 'His knowledge of garden plants was wide and deep, and both scientific and practical. Throughout his long life he had lived at Myddelton House and had grown there most plants of any merit which will survive out of doors in the Home Counties. About each plant he knew not only practically everything which is to be found in literature, but also those things which are learned only by those who garden with their own hands. He could, and did, talk about plants in a most entertaining manner, and it was virtually impossible for anyone, however knowledgeable, to spend many minutes with Bowles in his garden without being impressed by the vastness of his knowledge, and without acquiring some interesting and worth-while information. As might be expected, his garden was full of choice and uncommon plants, and nothing gave Bowles greater pleasure than to share them with others who would appreciate their worth. He was accustomed to greet an unexpected visitor with, "I hope you've brought a basket", for he did not like any fellow gardener to go away empty-handed. Then, with his visitor, he would set out on a tour of the garden armed with an old digging fork which had been cut down to two tines to adapt it for lifting pieces of plants without causing undue disturbance.'*

The Society's Treasurer also wrote a memoir of Mr Bowles, which appeared in the *RHS Journal*, LXXIX, 1954.

> 'His interest in plants embraced not only plants from the humblest weed to the most sophisticated orchid—with something of a bias in favour of the weed—but everything connected with botany as a living science. He would always put great emphasis on the word "living"; with herbarium specimens he was inclined to be impatient—"mummies" he called them.
>
> 'Those who have read his delightful books, *My Garden in Spring*, *Summer*, and *Autumn*, will remember that he came of French Huguenot

* *Gardener's Chronicle*, 1954.

stock, and that his family were connected with the "New River" of which a loop, subsequently by-passed by the Metropolitan Water Board, flowed through the gardens of Myddelton House. He was brought up and educated with a view to taking orders in the Church of England, and, although the onset of severe attacks of asthma frustrated this intention, he remained a duly licensed lay reader, and to the end of his long life took part of the duty at the parish church. It was these severe attacks of asthma that first drove him to the high Alps and started him on the annual exiles in late spring from which he never returned without a heavy cargo of plants which he had himself collected in the wild, and which were duly ensconced in the garden at Myddelton House, whence they have been carried far and wide by all those friends, and even strangers, who visited his garden. In middle age the attacks of asthma diminished in severity and finally ceased altogether.

'Bowles used to say that it was Canon Ellacombe who had first aroused his enthusiasm for gardening. The garden at Bitton, he maintained, was the most interesting garden he had ever seen, and many of the more uncommon plants at Myddelton House came originally from that garden. For all his learning and astounding knowledge, Bowles was first and foremost a gardener and not a scientist. He had all the artist's delight in form and colour. Those who saw his garden when *Crocus speciosus* and *Cyclamen neapolitanum* were in flower knew that he could use colour lavishly, but it is debatable whether he himself did not lay even more stress on form. He would spend infinite care in pruning ivies and conifers planted by the front door to the exact form that satisfied his sense of beauty. His instinct was to be restrained in the use of colour, but he loved leaf form and all sorts of variegations and used them to great effect. His bed of acanthus and another one composed entirely of grasses and sedges, some gold, some silver, some glaucous and some green, were good examples of his genius in this direction. For Bowles was an artist. His flower paintings were of no mean order. He used to refer to what he called "the early Bowles's" which hung rather like a stamp collection all over the wall of the staircase at Myddelton House. The series of pictures which he made of Crocus and Galanthus are among the best flower illustrations of the present day.

'His own personal habits were of the most spartan sort. A lifelong bachelor, he lived in Myddelton House just as his parents had left it to him. Although so near to London it boasted neither central heating, electric light nor telephone, and when, as some concession to modern luxury, he installed gas in the kitchen, he berated workmen who laid the pipe for their lack of care in digging up his lawn. There are vivid recollections of staying with him one February during the war, when his house was without window panes, and the evening was spent in looking up in his very good private library some recondite points in the nomenclature of cyclamen (in greatcoats by the light of one minute oil lamp over a minute wood fire), to the accompaniment of occasional explosions of V-bombs which shook the house. He would work in the garden in all temperatures and all weathers, making only minor concessions to the elements in matters of dress, and nearly always in a stiff collar. When he came to London he invariably donned the same blue suit and bowler hat which made him such a familiar figure at Chelsea and at the fortnightly shows of the RHS.

'Bowles was a man of profound learning. Throughout a long life he had studied to acquire knowledge on those subjects that interested him. He was a recognized authority on certain genera of plants, notably Crocus, Colchicum, Galanthus, Narcissus and Anemone, and his general knowledge of plants was encyclopaedic. He was very rarely wrong in his facts. He had too a very good knowledge of botanical and horticultural literature from classical times down to the present day. In early life he had collected together a wonderful library full of rare books and early herbals, with all of which he was thoroughly acquainted. In his writings and his speech he was most particular in his choice of words, and had in a marked degree the scholar's desire to find the precise word that expressed his meaning.

'But it was in his garden or those of his friends that the human quality of his learning came out—learning absorbed not only from books but from his observations made in continually working with his hands among plants. Plants were almost personalities to him. He seemed always to know all about them, and to be able to recognize them not only by taste (on which he frequently relied), but by some sort of sixth sense. Long after his eyesight had begun to fail he had an uncanny power of recognizing plants at a distance, when those with perfect sight were at fault. In his own garden he knew to a nicety where his plants were, whether they were flowering or dormant. Pointing with his two-pronged fork, he would indicate exactly where a bulb was to be found, and even whether it was in the first, second or third layer—for his bulbs frequently grew one on top of the other, two or three deep. It was a rich education to go round with him and absorb, now a piece of botanical information, and now an historical anecdote, then a culinary recipe—for he was something of an epicure—or even a fascinating trick like making the pig-squeak on leaves of Bergenia, which was a joy to old and young alike.

'The only visitor who was not welcome was the person, male or female, who cared not at all for plants, but chattered about something else all the way round the garden. He would suffer fools, or what passed with him for fools, with only a very moderate amount of gladness. In human beings the qualities he most valued were accuracy, sincerity and humility, and people who failed to come up to his rather exacting standards in this respect sometimes found that he had an acid side to his tongue. Those who experienced it, however, were conscious that it was seldom unjustly applied. At his passing a large church was filled to capacity with all sorts and conditions who had come to his funeral. There can be few near-nonagenarians—or "octogeraniums" as he himself would always call them—to whom such a tribute is paid.'

Mrs Frances Perry, herself a native of Enfield, and brought up close to Myddelton House, says that she absorbed a lot of plant-lore from Mr Bowles in her young days. She tells one of his stories in her lively lectures on plants, a story worth repeating. Mr Bowles is describing a fine plant of Hemlock which, although a poisonous drug, he cultivated for its quality as a plant.

'It is unfortunately biennial or at any rate monocarpic, but makes the most of its short life by keeping brilliantly green through the winter. The leaves are as exquisitely cut as any I know of, and wonderfully glossy. All through last winter these large leaves and the already developing central shoot were as beautiful as anything in the garden, and then from early spring till the seeds were ripe in July this fine specimen was always a thing of beauty.

'Gerard denounced it root and branch, saying: "The greate Hemlock doubtlesse is not possessed with any one good facultie, as appeareth by his lothsome smell, and other apparent signes and therefore not to be used in physicke." But both leaves and seeds are still used to yield the alkaloid coniine, which has a peculiar sedative action on the motor nerves, and is therefore occasionally prescribed' [The story quoted by Mrs Perry is of] 'an old man who used to supply a great firm of druggists with the dried plant at a much lower rate than they could obtain it from any other source. When through age he announced that he must give up the business, he was asked how he had always managed to undersell others, and he told a delightful tale of cunning practice. He used to wander about the eastern counties sowing Hemlock seeds in any waste corner near cultivated lands. Then when the plant was fully grown he used to call upon the farmer and tell him that a dreadfully poisonous plant grew upon his land, and would kill beasts if eaten by them, and that for a small sum he would clear it away.

He was generally paid for collecting his harvest, grown rent free on other folks' land, and therefore could afford to sell it so cheaply.'*

Mr Bowles's first book, *My Garden in Spring*, is perhaps my favourite, but all three are full of good things. The dedication 'To my father Henry C. B. Bowles who has so kindly and patiently allowed me to experiment with his garden for the last twenty-five years' shows that he had a home sympathetic to his horticultural talents. Here is a typical burst of enthusiasm:

> 'I wish I could show you the Crocus frame and the seed-beds on a sunny morning in early February, that you might see these gems in the flesh instead of through the printed page. Let us be childish enough to "make believe" we are doing it. I will take my garden basket and all its contents, almost as varied a collection as Alice's White Knight had, but certainly more useful, even the mouse-trap on too frequent occasions, while the cook's forks to extract new treasures, and painted wooden labels to mark them withal, are indispensable. . . . You must not mind if I suddenly yell with joy, for perhaps yesterday was an RHS day, and I was in Vincent Square from early until late, and Monday was wet and no crocuses open, and Sunday had so many services and Sunday-school classes, I have not seen my seedlings since Saturday. So, if there is an extra fine white flower with orange throat, a deeper blue self than ever before, or some especially peacocky chameleon with an inventive genius for external markings, I shall shout and flop on my knees regardless of mud and my best knickers donned for visitors, and the cook's fork will tenderly extract the prize, and you can admire it without going on the knee, while I am writing a label for it, and before it goes into a place of honour in the frame.
>
> 'Following close on the heels of the crocuses come *Scilla bifolia* and *Chionodoxa sardensis* racing *Anemone blanda* for the honour of forming the first blue carpeting of the year, for not one of these is much use as dots or stiff little rings in front of a large label, and all are quite unsuitable for the modern millionaire's made-by-contract, opulent style of gardening—a thing I hate rather than envy, so don't make mental remarks about the proverbial acidity of the immature fruit of the vine. The filling of so many square yards of prepared yards of prepared soil with so many thousands of expensive bulbs, to yield a certain shade of colour for a fortnight and then to be pulled up to make place for another massing, gives me a sort of gardening bilious attack, and a feeling of pity for the plants and contempt

* E. A. Bowles, *My Garden in Spring*, (1914).

for the gardening skill that relies upon Bank of England notes for manure. But I love a large colony of some good plant that you can see has spread naturally in a congenial home, aided by the loving care of an observant owner. It has the same charm of refinement and antiquity that one gets from an old house where the Chippendale chairs and cabinets have stood on the same polished boards and time-toned carpets ever since they were new. It is a case of good taste and knowledge from the first, and watchful care and appreciation and absence of the weathercock giddiness that is influenced by gusty Fashion with a large F if you please.

'Buy as many *Scilla bifolia* as you can afford, then, but choose them a permanent home. Among the roots of a wildish group of briar roses is a good situation, or even among dwarf heaths, so long as they are not the red *Carnea*—the flowering periods of these two coinciding and proving somewhat too competitive to please me; but almost anywhere will do among permanently planted larger plants that can stand a spring carpet of blue at their feet. Then leave them alone to seed and multiply and replenish the earth. There is a great charm about the red, polished noses they thrust through so early, and which, on a sunny day, suddenly split asunder and reveal the neatly-packed flower-buds, looking like a blue ear of wheat. This is only promise, and the reward comes when the two leaves lie close to the ground, and the blue spikes are feathery sprays.

'It sometimes happens that the collected bulbs have a few Chionodoxas mixed among them, but there is no harm in this, as the colours do not fight at all, and the Chionodoxas carry on flowering for a week or two. I have purposely mixed them in a large bed of briar roses that I am allowing to carpet itself with them. The Scilla comes first, then *C. sardensis*, followed by the interesting bi-generic hybrid forms known as Chionoscillas, which are sure to appear wherever the two genera are grown together. The most easily noticed distinction between Scilla and Chionodoxa is the difference of the filments of their stamens; in Scilla they are filiform, that is, slender and threadlike, but in Chionodoxa they are flattened out, wide at the base, and tapering upwards, so that they lie close to one another, forming a cone in the mouth of the flower, and are conspicuously white. In the hybrids they are of every intermediate width, and readily catch the eye even if they are the only mark that shows the mixed parentage . . .

'*Hyacinthus azureus* is one of the most exquisite of the small and earlies, but like eating soup with a fork, one never gets enough of it. It is cheap enough, only three shillings a hundred; yet I never saw a garden that could show so many. I vow that next season I will let six sixpences go bang and try to grow a century of spikes of its pure turquoise bells. It is very lovely grown beside *Crocus aureus*; their colours are not too violent in contrast, as at their early appearance there is plenty of brown earth for background. Are you nervous of scorpions? If so, plant a wide ring of Winter Aconite, and during its growing season at any rate you can feel safe in the centre of this magic circle, for Gerard tells us quite gravely it "is of such force, that if the scorpion passe by where it groweth and touche the same, presently he becometh dull, heavy and senseless, and if the same scorpion by chance touch the White Hellebor he is presently delivered from his drowsinesse". What fertile imaginations those old gentlemen had!'

Mr Bowles's description of biting east winds in March, and the havoc they make of plants, sounds to me more like my present home in the Eastern Border country than the London area; but it is of Enfield that he writes with a pen dipped in gall.

'A peck of dust in March, we have all been taught, is worth a king's ransom. The farmer may find it so; he generally wants it dry when others would like it wet, and then grumbles because some crop has not grown. He is always waiting for dry weather to get on the land himself or to get something off it, so he may put that hateful peck of what the schoolboy defined as *mud with the juice squeezed out*, on his credit side, but I do not suppose I am alone among gardeners in feeling it is more likely to cost a king's ransom to renew the plants it kills. Those cruel drying March winds do so much terrible damage, or at least they put a finishing stroke to many a struggling invalid, shaken but not killed by the winter's frosts. If only they could tide over another week or two, the warmer ground would help along the growth of their new roots, and enough sap would run up to equalize their loss by transpiration; but with imperfect roots and an east wind they shrivel and give up the struggle in an hour or two. It is an anxious and a trying time, not only because it roughens one's own skin, making shaving a painful bore, and the corners of one's smile less expansive, but it is then one notes day by day some pet plant's failure to put in an appearance, or the flagging and browning of a cherished specimen.

'I hate the grey, sapless look of the pastures during this spell of dry cold, and the arrest of progress in the flower beds. They look emptier than a week before, and plants seem to shrink, and the ground turns lighter in colour and shows out more conspicuously. There is no scent of growth or pine trees on the wind, and often a numbing suggestion of snow that seems to paralyse one's nose just below the bridge. Spring has come; but one cannot enjoy it or feel that any plant is safe, for any night the temperature may drop low enough to kill treasures January and February have spared. Here nothing lies between us and the North Pole to take the teeth out of the north-east wind. By the time it has bitten and shaken our tender things it has lost much venom, and before it reaches the West of England is by comparison a refreshing breeze. Or so it seems to me, when I leave my wind-scorched garden and go west of Swindon, and find everything green and smiling. . . .'

The author had a sensitive nose and a great gift for describing smells, as is shown when he embarks on the Crown Imperial, in his April chapter.

'Crown Imperials (*Fritillaria imperialis*) now shoot up another foot and take on their full beauty. The two best are those known as *maxima lutea* and *m. rubra.* I prefer the yellow one, but that may be because it does not grow so well here as the red, and one always loves most the delicate child. The old red one does well anywhere I put it, and increases only too fast, necessitating lifting and dividing the clumps oftener than I like, for the right moment to do this comes when one is full of other work, and it is unwise to touch them at all if it cannot be done soon after the leaves turn yellow, as they root very early, and soon deteriorate if kept out of the ground. I have the scentless form, *F. imperialis inodora*, but it has never done very well and is always a dwarf plant . . . A good race of scentless Crown Imperials would be worth working for. Surely some student of Mendelism might investigate the family to see whether tall, scentless, and yellow may not be a possible combination of Mendelian characters. The old forms possess such an awful stink, a mixture of mangy fox, dirty dog-kennel, the small cat's house at the Zoo, and Exeter Railway Station, where for some unknown reason the trains let out their superfluous gas to poison the travellers.

'But I cannot forego Crown Imperials even though I have sometimes to hold my nose when near them. I love showing children the tears in a Crown Imperial's eyes, and of all the monkish legends I like best that which tells of the origin of these. How that when our Saviour entered the garden of Gethsemane all the flowers bowed their heads, save the Crown Imperial, which was too proud of its green crown and upright circle of milk-white blossoms to show humility, but on the other hand expected admiration. When gently reproved by its Creator, it saw its error and bowed its head, flushing red with shame, and has ever since held this position and carried tears in its eyes. These honey drops are very curious, and though the cavities which distil them and in which they hang are to be found in some degree in other Fritillarias, they reach their highest development in *F. imperialis*, and being lined with white they have a wonderfully pearly effect when filled with honey. What animal in its native Persia looks up into the flowers and is attracted by these glistening drops? Observers have watched the honey-bees alight on the stigma and crawl up it to reach the honey, and as this flower is protogynous it can only receive pollen from an older flower, thus ensuring cross-fertilisation. These observations were made in gardens in Germany, but surely this tall drink, this pool of nectar, is not so cunningly arranged for nothing larger than honey-bees.'

Mr Bowles takes a deep interest in queer plants, such as the 'Corkscrew Hazel'; a fastigiate form of the common Elder, 'the wood of which is as stiff and upright as a grenadier'; Laburnum trees whose foliage went off the rails, one pretending to be an oak, the other having every leaflet rolled inward; an Ash, very dwarf, with 'crimped leaves, nearly black and beautifully polished'; all these and many more he put together in a corner named the 'Lunatic Asylum'. The Euphorbias apparently frighten some folk, but at Myddelton House they were not regarded as certifiable. '*Euphorbia wulfenii* makes a handsome bush and a fine dark mass when out of flower, but now with the great yellow-green heads rising up out of almost indigo blue foliage it is a very fine object. The stems turn over at the tips in autumn if they mean to flower next year, and then the heart leaves of these shoots take on red stripes, and the display gradually unfolds all through the winter until it ends in immense heads of bloom'.

The month of May for this writer brings the culmination of garden glory:

'If a fairy godmother or a talking fish offered me three wishes, I think one would be to have the clock stopped for six months on a fine morning towards the end of May. Then, perhaps, I might have time to enjoy the supreme moment of the garden. And I am not at all sure the second wish would not be used to extend the period. It must be after those plaguey Ice Saints have finished playing the fool with the weather, and when there comes a spell that is neither too hot nor too cold, but just the climate one would expect to meet with in Heaven, and in England sometimes comes to us in late May and September. The tall tulips would be at their best, *Iris florentina* and its early companions in full glory, Lilacs and Apple-blossom, Hawthorn and Laburnum, all masses of flower. Trees full of tender green, yet not too densely clad to prevent our seeing the architecture of the boughs. The Mulberry would be in a leaf and showing that frosts have ceased, for it is the wisest of all trees, and always waits till it is quite safe before it opens its buds.'

Dear Mr Bowles, you were the wisest of all gardeners, and I hope you are enjoying perpetual late May in Heaven; but unless I pull on the reins you will bolt with this entire book and make it your own. The Royal Horticultural Society is planning to have a full-length biography of you prepared for publication, a tribute long overdue.

V. Sackville-West

'VITA' SACKVILLE-WEST (1892–1962) was a very distinguished woman, who made a mark in two distinct fields of creative activity—as an author of novels, biographies and poems, and as a gardener. She went on to achieve her greatest popular success by fusing both these talents in her work as a garden writer, when at the age of fifty-five she became garden correspondent of the *Observer*. It is in this capacity, as a well-known writer in the world of London newspapers, that she figures here; for her wonderful garden at Sissinghurst is too far from the metropolis to qualify for inclusion in its own right. With the help of her husband, diplomatist Harold Nicolson, she began to lay out the wilderness of land round the half-ruined castle in 1930, and in 1931 she published her poem *Sissinghurst*, which shows her total involvement with this neglected domain set in the lush pastoral country of the Weald of Kent.

This husbandry, this castle, and this I
Moving within the deeps,
Shall be content within our timeless spell,
Assembled fragments of an age gone by,
While still the sower sows, the reaper reaps,
Beneath the snowy mountains of the sky,
And meadows dimple to the village bell.
So plods the stallion up my evening lane
And fills me with a mindless deep repose,
Wherein I find in chain
The castle, and the pasture, and the rose.

She lived an intensely imaginative life, caring little for society, whether written with a big or a small 's'. Her husband and two sons, Ben and Nigel Nicolson, and a few chosen friends were sufficient; and when the boys were at school and university and her husband busy in London or elsewhere, she would spend long days happily alone in her garden:

For here, where days and years have lost their number,
I let a plummet down in lieu of date,
And lose myself within a slumber
Submerged, elate.

Four years before the purchase of Sissinghurst she had won the Hawthornden Prize with her long poem *The Land*. In 1946 another long poem, *The Garden*, won for her the Heinemann Prize.

Small pleasures must correct great tragedies,
Therefore of gardens in the midst of war
I boldly tell . . .
Yet shall the garden with the state of war
Aptly contrast, a miniature endeavour
To hold the graces and the courtesies
Against a horrid wilderness. The civil
Ever opposed the rude, as centuries'
Slow progress laboured forward, then the check,
Then the slow uphill climb again, the slide
Back to the pit, the climb out of the pit,
Advance, relapse, advance, relapse, advance,
Regular as the measure of a dance;
So does the gardener in little way
Maintain the bastion of his opposition
And by a symbol keep civility;
So does the brave man strive
To keep enjoyment in his breast alive
When all is dark and even in the heart
Of beauty feeds the pallid worm of death.

This writer held the graces and the courtesies through every difficulty and discouragement. Her first achievement, so far as the garden was concerned, lay in seeing what could be done at Sissinghurst when it gave no hint of glory to come, except to her peculiar blend of foresight, hindsight and romantic imagination. In 1937 Harold Nicolson wrote to her from France: 'I confess that I never foresaw that Sissinghurst would combine dignity with loveliness. You foresaw these things. I really believe that you will be able to make it something that will render all vulgarity foolish.'

Brought up in the great house of Knole near Sevenoaks in the same county of Kent, the only child of the Third Baron Sackville, the Hon. Victoria Mary Sackville-West was debarred by her sex from inheriting her beloved birthplace. This grievous deprivation probably spurred her into taking up the challenge of the derelict castle which had been built in the sixteenth century by Sir John Barker, whose daughter Cecily married Sir Thomas Sackville, first Earl of Dorset; through this far-off connection it became to her in a sense a family home, so that some part at least of her deep-rooted love for Knole could be transplanted with greater success than would have been possible in an entirely new setting.

She wrote of her first impressions:

> 'The site of Sissinghurst was not a new one: it went back to the reign of Henry VIII. This was an advantage in many ways. Some high Tudor walls of pink brick remained as the anatomy of the garden-to-be, and two stretches of a much older moat provided a black mirror of quiet water in the distance. The soil had been cultivated for at least four hundred years, and it was not a bad soil to start with, being in the main what is geologically called Tunbridge Wells Sand: a somewhat misleading name, since it was not sandy but consisted of a top spit of decently friable loam with a clay bottom, if we were so unwise as to turn up the subsoil two spits deep.
>
> 'These were the advantages, and I would not denigrate them. But in self-justification I must also draw attention to the disadvantages. The major nuisance was the truly appalling mess of rubbish to be cleared away before we could undertake any planting at all. The place had been in the market for several years since the death of the last owner, a farmer, who naturally had not regarded the surroundings of the old castle as a garden, but merely as a convenient dump for his rusty iron, or as allotments for his labourers, or as runs for their chickens. The amount of old bedsteads, old plough-shares, old cabbage stalks, old broken-down earth closets, old matted wire, and mountains of sardine tins, all muddled up in a tangle of bindweed, nettles and ground elder, should have sufficed to daunt anybody.
>
> 'Yet the place, when I first saw it on a spring day in 1930, caught instantly at my heart and my imagination. I fell in love; love at first sight. I saw what might be made of it. It was Sleeping Beauty's castle: but a castle running away into sordidness and squalor; a garden crying out for rescue. It was easy to foresee, even then, what a struggle we should have to redeem it.'

The Nicolsons began the work of restoration by making the tower habitable. In those days workmen could be summoned by a click of the fingers, and there was no queueing up for attention in the builders' surgery. Even so, it took two months to make this part of the dilapidated fabric safe to picnic in, and it was not until mid-October that they spent their first night at Sissinghurst—camping in the tower on folding beds and reading by the light of candles. Vita had already spent two days there, using well water and doing without such trifles as windows and doors. By the end of the year the small building known as South Cottage was ready to live in, and they had dammed up a stream and made a lake in the grounds.

It took them over two years, with the help of one old man and part-time assistance from his son, to clear the ground of rubbish. Gradually they planned the garden and began to plant it, putting in hedges of yew and hornbeam, climbers to clothe the walls, roses, herbaceous plants, bulbs. The planning gave the pair great happiness. V.S.-W. wrote of their collaboration at this time:*

> 'The walls were not all at right-angles to one another: the courtyard was not rectangular but coffin-shaped; the tower was not opposite the main entrance; the moat-walk, with its supporting wall, ran away on so queer a bias that the statue we placed on the bank behind the moat stood opposite both to the tower and to the seat at the upper end of the moat-walk. All this was disconcerting, and there were also minor crookednesses which had somehow to be camouflaged. I do not think that you would notice them from ground-level now; though if you ascended the tower and looked down, you might still give a sympathetic thought to the worried designer, with his immense sheets of ruled paper and his measuring tapes and his indiarubbers, pushing his fingers through his rumpled hair, trying to get the puzzle worked out.
>
> 'I could never have done it myself. Fortunately I had acquired, through marriage, the ideal collaborator. Harold Nicolson should have been a garden-architect in another life. He has a natural taste for symmetry, and an ingenuity for forcing focal points or long-distance views where everything seems against him, a capacity I totally lack. After weeks of paper struggle he would come home to discover that I had stuck some tree or shrub bang in the middle of his projected path or gateway.
>
> 'We did, however, agree entirely on what was to be the main principle of the garden: a combination of long axial walks, running north and south, east and west, usually with terminal points such as a statue or an archway

* *Journal of the RHS*, November 1953.

or a pair of sentinel poplars, and the more intimate surprise of small geometrical gardens opening off them, rather as the rooms of an enormous house would open off the arterial corridors. There should be the strictest formality of design with the maximum informality in planting. This is what we aimed at, and is, I hope, what we have achieved.'

Elsewhere she expressed the idea in different words: 'Profusion, even extravagance, and exuberance, within the confines of utmost linear severity.'

In his diary for March 1932* Harold Nicolson gives a detailed account of his difficulties.

'Vita and I measure the kitchen-garden [this later became a rose-garden] to discover how much paling will be required to make it square. I fiddle about with this vista problem. Obviously what would be good in a teleological sense would be to put the end of the main nuttery walk at the end of the main vista running from the new angle of the kitchen-garden, past the cottage garden and thus perspectively to what is now a gate into a field, but which one day will be a classic statue erect among cherry trees. Only this cuts angularly across the holly hedge in our own little cottage garden and fits in obtusely with the rest of the design. That is what is such a bore about Sissinghurst. It is magnificent but constantly obtuse.'

By August 1934 the main work of construction in the garden had been completed. Soon after that my mother and I took possession of the Priest's House at Smallhythe, lent to us by Ellen Terry's daughter Edith Craig. 'Edy' was always very kind to me; I believe she thought that life in a tiny Kentish hamlet must be dull for a girl of my age. One day she took me to a lecture on *English Gardens since Roman Times*, given by V. Sackville-West in the little town of Tenterden. V.S.-W., looking a trifle shy and yet quite at ease, came to a reading-desk on the platform and said that she *must* read her lecture, because otherwise she would forget what she had intended to say. Afterwards 'Edy' took me up and introduced me. Hearing of my rides on a stout mare about the local lanes, Vita promptly invited me to call in at her castle when next in that direction. 'Edy' trumped up some excuse to send me there, knowing that I would not venture unaided. I shall never forget the sight of V.S.-W. standing in the garden, with her Elizabethan tower, rosy pink, tall, very English, like herself, and yet unworldly, behind her—both having a touch of that 'excellent beauty that hath

* *Harold Nicolson's Diaries 1930–39*, edited by Nigel Nicolson (1966).

some strangeness in the proportion' of which Bacon wrote. I cannot recall a single word she said—only the richness of the picture she made in her antique frame.

By the year 1947, when V.S.-W. began her work as Gardening Correspondent of the *Observer*, her own garden at Sissinghurst had become well established, and well known to a discriminating band of horticulturists; while the experience gained over the seventeen years since the inception of this project had turned the writer into a remarkably well informed practical gardener. Reprints of the popular 'In Your Garden' articles were issued by Michael Joseph (1951–8) in four parts, and after the author's death a selection under the title *V. Sackville-West's Garden Book* appeared in 1968.

I cannot be the only gardener in existence to have taken the paper for fourteen years solely for the purpose of reading those articles each Sunday:* but I may be unique in having been transformed from a purely practical gardener into one with a deep and ever growing interest in the history of plants under their influence. That which weary years of classroom study in history books failed to achieve, was accomplished painlessly by the weekly enjoyment of a short article on the subject of gardening. What a surprise for those who tried, without success, to develop some historical sense in my school-girl brain, were any of them alive to read this admission. Here is one of the articles which suddenly brought English history alive for me. It was issued in August 1954.

> 'I was writing about the brooms, and I said I would return to the subject. Having thus provided myself with a return ticket, I now use the second half.
>
> 'The brooms I wrote about were mostly in the rich, sumptuous colours of the reds and yellows and orange, the colours one associates with a westering sunset sky.
>
> 'The ones I want to write about now are the paler ones; the white ones; the virginal ones, the moonlit ones, the ones that look moonlit even when the sun is high. There is *Genista praecox*, a little shrub smothered in butterfly flowers in April, as pretty as a child going to her dancing class. Then there is the broom rightly called Moonlight; its name tells you what it is like, and suggests the nocturnal illumination which shows it up at its best. A full moon high in the heavens, gently diffusing its strange magical light, so different from the strong masculine light of the sun; a blending of moonlight with the white broom, a union of ghosts to be seen, not to be described.

* No disrespect to the paper, for I do not usually read the Sunday press.

'It reminds me of the old music-hall song, forgotten now:

Who were you with last night, last night,
Who was that peachy, creamy, dreamy
Vision of pure delight?

'The old song brings nostalgic memories, brought by the white broom called Moonlight vividly to mind.

'The brooms have many other romantic associations, going right back into the early centuries of our English history and our Kings. The name Plantagenet derives from *planta genista*, the Latin for broom, because a Count of Anjou, pilgrim to the Holy Land, adopted a sprig of broom as his crest and symbol. It was then thought to be a symbol of humility, but by the time Shakespeare came to handle it a royal dignity had attached itself to the humble broom:

Famous Plantagenet, most gracious Prince . . .

'The moment one touches Shakespeare, one begins to marvel at how much he exactly knew. When for instance, he wrote in *Henry VI*

I'll plant Plantagenet: root him out who dares . . .

did he know, as any gardener would know, that the brooms, *planta genista*, will not endure being dug up? Root him up who dares. Practical moral: insist on your nurseryman giving you your brooms in pots.'

Like Theresa Earle towards the end of the nineteenth century, and Elizabeth Coxhead in 1971, V. Sackville-West often refers to the Royal Horticultural Society and its Shows. She describes an unusual incident in March 1952:

'The other evening I had a strange and lovely experience. I found myself, never mind how or why, completely alone in the Royal Horticultural Society's hall in Vincent Square after the fortnightly show had been closed to the public for the night. There I was, by myself, with not so much as a stray kitten wandering about. The lights were on, turning that vast hall into a raftered church overhead, and shining down on the silent flowers beneath. It was like being in a cathedral paved with flowers, with the scent of thousands of flowers taking the place of incense. An old phrase from the fifteenth century came into my mind: "The fair flourished fields of flowers and herbs, whereof the breath as of balm blows in our nose, that ilk sensitive soul must surely delight." '

In August that year she wrote of myrtle:

'I have a myrtle growing on a wall. It is only the common myrtle, *Myrtus communis*, but I think you would have to travel far afield to find a lovelier shrub for July and August flowering. The small, pointed dark-green leaves are smothered at this time of year by a mass of white flowers with quivering centres of the palest green-yellow, so delicate in their white and gold that it appears as though a cloud of butterflies had alighted on the dark shrub.

'The myrtle is a plant full of romantic associations in mythology and poetry, the sacred emblem of Venus and of love, though why Milton called it brown I never could understand, unless he was referring to the fact that the leaves, which are by way of being evergreen, do turn brown in frosty weather or under a cold wind. Even if it gets cut down in winter there is nothing to worry about, for it springs up again, at any rate in the South of England. In the north it might be grateful for a covering of ashes or fir branches over the roots. It strikes very easily from cuttings, and a plant in a pot is a pretty thing to possess, especially if it can be stood near the house-door, where the aromatic leaves may be pinched as you go in and out. In very mild counties, such as Cornwall, it should not require the protection of a wall, but may be grown as a bush or small tree in the open, or even, which I think should be the most charming of all, in a small grove suggestive of Greece and her nymphs. The flowers are followed by little inky berries, which in their turn are quite decorative, and would probably grow if you sowed a handful of them.'

I will end with a quotation from *Even More for Your Garden*, written in October 1956:

'Topiary is a question on which opinions differ. Some people dislike seeing yew or box tortured into unnatural shapes; a tree, they contend, is a tree, not a pheasant or a rabbit or even a peacock or a teapot, and I suppose there is something to be said for their argument. Besides, topiary can so easily be overdone, when it becomes fussy and unrestful to the eye.

'Other people, on the contrary, contend that clipped yew, properly used, adds greatly to the architectural design of a garden. Surely everyone here will be in agreement. We should stipulate, however, that the masses must be bold. The essential character of yew is its noble darkness, a darkness which gives solidity and throws into relief the more frivolous gaiety of the coloured flowers. Yew is grave and masculine. Let us therefore aim at heavy and sombre archways, or at huge balls and obelisks, and let it not be said that these demand the generosity of a large garden: many a modest garden would gain in dignity from their judicious use. How many small plots, for example, are divided between the flower garden and the kitchen garden; there must be a break, which could not be better accentuated than by a dark mysterious porch, never minding if it gives access only to the cabbages. Ah, you will say, yew is too slow of growth. Not so slow as most people suppose. True, it is far too slow for a temporary tenancy, but not too slow for any holding that is yours for life, when you can afford to think in terms of fifteen to twenty years. I planted a yew hedge in my own garden, and in fifteen years' time people assumed that it must be a century old. Expensive? Well, yes . . .

'Topiary has a very ancient history behind it, giving it a sort of traditional authority. The Romans practised it in great elaboration in their villas in Italy; and it is not too fanciful to suppose that when they settled in Britain and found our native yew ready to their hand, they employed it in their English villas as they had done at home. We may thus imagine the carefully trained peacock of our cottage gardens to come in direct descent from some homesick Roman legionary, a pleasing thought. I saw recently an ingenious use made of an old yew hedge in a French garden. A section of it had been allowed to grow forward into the shape of a huge arm-chair. It looked so soft and comfortable that one was tempted to sink down into it. There was nothing fussy about this; it suggested only a large dark-green piece of furniture moved out of the house into the garden. With a little more ingenuity, one could have added a table in front of it, made out of one trunk or leg of yew with a flat clipped top.'

I cannot resist quoting a few more lines from *The Garden*:

The gardener half artist must depend
On that slight chance, that touch beyond control
Which all his paper planning will transcend;
He knows his means but cannot rule his end;
He makes the body: who supplies the soul?

Sometimes, as poet feels his pencil held,
Sculptor his chisel cutting effortless,
Painter his brush behind his grasp impelled,
Unerring guidance, theory excelled,
When rare Perfection gives a rounded Yes,

So does some magic in his humbler sphere,
Some trick of Nature, slant of curious light,
Some grouped proportion, splendid or severe
In feast of Summer or the Winter sere,
Show the designer one thing wholely right . . .

The Morning Glory climbs towards the sun
As we by nature sadly born to strive
And our unending race of search to run,
Forever started, never to be won,
—And might be disappointed to arrive.

SECTION FOUR

Market Gardeners and Nurserymen

Market Gardeners and Nurserymen of the 16th, 17th and 18th Centuries

LONDON is now a great centre for the marketing of fruit, flowers and vegetables, both home-grown and imported from continental and other countries, as is well known; but few people realize that until the industrial revolution and the advent of steam railways, England's capital itself produced fruit and vegetables in abundance. Up to the close of the Middle Ages, such unlikely-sounding places as Shoreditch, Stepney, Bermondsey, Holborn, Finsbury and Westminster were more or less open country, and largely under cultivation. Even in those days the centre of London was a built-up city, and not all its residents possessed sufficient ground to supply their own needs; so there was a constant demand for surplus crops from the gardens of ecclesiastical and noble houses. The change to commercial culture arose gradually, and over a long period London's markets were filled with fruit and vegetables from a mixture of sources. As far back as the end of the thirteenth century there was a forerunner of today's 'barrow boy' named *Gerin the Fruter*.

In the reign of Henry VIII a gardener named Cawsway had some ground under cultivation in Houndsditch, from which he served markets with root vegetables and potherbs. By this time land in the district was in great demand for building, and little open ground remained for horticulture. The huge ditch where the populace had been accustomed to throw dead dogs and other discarded possessions—a nauseous medieval midden which gave its name to the locality—was filled in, and the site developed for housing. Soon Cawsway had to go; his market garden was 'parcelled into gardens wherein are many fair houses of pleasure'. Another sixteenth-century grower, unnamed, plied his trade at the Minories near Tower Hill, using land which had belonged to the nunnery of the Order of St Clare from 1293 until it was annexed by Henry VIII in 1539. A man called Goodman, who farmed the old nunnery ground, leased a portion to the anonymous market gardener. In Goodman's Yard, E.1, we still preserve the name of the farmer.

A famous garden of the period, that belonging to John Gerard, included some orchard plantings, but was chiefly devoted to herbs. A very large variety of herb plants, some cultivated, others gathered in their wild state, were used medicinally and in the kitchen to improve the flavour of meats. Keeping facilities were poor, so that in summer meat was often over-ripe, and in winter rather unpalatable from being salted down. Gerard, originally a barber-surgeon, became a brilliant gardener and was employed by Lord Burleigh in his gardens at Theobalds in Hertfordshire and in the Strand. In 1597 Gerard possessed over a thousand herb plants in his own garden in Holborn, many of them rare species brought from overseas by friends of Burleigh's and shared with his employee. Gerard also used land at Old Street, and in 1602 leased two acres on the east side of Somerset House, 'abutting on the south upon the bank or wall of the Thames, and on the north upon the back of tenements standing in the High Street called "The Strand" '. It is a pleasant diversion to regard The Strand as London's High Street; one can even think of the shops and offices as 'tenements'; but it is beyond my imagination to picture Gerard's herb garden beside Somerset House, much less smell the aromatic fragrance that must have wafted over the street in his time.

The Earl of Lincoln had a forty-acre garden on the site of what are now Lincoln's Inn Fields, where grew apples, pears, cherries, nuts; beans, onions, garlic and leeks; also vines and many roses. The large household consumed a great deal of the fruit and vegetables, but even so a considerable surplus was sold in the markets each year. The medieval consumption of such produce seems to have fluctuated. In Harrison's *Description of England* (1577) the author speaks of 'herbes fruits and roots' as being plentiful in the time of Edward I and for a while after his death; but in the process of time they grew to be neglected, so that from 'Henrie the fourth until the latter end of Henrie the seventh and beginning of Henrie the eight, there was little use of them in England, but they remained either unknowne, or supposed as food more meet for hogs and savage beasts to feed upon, than mankind'. Seemingly this referred more particularly to the country as a whole than to London. The somewhat restricted choice of 'parsenepys, turnepez, karettes and betes', together with the everlasting English cabbage, plus onions and leeks, widened in the reign of Henry VIII to include melon, pompion (pumpkin), and gourd; garlic, globe artichoke, cauliflower and a good range of soft and stone fruit, all now considered suitable food for human consumption.

By the end of the sixteenth century the culture of fruits and vegetables had advanced, not only in market gardens and those attached to great establishments, but in humble plots as well. Demand for fresh produce grew rapidly, and imports from Europe increased. Flemish onions and Dutch salads became highly popular in England. In the reign of Elizabeth I there was an influx of Protestant refugees from the Low Countries, many of them skilled in the production of early vegetables. To begin with they set themselves up as market gardeners in the decayed port of Sandwich, and other places on the south-east coast of Britain. Then, as demand rose in the capital for their wares, they removed to London—to such districts as Wandsworth, Battersea, Bermondsey—in order to be near the best markets.

A company of 'Free Gardeners' had existed since the fourteenth century, and some of their scrapbooks are extant; but how much produce was then sold, or which crops predominated, are details not disclosed. In 1605 the organization was supplanted by the new Gardeners' Company, empowered to control the trade; its charter specifies 'the trade, crafte or mysterie of gardening; planting, grafting, setting, sowing, cutting, arboring, rocking, mounting, covering, fencing, and removing of plantes, herbes, seedes, fruites, trees, stocks, setts, and of contryving the conveyances of the same belonging'. One of the aims of the Company of Gardeners was to 'inspect the worth of others, who tended to practise without knowledge, or should offer to invade their customs'. It is clear that the growers from the Low Countries were not obstructed in London, for there is a petition from the Gardeners' Company to the Lord Mayor stating that they 'desire not . . . to restrain any forreyners to bringe into the cittie anie such commodities as they sell, for the fundamental lawes of this land give to all men whatsoever, libertie soe to doe in regard that they bring victuall wholesome and according to the lawes'.

A Surrey writer named Fuller* described in 1660 how gardening was 'first brought into England for profit about 70 years ago, before which we fetched most of our cherries from Holland, apples from France, and had hardly a mess of rath [early] ripe peas but from Holland, which were dainties for ladies, they came so far, and cost so dear. Since, gardening hath crept out of Holland to Sandwich, Kent, and thence to Surrey, where, though they have given £6 an acre and upwards, they have made their rent, lived comfortably, and set many people on work'. One of the novelties brought from Holland was asparagus, known then as 'Dutch asparagus'. It was extensively grown in the seventeenth century, but had never before been seen as a cultivated vegetable in Britain. A

* Market Gardening in Kent and Surrey.

variety of this plant was recorded as flourishing in the wild around Bristol in 1677; it has always been very localized. In the nineteen-thirties I can remember gipsies bringing baskets of wild asparagus to the Bath markets, and poorer people were able to buy the little bundles for a few pennies. I found this plant, *Ornithogalum pyrenaicum*, the Spiked Star of Bethlehem, growing near Conkwell above the Limpley Stoke Valley. It is cooked and eaten in bud; but the greenish-white flowers when open are attractive, and I was able to use them in a herb exhibition at the American Museum at Claverton near Bath in 1964.

If one cannot re-create the scent of Gerard's herb gardens in Holborn or the Strand, it is, in 1971, still possible to smell real fruits and vegetables on the site of a garden tilled (before Henry VIII and his ecclesiastical purges) by the monks of Westminster. For their convent garden became in the seventeenth century 'Covent Garden', site of what is now the largest market for horticultural produce the world has seen—a stupendous eruption of flower, fruit and vegetable in the heart of West Central London. The display will not be there much longer. In 1973 it is to be removed to Nine Elms on the south side of the Thames, to free its present site from the lorry traffic needed to supply traders with produce. This unique market place, where for over three hundred years the gentry and the *cognoscenti* were jostled by sellers of the homely potato and the lordly orchid, will have vanished for ever. That melancholy prospect is my excuse for presently devoting more pages to its history than might be expected in a book of gardeners and gardening.

Some other places used in the past for trading in the produce of commercial and private gardens were situated at Spitalfields and all along the north bank of the Thames from Queenhithe to Three Crane Stairs. The river served not only as a natural highway for the transport of perishable goods to the centre of trade; boats on return trips also ferried cargoes of horse manure, street sweepings, ashes and bones to the growers to fertilize their land. From Billingsgate, where large quantities of cherries were landed in the season, London refuse was taken away to the orchards of Kent. Manure boats also plied up the River Lea to Enfield, bringing back produce from market gardens being developed in that district as London expanded.

An account of English horticultural methods written in the late seventeenth century mentions cabbages weighing up to 28 pounds apiece, and describes how gravelly soil in the environs of London was made sufficiently fertile to produce heavy crops. The gravel was first taken out to a depth of three or four feet, the pits being filled up with 'the filth of the city'. This served as excellent manure,

34. Covent Garden market today

35. St Paul's Church, Covent Garden

36. The Royal Exotic Nursery at South Kensington, 19th century

37. The Great Conservatory at Syon Park

38. Flora's Lawn, Syon Park

39. Old Catalpa tree, Syon Park

'rich and black like treacle'. Having thus nourished their land, the owners then enclosed it with fences, deep ditches, or mud walls thatched with straw. In our own time we seem to be swinging round the circle, away from the supposedly essential twentieth-century hygiene of piping human excrement and other wastes out of built-up areas and, after treating it at filter plants, running off effluent into rivers or direct into the sea. The latest method, developed in Scandinavia, is to recoup the loss of fertilizing elements by treating the waste products to form compost, free from danger of infection, for use on the soil.

The coming of railways in the mid-nineteenth century brought immense change to market gardening. Much land in and around London was taken for the laying of multiple tracks, which had the effect of pushing growers further out to districts where, before the advent of rail transport, it had not paid them to raise perishable crops for consumption in the city. Early potatoes, cauliflowers, strawberries and spring flowers grown in Cornwall and the Isles of Scilly, which had formerly been shipped to Plymouth and other south coast ports, now reached London overnight in prime condition, as did the orchard produce of Worcestershire and the famous Evesham asparagus. Soon another novelty came to change the growers' habits: the large commercial glasshouse. The heated house was not new, for it had been used by the Romans; but it took centuries to develop. The Apothecaries' Garden in Chelsea had one of the earliest examples known in Britain, in the year 1681. This was more or less a heated room with extra large windows. During the eighteenth century greenhouses and conservatories, most of them heated by stoves and commonly called 'stoves', were used in nurseries and the gardens of great houses for the culture of exotic plants and for housing such popular subjects as orange trees and myrtles in winter time; but the huge glasshouse with minimal framing and large areas of glazing was not brought into use for market gardening until quite late in the nineteenth century. These at first made a nine-days' wonder for the residents of Tottenham, Enfield and Finchley. As the growth of London consumed more and more land for housing, market gardeners shifted to rural areas in the Lea Valley and to Hampton in Middlesex. By 1870 the glasshouse for raising crops had spread down into Kent.

Just as the gardens of great religious houses—of the Austin Friars who gardened from London Wall to Lothbury and Broad Street, and the Grey Friars who cultivated soil between Newgate and St Martin's-Le-Grand—disappeared during the Tudor régime, so the terrain of seventeenth- and eighteenth-century growers was swallowed up by nineteenth- and twentieth-century urban expansion. Few people in the crowds thronging the great Olympia exhibition halls in West London would credit an account of the vineyard which flourished on the site in the seventeenth century (and probably long before that), or have ever heard of the well-stocked nursery garden of James Lee and Lewis Kennedy which supplanted the vineyard in the eighteenth century and which their descendants maintained as a going concern until about 1890.

As the commercial growing of food crops expanded to meet an increasing demand, the production of seeds and plants for market gardeners became a separate industry. In his book *Five Hundred Points of Good Husbandry*, published in 1557, Thomas Tusser described how the good housewife would cherish and gather seeds from her own plants for the next season's sowing. Neighbours no doubt exchanged seeds with one another; but seedsmen from whom such necessities could be purchased were then virtually unknown. One of the first merchants to see possibilities in the business was a man named Child, who set up a seed shop in London's Pudding Lane. (Having assumed that this little alley had been named because its occupants baked puddings and pies, I was disconcerted to discover that butchers had scalding-houses for hogs there, and the excreta or 'pudding' voided by the beasts was collected and taken thence to manure-boats on the Thames.) Child began his trade in seeds a few years after Tusser's book appeared. Later in the sixteenth century, the Flemish refugees who practised market gardening over here also dealt in seeds and onion sets, being renowned for their remarkably fine onions. Another firm to engage in the seed business, Minier, had a shop in the Strand not far from Covent Garden early in the eighteenth century. By that time the market had become of paramount importance to buyers and sellers of garden produce, and the growers found Minier's shop handy. It lasted on the same site in the Strand for over a hundred years. The most favoured districts for seed raising were in the eastern counties, whose drier climate allowed the pods to ripen well. This was a separate trade, run to supply the seedsmen, few of whom were engaged in any form of horticulture.

The enormous interest in pleasure gardening, which was stimulated during the eighteenth century by the increase in plants and trees made available through the exertions of widely travelled collectors, opened up new possibilities of trade to nurserymen. One of them, James Lee, a Scotsman from Selkirk, had in his Hammersmith nursery ('The Vineyard', already mentioned) a range of plants brought to England from all over the world, many kept in 'stoves', or heated greenhouses. It is said that Lee introduced 135 new plants to British gardens during his lifetime. Queer plants from 'New Holland' (Australia) were exhibited to fascinated visitors at 'The Vineyard', along with a fine collection of English roses. Here the first standard rose was produced in England. Judging by its 76-page catalogue dated 1774, this nursery could be classed as a forerunner of the modern garden centre, being stocked not only with seeds and plants of all descriptions, but with tools and equipment as well. Nursery visiting was a popular and fashionable diversion throughout the existence of 'The Vineyard', from 1745 to 1890, and it is possible that in its time as many sightseers, in proportion to the total population, were drawn to its novelties as are commonly seen in the Olympia of today. It even crept into literature. In *Vanity Fair* Thackeray wrote: 'For a kiss from such a dear creature as Amelia I would purchase all Mr Lees' conservatories out of hand'. This would have been a costly deal. The collection of plants at 'The Vineyard' was regarded by botanists as second only to that at Kew, and in 1822 J. C. Loudon described it in his *Encyclopaedia* as 'unquestionably the first nursery in Britain, or rather the world'.

It is likely that the poor Scots lad, James Lee from the Borders, worked his way to fame through the patronage of the Third Duke of Argyll, who at Whitton Place near Twickenham (a house built for him by James Gibbs in 1725) employed Lee as a gardener. Accounts of the young man's early life are confused, some maintaining that he worked first in the Chelsea Physic Garden under Philip Miller, author of *The Gardener's Dictionary*, others that the duke gave him a start in London. That Lee worked at some time for Argyll seems certain. The latter, called by Horace Walpole a 'tree-monger', had a profound knowledge of silviculture; after his death in 1761 William Aiton, then in charge at Kew, acquired some of the Whitton Place plants for the Royal Botanic Gardens, and turned to James Lee for information about them. At some stage in his career Lee also worked in the ducal gardens of Syon House at Brentford; but details of that assignment are lacking. It is certain that Lee could not have dreamed that Syon itself was in future years to become the biggest nursery and sales centre for gardeners in London—perhaps in the world.

Together with Lewis Kennedy, he started up his own business as a nurseryman in 1745. According to contemporary accounts, the district was then a straggling place, noted for its gardens and public houses, depending much on 'the high Western road from London', and containing several 'very handsome seats belonging to the gentry and citizens of London'. The nursery garden, which in 1829 amounted to eighteen acres, lay between the parish boundary of Fulham with Kensington at Countess Bridge, and the turnpike gate on the north side of the road to Brentford. Much of this land, now in Hammersmith—which did not exist as a separate parish until 1834—is now beneath Olympia.

That 'The Vineyard' in earlier times really was used for viticulture seems to be well authenticated, although details of its history are few. In 1628 a cottage called 'Vynehouse' existed on the site, and a wine cooper was connected with the place in 1686. There are references in *The Compleat Treatise of Practical Husbandry* (Hales) to 'wines made from a little vineyard in Kensington which equal many of the lighter wines of France', and of a vineyard at Hammersmith from which 'a great deal of very good wine was obtained for sale, though neither of these were favourable plots'. Another writer, H. M. Todd, in his book *Vine Growing in England* (1911) states that a considerable amount of Burgundy wine was made here every year. 'Somewhere I have read that 100 hogsheads was not unusual. Be that as it may, various writers have agreed in describing the wine as good, very good, and excellent.'

Vine growing out-of-doors was introduced into England by the Romans in about A.D. 280; nobody seems quite sure why it died out. Some worsening of climatic conditions, and the importation of cheap wines from across the Channel, are thought to have made the wine trade unprofitable here. In the sixteenth century the Dissolution of the Monasteries dealt a severe blow to the art of viticulture, for the monks had almost a monopoly of knowledge and skill in this field of cultivation and in the production of wine. Only a very few London vineyards survived these troubles, among them those at Hammersmith and Kensington.

Whether the medieval monks deliberately kept their technical skill in vine growing secret or not, some eighteenth-century plantsmen are known to have jealously guarded details of species which had newly arrived in this country, so that botany acquired a cloak-and-dagger aura of mystery in their hands. Philip Miller of the Chelsea Physic Garden was one such uncommunicative savant who wished to maintain a reputation for superior knowledge. Dr Robert Thornton, renowned for his lovely book *The Temple of Flora*, related how Miller once threw into the Thames a number of empty packets, which had contained seed brought to him from abroad by a collector, and how some watchful and astute bystander swam and dived after these before they disintegrated in the water, to disclose (no doubt for a fee) the names and descriptions of novelties in the plant world to Miller's rivals. It is a good story; but as other writers have questioned Thornton's veracity, it must remain in the limbo between fact and fiction. There is assuredly some truth in the point it illustrates, for rivalry over plants and plant-lore was then at its fiercest.

In 1760 James Lee acquired scholarly fame, surpassing that of Philip Miller, by his translation of the work of the great Swedish botanist Dr Karl Linnaeus into English. Linnaeus invented the binomial method for naming plant species, now universally adopted, and known as the Linnean system. Modern gardeners who deplore the long Latin names found in horticultural dictionaries would have had greater cause for dismay if confronted with the much more involved Latin descriptions in vogue before the binomial ones existed. By comparison, the ideas of Linnaeus are beautifully simple. He divided plants into classes, orders, genus and species by the number, or some obvious characteristic, of their stamens, and subdivided them by the number of pistils in each flower; a method described as the 'sexual system'. Lee's translation of the *Philosophia Botanica* of Linnaeus was distinguished by the abundance of examples the nurseryman was able to give, drawn from his wide experience of both native and foreign plants. It was regarded as a standard work of reference in England for at least fifty years.

According to J. C. Loudon, some 5,000 new species were introduced into Britain during the eighteenth century. One of these plants, on which hangs another of James Lee's claims to be remembered, was the Fuchsia. It is only one among 135 named in *Hortus Kewensis* as having been introduced in, or first cultivated by, The Vineyard during its period as a nursery under Lee's direction; but it has an unusual story attached to it. It also bears a more attractive name than the *Slender-stemmed Pogonia* or the *Cape-Marigold-leaved Goodenia*, which seem better suited to a skit by Ruth Draper than to a sober garden catalogue. That popular plant, the Fuchsia, was named after a learned botanist, Leonard Fuchs. Although Lee did not introduce it, he was the first man to propagate it and offer it for sale.

The Lincoln Herald for 4 November 1831 printed the story thus:

> 'Old Mr Lee, a nurseryman and gardener near London, well-known fifty or sixty years ago, was one day showing his variegated treasures to a friend, who suddenly turned to him and declared, "Well, you have not in your collection a prettier flower than I saw this morning at Wapping." "No! and pray what is this phoenix like?" "Why, the plant was elegant, and the flowers hung in rows like tassels from the pendant branches, their colour the richest crimson, in the centre a fold of deep purple," and so forth. Particular directions being demanded and given, Mr Lee posted off to the place, where he saw, and at once perceived, that the plant was new in this part of the world. He saw and admired. Entering the house, "My good

woman, this is a nice plant. I should like to buy it." "Ah sir, I could not sell it for no money, for it was brought me from the West Indies by my husband, who has now left again and I must keep it for his sake." "But I must have it!" "No, Sir!" "Here" (emptying his pockets) "here is gold, silver and copper"—his stock was something more than eight guineas. "Well-a-day, but this is a power of money, sure and sure." " 'Tis yours, and the plant is mine, and my good dame shall have one of the first young ones I rear to keep for your husband's sake." "Alack, alack!" "You shall, I say." A coach was called in which was safely deposited our florist and his seemingly dear purchase. His first work was to pull off and utterly destroy every vestige of blossom and blossom-bud, it was divided into cuttings which were forced into bark beds and hot beds, were re-divided and sub-divided. Every effort was used to multiply the plant. By the commencement of the next flowering season Mr Lee was the delighted possessor of three hundred fuchsia plants, all giving promise of blossom. Two which opened first were removed to his show-house. A lady came. "Why, Mr Lee, my dear Mr Lee, where did you get this charming flower?" "Hem! 'tis a new thing, my lady—pretty! 'tis lovely." "It's price?" "A guinea; thank your ladyship," and one of the two plants stood proudly in her ladyship's boudoir. "My dear Charlotte! Where did you get" etc. "Oh, 'tis a new thing I saw at old Mr Lee's. Pretty, is it not?" "Pretty! 'tis beautiful! Its price?" "A guinea; there is another left." The visitor's horse smoked off to the suburb; a third flowering plant stood on the spot where the first had been taken. The second guinea was paid and the second chosen fuchsia adorned the drawing room of her second ladyship. The scene was repeated as newcomers saw and were attracted by the beauty of the plant. New chariots flew to the gates of old Lee's nursery grounds. Two fuchsias, young, graceful and bursting into healthy flower, were constantly seen in the same spot in his repository. He neglected not to gladden the faithful sailor's wife by the promised gift, but ere the flower season closed three hundred golden guineas clinked in his purse, the produce of a single shrub of the widow in Wapping, the reward of the taste, decision, skill and perseverance of old Mr Lee.'

A story not very well authenticated, and probably owing something to journalistic fervour; the quick change from wife to widow is not explained; nevertheless, it appears that James Lee did 'corner the market' in the Fuchsia and do very well out of it. The plant he chose to propagate is thought to be the *Fuchsia coccinea* from Chile. A Captain Firth gave a specimen of this to Kew in 1788.

James Lee died in 1795 and was buried in Hammersmith. Among the possessions left to his son James was a sword made by Andrea Ferrara which he had brought from Scotland on his first journey to seek his fortune in London, and a portrait in oils by an unknown artist. This shows the nurseryman in middle life, examining a flower through a magnifying glass.* It now hangs in the Hammersmith Public Library. James Lee the younger was forty-one when he inherited his father's interest in The Vineyard Nursery, of which he subsequently became sole proprietor. It survived in the hands of his children right up to the 1890s. Among its distinguished customers, the Empress Josephine earlier in the century had ordered large quantities of plants for her gardens at Malmaison. Two of these orders, totalling over £3,000, were mentioned in *The Gentleman's Magazine* for 14 November 1811.

The lives of James Lee in the eighteenth and of his son in the nineteenth century were not in essence very different from those of most sober businessmen in London; but Tradescant Road in Lambeth, not far from The Oval Cricket ground, commemorates an earlier father and son who not only traded in and cultivated rare plants, but travelled themselves to distant lands in search of material. The first John Tradescant was born in the capital towards the close of the sixteenth century, and married a woman of Kent at Meopham in 1607. The post of gardener to the Earl of Salisbury at Hatfield House gave him his first opportunity for foreign travel. The Earl, a keen plantsman, sent him to Holland, where in Haarlem he bought '32 rathe [early] ripe cherries at 4s. each, 1 Spanish pear 2s., 1 apple quince 3s., 1 rathe ripe cherry 3s., 2 mulberries 6s., 6 messenger trees 3s., 6 red currants 1s., 2 arbor vita trees 1s., anemones 5s., 16 Province roses 8s.' The 'messenger tree' was a *Daphne mezereum*, and the name is too charming to be forgotten.

Tradescant went also to Delft, Rotterdam, Antwerp and Brussels, buying a quantity of cherries, pears, quinces, medlars, apples, apricots, peaches and walnuts. He also acquired narcissus bulbs and fritillaries, along with garden baskets and scythes. Next he went to Paris, where he met the royal gardener, Jean Robin, from whom the false Acacia takes its name of Robinia. Robin supplied pomegranate, fig, oleander and myrtle trees, and plants of '*genista hispanyca*'. In France alone Tradescant purchased 500 trees; a similar consignment came from Belgium and Holland. The transport in those days of such a large and perishable cargo presented difficulties, but no sooner were these plants safely installed at Hatfield than the gardener was off again to France, in search of roses for the

* See plate 33.

garden of Salisbury House in the Strand. He returned with 800 sweet briars, 600 'long briars' and 20 white roses grown as standards. More than a century was to pass before James Lee raised the first English standard roses at The Vineyard.

Later journeys took Tradescant to Russia and to north Africa, where he found the 'corne flagge' or Gladiolus. The naval vessel in which he sailed was supposedly on a mission against Algerian corsairs, but Tradescant saw no fighting, and placidly pursued his search for such treasures as the 'golden Barbarie apricocke' and new varieties of peach and plum. In 1625 he changed his job, accepting the appointment of gardener to the Duke of Buckingham at Newhall in Essex. Thirty years later the diarist John Evelyn referred to the place in these terms:

> 'A faire old house built with brick, low, being only of 2 stories, as the manner then was; the Gate-house better; the Court large and pretty; the staire-case of extraordinary wideness, with a piece representing *Sir F. Drake's action* in the year 1580, an excellent sea-piece; the galleries are trifling; the hall is noble; the garden a faire plot, the whole seat well accomadated [*sic*] with water; but above all I admird the faire avenue planted with stately lime-trees in 4 rowes, for neere a mile in length. It has three descents, which is the only fault, and may be reform'd. There is another faire walk of the same at the mall and wildernesse, with a tennis-court, and pleasant terrace towards the park, which was well stor'd with deere and ponds.'

As Tradescant had been re-designing and planting the Duke's gardens since 1625, Evelyn's entry in the year 1656 doubtless referred to his work.

In 1627 Tradescant again went on a service mission, this time the Duke of Buckingham's expedition to liberate La Rochelle. Despite heavy fighting, the gardener was able to explore the terrain and collect two novelties: the poppy from which our showy Shirley strain was evolved, and the forerunner of today's ten-week stock. In 1630 he was appointed Keeper of His Majesty's Gardens, Vines and Silkworms at Oatland. This palace, one of the many hunting lodges near London used by Henry VIII, was in use as a royal palace until destroyed by Cromwell.

Meantime the Tradescant family had leased from the Dean and Chapter of Canterbury a dwelling in what was then part of Surrey, later to be absorbed by the tentacles of London. Turret House in Lambeth was a peaceful rural retreat, from whose tower Evelyn admired a very fine view, 'it being so near London and yet not discovering any house about the country'. To the north lay Lambeth Palace, to the east a deer forest, and to the south open country and the hamlet of Brixton. The gardens, over four acres in extent, became a wonderland of rare and beautiful plants, matched by an extraordinary collection of museum-pieces within the house, which soon acquired from frequenters the name of 'The Ark'. On his father's death in 1638 John Tradescant the younger succeeded to the post of royal gardener to Charles I, which he held until the king's death in 1649. The remaining thirteen years of Tradescant's life were spent at work in the Lambeth garden and museum, where he drew up an impressive illustrated catalogue of the animals, birds, fish, insects, coins and medals, strange fruits, paintings, garments, weapons and household goods. Certain items must have been difficult to classify, such as 'flea-chains of silver and gold with 300 links apiece and yet but an inch long'. Into such strange by-ways could the search for rare plants lead an enterprising gardener long ago.

By rather dubious means the contents of The Ark were obtained from Tradescant's widow by one Elias Ashmole, who subsequently left the collection to Oxford University. His name is perpetuated in the Ashmolean Museum, while the Tradescants have to rest content with a road in Lambeth and some plants of Spider-wort—the potted favourite known as 'Wandering Jew' (*Tradescantia fluminensis*) and that old garden stand-by, *T. virginiana.* American Gardening Societies did their best to redress the wrong by putting a stained glass window to Tradescant in the Ashmolean Museum, and the London Gardens Society awards a Tradescant Trophy each year to the best-kept Police garden.

Alfred Smith

EVEN in Victorian days there was scope for a great variety of characters in the world of professional horticulture. Alfred William Smith, familiarly known as 'The Cabbage King', was far from being a cabbage himself. His father, Henry Smith, had a market garden in Feltham, and there Alfred was employed on leaving school in 1864 at the age of nine. He received neither wages nor holidays until he was married. For that event he was allowed a day off. He did not drink, smoke or swear (he could hardly have afforded the first two vices), and when he started up in business on his own account the employees were strictly forbidden to indulge in tobacco, alcohol or bad language. He began with a horse, a van, and implements bought cheaply at local sales. Somebody leased him 40 acres of fruit garden at Bedfont, and so without any capital behind him he built up a thriving enterprise. Sheer hard work and concentration led to success; an achievement which, the professional growers say, would be impossible for a penniless man in modern conditions.

A century ago, the production of green vegetables, fruit and flowers was commonly divided into three categories: farming, market-gardening (roots and salads) and the glasshouse cultivation of tomatoes, cucumbers and cut flowers. Before long Smith managed to combine outdoor market gardening with glasshouse cultivation. To start with, he grew flowers beneath his orchard trees: violets, stocks and wallflowers for sale in bunches at Covent Garden. He habitually toiled on the land all day, then travelled to London to be on his stand in the market by 3 a.m. This gruelling activity prospered, and from the proceeds he was able to acquire more land. First of all he took up 40 acres on the Walton Road, then another property of similar acreage came into his hands at Feltham Hill. This became his headquarters, having good stabling and buildings suitable for use as packing sheds. At this stage he had to give up manual labour in order to supervise the workers on all three sites. Everything had to be paid for as he went along, for he had no cash reserves. There was no room for failure at any point in the chain of operations.

A nephew of Smith's wife, young Alfred Lucas, became apprenticed to the business. Some years ago he described* how he learned to use tools, to grade, bunch and pack produce, to care for trees and to look after horses. His employer constantly exhorted him to show the men how things should be done, and not to be content with passing on orders from above. Lucas was being trained to take over part control, by the same path that Alfred Smith had followed. A youngster had to work hard and obey orders if he wished to get on. The same applied to all workers. Good labour was easy enough to find, for jobs were scarce and there was no unemployment benefit. The average wages were 18 shillings weekly for a man and 12 shillings for a woman. This rate applied to a stint of 62 hours, with overtime paid extra at fourpence an hour. The slightest unpunctuality was subjected to a fine, as also was such a trivial offence as eating a plum without permission: penalty sixpence.

Land was ploughed with single-furrow two-horse ploughs at the rate of one acre a day. When Smith came across seventy acres of land at Ashford, seeing that it had been allowed to fall into a very bad state, he bid only £25 an acre for it. Having received an acceptance from the owner, he went to his bank for a loan, and on valuation was able to get £100 an acre. For the first time he had capital in hand, and from that moment he went on buying land until he had 1,000 acres under the plough. In one season he put in a million cabbage plants. He was now the largest producer of greenstuff in England, which accounted for his nickname 'The Cabbage King'.

According to Alfred Lucas, Smith had no truck with unions or labour restrictions. Each man and woman was valued and paid, latterly, according to his or her knowledge and worth. Labourers had to build up personal reputations, and only the best workers were retained. Very few ceased work because of rain or other discomforts. Sacks were tied round the waist and pulled over head and shoulders for protection, there being no macintoshes available then, and no plastic rainguards. All shabby tricks, such as the hiding of inferior produce beneath a layer of top quality goods, were absolutely banned. Buyers at Covent Garden learned to accept Smith's graded produce without examination or query, so reliable was his reputation for fair dealing.

His understanding of plants owed nothing to books, for he often asserted that he had never read one in his life. He had great insight, and a genius for predicting what would succeed in horticulture. He demonstrated that the cabbage could be successfully raised under glass, so lengthening the supply by two months, when other growers had been convinced that the plants would bolt and

* *The Countryman*, Winter 1956.

be useless. He was a pioneer of early raising under glass, getting his plants established by this means outside before drought conditions came to set back the newly-planted stock of his rivals. He decided that mushrooms, contrary to current practice, did not need darkness or artificial heat, and proved this by growing record crops under two acres of glass. He also made a name for himself as a tomato grower, being one of the first men to appreciate the potentiality of a crop new to Britain. Twenty glasshouses were put up, covering ten acres of land. He used no more timber than was absolutely necessary to support the panes, thus reducing shade to a minimum. When finished, this was probably the largest block of tomato houses in the world. It cost Smith £13,500.

He was firm believer in farmyard manure, using as much as 200 tons a week when his holdings were in maximum production. So fertile was his land that he could with safety plant the same crop on one site for several years in succession. Present-day advocates of organic farming and gardening have been known to obtain similar results, although the quantity of farmyard dung used by Smith would be hard to come by now. In his hey-day he sent a score of loaded pair-horse wagons to London every night. While one was being unloaded the others had to wait in side roads. Regular buyers included Harrods and the Army and Navy Stores, by whom only the finest produce was accepted.

Alfred Smith died suddenly in 1927, following an attack of the severe type of influenza then prevalent. He was 72; his fortune amounted to £170,000. With foreign foodstuffs arriving in ever-increasing quantity, he considered that market gardening had passed its peak period in Britain, and must inevitably decline. According to Alfred Lucas, he was the greatest grower this country ever had; yet few have ever heard his name.

R. D. Blackmore

IT IS otherwise with R. D. Blackmore, whose name is familiar throughout the English-speaking world and beyond as the author of *Lorna Doone*. But he is known solely for his work as a writer, and the forty-odd years he spent as a fruit-grower are forgotten. For most of that time, from 1857 until 1899, he worked manually in orchard and vine-house, and for many years he also attended to the marketing of his produce at Covent Garden. Would that his pen had been employed on a description of 'The Cabbage King', for the two men must at some time have set eyes on one another, and Blackmore might well have given Alfred Smith more than a passing glance. Several of the novels (*Kit and Kitty*, *Christowell*, *Alice Lorraine*) make use of his experiences as a grower and salesman; most of their pages are inferior to *Lorna Doone* and almost unreadable today. Efforts made to unearth a character which could be linked with Smith have not been successful.

The story of Richard Doddridge Blackmore is a strange one. Born in 1825 and left motherless when only four months old, he was taken by his father, the Reverend John Blackmore, from his birthplace in Berkshire to the North Devon homeland of the family. At the age of twelve the boy was sent, as earlier Blackmores had been, to Blundell's School at Tiverton, where he was the recipient of an excellent classical education and many less advantageous physical blows. Of the classrooms he wrote:

> 'This was the place to learn things in, with some possibility of keeping them, and herein lay the wisdom of our ancestors. Could they ever have known half as much as they did, and ten times as much as we know, if they had let the sun come in, to dry it all up, as we do? Will even the fourteen-coated onion root, with its bottom exposed to the sun, or will a clever puppy grow long ears, in the power of strong daylight? The nature and nurture of solid learning were better understood when schools were built from which came Shakespeare, and Bacon, and Raleigh; and the glare of the sun was not let in, to baffle the light of the ages upon the mind. And another consideration is, that wherever there is light, boys make a

noise, which conduces but little to doctrine; whereas in soft shadow their muscles relax, and their minds become apprehensive. Thus had this ancient grammar-school fostered many scholars, some of whom had written grammars for themselves and their posterity.'

Judging by this, written when schools were just beginning to look a little less like prisons, Blackmore would have viewed the modern picture-window classrooms with dismay; perhaps the increasing noisy unruliness of school children could be tempered by the introduction of sunblinds. On the matter of physical punishment and bullying the author was reticent; but there are hints that the epileptic seizures which afflicted him in early manhood may have derived from brain damage caused by maltreatment at school. In spite of that serious handicap, he took his BA at Oxford in 1847, and after a spell at the Middle Temple was called to the Bar in 1855.

Finding that his seizures made the legal profession impossible, he rather surprisingly took a post as schoolmaster in Twickenham. Why this change of occupation was considered to be an advantage, or how an epileptic managed to control and teach groups of boys, is a mystery; yet Blackmore retained the position for several terms. A substantial legacy received from an uncle in 1857 allowed him to carry out a secret ambition to set himself up as a fruit-grower, in the hope that a free open-air life would cure his malady. That this hope was realized, to a great extent, seemed worth investigation. In response to my inquiry as to the effect of outdoor manual work, the Senior Physician to the National Society for Epileptics at Chalfont St Peter wrote: 'It is very difficult to answer your questions since so much depends on individual cases. However, in general people with epilepsy are rather less likely to have attacks if they are working and occupied. Epilepsy is a very variable condition and many people stop having attacks either as a result of drug treatment or in the natural course of the condition.' We shall therefore never know whether fruit-culture cured the author, or whether he would have grown out of the trouble in any case.

That Blackmore at thirty-two was extremely happy in the acquisition of his sixteen acres at Teddington is beyond doubt. There he built a residence named Gomer House for himself and his wife, and there he remained until his death in 1900. The property was sold by auction before the outbreak of the Second World War, and, following demolition of the house, the land was used for building. 'Blackmore's Grove' perpetuates his memory today. How many residents, at work in their little gardens, ever give a thought to the tall, broad-shouldered, farmer-like man with genial whiskered face and old-fashioned courtesy of manner, who tilled the same soil and wrote the much-loved story *Lorna Doone* there?

When Blackmore purchased his land, Teddington was still a country village, well away from the smoke of London. It was a parcel of ground conveniently situated for Bushey Park—the Lion Gate being a short walk away—and within easy reach of both Hampton Court and the Royal Botanic Gardens at Kew. The Twickenham of Alexander Pope, and Horace Walpole's Strawberry Hill were near enough to keep him in mind of their literary associations with the neighbourhood. That he had seriously studied fruit-growing as well as the classics seems clear, but nobody seems to know just where he acquired his knowledge of botany and agricultural chemistry. His friend Professor Richard Owen may have instilled in him a scientific attitude to horticulture; possibly Blackmore attended lectures on the chemistry of soils at the University of London. These are mere speculations, for his studies have not been recorded. All we know is that he was not an amateur, content to plant and pick haphazardly. From the start he showed a scientific bent.

Describing his search for land 'suitable for pear culture for Covent Garden Market, which was not then well supplied', he wrote of the sixteen-acre plot near the Lion entrance to Bushey Park, only twelve miles from the Market, which could be purchased in fee-simple: 'I secured samples of the soil, and the analysis proving it to possess the requisite qualities in iron, etc., I decided to purchase it.' He made no mistake about the soil. It grew splendid fruit under his care; in September 1865 he reported that two apples weighed 15¾ and 15½ ounces apiece, while peaches grown on a standard tree were 10 ounces and 8 ounces, the first being eleven inches in girth. At the business of selling he was less expert; profit always seemed to elude him. He told a friend, after some thirty years' experience, that his orchards cost him £500 a year and had often brought him only one-fifth of that sum. Although he tried different kinds of fruit, he said at the end of his life: 'I am thinking of writing a "Pyriad"—my life has been offered up to pears.'

Although he worked hard for long hours himself, and labour was cheap, it may be that the six permanent men he employed, and up to twelve in busy seasons, was too large a force to be supported on sixteen acres at a time when prices obtained at Covent Garden were going down. In that forgotten novel, *Kit and Kitty*, his hero and heroine, who were engaged in fruit-farming, expressed his own feelings: 'Few things vexed them much, except to find things sold below their value; and that far less for the love of money than from the sense of justice.' A friend named William Rideing wrote of Blackmore's produce: 'It was exceptionally fine fruit that filled the round wicker baskets of familiar pattern which, bearing his name in big black letters, were trundled down to market . . . to meet, where the Isleworth Road connects with the Hounslow Road, the similar produce of another novelist, a friend of his, George Manville Fenn. Better fruit than that of R.D.B. and G.M.F. was never sent to market; nor ever had the brotherhood of gardeners more honest or more enthusiastic followers than they.'

Visitors were often taken into the gardens by Blackmore, who was invariably armed with shears and pruning knife, which he used as the tour progressed. He talked more of his fruit than of his novels, being very shy about his work as an author. He wrote to one friend:

> 'My vines are going on gloriously, white bunches hang like water-spouts and black ones like thunder-clouds. Anyone looking at my vines would say, "This is your role my good fellow, stick to it; any ass can write novels (at least in the opinion of the publishers); but to make a vine needs intellect." '

In his young days Blackmore was well over six feet tall, and even when his shoulders sagged with the years he still seemed a giant. His large head, festooned with whiskers, had a rustic look which was matched by loose-fitting clothes; his rosy face and shrewd twinkling eyes were those of a placid, old-fashioned West-Country farmer. He would have looked more at home in Devonshire, against a background of red earth and russet cattle, than in the environs of London.

In 1879 he took a young American admirer, Lucy Derby, round his gardens. She wrote of how the author 'kindled with genuine love and enthusiasm for his chosen avocation, as he showed a great magnolia tree, trained against the face of his mansion, which at his bidding had become a vine, winding and twisting about the many windows'. Gomer House must have been a large building. Blackmore told the young lady that it was a great satisfaction to him to subject a tree to his will 'and watch it thrive in its new obedience'. Lucy described the spacious, sunny drawing-room where she feasted upon strawberries finer than any she had hitherto seen. In the garden Blackmore gathered for her roses and lilies and pansies, while he drew attention to the beauty and variety of foliage borne by the various bushes, and to the wonderful intricacies of the ferns. He knew the birds individually, and remembered them from one season to another. Numbers came through the windows into his study when he called to them. Though the birds made havoc with his fruit, he welcomed them all save starlings. 'These swept down in a great flock from Bushey Park upon his garden, and remained for some two hours each afternoon, and to them he sometimes felt obliged to take his gun.' He had great sympathy for all forms of life, and would frequently harbour stray cats and dogs, nursing sick ones back to health.

Blackmore's activities were certainly varied, as was the fruit he grew. By 1884 he had tried out nearly eighty varieties of pear and twenty different peaches. According to his friend Dr Robert Hogg, then President of the Royal Horticultural Society, every kind of hardy fruit could be grown in its greatest perfection on the fertile land round about Teddington. The trouble was that so small a proportion was able to reach perfection. Birds, insects, and rough weather accounted for a high percentage of waste. In one year it was estimated that eighty bushels of pears lay on the ground, unsaleable because of insect pests. In 1897 Blackmore wrote jokingly about a wonderful plague of maggots, 'so plentiful that they cannot find a pear apiece to live in, and are obliged to chum together'. He had nobody to advise him on control of pear midge. Yet he was an acknowledged authority on the growing of pears and peaches, and served as Vice-Chairman of the Royal Horticultural Society's Fruit Committee. Pest control had not been developed by scientists in Blackmore's day.

In September 1894 he wrote to *The Times* setting out the poor wholesale prices obtained for some of his fruits at Covent Garden—grapes at 9d. to 2s. a pound, outdoor peaches 1s. to 3s. a dozen, pears only 2s. 6d. to 4s. per bushel. These were gross receipts. At least 20 per cent must be deducted to cover carriage and commission. He asked if any man could produce fruit with profit on these terms. When apples were in good supply, the prices sank to a contemptible level. One year he had parted with 60 bushels at 1s. a bushel, and lost his baskets in the deal. In a recent article on Blackmore,* Mr Macer Wright mentioned a certain Mr White, who suggested that The Gomer House fruit was of inferior quality—he called it 'sponge and water', and 'bath water' at that. (He tried to promote imported Bartlett pears, and it may be that he was not a disinterested observer.) At all events Blackmore was not to be defeated in the debate. He took on Mr Gladstone, and later the Lord Mayor of London; but his pen was apparently mightier than his flair for commerce. After running the

* *Country Life*, April 1969.

business for over thirty years he had to admit that it had stuck fast on the wrong side of the balance sheet, whatever politicians and pundits might say about the profitability of what the Grand Old Man called 'fructiculture'.

Nevertheless, it was all a labour of love; he lived in harmony with his growing things, and gained that contentment which outweighs riches. The epileptic seizures of his youth were forgotten, except in one of his novels—*Clara Vaughan*, wherein the onset of a fit is described as only one who had experienced the misery himself could have written it. Whenever Blackmore was asked why he continued to toil at horticulture in the face of heavy losses, he replied that it was his way of obtaining both health and pleasure. Luckily for him, he was not obliged to earn his living by the produce of his land. As he put it, 'I must ply the pen to pay for the spade'.

At first the pen was not very profitable either. He laboured for seven years to turn the *Georgics* of Virgil into English, published several volumes of verse, and a small manual called *The Farm and Fruit of Old.* His first work of fiction, *Clara Vaughan*, was issued by Macmillan in 1864, *Cradock Nowell* in 1866 by Chapman and Hall, and the now famous *Lorna Doone* by Sampson Low in 1869. The success story of this book is more like wild fiction than the tale itself. Of the first 500 copies printed, only 300 were sold, the rest being sent abroad at a cheap price. Then Sampson Low Junior decided to risk it in a 6s. edition, against the wishes of the rest of his firm. It so happened that the Marquis of Lorne had recently married Queen Victoria's daughter Princess Louise, a marriage which created a great deal of interest because it was a break with tradition for a queen's daughter to marry one not of royal blood.

Princess Louise announced her engagement in October 1870, and was married in the following March. Meanwhile Low had produced the cheap edition of *Lorna Doone.* Some ill-informed book reviewer stated that this story concerned the forebears of Lord Lorne, and by his weird blunder caused a run on the book. Everybody who read books wanted to see what this one was about, and in a very short time twenty editions were sold out. Later on, the author wrote to Low: 'But for you, *Lorna Doone* might never have seen the light. All the magazines rejected her, and Smith and Elder refused to give me £200 for the copyright.' Publisher, reviewer and royal couple managed between them to make the fortunes of *Lorna Doone*, which became a minor classic, still in demand a century afterwards.

That story was never a magazine serial; but many other novels by Blackmore appeared in *Blackwood's*, *Fraser's* and *Harper's*, also in a popular journal called

Good Words. My own mother received bound annuals of the latter every Christmas as a present from the rector of her family's parish. She told me that it was more entertaining than the title might suggest. Blackmore's tale *Christowell* contains the following words: 'The finest gardener, that ever grew, knows well that he cannot command success, and has long survived young arrogance. Still he continues to hope for the best; for the essence of the gentle craft is hope, rooted in labour, and trained by love.' This story, published in 1881, appeared in *Good Words*. The earlier *Alice Lorraine*, which appeared in *Blackwood's*, contains descriptions of the author's experiences at Covent Garden. 'The early sun was up and shining bright upon London house-tops' as the van and its four men finished their night drive to London. Then came the arrival at Covent Garden Market. 'Here was the wondrous reek of men before the night had spent itself. Such a babel, of a market morning in the berry season.' All Blackmore's fiction was written in violet ink, which he found in a little country shop as a young man and used ever after.

That ink provided the only purple patches in all his books, but he could be slightly caustic at times in letters to his friends. The first Baron Avebury, whose name was Lubbock, sponsored the Bank Holidays Act of 1871 and for this social service became affectionately known as 'Saint Lubbock'. Until recent years the August Bank Holiday occurred on the first Monday in August, and was for long known as 'St Lubbock's Day'. In August 1882 Blackmore wrote to an acquaintance, Francis Armstrong, that 'No Briton does anything for a fortnight, after duly *Lubbocking*'.

Although he never experienced the joy and anxiety of parenthood, Blackmore had great affection for children and was much in demand as a godfather. His old friend Violet Veitch, who married Arthur Coward and lived at Teddington, persuaded him to act in that capacity when her first boy, Russell, was christened. A frequent visitor in the Coward home, Blackmore grew very fond of the child, and it was a bitter sorrow when meningitis ended his life in 1898, at the age of seven. The next son, born a year later, received the name of Noël, but without the author's sponsorship. When asked to officiate, Blackmore replied that too many of his godchildren had died young for him to act as godfather again. So the now famous actor and dramatist Noël Coward missed having the author of *Lorna Doone* in that relationship. As Blackmore died little more than a month after the child's birth, they can scarcely be said to have known one another.

Mrs Blackmore, a shadowy figure who suffered from delicate health and in later years became a chronic invalid, died in 1888, after which two devoted nieces kept house for the widower. He was for long partially disabled by some form of paralysis, and wrote in 1892, on retiring from the Vice-Chairmanship of the RHS Fruit Committee, 'I have had to give up . . . being a pronounced limper (and not a good one) for the rest of my pilgrimage.' During his term of office he made friends with Dr Robert Hogg, sometime Vice-President and later Secretary of the Royal Horticultural Society, and Editor of the *Journal of Horticulture*, and was ever an admirer of Hogg's work, *The Fruit Manual, a guide to the fruits and fruit trees of Great Britain*, first published in 1860, with a fifth edition in 1884. This is possibly the only work of its kind ever to be quoted in a work of fiction—*Alice Lorraine*. It is thought probable that Blackmore himself revised the section on Pears and Peaches in the fifth edition of Hogg's *Fruit Manual*.

Richard Doddridge Blackmore died in January 1900. Both he and his wife were buried at Teddington. In 1904 a window was unveiled in Exeter Cathedral to his memory, with an address given by another West-Country author, Eden Philpotts.

The Rochfords

THE Rochford family has recently had a whole book devoted to it*—but that is no reason for omitting it; in fact, a book on horticulture in and around London which left the Rochford enterprises out would be like a vine without tendrils. The Rochford tendrils have, in just over a century, reached out far and wide, and maybe they have not stopped growing yet. Everyone who visits the Chelsea Flower Show sees a gorgeous display of this firm's house-plants, and the large conservatory at Syon Park houses a permanent display of great range and variety—a display grown for flowers rather than foliage, and therefore expendable. The exhibit was designed and presented by Mrs Thomas Rochford. Among the less showy subjects are a number of the well-known Rochford house-plants, mostly foliage plants which will last for years in a room. The fashion for these, which has grown apace since the last war, owes much to the skill and business acumen of this firm. The Rochford label is a guarantee of quality, and the cultural hints, notes on country of origin, and names, botanical and vernacular, have interested and educated the purchasers to a remarkable degree.

Our story of this green-fingered family begins towards the close of the nineteenth century, when the Lea Valley became an important centre of glasshouse cultivation. The soil was good, much of it silt brought down by the River Lea, and the newly built Great Eastern Railway provided swift transport for produce. The price of land was modest, by today's standards. Tom and Joseph Rochford, who in 1882 acquired a large house and eight acres of land for the sum of £2,000, could not have guessed that from this small investment would spring a huge modern business of the twentieth century. The village where it all began, Turnford, was at their coming little more than a hamlet of thatched cottages. By 1895 the brothers employed sixty men and boys, and in 1901 they took in enough land to build seventy acres of glasshouses, while the homes needed for their workers increased local housing tenfold.

To begin with, both brothers planted grapes in their greenhouses, to which

* Mea Allen, *Tom's Weeds*, (1970).

Joseph added the growing of cut flowers and Tom the cultivation of pot-plants. Then Joseph saw a future in tomato culture, and turned his attention mainly to that fruit. It had become popular fairly late in the nineteenth century in Britain, and at the time most of our supply had to be imported from the Continent—chiefly from Italy. While Joseph concentrated on building up his tomato business, Tom stayed faithful to house-plants. He made many experiments, among them the keeping of Lily-of-the-Valley crowns in cold storage and bringing them forward in relays, so as to ensure a constant supply throughout the year of this popular Victorian pot-plant. Similar methods were applied to *Lilium longiflorum* and Spiraea; even vegetables were subjected to a freezing period, out of which Rochford thawed them at the moment when ordinary supplies fell off.

Every plant in his nursery had to be brought to a state of perfection before he would allow it to be sold—a policy still rigorously maintained by the firm of Rochford. Michael Rochford, the father of Tom and Joseph, who had a successful nursery and market garden in Tottenham, is said to have had a great love of plants and an understanding of their needs. Between them, this extraordinary family of horticulturists developed an instinct for plants never equalled in the garden world in Britain. Only the great Vilmorin family in France can compare with it.

The success of the Rochford enterprises was closely linked with the development of sheet glass, an invention which encouraged Joseph Paxton to put up the great Chatsworth conservatory, followed by the Crystal Palace. Although it ended up at Sydenham, the Crystal Palace was designed originally to house the Great Exhibition of 1851 in Hyde Park, and commercial growers took a decade to grasp the possibilities of large areas under glass for the cultivation of crops. Heating was a problem until the horizontal tubular boiler, with whose development the Rochfords were closely associated, came into use. This family was also a pioneer of modern systems of ventilation, and constructed some of the first overhead tanks for watering glasshouses by hose.

In a world of rapid change, where traditions are constantly being submerged in the name of 'progress', it is good to know that the present head of the huge Rochford enterprise, Tom the Third, great-grandson of Michael, has a son, Thomas Christopher, who is already at work in the nurseries. The wife of Tom the Third, Betty Rochford, has a brilliant flair for arranging plants—not so much the smaller art of the wedding or dinner-table, but displays on those vast and formidable stages at Chelsea and the Paris Floralies, where as many as 2,000 pot-plants are arranged by her. These exhibits have brought the firm countless prizes and medals, and when in 1964 Lord Aberconway, President of the Royal Horticultural Society, presented Tom with the Victoria Medal of Honour, he said he wished he could divide the medal, giving half to Tom and half to Betty.

> 'I have seen so often the two of them setting up their fascinating exhibits of stove plants at Chelsea and in our halls, maybe altering slightly, but with telling effect, the particular angle of a rotting log. Between them with their exhibits they have given immense pleasure to many, have opened for many new vistas, new possibilities of growing plants, in London gardens, London window-boxes, even in London rooms. But whoever is really responsible for all this, Mr and Mrs Rochford, it is a man's world.'

Games and market gardening are curiously linked in London. Part of Michael Rochford's original nursery is now the site of Tottenham Hotspur's football ground, and a member of the Huguenot family of Poupart, a name still of high repute at Covent Garden, had land connected with the present day Twickenham rugby ground, and in 1776 Jacques Poupart developed a market garden on what is now the Stamford Bridge ground of the Chelsea Football Club. Cricket, too, makes use of nursery and market garden land. The branch nursery in St John's Wood of Arthur Henderson, who had a famous pineapple nursery off the Edgware Road, was bought in 1889 by the Marylebone Cricket Club, and is now familiar to all under the name of 'Lord's'. This ground still has its 'nursery end'.

Arthur Henderson's assistant, John Wills, left to join the business of Segar, at premises known as 'The Royal Exotic Nursery', opposite the present South Kensington Underground station. Under the joint names of Wills and Segar, this firm carried on an enormous trade in palms, pot plants, and the regular supply of floral arrangements for great London houses from Buckingham Palace downwards. It was an era of lavish entertaining, and huge sums were expended on the decoration of ballrooms, dining tables and conservatories. In the first year of the First World War, Wills and Segar bought part of the Royal Nurseries at Feltham. This had belonged to another famous firm, Veitch of Chelsea, whose founder (like so many London gardeners) came from Scotland. A native of Jedburgh, he went south to Devon at the end of the eighteenth century, and in 1833 his sons bought the firm of Knight and Perry in Chelsea. The most famous member of the Veitch family became Sir Harry Veitch. After training with the

Vilmorins in France, he ran the Veitch business until part of the land was sold to Wills and Segar. Sir Harry's father, James Veitch, who died in 1869, is commemorated by the Royal Horticultural Society's Veitch Memorial Medals and Prizes, which are awarded annually for outstanding work in some field of horticulture.

5

Covent Garden Market

OUT of a huddle of sheds and stalls against the wall of the Earl of Bedford's garden, where sellers of fruit and vegetables plied their trade over 300 years ago, grew the great and famous market of 'Covent Garden'. Nothing lives for ever; the days of this venerable trading centre are already numbered; but at the time of writing it is still very much alive and worth recording. The area we know as Covent Garden (or to Londoners oftener just 'The Garden') is more or less bounded by the Strand, St Martin's Lane, Long Acre and Drury Lane, and was once a large garden belonging to Westminster Abbey. This convent garden was part of a vast domain stretching from the City Wall at Ludgate in the east to the wilds of Bayswater and Kensington in the west, and from Tybourne south to the Thames at Chelsea. The thirteenth century saw squabbles between the Bishop of London, who was establishing new parishes outside the city, and the Abbot over some of his lands; but a papal commission allowed the Abbey to retain its garden. The soil was light and friable, of a reddish colour, named 'brick earth'. As it warmed up quickly in springtime, it produced valuable early crops. No wonder the monks wished to keep it. It is probable that the original St Martin-in-the-Fields was a chapel built for the use of convent gardeners.

In 1536 Henry VIII took possession of the garden and the adjacent seven-acre field—the 'long acre'—from which the modern thoroughfare was named. During the reign of Edward VI these lands were given to, or annexed by, the Protector Somerset, and after his execution they passed to the Earl of Bedford. In 1627 the 4th Earl, striving to restore his family's depleted fortunes, set out to develop the convent garden site on a grand scale, with the assistance of that brilliant architect Inigo Jones. Charles I, who had instituted a Commission for Building, empowered to enforce standards and limit development, lent a sympathetic ear to the Earl's scheme. This comprised a large piazza with church at one end, bordered by spacious mansions with projecting upper floors to form covered walks below; there were also fine streets converging on the open square. Everything was designed with the utmost elegance in classical style, having well-proportioned rooms and decorations of Italian plaster work. When the people of London saw this Italian-style piazza going up in their midst there was considerable excitement, and before long Covent Garden became one of the most sought-after residential districts. Like many architectural projects, it cost more than expected, and when it came to building the church the Earl told Inigo Jones to economize, saying that it need not be much better than a barn. His architect is supposed to have replied, 'Well, then you shall have the handsomest barn in England.' It still stands, though considerably altered, and as a barn is certainly in a class by itself.

While the place swarmed with bricklayers, plasterers, carpenters and glaziers, and the cultivated land disappeared for ever beneath buildings, the sellers of fruit and vegetables multiplied rapidly, putting up a clutter of mean sheds along the garden wall of Bedford House in order to exploit the increasing trade brought by the new development. Soon members of the nobility took up residence on the Piazza, and to the newly built streets leading up to it there came gentry and professional people, in particular artists and writers. So it was that those engaged in the gentler arts and graces of life rubbed shoulders with the less polished traders in market garden produce, to form a rich and strange mixture of humanity unique in the annals of London.

The terrible Plague of 1664–5 claimed its first victim in Long Acre. The Rector of St Paul's Church, Covent Garden, who proved himself a hero during this epidemic, went about ministering to his people regardless of his own safety. This endearing character, who was known, in happier times, to be exceedingly nervous of catching a common cold, later became Bishop of Ely. Inhabitants of the new houses round the Piazza benefited from the more hygienic conditions, suffering less from the incidence of Plague than the people in densely crowded tenements of older date. When the Great Fire of 1666 swept many of those wretched dwellings away, Covent Garden escaped the flames and served as a storehouse for goods salvaged from stricken areas. A number of street markets vanished in the blaze, causing a still greater concentration of trade at The Garden.

By this time the fruits cultivated in Britain were being sold under varietal names. The Costard, a large and very popular kind of apple, gave its name to the apple-sellers or costard-mongers, and from that was derived the costermonger's title still used today. The Warden pear, raised by the Cistercians of Warden Abbey in Bedfordshire, gave its name to the delicious 'Warden pies' mentioned by Shakespeare, and the cherries known as Gaskins (Gascoynes) were brought here by Joan of Kent, who accompanied her husband the Black Prince to the battlefields of Gascony. Gean—a word often used in Scotland for cherry—probably came from Guienne at the same period, while May Duke may be a corruption of Medoc. The gooseberry was sold in named sorts, as 'Blue', 'Red' and 'Prickly Hedgehog'. Our luxuries, the peach and apricot, were regarded with some suspicion, as was the melicoton, a cross between peach and quince. Italians called these *Mazzofranchese*—'Kill Frenchmen'.

Tomatoes were in rather bad odour in their early days in Britain, being suspected of causing cancer. Some braved this risk because of their supposed virtue as an aphrodisiac. In general, vegetables were back in favour in the seventeenth century after a period of neglect. Cabbages, carrots, onions, leeks and garlic were sold, also the turnip—hitherto regarded as food for cattle or starving peasantry. The potato, still very small, was looked upon as a luxury. Tender green peas were developed from the old, coarse field pea, and a large yellow cucumber was so esteemed that one of Pepys's friends died of a surfeit of 'cowcumber'. Asparagus was popular; the 'sparrowgrass' grown in quantity at Battersea used to be sold as 'Battersea bundles'. Watercress was gathered wild, also many herbs used in cookery and medicine. The lettuce was regarded as a medicinal plant. It was taken with oil and salt to cool the blood and as a cure for insomnia.

By the middle of the century market gardening had become an important profession, and the Worshipful Company of Gardeners, awarded its first charter in 1605 and a second in 1616, worked actively for the maintenance of high standards. In 1649 the Company itself owned a large garden outside the city, with a labour force of some 1,500 men, women and children and 400 apprentices. Another area of market garden ground, famous for two centuries, bore the name of Neat House Gardens, and ran from Vauxhall Bridge alongside the Thames to Chelsea. Here were grown fine crops of asparagus, artichokes, cauliflowers, melons and salad vegetables, on soil kept well dunged with the waste products of London, brought down by barge. Richard Bradley in 1706 wrote of the early forcing that took place here. 'Kitchen Gardens which are first and exceed all other gardens in Europe for wholesome produce and variety of Herbs are those at the Neat-houses near the Tuttle Fields, Westminster, which abound in Salads, early Cucumbers, Colliflowers, Melons, Winter Asparagus and almost every Herb fitting the table.'

Neat derives from Neyte (a name that appears in Domesday Book), which formed a Manor of the Abbots of Westminster until the Dissolution. It probably signified that the place was in use as a depot for cattle.* After the Abbot's grange went, a collection of small houses was erected on part of the land, one of which became a tea-garden in the seventeenth century. Pepys records a visit he paid to the place with an actress named Knipp. 'To the Neat Houses in the way of Chelsea; where in a box in a tree we sat and sang, and talked and eat; my wife out of humour, as she always is when this woman is by.' The mother of Nell Gwyn kept a house of refreshment hereabouts, and on 29 July 1679 was found lying dead, face downwards in her own fishpond. She was known to be fond of brandy, and some ascribed her end more to that fluid than to the shallow water of the pool.

The first charter for a market at Covent Garden was granted by Charles II in 1670 to William, Earl of Bedford. It specified the right to hold a market for fruit, vegetables and other produce 'on every day of the year except Sundays and the Feast of the Nativity, in a place commonly called the Piazza near the church of St Paul, Covent Garden'. Having obtained this document the Earl made little use of it for the next eight years, and after that the running of the market passed into the hands of men named Pigott and Day. In 1704 the whole of the Bedford House was leased for building, and the great house, left empty for several years, was demolished in 1705.

While Tavistock Row went up along the front of the old Bedford garden wall, stallholders who were ejected to make way for the development were allowed to set up their booths further in, so that the great open square began to shrink. The original market expanded steadily with the population—still small by our standards, for when Inigo Jones built St Paul's Church there were only a quarter of a million people in London. Commerce was rapidly ousting Society. Coffee houses were set up, sellers of wares other than garden produce joined the throng, streets were congested with vehicles. Protests were made, but they proved unavailing. There was mention in 1748 of bakers, haberdashers, cookshops, sellers of spirituous liquors, who between them made 'a stench and offensive smoke'. As might be surmised, the once-fashionable residences had lost their glamour and their value in hard cash.

Yet the crowded square was still used for games. John Gay referred to the 'Furies of Football War', which suggests that football has not changed much through the centuries. There were firework displays, bonfires, puppet shows, punchinello and such lurid real-life dramas as hangings and pillory whippings. In 1730 one Mary Williams was whipped at the cart's tail thrice round Covent

* *Neat-herd*, cattleman; *Neat-house*, cattle shed.

Garden Market for stealing oranges out of Mrs Vernon's greenhouse at Twickenham. In the Piazza was a curious four-sided sundial, mounted upon a stone pillar which in turn was raised on a stepped plinth. Here sat the sellers of barley broth and rice porridge, and quack doctors with nostrums to cure the indispositions brought on by over-indulgence. The inns, too, sold home-made potions with medicinal properties; at the corner of Henrietta Street, one public house sold scurvy grass ale and 'saloop', a cure for inebriates made from sassafras and cuckoo flower boiled to make a tea. This was taken with milk and sugar.

The nobility faded out from the scene, all having left by 1750, while gentry and professional people continued to live around the market until the end of the century. The arcades fell into decay and were not repaired, for this Italian street architecture was not really suitable for the less sunny climate of London. The first Covent Garden theatre opened in 1733 with Congreve's *Way of the World*. It was destroyed by fire in 1808 and again in 1856; but this phoenix has never failed to rise again from the ashes. The Theatre Royal, Drury Lane, was considerably older, having obtained its Charter from Charles II at a time when theatres had hitherto been kept outside the city, with men acting women's parts. Women were permitted to act at Drury Lane, and Nell Gwyn, who started life selling oranges to the audiences, appeared on the boards at the age of fifteen. By seventeen she was the king's mistress, and had several children by him.

In 1763 Boswell, who frequented the many taverns and coffee-houses, recorded an adventure in Covent Garden. Being solicited by two amorous girls, he declared that, being poor, he could offer no money. 'But if you choose to have a glass of wine and my company and let us be gay and obliging to each other without money, I am your man.' They agreed, so back to the Shakespeare tavern the trio went.

'We were shown into a good room and had a bottle of sherry before us in a minute. I surveyed my seraglio and finding them good subjects for amorous play I toyed with them, and then I solaced my existence with them, one after the other, according to their seniority.' An extraordinary mixture of promiscuity and punctiliousness which only Boswell could have employed. In that same year occurred a more momentous contact, when Boswell met the great Dr Johnson in a Russell Street bookshop. The Doctor knew the district well, for in 1737 he took his first London lodging in Exeter Street, Covent Garden. In that melting-pot these oddly assorted characters met, and out of their companionship came Boswell's *Life of Johnson* and *Journal of a Tour to the Hebrides*. What would

Johnson's *Life of Boswell* have been like? A lady in a train assured me that she had read it.

Kneller and Hogarth, Dryden and Pepys, Congreve, Swift, Addison and Steele, Pope and Fielding, Walpole, Goldsmith, Sheridan, Turner—each in his time frequented The Garden. There were plenty of places where such men could meet and talk. One famous house, Swan's Grand Hotel, Music and Supper Rooms, which Thackeray knew, existed for many years under different proprietors and a variety of names. Some of the original great houses were turned into gambling dens, brothels, or so-called Turkish Baths, often bawdy houses in disguise. The Hummums, a genuine bathing establishment, afterwards became a hotel, which perpetuated the old name. Crabbe and Tennyson both stayed in it. After its closure in 1865 a second Hummum's Hotel was built next door and survived until 1900.

In 1712 Steele in *The Spectator* described a journey he made by boat from Richmond with a number of market gardeners, calling in at 'Nine Elmes' to take on board a cargo of melons consigned to Sarah Sewell and Company at their stall in Covent Garden. Nine Elms is the site chosen for the new market to take the place of Covent Garden when that great centre for the buying and selling of market garden produce fades out—a melancholy event scheduled for 1973. It is said that the traffic congestion is no longer supportable in this area. For centuries produce has converged on this place by sea, river, packhorse, wagon, cart, dray, train, van, and carried in baskets upon the heads of women. As many as a hundred women would bring strawberries from Fulham and adjacent districts in this manner. There was always congestion around and in the market; but the huge modern lorry and its fumes appears to have delivered a final, fatal blow.

The baskets used for holding produce deserve a study to themselves. They were formerly made by colonies of basket-makers in Fulham and Staines, from osiers growing along the marshy verges of the Thames before the embankments were built, and on islands in the river. Prior to the Dissolution, the monks of Westminster earned ten shillings a year from the osier beds on Abbey lands. The 'pottle' was a small tapered basket of fine wicker work, made to hold about half a pound of strawberries. A number of these fitted into a much larger one called a 'marne', 42 inches in diameter and 27 inches deep. This, full of pottles, was carried on the head. The 'pad' was a small rectangular basket with a hinged lid, used for such tender delicacies as ripe peaches. The Irish 'basket-women' who carried heavy loads at the Garden in the nineteenth century acquired a bad reputation for their vile language and heavy drinking. By the time they came upon the scene the commerce of the market had grown enormously; but as a social centre the great days were over. Dickens saw it in his youth, and described what he saw in *Sketches by Boz.*

Among the choice fruits grown under glass at this time we hear of grapes being on sale from June to November, and of sixty ripe pineapples cut by Isaac Andrews of Lambeth at the Coronation of George IV. The Garden could also supply such odd trifles as silkworms (from fourpence to a shilling a dozen), garden snails, goldfish, frogs, snakes, leeches, morels and truffles.

The subject of trees is not one often associated with The Garden, yet in the mid-eighteenth century the wood of a West Indian tree made its first appearance in Britain at a house in King Street. An eminent physician, Doctor Gibbons, was having a house built when his brother, captain of a vessel plying with the West Indies, brought back some wood as ballast and offered it for use in the construction. The carpenters, finding it excessively hard, refused to have anything to do with it. The doctor then persuaded his cabinet-maker to fashion a candle-box for his wife, and the result was greatly admired for its rich colour and polish. Among the visitors to the Gibbons's house, the Duchess of Buckingham took a fancy to the unusual wood, and she so ardently praised it to all her circle that mahogany became the rage. After 1753 it was imported in large quantities and used by the Adam brothers, Sheraton, Hepplewhite and Chippendale. The latter had workshops in St Martin's Lane. Some of the old houses in and around Covent Garden still have mahogany doors, exterior and interior.

The Market itself, which continued slowly but steadily to oust nobility, gentry, and the artistic fraternity as it expanded, became in the nineteenth century the dominant force, so that 'Covent Garden' signified the great exchange for fruit, vegetables and flowers in the mind of everyone hearing those two words. Old buildings and sheds disappeared fast, and in 1828, when the Act 'for the Improvement and Regulation of Covent Garden Market' became law, an entirely new look was given to the place. A fine central covered arcade with two-storey shops intersected a smaller one at right angles, the whole covering $1\frac{1}{2}$ acres. The Duke of Bedford was now invested with the right to let shops, impose market tolls, and make bye-laws for the ordering of affairs within the market area.

During the second rebuilding of the Opera House after the fire of 1856, a 'Floral Hall' was erected against the south wall of the theatre, with its entrance in Bow Street. This hall was in reality a giant conservatory, 227 feet long and

100 feet wide, made from left-over material salvaged when the Crystal Palace was moved from Hyde Park to Sydenham after the Great Exhibition of 1851. For some reason the new structure did not thrive as a flower market; it became popular for music and other entertainment instead, and another hall went up soon afterwards for the flower trade, with an entrance in Wellington Street.

By 1890 there were loud complaints of congestion in and around Covent Garden, but nothing could stem the tide of commerce there. The Russell Street extension went up, then the Jubilee Market. Today the premises used for the buying and selling of produce stretch far beyond the original market precincts, overflowing into Long Acre, Russell, Hart, King and Tavistock Streets. After the First World War the family of the Dukes of Bedford disposed of the trading rights, and the Market was run by a company until, in 1962, the Covent Garden Market Authority was set up by the Government to take over responsibility. Its jurisdiction extends over 6½ acres, and it has been charged with the task of improving existing facilities or providing better ones.

This market is now one of the largest in the world, handling over 70 million pounds worth of fruit and vegetables and 10 million pounds worth of flowers and plants in a year. It employs upwards of 4,000 people, and about 1,000 lorries roll in each day with the produce—two thirds of which, in value, is imported. Three times as many vehicles take the goods away to secondary wholesalers and to retailers all over the kingdom. All this will soon disappear. What is going to take its place in The Garden? That is the question everyone asks and nobody can answer properly. Even when every building and road has been planned in detail on paper, the tale is not told. It is scarcely begun. The people and their interests; their behaviour; the atmosphere they will create—such matters are unpredictable.

One thing is certain. The fruits of the earth will no longer occupy this piazza. One of the charms of my publisher's office* has been the sight of enormous loads coming in, often parked so close to the entrance that a hand outstretched from the editorial window might have filched the occasional sweet orange or carrot, had not these been imprisoned in the gaudy nets now worn by fashionable fruits and roots. No more will the wholesome smells of earth and orchard rise to blend with the printers' ink, or the shouts of vendors and porters mingle with bookish accents within doors. It will still be possible to walk across to King Street for an editorial luncheon, dizzied by thoughts of how my undistinguished feet may at any moment be slotting into invisible prints left there by Dryden, Congreve,

* This was removed from Covent Garden in 1972.

Goldsmith, Sheridan, Swift or Doctor Johnson long ago; but never again will such heady dreams be brought to an abrupt end by the discarded carrot or handful of rotten sprouts whizzing happily past my ear.

The church will remain: that place of waiting when too much time has been allowed before an appointment; the handsome barn where a modest casket in the wall bearing the name of Ellen Terry seems so extraordinarily potent that one is forced to regard physical death as a matter of little importance. Here are the mortal remains and immortal memories of Grinling Gibbons (and one of his carvings); of Samuel Butler, Sir Peter Lely, Thomas Girtin, William Wycherly, and others. Among those commemorated by modern tablets are Ben Webster, Dame May Whitty, C. B. Cochran, Ivor Novello, Leslie Henson, Bransby Williams and Clemence Dane, who lived in The Garden and wrote a book about it.* Last but not least, there is a tablet inscribed:

Thomas Arne musician and parishioner 1710–1778
Baptized in this church Buried in this churchyard
Rule Britannia

* *London Has a Garden* (1964).

The Gardening Centre, Syon Park

MOST people travel to this great new exhibition of gardening by car; but, having found that British Rail provided a combined rail and admission ticket at a cost of sixty new pence from Waterloo, I took advantage of this package deal. Trains run frequently to Syon Lane Station—a half-hour's journey—and the walk to the entrance gate took me ten minutes. My sole difficulty lay in the regrettable absence of signs to direct passengers to the Gardening Centre, which is not visible from the station exit. When a way in had been found, it turned out to be the Brent Lea Gate (for pedestrians only), situated in a narrow lane off the London Road at Brentford. Nothing is seen of Syon House or the great dome of the conservatory until the visitor has advanced some distance within the massive walls which enclose the estate.

The story of Syon Park extends far back into legendary times before history was written. There are prehistoric remains, and Julius Caesar is said to have crossed the Thames near the point now known as 'Old England', on his second visit, in 54 B.C., when he fought the Britons led by Cassivelaunus. Recorded history does not begin until the fifteenth century, when Henry V founded two monasteries, one being at Sheen. The other, named 'Syon Monastery' after the hill outside Jerusalem, was built at Twickenham in 1415 for the Order of the Most Holy Saviour, the English Bridgettines. These nuns moved in 1431 to the site of the present Syon House. Remnants of their nunnery still in existence include some good Tudor brickwork in the west wall of the barn, now exposed after one hundred years of concealment. This wall may be seen opposite the Gardening Centre car park.

After the suppression of the monasteries by Henry VIII in 1539, the estate and buildings of Syon fell into a state of decay until, with the monarch's death, they were granted to the 'Protector', Duke of Somerset, who replaced most of the monastic block with a fine Tudor mansion, much of which is incorporated in the present Syon House. The 'Protector' had his park encircled with high walls, and a raised triangular terrace constructed on the south-west side of the mansion. This unusual structure was regarded by his supicious enemies as token of an incipient desire to fortify the place. In 1552 they triumphed over him, and Somerset was executed for treason. Syon came next into the possession of a Duke of Northumberland—not of the Percy family, as are the present holders of that title. If the Protector's reign was short, it made its mark in horticultural history. His protégé, Dr William Turner (known as the 'father of English botany'), created in a formal area near the house one of the first botanical gardens to be made in England, and his book *The Names of Herbes* was partly written at Syon in 1548.

William Turner, born at Morpeth in Northumberland in about 1508, was a true observer in the modern scientific sense, sceptical about the romantic legends and misconceptions indulged in by earlier naturalists, not excepting Aristotle. The latter's assumption that robins in winter turned into redstarts was dismissed by Turner in these words: 'Both the birds are seen at the same time.' A Protestant of extreme Puritan persuasion, he found it expedient to spend much of his time abroad, returning to England only when the climate of opinion was favourable to his views. He became Dean of Wells in Somerset.

Like Turner's patron Somerset, Northumberland and the latter's unhappy daughter-in-law, Lady Jane Grey, lost their heads on Tower Hill, and the lands of Syon came once more into the possession of the Crown. In 1557 Queen Mary restored it to the Bridgettine Order; but those were troublous times, and their stay of short duration. On her accession Elizabeth I promptly dissolved all monastic houses by Act of Parliament, and annexed the lands. Before the close of the century Henry Percy, ninth Earl of Northumberland, obtained a lease of Syon, and in 1603 he was granted the freehold. It is still a Percy residence. The displaced Bridgettines, after many wanderings abroad, came at last to Syon Abbey in Devon, where they have been settled since 1861. This is the only English community of religious women to have had continuous existence since the time of Mary I. At Syon House, the tenth Earl had the Inigo Jones colonnade added to the east front, and introduced many exotic plants into his gardens, so that for a second time the name of Syon was well known in the horticultural world.

His successor died in 1670, to be followed by his son-in-law, the sixth Duke of Somerset, whose wealthy grandson-in-law (created first Duke of Northumberland in 1766), had the entire place refurbished. The brothers Adam reconstructed the interior of the great house, while outside the new owner had all the formal Tudor terraces and walled enclosures swept away. He then called in the famous Lancelot Brown, known as 'Capability', to landscape the sixty-three acres of pleasure garden in the informal manner of the period. It is said that Brown's fee for this work amounted to nearly two thousand pounds—a large sum in those days. On the south and south-west sides of the house many existing trees are probably relics of this conception. A number of introduced trees, such as cedars and chestnuts, with oaks and beeches, were almost certainly of his planting, although detailed records are not available.

To the north and north-west Brown cleared away fifteen acres of orchard, and set many more trees and shrubs; amid these was a botanical garden, and a wide sweep of lawn with a Doric column surmounted by a statue of Flora. A man-made river, originally created to provide water for an explosives factory, was used to form a lake, about a quarter of a mile long and forty yards wide, which makes a charming and peaceful feature within the area now occupied by the Gardening Centre; the use of this water for ornamental purposes may be regarded as a horticultural equivalent of turning swords into ploughshares. Those who walk along the lakeside in early summer would do well, if they care for waterfowl, to take a few morsels of sandwich with them. Delightful little ducklings, round-eyed and confident, silently plead for largesse, and look indescribably wounded if the visitor has nothing edible to offer.

The great conservatory, built between 1820 and 1822 by Charles Fowler for the third Duke of Northumberland, was used by Paxton as a model for his famous glasshouse at Chatsworth, and later for the Crystal Palace. The Syon conservatory is 382 feet long and 65 feet high to the top of the dome, and is constructed of Bath stone and gunmetal, with interior supporting columns and tracery of cast iron. In addition, extensive vegetable grounds and hot-houses were at this period developed in the northern corner of the estate, and under glass were ripened exotic fruits, such as mangosteens and pineapples. By the middle of the nineteenth century Syon had again achieved a high reputation for horticulture, which was maintained until in the mid-1960s the effect of two world wars and changing economic conditions made full upkeep of these great gardens impossible for the owner. With the leasing of fifty-five acres to ICI's subsidiary, Plant Protection Ltd in 1965, the present duke allowed this area to become a national centre of gardening, where our 'nation of gardeners' may study and enjoy all that is best in horticulture for the million. The Centre was officially opened by Queen Elizabeth The Queen Mother on 12 June 1968; thus was added to Syon's 450 years of garden history a novel and unexpected twist.

The history of silviculture in England is closely linked with this estate: a subject at once apparent to those who arrive by car, when an enormous Black Walnut comes into view at the back of the car park. This species was introduced into Britain from North America in 1630; the tree at Syon is very likely of 'Capability' Brown's planting, around 1770. It now has a girth of 16 feet 10 inches, which has been exceeded by only one other specimen in this country. Two fine London Planes (*Platanus acerifolia*) near the walnut are probably of the same age. Both have attained a height of nearly 100 feet. Beside the lake an Indian Bean tree (*Catalpa bignonoides*) leans athwart the shore with an air of ancient fatigue. It dates from 1726, and still flowers in spite of its age and lethargic look. Tree specialists have told me that the Catalpa abhors the proximity of other trees, and that it leans or flops in order to avoid being touched by their branches. Behind the woodland garden a Liquidambar, the tallest specimen in Britain, has reached 93 feet, and a Turkish Hazel holds the record for its species in girth—a waist measure of 9 feet 1 inch, which vital statistic is considered no disgrace in a tree. The species of tree that most of us consider to be the typical adjunct of an old English garden, Cedar of Lebanon, is well represented in the Rose Garden. Although so picturesque, it is deceptive as to age, being a fast grower and quick to assume the appearance of venerable seniority. Many of the biggest specimens were planted not earlier than 1800.

The six-acre Rose Garden is separated from the rest of the Gardening Centre, with Syon House and its precincts between the two sections of ground open to the public. To explore both areas thoroughly at one visit requires either a superior pair of feet, or a long day given to the business, with time allowed for several periods of rest and refreshment between walks. There are plenty of facilities for these essential interludes, sited with ingenuity; unobtrusive, but convenient and easy to locate. The Rose Garden, which occupies almost the same area as the earlier Tudor garden, is pleasantly shaded to the west, with open views over the Syon Park water meadows to Kew Gardens beyond. More than 14,000 rose bushes in 400 varieties may be seen, the hybrid teas and floribundas massed in large, named beds in full sun, with the shrub and species roses planted less formally in open glades between the trees. A semi-circular pergola is furnished with climbers and ramblers, each with an attendant clematis to provide alternative floral display. The natural soil of Syon is too thin and sharply drained to be ideal rose ground, but peat and other humus-forming material is added frequently, and the wealth of blossom when I saw it in June showed what could be achieved by this means.

To describe the main part of the Gardening Centre (or National Exhibition of Gardening, as the promoters now call it) in full detail would be to produce a catalogue. Probably nine out of ten visitors are content to gain an impression of the fine old trees of Syon, the lake and Woodland Garden and the newly-made Rose Garden, with deliberate concentration on certain chosen aspects of the exhibition sites and pavilions. Only the youngest and most ardent gardener would take time to examine all the machinery, greenhouses and frames, chalets, garden furniture, tubs and pots, tools, netting and trellis, incinerators, hoses and cans, plant foods, pesticides, paving materials, wheelbarrows and trucks, aviaries, wrought-iron work, and the rest; while even the keenest plantsman or woman could hardly expect to take in at one visit the name of every plant, shrub and tree on show here.

All are clearly named, so that there is no frustration when it comes to taking note of 'that silver plant' in Mrs Desmond Underwood's grey bed near the conservatory, or of some dwarf conifer from the Wansdyke Nursery on Flora's Lawn, or of favourite blooms in the Rose Garden. From the living plants it is easy to speed away to the Selling Area in the old stables, there to place an order or to obtain a catalogue. There is also an Information Centre, a Technical Information Centre, and a bookshop full of horticultural publications and coloured slides. At the Technical Information Centre experts will identify your plants, or any pests and diseases afflicting them, without charge.

Of all the 'special' gardens laid out and planted at the Centre (among them an 'Electric' garden, showing how electricity can be harnessed to reduce work to a minimum; a 'Sleeper' garden: not for the somnolent, but made with old railway sleepers forming raised beds, steps, wall beams and a garden seat; a garden for the disabled and handicapped, and an Allotment garden), the ingenious five-in-one scheme devised by Violet Stevenson in association with Mary Dene particularly held my attention. It is beautifully simple and highly practical, as might be expected of a design planned for the readers of *Woman's Realm* Magazine. The area is divided into five self-contained sections which would all combine into a harmonious whole if one had sufficient room. Singly, or in part, they may be adapted to the smallest plot of ground. A long rectangular space, 100 feet by 30 feet, has been split into three. First, there is a courtyard with sun-lounge and pool, then a small lawn and border, and lastly a section for vegetables and fruit. Alongside these plots are odd-shaped pieces of land laid out in less formal ways. Occupants of corner sites often have such unsymmetrical shapes to deal with. The front plot has been cut up into island beds, with a mixed border of shrubs, scented herbs, and roses. Beyond it is a rock and water garden, edged by a long raised mound of peat blocks, where lime-hating plants will thrive, their artificial bank serving also to shelter plants below it. Both vegetables and fruit are safely housed within a portable cage, 16 feet square, with a neat greenhouse and small shed adjoining it and a compost bin close at hand. Where birds are a nuisance, these light, portable cages, which can be erected and taken down with ease, will soon earn their modest cost. It was interesting to see, used here in a border, the decorative grey-green, cream and mauve variegated Borecole. In the last century a Scottish lady, the Gertrude Jekyll of Edinburgh, named Frances Jane Hope, introduced this plant as a foliage foil to flowers in her borders, to the astonishment of more conventional neighbours. It is of course edible as well as attractive to look at, which should appeal to thrifty Scotswomen—and others.

The Garden for the Handicapped was looking a little dispirited when I saw it. To inspire and encourage those who garden against difficulties, all those raised beds should really be crammed with treasures. There was a good array of special tools, wide, smooth paths to take wheelchairs, and the planting areas were very easy to reach from all sides. Would that every place where elderly, disabled or even temporarily handicapped people dwell could have a garden like this to occupy them and help to overcome invalidism! The therapeutic value is beyond price.

The great conservatory forms an exhibit which makes Syon worth visiting for itself and its contents alone. Beneath the dome an area of nearly 3,000 square feet houses plants that require a minimum temperature of 60° Fahrenheit. Among these are the Saintpaulia (African Violet), Bougainvillea, ornamental Fig, Castor Oil Plant, Stagshorn Fern, *Citrus mitis*—hung with mini-oranges, Bromeliad and Hoya. The last-named commemorates Thomas Hoy, who was gardener to the first Duke of Northumberland for forty years. In the west pavilion, amid mosses and rocks and moving water, certain kinds of orchid are beautifully displayed—to demonstrate that Cypripedium and Cymbidium can be managed fairly easily by the owner of a cool greenhouse, or even a window-sill where the temperature does not fall below 55°. (It is a common mistake to assume that *all* orchids are best left to the care of trained gardeners.) Of course there are plenty of cacti and succulents on show, and the display of fuchsias proves how far we have progressed since that day when James Lee first propagated the novelty which he had cajoled from a sailor's wife in Wapping.

In the west wing also are some young vines. They are worthy of notice, for they remind visitors of an important piece of gardening history. In 1831 a young man named James Busby—born in Scotland and later resident in Alnwick—took a collection of vine cuttings out to Australia. He had emigrated to that country in 1824; published a treatise on viticulture; was asked to teach the craft to settlers; and finally returned to Britain to obtain plants of many varieties of vine, thirty-six of which came from Syon. The vast vineyards of New South Wales, Victoria and South Australia owe their inception to his knowledge and foresight. Wine production in Australia is now an industry of great importance to the country's economy, and to commemorate the original donation of vine cuttings from Syon, the High Commissioner in 1962 reversed the process, presenting a number of cuttings which were planted in the conservatory by the present Duke of Northumberland in November of that year.

In addition to all these permanent exhibits, and many more which cannot be mentioned here, Syon provides a series of special events throughout the summer season. Flower Shows, Flower Arranging Contests, Rural Craft Demonstrations, Rose Weeks and Autumn Planting Weeks, Folk Dance and Song Festivals, even a Horse Show and a Puppet Festival, have been held at various times. Details may be had each year from the Gardening Centre Ltd, Syon Park, Brentford, Middlesex. There are special quotations for parties.

One thing is missing. I felt that a well-designed herb garden, enclosed in wattle or other fencing to shelter the plants and contain their fragrance, would be a great asset. There is at present only a small group of the better-known culinary herbs in the Allotment Garden, and some lavender and other fragrant plants, and Angelica, used decoratively in the *Woman's Realm* Garden. A real herb enclosure, containing a comprehensive collection of culinary, fragrant, old medicinal and dye-herbs, would be singularly appropriate at Syon—where the great Dr William Turner, the 'father of English Botany', grew such plants and wrote about them in the sixteenth century.

Detailed information should be available on the cultivation and use of all kinds of herb plants. How many gardeners know that Lovage is an easily grown perennial whose foliage may be dried and stored without difficulty, to provide delicious celery-type flavouring for many dishes? Or that young leaves of Borage taste like cucumber? Or that Spearmint is not the only variety to be cooked with potatoes or peas? Some people uproot and banish the common garden mint because it is prone to rust disease, not knowing that other culinary kinds are rust-free: *Mentha rubra raripila* is one with smooth green leaves, and the tall woolly Applemint or 'Monk's Herb' another, both of excellent flavour. The handsome and heavily scented Bergamot Mint is not for the kitchen, but dries well for sweet-bags and pot-pourri; silver variegated Applemint makes a cheerful edging plant and provides lacing for fruit drinks in summer, and Alecost (or Costmary) may be used in salads, in place of the usual Spearmint with peas and potatoes, or dried for sweet-bags and the like.

The grey-green Camphor Plant when dried acts as a moth-deterrent, along with the decorative fine-curled Tansy—Miss Jekyll's favourite, *Tanacetum vulgare* var. *crispum* should be chosen—and some Wormwood or Southernwood. The gorgeous Bergamot makes what Americans call 'Oswego Tea'; this really does taste very like China tea; while elderberries, fruit of the bush traditionally known as the 'Elder Mother' of all herbs, can be used for making a thick syrup which is soothing for winter coughs.* Elder flowers, too, have great value when turned into Elder Flower Water; this works wonders in skin complaints. The stately biennial Woad, although the extraction of blue dye is too long and messy a process for most of us today, gives a bonus of pendant black seeds for flower-arrangements.

Yes, Syon needs a good old-fashioned herb garden, with a sundial, and old varieties of rose, and seats where tired people may inhale the restorative scents of Dr William Turner's 'herbes'.

* The Golden Elder looks decorative in a herb garden; and there is a cut-leaved variety.

pumpkins and heavily scented [illegible] Mint is fine for the kitchen or bedside walk. The sweet fine-and-[illegible] 'Silver' [illegible] Apple Mint [illegible] leaves are [illegible] and provides [illegible] for fruit drinks or [illegible], and Mint [illegible] Costmary may be used in salads, in place of mint and [illegible] with meat and potatoes, or in [illegible] and [illegible].

The [illegible] Compass [illegible] which [illegible] [illegible] among [illegible] Tansy. Miss [illegible] [illegible]. [illegible] [illegible] [illegible] and some [illegible] Tansy, and Bergamot makes what Americans call [illegible] Tea [illegible] [illegible] the [illegible] white [illegible] [illegible] Known as the Rose Mallow [illegible], can be used for making a [illegible] which is soothing for sore throats. Elder flowers, too, have [illegible] [illegible] Elder Flower Water [illegible] works wonders to [illegible]. [illegible] [illegible] Woad, although [illegible] of [illegible] is [illegible] and [illegible] [illegible] of [illegible] plants [illegible] [illegible] [illegible].

[illegible] [illegible] a [illegible] [illegible] herb garden, with a [illegible] [illegible] [illegible] and [illegible]. [illegible] may [illegible] the [illegible] [illegible] William Turner's [illegible].

[illegible]

SECTION FIVE

Parks and Pleasure Gardens

Hyde Park and its Neighbours

ORIGINALLY part of the manor of Hyde, with arable sectors under the plough, then for centuries a royal chase, Hyde Park today seems at first sight a rather tame stretch of grass and trees, where crowds stroll, run, sit, lie, cuddle, play games, exercise dogs and children, and generally take the air. The boundaries to north and east, now Bayswater Road and Park Lane, are more or less aligned with the Roman *Via Trimobantina* and Watling Street. The latter used to fork, one leg going east to the city by the route of what is now Oxford Street, the other running south on the line of Park Lane, through St James's Park down to the Thames, which was crossed by a ford at Westminster.

This park was never listed as common or waste land. It must have been cleared and cultivated at a very early date. In Domesday Book it is shown as plough and pasture land, with villeins living there. The river formed the southern boundary of the great manor of Eia, which embraced Hyde, Ebury and Neyte. From the Norman Conquest to the Reformation all these lands belonged to the Abbey of Westminster; the first sell-out to royalty occurred in 1531–2, when Abbot Islip exchanged some 100 acres between Charing Cross and St James's Palace, and meadows between St James's and Westminster, with Henry VIII. Soon after that deal the Abbot expired in his manor house of Neyte. Five years later, at the Dissolution, the monks of Westminster were required to give up the rest of their manor.

From his palace Henry could indulge in his favourite pastime, the hunt, across Hyde and St James's to Marylebone and up as far north as Hampstead without hindrance. Hyde was 'emparked', 'empayled', and a herd of deer installed; there was now jealous preservation of sporting rights. Queen Elizabeth also enjoyed the chase. Sometimes she joined in herself; on other occasions she watched from a 'princelye stande' or pavilion, and later regaled the assembly in the grand banqueting house. Royal party and guests entered the park by the old lodge, which stood at the spot we know as Hyde Park Corner. Inside its gates the park would have looked much as unspoilt quarters of the New Forest do now. No high buildings, no incongruous structures marred rural vistas through the trees.

Even the distant pile of the Abbey lacked its conspicuous towers, for these were not completed until 1714.

During the troublous times of Charles I and the Commonwealth these acres of parkland took on a warlike aspect, with trenches dug and fortifications built by citizens of both sexes. Samuel Butler's description of these efforts in *Hudibras* suggests the French Revolution. But there was no guillotine in London, and the monarchy did not go out of office for long, despite the machinations of Roundheads who lay in wait in the deepest thickets to intercept the king's messengers. Fairfax at the head of Parliamentary troops marched through Hyde Park in 1647 to meet the Mayor and Sheriffs of the city, and two years later the parks were declared to be Commonwealth property and open to the public. This state of affairs did not last for more than three years. Hyde Park was then put up to auction in three lots. To the north was a wooded stretch, to the west a section of mainly pasture land, and the third lot contained the lodge, banqueting house, and the ring where races were held.

The new owners levied a toll, as Evelyn recorded: 'Went to take the aire in Hide Park, when every coach was made to pay a shilling, and every horse sixpence, by the sordid fellow who had purchas'd it of the State, as they were call'd.' Cromwell used to take exercise by galloping round the ring, watched by large crowds. The ring was a railed-in enclosure encircled by a wide roadway. It was described at the time as 'a ring railed in, round wch a gravel way, yt would admitt of twelve if not more rowes of coaches, wch the Gentry to take the aire and see each other Comes and drives round and round; one row going contrary to each other affords a pleaseing diversion.' Pleasure seekers who gathered to drive round, or to watch races, occasionally met other excitements. One thrilling day a well-known highwayman, for a wager, rode into the ring and robbed a coach in full view of the crowds. Hotly pursued, he made his escape by taking sanctuary in St James's, wherein only a traitor could be apprehended. He got away with about £100, and exclaimed afterwards that it was the most dearly earned in all his life.

With the Restoration, fashionable people once more thronged the park, to the exclusion of poorer citizens, who for the most part saw only the trees above palings, forming a background to the gibbet at Tyburn. But they were the inarticulate, mostly illiterate majority. Historians of the future will have books and tape-recordings made by every section of the community. We have only the upper crust to rely upon for news of the centuries before free education and the 'mass media' gave opportunity for self-expression to everyone alike.

One very prolific source of information in the seventeenth century was, of course, Samuel Pepys. His *Diary* contains many a reference to Hyde Park. An entry describes how, having no coach of his own, he took his wife and a friend in a hackney, and they not in smart clothes, so he felt 'ashamed to go into the tour' (Ring) 'but went around the Park, and so with pleasure home'. At last he acquired the grandeur of a coach, varnished many times to 'make it more and more yellow'. On May Day 1669 his wife made herself 'extraordinary fine with her flowered tabby gown . . . laced exceeding pretty; and she would have me put on my fine suit'. The manes and tails of their horses were also dressed up, 'tied with red ribbons, and the standards gilt with varnish, and green reins, that people did mightily look upon us; the truth is, I did not see any coach more pretty than ours, all that day'. They met some friends and took them to the lodge for syllabub and other things, which cost Pepys 12s., 'and pretty merry' for it. This lodge was also known as 'Cheesecake House', 'Cake House' or (after its proprietor) 'Price's Lodge'. It stood near the Ring and was a picturesque white cottage with latticed casements and gabled roof. A little stream ran in front of it, crossed by a plank bridge.

The park had some more serious uses at times. Soldiers camped here during the Great Plague, and many a duel was fought at a secluded spot gruesomely called the Field of Blood. A famous encounter which took place in 1712 ended in the death of both adversaries, Lord Mohun and the Duke of Hamilton. One of the last duels recorded in London was actually fought elsewhere, but the quarrel which led up to it took place in Hyde Park. The gentlemen concerned were exercising their dogs, which got into a fight. Their masters then exchanged such abusive language that the matter had to be settled by a duel. One of the men was killed, and the other had to face a trial for manslaughter. He was acquitted.

Fear of a Jacobite rebellion in 1715 turned Hyde Park into an armed camp, and at the time of the Gordon Riots (1780) six regiments of militia were stationed here. After the Restoration in 1666, one James Hamilton was appointed Keeper of the Park, and the site of his house and garden is still commemorated by Hamilton Place. He was allowed to enclose fifty-five acres of the park to make an apple orchard, and in return for this favour had to keep the king supplied with cider. A wall was now built to make a safe preserve, and the park again stocked with deer. That wall lasted until 1726, when it was rebuilt, to be replaced by iron railings a century later. The deer were gradually restricted to smaller parcels of land, but still hunted in the eighteenth century. In 1704 a hundred brace of the finest coloured deer were transferred to St James's Park from Hampton Court. The last royal hunt is believed to have taken place in 1768. By 1840 all the deer had gone.

For a long time the roads through Hyde Park were primitive tracks, preyed upon by highwaymen and unsafe in the dark for lumbering coaches. The Duke of Grafton and his coachman were injured when, on a bad night, the coach went off the track and overturned in 'a deep and large pit'. After his purchase of Kensington Palace from the Earl of Nottingham, William III took this matter in hand, and a fine new approach road was made through the park, wide enough for several coaches abreast and lit by 150 lanthorns on each side. Celia Fiennes described it in her diary about 1695:

> 'Ye whole length of this parke there is a high Causey of a good breadth, 3 Coaches may pass, and on each side are Rowes of posts on which are glasses—Cases for Lamps wch are Lighted in ye Evening and appeares very fine as well as safe for ye passenger. This is only a private roade ye King had wch reaches to Kensington, where for aire our Great King Wm. bought a house and fitted it for a Retirement with pretty gardens.'

King William's road did not last forever. This *Route du Roi*, which gave its name—after a fashion—to our Rotten Row, became in the eighteenth century 'the King's Old Road', and George II made 'the King's New Road' to the south of it. The old road fell into disrepair before the new one was usable, so that Lord Hervey in 1736 wrote disgustedly of 'a great impassable gulf of mud' between London and Kensington Palace. Horace Walpole was robbed in 1749, and stunned by a near-miss from the thief's pistol. We can hardly imagine what road travel was like before the nineteenth and twentieth century inventions of tar macadam and concrete surfaces; yet it is clear that, if we had to endure anything approaching such conditions now, the driving of cars would be so impeded as to reduce the fatal accident rate to negligible proportions. It is not easy to determine the precise point at which what we call progress ceases to enhance the quality of human life; but every time there are gruesome pile-ups in fog on the new motorways I am inclined to opt for a slow coach in the mud.

Roads were often planted with trees on either side to form avenues, but records of road making are usually to be found with far less difficulty than precise accounts of tree planting. Three exceptional trees appear in every essay on Hyde Park; they stood on the site chosen for Paxton's construction of

40. St James's Park

41. Rotten Row

42. Queen Mary's Rose Garden, Regent's Park

43. Royal Naval College, Greenwich

44. Old Spanish Chestnuts, Greenwich Park

45. Title page, catalogue of the Society of Gardeners, 1730

iron and glass known as the Crystal Palace, when this was first erected in the park for the Great Exhibition of 1851. It was stipulated that the trio of great elms was not to be disturbed or mutilated, so the huge glasshouse was built around and over them. After the Prince Consort's death, when the site had been selected for the Albert Memorial, an avenue of elm and plane trees was planted to lead up to the shrine. Sir Gilbert Scott intended his concept to suggest a medieval reliquary or shrine on a gigantic scale.

Alicia Amherst lists 570 varieties of trees and shrubs planted in Hyde Park and Kensington Gardens, of which a score (mostly conifers) had disappeared by the time she made her study in 1906–7. In Webster's *Trees of London*, published in 1920, the author mentions upwards of 220 distinct species of trees grown in these two parks alone. Mr Miles Hadfield, in a lecture to the Metropolitan Public Gardens Association's Tree Conference in 1965, remarked that there were probably more now, for in 1920 we had not got all the Japanese and Chinese trees cultivated today. 'It gives you an idea of the immense variety of trees that seem to thrive in London.'*

Two names famous in French horticulture, those of André and Gabriel Mollet, were also familiar to the English, for they became gardeners to Charles II. When that monarch put in hand his ambitious alterations to St James's Park, the Mollets laid out and planted a number of new avenues. Unhappily the acacias, which they used freely, did not stand up to wind, and their brittle boughs were soon mutilated. The plans for these transformations have disappeared, and it is not certain whether the great Le Notre really had anything to do with them, although his name is often mentioned. By 1666 John Rose had succeeded to the post of Keeper of St James's Garden. The Dutch painter Danckaerts produced a picture, which has often been reproduced, entitled *Rose, the Royal Gardener, presenting the first pine-apple grown in England to Charles II.* The trouble about this portrait is that there is no record of pine-apples being ripened in England until after the king's death, and Horace Walpole is thought to have invented the title. Such little conceits indulged in by great men make the lot of a future student difficult. It is a charming picture, but not sufficiently authenticated to be worth using here.

Whatever his faults and extravagances may have been, Charles II had a genuine passion for gardening and managed to inspire similar enthusiasm in many of his subjects; not entirely a new fashion, because Aubrey's opinion, that 'in the time of Charles II gardening was much improved and became common'

* *The London Gardener* (1965).

might really have been dated from earlier in the seventeenth century, when in fact Cromwell was a power. Sir Thomas Fairfax, the Parliamentarian General, had a splendid garden in Yorkshire, where Andrew Marvell came as tutor to young Miss Fairfax. Perhaps it was here that he found his 'green shade' and 'green thought'. Other military gardeners of Cromwell's army were Colonel John Hutchinson and General Lambert. In May 1652 the latter bought for £7,000 the Manor of Wimbledon, whose gardens had already been remodelled by Queen Henrietta Maria, her gardener being none other than Tradescant the Younger. In a Parliamentary survey of Wimbledon made in 1649, this 'parcel of the possessions of Henrietta Maria, relict and late Queen of Charles Stuart', contained 'one fair tree, called the Irish Arbutis [*sic*] standing in the middle of the said Kitchen Garden, very lovely to look upon, worth £1–10–0'. A poetic item to come across in an inventory. Lambert shared the current preoccupation with the culture of tulips, known as 'tulipomania', and his portrait appears on the eight of hearts in a pack of satirical playing cards of the time, inscribed *Lambert Kt. of ye Golden Tulip.*

Charles II was fond of many other things besides gardening, including water-fowl and other birds—winged kinds and what the younger generation know as *birds* today. The marshy lands of St James's had ever been populated by duck, and the monarch had their waterways improved. A canal was cut across the middle, with a decoy up at the end near the present Foreign Office. Birdcage Walk still exists, but the rows of aviaries which gave it the name have gone long since. Charles often took the air in St James's and was seen feeding his ducks. The large collection of waterfowl is a perpetual attraction to the public in this park, and the pelicans, ducks and geese are the only feature that Charles would find familiar today. Little attention was given to them after the king's death, until in 1841 the Prince Consort became Patron of the Ornithological Society, which had a cottage built on Duck Island for a Bird-keeper.

On 9 February 1665 Evelyn wrote of the creatures in St James's:

> 'I saw various animals, and examined the throat of the *Onocrotylus*, or pelican, a fowl between a stork and a swan; a melancholy water-fowl, brought from Astracan by the Russian Ambassador; it was diverting to see how he would toss up and turn a flat fish, plaice, or flounder, to get it right into his gullet at its lower beak, which, being filmy, stretches to a prodigious wideness when it devours a great fish. Here was also a small water-fowl, not bigger than a moorhen, that went almost quite erect, like the penguin of America; it would eat as much fish as its whole body

weighed; I never saw so insatiable a devourer, yet the body did not appear to swell the bigger. The Solan geese here are also great devourers, and are said soon to exhaust all the fish in a pond. Here was a curious sort of poultry not much exceeding the size of a tame pigeon, with legs so short as their crops seemed to touch the earth; a milk-white raven; a stork, which was a rarity at this season, seeing he was loose, and could fly loftily; two Balearian cranes, one of which having had one of his legs broken and cut off above the knee, had a wooden or boxen leg and thigh, with a joint so accurately made that the creature could walk and use it as well as if it had been natural; it was made by a soldier.

'The park was at this time stored with numerous flocks of several sorts of ordinary and extraordinary wild fowl, breeding about the Decoy, which for being so near a great city, and among such a concourse of soldiers and people, is a singular and diverting thing. There were also deer of several countries, white; spotted like leopards; antelopes, an elk, red deer, roebucks, stags, Guinea goats, Arabian sheep, etc. There were withy-pots, or nests, for the wild fowl to lay their eggs in, a little above the surface of the water.'

So bird-watching and the provision of nest-boxes were popular three hundred years ago. Duck-nesting baskets are still obtainable at a nursery in Wiltshire.

Cows used to be pastured in the central parks, and grazing was let to milkwomen, who sold milk over towards Whitehall. They paid half a crown a week for the right to keep cattle in the park; after 1772 the dues were raised to three shillings. Cows were tied to posts and milked, their product being sold at a penny the mug. Long after the genuine use of this pasture for herds had ceased, a few cows were kept at stalls. When the Mall was altered the beasts were finally removed, despite a newspaper campaign to retain them as survivals of long established custom. That was in 1905.

The game of *paille-maille*, an old French pastime, became popular in England in the seventeenth century, and Charles II was supposed to be a brilliant performer. It was first played in James I's time on the north of the street named after it, Pall Mall. Later a new ground was laid out, parallel to the old one, now known as The Mall. The game seems to have been a forerunner of croquet, played with ball and mallet, with hoops along the course and a peg at the end as target. The course, 600 yards long, was levelled and coated with fine crushed shells. Later, in 1712, Henry Wise undertook to sweep it and shell it with crushed cockle-shells for the sum of £50 a year. Charles must have spent a great deal of time in St James's Park, feeding his waterfowl, watching other creatures, playing *paille-maille*, dallying with Nell Gwyn—who had a garden alongside the park—and exercising and sometimes losing his pet dogs. Descriptions were circulated in the *Gazette*: 'Lost, a dogg of His Majestie's, full of blew spots, with a white cross on his forehead about the bigness of a tumbler'.

The Mall for over a hundred years was a popular place of assembly, used by the rich and fashionable and by those who came to look at the show. Through the reigns of Queen Anne, George I and George II everyone congregated there in the forenoon and after they had dined. Often young and lovely girls were jostled by the ruder class of citizen, and on one such occasion a beautiful Miss Gunning fainted and had to be carried home in a sedan chair. Apparently people were not much deterred by the weather. A Frenchman in 1765 remarked on the way Londoners disregarded fog and rain. On the 26 April St James's Park, 'incessantly covered with fogs, smoke and rain, that scarce left a possibility of distinguishing objects at a distance of four steps, was filled with walkers, who were an object of musing and admiration to me during the whole day'. There were wrestling matches, races and wagers, diversions of many kinds. On the Horse Guards Parade corporal punishment was administered to soldier miscreants in full view of the strolling public.

Only royalty or their favourites were allowed to drive through the park. In Queen Anne's day this privilege was restricted to 'coaches bearing the royal arms, and those of the Duke of Buckingham and the Earl of Bradford', while Henry Wise, the royal gardener, was the sole horseman with the Queen's permission to ride in St James's Park. Pedestrians were forbidden to wear pattens, or to walk on the grass, or to 'carry any sort of burthens'. They were not to enter the wilderness or the plantation where the deer lay, or to disturb fillies, colts or wildfowl. Nobody was to dry linen in the park, or attempt to sell any wares, and beggars and dogs were prohibited. Restrictions on the use of carriages lasted right up into the memory of older folk in my youth. A notice board stating that Members of Parliament during session might drive through the park was not removed until 1887, and Constitution Hill did not become a public highway until 1889.

Towards the last decade of the eighteenth century The Mall ceased to be used as a parade, and the Green Park came into favour instead. The promenaders were described as greatly changed, for the nobility and gentry had been succeeded by 'well-to-do tradesmen and citizens'. One elderly gentleman in 1817 wrote of tears starting to his eyes as he recalled the enchanting assemblage of beauty, rank and fashion which used to display itself in the centre Mall. 'Here could be seen, in one moving mass, extending the whole length of the Mall, 5,000 of the most lovely women in this country, all splendidly attired, and accompanied by as many well-dressed men. What a change a few years have wrought . . .' Of course elderly gentlemen always have said that the women of their youth were more attractive than those of today.

The Green Park had been favoured as far back as 1730 by Queen Caroline, who had a walk made parallel with the backs of houses in Arlington Street—the 'Queen's Walk'; but not quite where the present one is to be found. A pavilion, the 'Queen's Library', was erected in the park, where the royal ladies would go after their exercise. Following the peace of Aix-la-Chapelle another, much larger pavilion, in form like a Doric temple, was set up near the wall dividing the Green Park from St James's. Here a grand display of fireworks was arranged, preceded by an overture specially composed for the occasion by Mr Handel. Unhappily fire broke out, destroying the pavilion, injuring a number of people, and all the fireworks went up in smoke before they could be used in the way intended.

Changes had affected The Mall since its heyday as a resort of rank and fashion. The splendid gardens of St James's Palace, which had formerly run along the northern side as far as Whitehall, had been cut up and some of the land used for other purposes, including Carlton House, which was built in 1709 on part of it. This mansion had its own garden laid out by Kent some twenty years afterwards. Between The Mall and the garden wall of St James's Palace ran a green pathway, overarched by trees, known as 'Duke Humphrey's Walk'. The origin of that name is curious, for it began in old St Paul's, where a monument to Humphrey, Duke of Gloucester, in the centre aisle was for long in use as a gathering ground for idlers and malcontents. After this venue had been destroyed in the Great Fire, similar groups of underdogs took to passing their time in the walk beside The Mall, which Londoners then named 'Duke Humphrey's Walk' to maintain the tradition; this name lasted for at least a century.

When George III bought Buckingham House, then an old red-brick mansion, he had the wall between the Green Park and St James's replaced by railings. By this time the canal made for Charles II had been allowed to fall into disrepair, and the whole park was in a shabby unkempt state. The naturalistic ideas of Lancelot ('Capability') Brown became the rage all over England, and his appointment as royal gardener in 1761 set the seal on his success. Wholesale destruction of straight canals, avenues, terraces, parterres occurred, and everything formal in the design of gardens and parks was swept away. It is claimed that Brown was personally responsible for the complete transformation of 150 great gardens and estates, as well as having a major influence on the alteration of countless others.

The 'naturally' curved ornamental water in Hyde Park, the Serpentine, had been engineered before Brown's time, when Queen Caroline had a collection of small ponds and marshy places thrown into one twisting lake by John Bridgeman, who succeeded Wise as royal gardener in 1728. The change from straight canal to curving artificial naturalness in St James's Park came into being at a much later date, under W. T. Aiton's direction in the reign of George IV; a work involving tremendous destruction of avenues of fine old elm trees. The water was permanently bridged over at this time.

The straight canal of Charles II was used to display the first skates of modern type ever seen in London. In earlier times a kind of ice-shoe made from bone had been used at Moorfields. Evelyn and Pepys both record the new type of edge-skate in the year 1662. Two years later Pepys wrote with disapproval of the Duke of York skating on broken and dangerous ice: 'He would go slide upon his scates, which I did not like, but he slides very well.'

Early in the nineteenth century the innovation of gas lamps to light the Park caused excitement and some criticism, for the custom of locking up the gates every night was instituted at the same time. Some wag pinned the following lines of doggerel to the trunk of a tree:

The trees in the Park
Are illumined with gas,
But after it's dark
No creature can pass.

Ye sensible wights
Who govern our fates,
Extinguish your lights,
Or open your gates.

The last major change made to St James's and The Mall occurred when the Queen Victoria Memorial was erected in front of Buckingham Palace. Alicia Amherst has described it in a style redolent of the period:

'Yet once more has St James's Park been subjected to renovation. The work, which is a memorial to our late beloved Queen Victoria, is not yet completed, so its description must be imperfect. The design aims at drawing together the several quarters of the Park, towards Buckingham Palace and a central group of statuary. The Mall is now the scene of ceaseless traffic [this was written in 1906–7] and the sauntering pedestrian is a thing of the past. A wide road runs at right angles across the Green Park, and so once again more closely associates the Upper with the Lower St James's Park. Probably the greatest praise of the alterations would be to say that Le Notre would have approved of them. They seem to complete the design in a fitting manner, but they banish once and for all time the semi-rural character which for so many centuries clung to the Park.

'The design includes a series of formal parterres which are filled with bedding-out plants raised in Hyde Park. In the summer of 1906 they were planted with scarlet geraniums with an edging of grasses and foliage and a few golden privets, and on hot July days there were many people ready to pronounce the arrangement as extremely bad taste. It seemed a reversion to the days when a startling mass of colour was the only effect aimed at. As they appeared all through the mild October days, when a soft foggy light enveloped the world, and the trees looked dark and dreary, with their leaves, devoid of autumn tints, still struggling to hold on, the vivid colouring of the beds gave a very different impression. The charm of the warm red tone against the cold blue mists must have given a sensation of pleasure to any one sensitive to such contrasts. The Park in spring has nothing of the stiff, early Victorian gardening left. Under the trees crocuses raise their dainty heads, as cheerily as from out of Alpine snows, and the slopes of grass spangled with a "host of golden daffodils" are a delight to all beholders.'*

At the time there were 1,270 square yards of flower bed round the Victoria Memorial.

This same author gives figures for the cost of maintaining certain London Parks, including Hyde, St James's and the Green Parks, which she quotes as £69,269 in 1907–8. That sum includes £12,153 for police and park-keepers. I have tried without success to obtain comparable figures for 1970–1 or the previous year. Today things are aggregated; there are 'no figures available to indicate the running costs of individual parks, and since many benefit from the

* *London Parks and Gardens* (1907).

use of mobile equipment and staff this would be extremely difficult', says the G.L.C. Parks Department; while the Department of the Environment, which is responsible for the Royal Parks, seems unable to answer private inquiries. It has been said that what is now the G.L.C.'s Victoria Park, 217 acres to the south of Hackney Marsh, had a staff of 107 and cost £12,099 yearly to maintain in the first decade of this century. *Estimated* expenditure for 1971 on this park amounted to £154,000, not counting £11,000 for a new bowls pavilion. The acreage is unchanged, but the permanent staff has been reduced to 62. Public expenditure is an absorbing subject, and I regret that efforts made to discover more details have proved abortive. According to Richard Church, the cost of removing *litter* from this group of Royal Parks amounted to £14,000 a year at the time of writing his handbook.*

Alicia Amherst says that the high cost of maintaining the central group of Royal Parks, as compared with her figures for Victoria Park, is partially accounted for by the expense of police patrols in the former. Hyde Park had a police bill for £8,782 in 1907–8. For some reason this park is still controlled by the Metropolitan Police, while order is maintained in the others by uniformed park-keepers. Beneath the Quadriga at the Wellington Arch, a number of policeman are stationed, and patrols with dogs are in operation at night.

The setting up of a Lido in Hyde Park in 1930, the invention of George Lansbury, then First Commissioner of Works, turned the Serpentine into a bathing place from 6 a.m. to dusk for all sections of the public. Up to that time, bathing had been restricted to men, who could take their plunge only at an early hour of the day when few people were about. This innovation, which caused a stir when first mooted, has long been taken for granted, as is Epstein's bas-relief of Rima in the bird sanctuary, a memorial to W. H. Hudson. For some time this sculpture attracted the attention of vandals with cans of paint. Today it is unnoticeably orthodox, even tame, by comparison with vast constructions made from junk-shop materials, with which we are now familiar.

It is a short walk from Rima to Rennie's bridge, by which the pedestrian may cross into Kensington Gardens. Although the physical boundary is not sharply defined (many people do not even know that it runs from Alexandra Gate, over the bridge, along Buck Hill Walk to Victoria Gate), the atmosphere of Kensington Gardens still has a relaxed quality, some slight remnant of the palace grounds about it, in particular the lovely Flower Walk; while the abundance of bird life makes this a sanctuary in fact if not in name.

* *The Royal Parks of London* (1956).

Near the northern end of the Broad Walk is a children's playground, with swings given by J. M. Barrie. The famous statue of his best-loved creation, Peter Pan, stands on the western side of the Long Water, a continuation of the Serpentine. What would London be like without these parks, these trees, these flower-beds, stretches of grass and ornamental water?

A horrific film in the style of Hitchcock's *The Birds* could be developed from this idea, which has occasionally afflicted me in dreams. High-rise buildings, traffic-jammed roads, overpasses and underpasses and elevated railways smother every inch of the Green Park, St James's, Hyde Park and Kensington Gardens. Not a tree, not a flower, not a blade of grass, no birds to be seen or heard, nothing but man-made constructions, noise and stench. Only the Albert Memorial remains to bring nostalgic thoughts of the beauty that once formed its background. And Albert has been painted bright red. Let psychologists make what they like of this nightmare. Terrible while it lasts, it serves to produce immense pleasure and thankfulness when I next arrive at the Marble Arch or The Mall and perceive this great and lovely tract of 'gardener's London' still blessedly green and growing.

Regent's Park

THE history of this Royal Park is as long as those of Hyde Park or St James's, but for most of the time it was in use as agricultural and sporting land, being turned into a public recreation park in the nineteenth century. Originally part of the manor of Tybourne, it later became Mary le Bourne (Marylebone), the brook or burn being the Tyburn. As Crown property it was at various times leased out by the Sovereign. Cromwell sold it, with many other royal estates, but it reverted at the Restoration. Meantime it had been 'disparked', and the timber felled. The price paid for it was £13,215, which included £130 for the deer and £1,774 for timber. In addition to the trees sold, nearly 3,000 were earmarked for use in naval shipbuilding.

In 1793, when the Duke of Portland held a lease of the land, the Surveyor-General was approached by the Duke's architect with plans for improving the whole area. For fifty years streets and squares had been multiplying between Oxford Street and Marylebone. When the brothers Adam designed Portland Place in 1772 the street ended where No. 8 stood; beyond that were the buttercup meadows of Marylebone. At the time the acreage (roughly 543) was split between three farms of about 290, 135 and 120 acres. We are not told what became of the farmers; but the development went ahead, largely to designs submitted by Nash. The 8¾ miles of the Regent's Canal linking Paddington and Limehouse, constructed between 1812 and 1820, formed part of the same scheme, in which the Prince Regent took a great interest. It was therefore obvious that canal and park must bear his name.

The park suffers from a lack of vistas to take the eye beyond its confines, for it is mostly rather level ground, and the surrounding houses enclose it. Perhaps my feeling of being restricted is less troublesome to those not blessed with long sight. The buildings were all designed in the classical manner, and have at different periods been praised and condemned as taste in architecture changed. At least they have the merit of being designed for this site, and in one style, which is an advance upon the higgledy-piggledy eruption of houses in a variety of shapes and sizes with which city developers have so often burdened future generations. One special feature of the scheme was a number of separate villas standing in their own grounds. St Dunstan's Villa, St Katherine's Lodge, St John's Lodge, and South Villa were all set in charming gardens. The last named belonged to a Mr George Bishop, who erected an observatory there in 1837.

Soon there were no fewer than three Societies using sections of the parkland for their particular needs. First, the Toxophilite Society, which developed from the sixteenth-century Fraternitye or Gylde of Saint George, a body that used to loose its arrows in Spital Fields. At the time of the Spanish Armada the Honourable Artillery Company was formed, with a Company of Archers which continued for 200 years; there was also a society called the Finsbury Archers. When this came to an end in 1781 the Toxophilite Society, shooting on Blackheath, took up the tradition. As George IV was a member, it soon became the Royal Toxophilite Society, a title still very much alive. The ground in Regent's Park was taken into use in 1834.

The Royal Botanical Society of London, founded in 1839, at once acquired a share of the park for its garden, leasing a little over eighteen acres of the Inner Circle from the Commissioners of Woods and Forests. Robert Marnock, who won an open competition for laying out the garden, was also the Society's first curator. For thirty years its secretary was one J. de C. Sowerby, eldest son of the author of Sowerby's *English Botany*. William Robinson, author of that long-lived book *The English Flower Garden*, was employed for three years by Marnock when he first arrived in London from his Irish home. After ninety years of active life, the Royal Botanical Society declined, overshadowed by the combined work of the Royal Horticultural Society and the Royal Botanical Gardens at Kew. The lease of its land in Regent's Park was finally terminated in 1931. A tentative proposal that the Royal Horticultural Society should take over this garden was never endorsed.

The third Society to be associated with Regent's Park is by far the best known: the Zoological Society, which maintains the ever-popular London 'Zoo'. This should really have been put before the others, having settled in the park as early as 1826, at the instigation of Sir Thomas Raffles, president at that time. I must here declare my non-interest in zoos, derived from a mixture of principle and personal failure to enjoy myself in them. I dislike caged birds, even little birds in big aviaries, and feel positively shamefaced when the brooding eye of lion or tiger catches mine through the interstices of iron bars. The sight of an elephant restores my morale a little, for this great beast has an age-old partnership with man, and appears to have developed an elephantine philosophy so weighty that no indignity has power to disturb it. But all things in this world are relative, and if one *has* to have zoos the London example may be looked at with pride as having reached the top class.

Not only does it provide a five-star standard of amenity within the cages, but the horticulture and silviculture surrounding those apartments are superb. The 'Three Island Pond' would grace the grounds of a palace, with its great sweeping branches of willow caressing the water, its silver birches, catalpas, deciduous cypress and *Populus lasiocarpa*. The animated collection of waterfowl bustling to and fro through the leafy curtains might keep the visitor anchored beside their harbour for hours. Of course the birds on this pond are free, which adds greatly to the charm of the spectacle. Near at hand, around the unusual war memorial—a little white tower—are more fine trees, including a horse chestnut in whose deep shade stand benches, highly popular with steamed-up adults on a hot day. The sea-lions have a weeping willow overhanging the back of their pool, and an elegant semicircle of petunias bordering the front, while the dingoes are hedged in by low conifers.

Finding the restaurant full, I bought some portable food at a cafeteria and thought how pleasant it was to sit out of doors on the large forecourt, beneath another group of shade trees. Various squawks, quacks, caws, croaks, barks and roars mingled with the cooing of wild wood-pigeons to make a sustained accompaniment more congenial to my ears than canned 'pop' music and clatter within places designed for eating. But there were sparrows. No wonder it was said of old that not one sparrow fell to the ground without the Creator having knowledge of it. The London sparrow has no intention of being forgotten, and is the most persistent and importunate beggar in the world. Salvaging about half the sandwiches purchased for my own consumption, I bolted them and made off before being bullied into buying another lot for my tormentors.

Outside the zoo enclosure many more good trees may be found, including a manna ash and a magnificent weeping elm, which must be a very old resident. The large formal round pond with its memorial fountain has a striking background of Lombardy poplars arranged in a crescent shape. It is not common to find this tree so happily married to an English landscape. The large mixed borders make excellent use of *Rosa hugonis* and *R. californica plena* in enormous mounded bushes, demonstrating what one had long known in theory, that these roses need far more space to look their best than can be spared by most amateur gardeners. Foliage of golden Robinia and *Atriplex halimus*, a soft grey-blue, makes a splendid foil to flowering plants. I noticed with pleasure near the pool and cascade masses of double Soapwort, and that curiously docile 'Obedient Plant' whose blossoms will submit to being rotated by hand around the stem as if mounted on roller bearings or castors. An old-fashioned plant, now back in favour for its autumn flowering; but the trick that used to please our childhood seems to have been largely forgotten.

Mention Regent's Park, and most people will exclaim 'Queen Mary's Rose Garden': quite rightly, for it merits attention. One curious fact about the average Londoner came to my notice when I toured the London parks. As a people they are traditionally negligent about visiting the great national monuments which cluster like grapes for the Cockney hand to pluck. The Tower of London, St Paul's Cathedral, Westminster Abbey, the British Museum, the National Gallery, and the endless corridors of South Kensington, resound to every accent except that of the native—certainly it would be hard for a blindfolded visitor to guess whether he stood in Sydney, Auckland, Washington or Paris, unless one of the custodians gave the game away with his voice bred in Battersea or Stoke Newington. But the parks are a different story. Here the Londoners flock, while visitors from other lands are very seldom seen. Time and again I sat on benches beside local residents who seemed pleased to hold forth on the merits of their favourite park. A woman in the Rose Garden told me that she hardly ever missed coming to it at week-ends all the year round. She could not imagine life in London without refreshment supplied here by the charm of growing plants and trees.

It occurred to me that her obvious involvement with this great rose garden may have had deeper significance than she herself was aware of; but I did not wish to disturb the relaxed mood of the moment by probing. Had I inquired if she, like Saint Perpetua, ever heard the roses singing, she might have turned away from me aghast, fearful that her park pick-up was suffering from mental upset. Yet mystics in all ages have believed themselves to be in some sort of communication with plants. The Royal Horticultural Society has a rare copy of Ralph Austen's *The Spiritual Use of an Orchard*, in which this seventeenth-century gardener describes a 'dialogue between the husbandman and fruit trees'. I have met someone in Scotland—young and alert, not a drug addict or a drop-out—who is convinced that plants transfer their thoughts to her mind, although these messages need clothing in her words before other people can share them. This subject was the motive for some experiments in 1970, when a Mr Vogel of California wired a plant to a device he had made for measuring very small electrical impulses. Both man and plant, explained the inventor, emit minute electrical fields. When that generated by a person cuts into that of a plant, a response is produced which his device is able to measure. When he thought fiercely about destroying the plant, it reacted to his thought and the reaction showed up on the instrument. Even the sight of a 'Sensitive Plant' in Ceylon, which flinched away at my lightest touch, caused some expansion of my horizon. Perhaps the so-called 'green fingers' of the plant lover may be instruments transferring impulses helpful to growth, and possibly the hands of a 'healer' carry even greater electrical charges, with power to ease human suffering.

If we have power over plants, it is plain that they have more influence upon us than we usually give them credit for, and that not only by their effect on the air we breathe. In her recent book *The Rose-Garden Game*, Eithne Wilkins goes back to the very beginnings of garden history and legend:

> 'A garden is a secret place, at once closed, alive with a concentration of natural forces, and open to the sky. Its secrecy may result from its being a small place between high walls, or from its being surrounded by forest, or simply from its being difficult to find. One archetypal garden is the secret herb-garden of Artemis, twin sister of Apollo the Physician, who as the moon lady tends the magico-medicinal plants; to this correspond the Roman vegetable garden, the monkish herb-garden, and our own kitchen-garden, all of which are laid out in severe rectangles and serve a practical purpose. Another archetype is the apple-orchard, which even now still has vestiges of its archaic sacred character. Another is the clearing, the grove, a place graven out of the forest, which is the *nemeton* of the ancient Celts, a place of light and shade, a place apart, a temple of air. Here, and not among the nightshades and lettuce, nor among the golden apples, lies the origin of the pleasure-garden. For the pleasure-garden, which is not necessarily filled with flowers, is always a place apart, an enclosure where one may commune in air, light, and "delicious solitude"—until, as Marvell wrote, the contemplative mind transcends the correspondences with which it is filled, and annihilates "all that's made / To a green thought in a green shade".'

The beginnings of the rose-garden cannot be dated with certainty, but Homer extolled the rose, and as the plant is said to have thrived in Gaul when the Romans built villas there, they may have planted rose-gardens and perhaps have brought the fashion to England. There were roses in monastic gardens here in early Norman times, and when William Rufus visited young Matilda at the convent of Romsey he pretended that the roses and herbs of the nun's garden were the chief cause of his interest.

Before the Reformation our great churches had gardens attached to them, and priests were crowned with flowers, not only in processions but also when officiating at the altar. At the installation in 1405 of Bishop Roger de Walden, the Canons of St Paul's walked in procession wearing garlands of red roses. It is on record that a medieval Dean of St Paul's leased some land in Essex to a kinswoman for a yearly rent of 'a chaplet of roses at the Feast of St John the Baptist'. Another document in the Record Office states that the monks of Charterhouse, concerned at the neglected condition of a strip of land outside their walls, approached the Abbot of Westminster for permission to cultivate it. This was granted, in consideration of the 'rendering of a red rose and the saying of a Mass annually for the sacred King and Confessor, Edward'. The roses of York and Lancaster were united in the Tudor rose of heraldry, and in medieval France a whole way of life was founded upon the cult of the rose; while the rosary was originally a string of fragrant beads made from pounded rose-petals. This vast subject requires a volume to itself, and that Eithne Wilkins has compiled for readers who wish to study it in detail.

Returning to my chance companion on the park seat, she who felt so grateful for the benefits conferred on her by this place, I shall never know whether the fact that Marvell's garden was a round one, and that Queen Mary's Rose Garden is also circular—'a *rond-point* in a place of recreation'—would have any significance to a practical business woman in London, or whether to her, as to Gertrude Stein, a rose is a rose is a rose. At all events, these modern roses in their hundredfold array are splendid when in full bloom, and their setting is carefully planned, with pergolas and little arbours for seats where each individual (or two or three together) may feel set apart from passers-by, in a spot as nearly private as any in a public park could well be. The appreciative lady told me that her daughter worked as an air hostess, flying all over the world. No doubt many stay-at-homes envy the young woman her varied and exciting career. On reflection, I would rather opt for her mother's life, steadily centred upon a garden of roses in the heart of London.

Greenwich Park

Among all the London Parks, Greenwich Park, as Alicia Amherst truly observed in 1907 in *London Parks and Gardens*, is one of the most fascinating, both for material features and historic interest. To these old-established charms have been added in our own time some unusually imaginative and successful plantings by the Superintendent, Mr John Murray. The exercise of royal prerogative in the fifteenth century led to its present title: for this land had been part of the Common of Blackheath until (*circa* 1432) Henry VI gave his uncle, Humphrey, Duke of Gloucester, licence to enclose 200 acres of wood and heath 'to make a park in Greenwich'. So, in a period of over four centuries, the story slowly turned full circle—or nearly so—from common land to privileged enclosure, restored in Victorian times to public use with free access in daylight hours. But it is still classified as a 'Royal Park', enjoying the same status as Hyde Park, St James's, Kensington Gardens and Regent's Park.

Long before royalty annexed it, this place, situated on elevated ground above the Thames and close to the important highway of Watling Street, had attracted the attention of Roman settlers, who built a villa here. Coins dating from 35 B.C. to A.D. 423 have been unearthed on the site, together with pottery, bronzes, tessellated paving and scraps of painted plaster. The building appears to have been destroyed by fire. No doubt the inhabitants made themselves a garden round about it, with box hedging, trees, fountains, and a terrace where they could sit watching the Roman galleys being rowed to and fro on the river below. Roman gave place to Dane, a band of whom in 1012 slew Alphege, Archbishop of Canterbury, at the spot (it is said) where the parish church of Greenwich now stands. Pilgrims on their way to pray at the shrine of another murdered Archbishop, Thomas à Becket, crossed over Blackheath, as Chaucer, who worked as a clerk near by in the Palace of Eltham, described in his *Canterbury Tales*.

There was a royal residence of some sort at Greenwich before Duke Humphrey enclosed his park, but the Palace of Placentia, so favoured by the Tudors, dates from the time when the king's uncle was licensed to enclose and to erect inside the fence 'towers of stone and lime'. Its guardian castle stood upon the hill, and was demolished after 250 years to make way for Wren's elegant Observatory, designed for Charles II in 1675, which still stands. In those early days of astronomy Flamsteed had a well, 100 feet deep, sunk to form a kind of underground telescope, at the bottom of which he lay on his back to observe the night sky. This primitive arrangement is not open for public inspection—if indeed it still exists—but the Observatory is now in use as a Museum of Astronomy and Navigation, forming a section of the Maritime Museum. John Harrison's first satisfactory marine chronometer, used by Captain Cook on his second voyage to Australia in 1772, may be seen here, still working perfectly. To celebrate Britain's return to Greenwich Mean Time on Sunday, 31 October 1971, after a three-year experiment with Continental time, the Old Royal Observatory restored the Airy transit circle, built in 1851. It was designed by Sir George Airy, Astronomer Royal from 1835–81, and is a telescope for measuring the time when a star passes across the meridian. This instrument is now on view in the Museum.

Henry VIII and Elizabeth I were often at their Palace of Placentia, and both monarchs enjoyed pageants, jousts, tournaments and revels in the park of Greenwich. The Venetian Ambassador, early in the turbulent reign of Henry, recorded his impressions of a May Day frolic, when Queen Catherine of Aragon, richly attired, rode out into the woodland with twenty-five damsels on white palfreys. In a leafy glade they found the king, guarded by men dressed like trees, in green livery and carrying boughs in their hands. There was an open-air banquet, with music, and afterwards the procession returned to Placentia under the admiring gaze of some 25,000 subjects. The ancient oak in whose shade Henry VIII is said to have danced with Catherine's successor, Anne Boleyn, still exists, a decayed shell of moribund wood, bound up and supported by a great mass of ivy. This tree is sometimes known as 'Queen Elizabeth's Oak', for the Virgin Queen is popularly supposed to have taken refreshments in its hollow centre. At one time that chamber was fitted with a door and used as a gaol for felons who broke the rules of Greenwich Park.

Anne Boleyn made her last dreadful journey up river to the Tower from Greenwich, and Queen Elizabeth was rowed to and fro from London by state barge on many happier occasions. On one of these Sir Walter Raleigh is said to have spread his cloak on the ground before Her Majesty, to preserve her feet from the mud of Greenwich. In her day, it was customary to build 'banqueting houses' in the park, using fir poles decked with birch boughs and flowers of many kinds, the floors strewn with rushes and herbs. Many a brilliant pageant was given under the trees, while Shakespeare himself acted inside the palace on occasion. The queen's death ended a long series of gay and sumptuous entertainments at Greenwich.

James I replaced the original wooden fencing by a massive brick wall, twelve feet high and two miles round, much of which survives today. He also began the building known as 'Queen's House', which Inigo Jones completed for Henrietta Maria. During the Commonwealth, Parliament actually planned to sell Greenwich Park; for some reason the deal was never completed. So valuable was the fine herd of deer, that soldiers were placed on watch in the castle to preserve them from thieves. After that, no significant changes took place until Charles II decided to remodel the park and have the old Placentia Palace removed to make way for a splendid building designed by Webb, nephew and pupil of Inigo Jones. Only one wing of this was completed in his reign, and of it Pepys shrewdly commented in 1664: 'At Greenwich I observed the foundation laying of a very great house for the King, which will cost a great deal of money'. Within five years the money gave out, and Charles lost interest in his grandiose scheme for building a 'King's House' at Greenwich.

He was more successful in the project for remodelling the park, which was carried through in his time. It was not, it seems, supervised in person by the famous Le Notre of Versailles—although his name appears as its architect in many books—but, more probably, engineered by his friend and disciple Mollet acting on sketches devised by Le Notre. According to an official guide to Greenwich Palace, the trees in this scheme were planted by William Boreham of Greenwich in 1661–2; but John Evelyn, whose house and garden of Sayes Court, Deptford, were situated close at hand, says that elms were put in a little later, in 1664, together with 'the avenues and all the fine Sweet Chestnuts'.

A series of terraces, cut on the contour lines along the riverward slope of the castle hill, formed an important part of the new lay-out; their outlines may still be traced in places below the Observatory, with Wolfe's statue towering up on the topmost one. Each terrace is said to have been forty yards wide, and on either side plantations were made of fir trees brought from Scotland by General Monk. Some of these survived for about two hundred years; but London smoke told on them with more deadly effect than on deciduous trees of similar age, which were able to renew their foliage completely every year. The last dead stumps of the conifers were removed at the close of the nineteenth century. Mr Murray told me that there had recently been some suggestion of remaking the terraces. So far, the difficulty of providing adequate funds for this large undertaking has held up the project.

46. 'The Citizen at Vauxhall,' 1755

The Royal Observatory, which so impressively crowns the hill where the castle used to stand, is the original Wren structure, built for Charles II 'in order to the finding out of the longitude of places for perfecting navigation and astronomy'. The first Astronomer Royal, Flamsteed, did not achieve this end, and it was left to John Harrison, working on his own account, to invent a chronometer which did perfect the means of obtaining longitude. Halley, famous for the comet which bears his name, succeeded Flamsteed. The Observatory came under the direction of the Admiralty early in the nineteenth century. It had long been celebrated for the measurement of time, and in 1880 Greenwich Mean Time was made the legal time of Great Britain. As far back as the eighteenth century the Prime Meridian was recognized here as passing through the building: a fact that was granted international status under an agreement made in Washington in 1884. In 1833 the Observatory provided the first public time signal, when a large time ball was 'dropped every day from the top of a pole on the Eastern Turret at the moment of 1 o'c. p.m. mean solar time', as an Admiralty Order expressed it. This time signal is still in daily use, although the Observatory itself has been moved to Herstmonceux Castle in Sussex, where the clearer atmosphere provides better conditions for astronomical work.

There can be no doubt that the appearance and interest of this early Observatory add greatly to the attraction of Greenwich Park. It is not a superimposed construction, but an intrinsic part of the landscaped terrain, pleasantly attended by trees without being crowded or hidden from view. Standing just below it, the visitor has a remarkable prospect down the grassy slope, over the magnificent buildings of Greenwich Palace and the tall masts of the *Cutty Sark*, in dry dock for ever beside the winding Thames. First a royal residence, then a hospital for aged seamen, now the Royal Naval College, the Palace of Greenwich had many architects, including Sir Christopher Wren, Vanbrugh and Hawksmoor. Nobody seems able to date the various sections of the present building with certainty, for the work proceeded by fits and starts over many years. The last blocks to be completed, Queen Anne and Queen Mary, were the work of Colin Campbell and Thomas Ripley. The chapel, destroyed by fire in 1779, was rebuilt by Stuart and opened ten years after the blaze. The palace resembles many a Gothic cathedral in that it shows the work of numerous hands over a long period. The resultant mixture forms a splendid and impressive architectural group; one of the finest to be seen anywhere in England. A crypt, or cellar, in the Queen Anne block is the only remnant above ground of the Tudor

Palace of Placentia; although, when drains are dug or foundations inspected, traces of enormously thick walls appear.*

When in 1869 this great pile fell into disuse as a hospital for seamen, the Admiralty acquired it for use as a naval college at an annual rent of £100. Before long the Royal Naval College expanded to include young officers of the Engineering Branch, Medical School and Royal School of Naval Architecture. It is a curious fact that, whereas it is customary to name and honour the architects of important (and lesser) buildings, this maritime nation with age-old pride in its navy seldom knows anything about the designers of those great ships whose names are familiar to all. People seem to imagine that a ship grows spontaneously from the keel upwards, like a tree, without plan or master-hand in control. My own father having been a member of the Royal Corps of Naval Constructors, a form of service which in 1915 cost him his life, I have reason to know that ship design in general, and warship design in particular, is an exacting scientific profession. In his case, the fine buildings of Greenwich College (as he called it), the splendid old trees and undulating parkland of its setting, were a major source of pleasure throughout his student years. There must be few among the vast number of naval personnel passing through this naval university who fail to find inspiration in such noble precincts.

No visitor to Britain should omit to spend a few hours in this historic and lovely place. The most rewarding way to make the journey is by river launch from Westminster Pier. Nothing could be simpler than to dive beneath the road, or continue by subway from the District and Circle railway station of Westminster, and walk straight on board a waiting boat. In the summer season a frequent service is maintained, and there is only a short pause before the launch glides off downstream towards Greenwich. At the time of writing the return fare for the trip was a modest 60p., in a comfortable vessel with restaurant and toilet facilities, and awnings to protect passengers from rain or scorching sun. The Thames in these sheltered reaches may be pledged not to upset the most squeamish traveller, and the varied sights of London as seen from the water are as unexpected as they are fascinating.

Not only are there uninterrupted views of the many bridges, of St Paul's Cathedral and the Tower of London, but also close-ups of Captain Scott's ship, HMS *Discovery*, and other naval vessels moored alongside the embankment below the Temple Gardens. In the Pool of London the cruiser *Belfast* now lies at her permanent anchorage. The launch passes innumerable wharves and ware-

* Considerable remains of fifteenth-century building were excavated in 1972.

houses, including the little dock called Queenhithe Quay, whose history goes back to Alfred the Great; historic buildings like Vintner's Hall, with its 500-year-old courtroom; the Cherry Gardens Pier, now no longer in a cherry orchard; one of the famous old riverside taverns, 'The Angel'. On the north bank at Wapping, headquarters of the Thames Division of the Metropolitan Police, a fleet of their businesslike black patrol launches is moored at the pier, and near by stands another old inn, the 'Prospect of Whitby'.

The river is full of shipping: strings of barges, heavy with cargoes, being shifted at speed by powerful tugs; other flotillas of blunt-nosed barges at anchor; passenger and police launches; private sailing dinghies and catamarans; speedboats, hydrofoils and, beyond London Bridge, the larger sea-going vessels which cannot come higher upstream than the Pool. The names of the barges range over a wide field, with some bizarre effects. *Tredegar*, *Arnheim*, *Kilsyth* and *India* make strangely assorted companions, and simple *Joan* and *Betsy* look somewhat shy of the *Duke of York*. The fishy ones—*Sturgeon*, *Coby* and the rest—reminded me of those flat coal trucks on the railway. How did *they* acquire such labels as *Dogfish*, *Catfish*, *Pilchard* and *Herring*? For that matter, how did a large modern vessel seen unloading at a Thames wharf come by the imposing name of *Dame Caroline Haslett*? Is she the only Dame afloat?

Soon the masts and spars of another, more picturesque ship are sighted—those of the *Cutty Sark*. As the boat enters Greenwich Reach, with the old naval victualling yard of Deptford to starboard, one remembers that older wooden walls were once built there, including some of the ships that defeated the Spanish Armada. Off Deptford in the *Golden Hind* Francis Drake received his knighthood. On the opposite bank another famous vessel is commemorated by a sign indicating that here Brunel's *Great Eastern* was built. The *Cutty Sark*, a clipper ship of 963 tons gross, built at Dumbarton by Scott and Linton and launched in 1869, was designed for the great yearly tea race from China, carrying the new season's crop. She cost £16,150—less than half the price paid in 1966 for Sir Francis Chichester's midget *Gypsy Moth IV*, which now lies in a permanent berth beneath the tall ship. The *Cutty Sark* was opened to the public by HM Queen Elizabeth II in June 1957, and *Gypsy Moth* was laid up in her adjacent dry dock a few years ago. Both ships now form a valuable adjunct to the National Maritime Museum in the Queen's House, which since 1934 has owned this fine example of early Palladian architecture. It was opened to the public in its present role in 1937.

The traveller by river launch disembarks at Greenwich Pier within sight of the Royal Naval College, and it is but a short walk uphill to the lower park entrance. The first planted area to catch the eye is a 'scented garden', which has been skilfully designed to fill an odd-shaped piece of ground. This garden was originally planned some three years ago as a fragrant haven for the special use of blind residents. Mr Murray, the Superintendent, who is never too grandly official to mix with inhabitants and elicit local opinion, discovered the interesting and significant fact that blind users of his park were not in need of a special section. One regular visitor put it in this way: he found so many enjoyable scents in the whole area of parkland, such as mown grass, dried grass, fresh spring foliage and dead autumn leaves, bulb and summer flower, winter bonfire, peat, compost and newly turned earth, that endless pleasure was already provided for the sensitive awareness of those without sight. Even the many varieties of tree could be distinguished by their individual scents. So the Scented Garden was made; but for all with a nose for fragrance, and not for the blind alone.

This is the only public park in which I have seen many kinds of old-fashioned herb and foliage plants used in groups in ordinary beds as well as in the fragrant garden. In the long flower border along the ha-ha behind the Queen's House there are good clumps of Miss Jekyll's favourite fern-leaved tansy, southernwood and wormwood, lady's mantle, *Crambe cordifolia*, gold-variegated lemon balm, sedums and herbaceous geraniums, together with Tradescantia 'Purple Dome'. This fine border must be among the largest in the kingdom, worthy to rank with that at Buckingham Palace, which measures 520 feet by 24 feet. The famous Evelyn terraces at Albury are situated on two levels, and the grass walks each measure a quarter of a mile, the two together making up the half mile so often mentioned when these grand walks are described in print. The accompanying flower borders are divided by a pool and steps and are not continuous. At a rough pacing I judged each section to measure slightly more than the 520 feet of Buckingham Palace, but the width of the Albury beds is only a little over half that of the Queen's grand herbaceous border. Mr Murray gives the measurements at Greenwich as 936 feet long and 12 feet wide.

Higher up the slope, there is a long avenue of ancient Spanish chestnuts linking Macartney House with Blackheath Avenue and the Observatory. All the Spanish chestnuts in Greenwich Park were topped at some period: an event of which no record can be traced. Whether these splendid veterans will survive much longer no one can foretell, but already provision has been made for their demise by planting young ones of the same species in lines parallel to the original avenues. It will be centuries before the newcomers develop the character of their seniors, many of which reminded me of elephants, having bark whose colour and texture suggested hide, and great knobs of basal root shaped like elephantine feet. It was a surprise to see strong tufts of new growth bristling up from these toes at ground level.

Around the lake in springtime a remarkable display is given by mature cherry trees, magnolias, ginkgo and *Acer palmatum*. The colour combination of the flowers with innumerable shades of green in the foliage of a wide variety of trees, seen to best advantage when looking north over the water through arches of golden weeping willow, is unforgettable.

Backed by the old brick wall of Macartney House, once the home of General Wolfe, is an enormous delphinium border, all of 150 feet long, interplanted with weeping cotoneaster; behind it, *Hydrangea petiolaris* and pyracantha clothe the wall. This looks like something one would expect to find within the precincts of such a stately house and garden as Wolfe's, not outside in a public park. Such incidents give great delight to the visitor, and deserve to be recorded. Higher up still, also on the western perimeter of the park, is the Ranger's House—once the home of Lord Chesterfield. This splendid early eighteenth-century mansion became Crown property in 1815 and was made the official residence of the Ranger of Greenwich Park. The Duchess of Brunswick, Lord Haddo (later Earl of Aberdeen), the Duke of Connaught and Sir Garnet Wolseley were all holders of that office. In 1900 the London County Council acquired the premises, laid out a bowling green in the grounds, and, many years afterwards, raised funds to restore the house to its present condition. It is now in use for concerts and exhibitions, and as a summer tea-room, and is well worth a visit. In front there is a fine display of roses in ninety beds.

Another tea-house, the charming little octagonal building to the east of the Observatory, is one of the mysteries of the place, for no record of its construction has ever come to light. At the top of the park are the impressive Blackheath Gates, opening to Charlton Way, with a wide stretch of common land beyond. At the gate Mr Murray has his office, opposite his house, and beyond that lie the flower gardens and deer enclosure. Only twenty-four now remain of the original herd that roamed free when the park was first enclosed, beasts considered so valuable that an armed guard was placed on them during the Commonwealth. About seventy men are regularly employed as gardeners here, and there are also the very smart Royal Parks Police, with green shoulder flashes. Sometimes one sees a beautiful Alsatian dog with its handler.

Mr Murray told me of the very marked improvement in trees and smaller plants under his care resulting from the Smoke Abatement Act; but when in 1969–70 a shortage of smokeless fuel led to some slackening of control, the deleterious effect of smoke was soon noticed, many different varieties being affected by the increased pollution of the atmosphere. Few among us, the ordinary consumers of household fuel, would have thought that what the Coal Board does—or fails to do—today may quickly react upon the well-being of a great park.

On the journey downstream to Greenwich my attention was held by bridges, boats, historic buildings and old wharves. Although the expedition was planned in connection with this study of horticulture and silviculture, the real purpose became overlaid by the excitement of river travel. It was otherwise on the return voyage. Now the sights which had been found so stimulating on the outward trip took second place, and the astonishing wealth of trees to be seen lining the great river (where embankments and wharves are of prime importance), made a deep impression—even though a few passing sighs were raised for the departed Cherry Gardens. These gave their name to the pier, whose watchmen inform the operators on Tower Bridge of the approach of large ships desirous of entering The Pool.

The north bank is particularly rich in parks and trees. First one sees Millwall Park and Island Gardens on the Isle of Dogs opposite Greenwich, a place reputedly used by Charles II to keep his hounds when he lived at the palace. Perhaps their baying disturbed him less when the Thames flowed between palace and kennels. Next come the Sir John McDougall Gardens in West Ferry Road, followed by the green churchyard of St Anne's Limehouse, whose tall white church tower used to provide a valuable aid to navigation for ships under sail. At Shadwell there is the King Edward Memorial Park, then the Wapping Gardens and Waterside Gardens, and after those are left astern the plane trees softening the grimness of Traitor's Gate and the Tower of London come into view. Most of the way from the Tower to Westminster Pier is lined with trees, and upriver past the Houses of Parliament too.

On the south bank, from Blackfriars Bridge along to the South Bank Gardens by County Hall, there are nearly continuous plantings. The very wide paved area of the South Bank Gardens contains a double row of young plane trees, each set in a grating some 2½ feet square, which apparently allows them sufficient moisture. In an age when many people fear that the reckless felling of big trees by farmers, who seldom make any effort to replant, will lead to a prairie-style countryside in Britain, it seems that if the trend is not checked, London may by the year 2,000 possess more trees to the acre than some agricultural districts.

Pleasure Gardens of the Eighteenth Century

THE fashion for spending one's leisure hours in Pleasure Gardens, at its height in the eighteenth century, had a beginning in the previous one; for Pepys in June 1665 records that on the hottest day he 'took water to the Spring Gardens in Fox-Hall, and there stayed pleasantly walking, spending but sixpence till nine at night'. The Spring Gardens which he enjoyed formed the nucleus, some seventy years later, of the popular Vauxhall Pleasure Gardens; by the middle of the eighteenth century the most elaborate entertainments, concerts, suppers and brightly lit walks had been developed there, an enterprise far removed from the simple gardens known to Pepys. Some other famous Pleasure Gardens of the eighteenth century had their beginnings in humble places dating from the period between the Restoration and the reign of Queen Anne.

Even before the Restoration, the Mulberry Garden near the present Buckingham Palace, which became a place of public recreation and refreshment after the failure of James I to develop the silkworm industry, and the Spring Gardens at Charing Cross, were in existence. In the early days no charge was made for admission to these places. The strollers spent money on light fare, such as cheese-cake and syllabub, bottled ale and pies, and the owners had to extract profit from sales. There is very little mention of music in those years, certainly nothing on the grand scale of Vauxhall and Ranelagh, but Pepys does refer to the sound of 'harp, fiddle and jew's trump' in the Spring Gardens. In this unpredictable island climate of ours, it is a wonder that so much profit and pleasure was obtained from amusements of a basically outdoor nature. Could the rapid rise in popularity of the Pleasure Garden, and its fairly sudden decline after the end of the eighteenth century, have been geared to a run of pleasant summers followed by a series of wet and cold ones?

This seems unlikely, but evidence in the form of weather records is almost non-existent. We know that rainfall in London is low compared with some other areas in Britain, and that the temperature in a city is usually a few degrees above that of the surrounding country, yet Londoners today are apt to arrange for alternative accommodation under cover when planning garden parties and fêtes. As to the business of forecasting weather, this is a modern occupation. Aristotle wrote on the subject in his *Meteorologica*, after which it made practically no progress for about 2,000 years. The Royal Meteorological Society of London was founded in 1850, and the Board of Trade became involved in weather recording and forecasting five years later. An interesting sidelight on this matter is the story of how Napoleon, infuriated by storm damage to his fleet in the Black Sea in the mid-eighteen-fifties, charged Leverrier with the task of organizing a system of weather forecasts. Of course modern telecommunications have given the work of the weathermen a tremendous boost, but as yet few care to rely wholly upon their predictions.

Pleasure Gardens may be broadly divided into places of outdoor recreation (with, in later years, 'Long Rooms' added for dancing, card-playing and the like), and those combining amusement with the serious business of 'taking the waters' at medicinal springs. Of the latter, Islington Spa, in use from 1684–1840, and Sadler's Wells (opened in 1683) were chalybeate waters, said to rival those of Tunbridge Wells. The Wells of Sadler were lost sight of early in the eighteenth century, and thereafter 'Sadler's Wells' became a place of indoor entertainment, with rope-dancing and pantomime enacted in the little theatre which preceded the Sadler's Wells Theatre of modern times. Other well-known London spas were the Wells of Bagnigge (1759–1841), the London Spa (opened in 1685), and St Chad's and St Pancras's Wells (*circa* 1697). At Old Street there were the 'Peerless Pools'; but these waters were apparently intended for bathers and anglers, and not for imbibing.

Further west, the bowling green and garden of Marylebone developed in 1728 into the famous Marylebone Gardens, while to the south, at Brompton, there was a novel combination of pleasure garden and nursery, known as the Florida or Cromwell's Gardens, where patrons could in season gather their own refreshment in the shape of ripe cherries, strawberries and other fruits. There were wells and a spring garden in Lambeth, and in St George's Fields the mineral springs of the notorious Dog and Duck, while Bermondsey Spa had, from about 1784, a grand walk illuminated by coloured lamps, and maintained its own poet and composer, an organist named Jonas Blewitt.

The spas and wells were usually day resorts, open early in the morning for breakfasts, dancing and music. Their waters were believed by many people to be infallible remedies for the politely-named 'rising of the vapours' (wind), scorbutic humours, and inveterate cancers. All these ills could, it was said, be cured by drinking copious draughts of rather unpalatable liquids on the spot; for those who could not manage personal visits to the spring, supplies might be purchased in bottles, authenticated by the seal of the proprietor. Islington Spa became a place of high fashion in 1733 when Princess Amelia took a course of treatment there, and the Dog and Duck (in the days of its respectability) was recommended to Mrs Thrale by no less a personage than Dr Johnson. Many astounding cures by 'purging and chalybeate' were solemnly attested here by a physician. At a later date it became a tea-garden and dancing saloon, and was in the end suppressed as the 'haunt of riff-raff and scum of the town'. There were also numerous small tea-gardens, set on the fringes of London and possessed of rural charm, such as Highbury Barn, Canonbury House, Hornsey and its Wood, Copenhagen House amid hayfields, where the season usually lasted from May to August or September.

The celebrated Vauxhall Gardens were in existence for about two hundred years (1661–1859), a longer life than any of the others enjoyed. To a great extent they avoided a difficulty which frequenters of some pleasure gardens had to face—the risk of attack by footpads and ruffians; for access to Vauxhall was by water, and less vulnerable to these parasites.* Advertisements for Ranelagh and Marylebone show that regular services of escorts were provided, at least on gala occasions, while one special night at Sadler's Wells was fixed when there would be 'moonlight, and horse-patrols to see patrons safely home to the City and West End'. Inside the gardens the pleasure-seekers at Vauxhall were no less subjected to the attentions of pickpockets than elsewhere, although watchmen and vigilantes did their best to exclude undesirable characters and keep order. At the opening 'Ridotto' at Vauxhall in 1732 a masquerader had fifty guineas stolen from his pocket. In this instance a watchman caught the thief.

From the year 1752 all Pleasure Gardens had to be licensed, and in order to obtain these licences it became of vital importance for the proprietors to ensure orderly conduct. A *Guide to Vauxhall* issued in the following year solemnly stated that 'even Bishops have been seen in this Recess without injuring their character'. The gardens occupied about twelve acres, laid out in gravel walks between rows of fine trees. The Grand, or Great, Walk, about 900 feet in length, passed between large elms to a boundary fence, beyond which were hayfields. At the eastern end there was at first a gilded statue of Aurora; later on, a Gothic obelisk replaced it. The Grand Cross-Walk intersected

* There was no coach-road to Vauxhall until about 1760.

the Avenue, and on the far side ran the Lovers' or Druids' Walk, well wooded, where nightingales, thrushes and blackbirds nested and sang.

On an eminence between pine trees and cypresses a statue of the poet Milton was placed, with illumination by lamps at night. Amid what were called 'musical bushes', a concealed band used to perform 'fairy music'. It did not last very long, for our climate produced a 'natural damp which was found prejudicial to the instruments'. (Presumably they were of more importance than the unfortunate musicians and their rheumatic hazards.)

Illuminations were always a great attraction at Vauxhall. Early engravings show many lamps arranged above archways and attached to trees by means of iron brackets all along the main walks. These lamps were oil-burning, and 'so contrived that illumination appeared to be instantaneous'. In the supper-boxes patrons were able to purchase wax tapers for additional light, but the general brightness of these gardens was a constant topic and source of admiration. Apparently the oil-lamps in London streets were given to sooting up their globes soon after they had been lit, which dimmed the light and gave an effect of murk, while those at Vauxhall stayed clear. From a contemporary description it appears that they were constructed with holes at the bottom, through which hung 'a little flax, used to communicate flame more suddenly to the wick'.* The second, unplanned use of the hole—that of admitting more air—served to prevent fouling of the globe. How exactly the attendants managed to set off so many lamps simultaneously is difficult to understand, especially as some were mounted on arches high overhead.

The supper boxes and orchestra were hung with coloured lights, and on gala nights festoons stretched between the trees. There were about 1,000 lamps in the 1750s, and that number was doubled before the end of the century.

At a masquerade in 1787 lamps were arranged in crowns, circles, and stars; on the recovery of the king in 1789 the words LONG LIVE THE KING were spelt out in lights. At an earlier date *England's Gazetteer* had reported that these gardens were laid out in so grand a taste that they were frequented by most of the nobility and gentry, and often honoured by members of the royal family, who were entertained with 'sweet song of a number of nightingales in concert with the best band of musick in England'. Here, says the *Gazetteer*, are fine pavilions and shady groves, and the most delightful walks, illuminated by above 1,000 lamps, 'so disposed that they all take fire together, almost as quick as lightning, and dart such a sudden blaze as is perfectly surprising'.

* J. G. Southworth, *Vauxhall Gardens* (1941).

Although favoured with the visits of royalty, Vauxhall was by no means a 'select' place of entertainment, but used by all sections of the London public. On 6 July 1737 Frederick, Prince of Wales, with ladies and gentlemen of his household, came by river from Kew, attended by musicians. He walked in the Grove, 'commanded several airs', and retired after taking supper in the Great Room. At this period a 'New Vauxhall' fan, painted with views of the walks, orchestra, grand pavilion and organ, was on sale to the ladies. (I have not been able to find and photograph an example of this product.) Regular patrons could obtain silver 'season tickets', some of which were designed by Hogarth, and are now to be seen in the British Museum. Even in those days prices rose. A season ticket cost one guinea in 1737, £1.5s. in 1742, and two guineas in 1748. Among the 'curious statues' to be seen was one 'of Mr Handel as Orpheus, in marble by Roubillac'.

The principal structure, a rotunda, was entered through a colonnade. Some seventy feet in diameter, it was elegantly fitted, and contained an orchestra where the band performed on wet evenings. This edifice was nicknamed 'The Umbrella', from the shape of its roof. In the latter part of the eighteenth century there was a tendency to stay later, until 11 pm or even 2 am, and by 1772 a good deal of rowdyism was reported. In *Evelina* young Braughton considers 'last night at Vauxhall' to have been the best of any—'there is always a riot—folks run about—then there's such a squealing a squalling and then all the lamps are broke . . . the women run skimper-scamper'. Evelina, the heroine of this novel by Fanny Burney (published in 1778) was herself surrounded by impudent young men in the Dark Walk. In 1782 the Prince of Wales and this party were recognized when the music stopped, and being surrounded, crushed, and pursued, had to beat a hasty retreat.

In spite of this rudery, the title of *Royal* Gardens was adopted in 1822 with the approval of George IV. By that time 20,000 lamps were in use, and constant variety shows were being staged, including a replica of the Battle of Waterloo with 1,000 horse and foot soldiers. At the eastern end of the garden a wood and canvas erection was installed, known as the 'Hermit's Cave', wherein 'all in transparency the hermit pursued his studies with the aid of a lamp, blazing fire and brightly shining moon'. By this time the Cross Walk had been lit with the fashionable Chinese lanterns and renamed the 'Chinese Walk'. In 1846 gas lamps took the place of oil, and the musicians ceased to wear cocked hats. In spite of all its novel attractions, the place declined in popularity, and in July 1859 the last show was held. Builders moved in, and before the end of the century the Pleasure Gardens were entirely built upon. Gye Street perpetuates the name of one of the proprietors.

The Marylebone (or 'Marybone' Gardens), which existed in a simple form from about 1650, were expanded and developed as a pleasure garden in the style of Vauxhall to attract people from the surrounding area. The grounds reached as far east as Harley Street, and when enlarged to the fullest extent in 1753 occupied eight acres, two-thirds the size of Vauxhall Gardens. The land belonged originally to the old Manor of Marylebone. As a garden and bowling green it was known in the seventeenth century, and described by Pepys in 1668 as having 'gravel walks and bowling green forming a central square. Walks double-set with quickset hedges, full grown and indented like town walls. On the outside a brick wall with fruit trees'. He considered this 'Marrowbone' a very pretty place, as no doubt it was. Up to the early years of the eighteenth century, these gardens probably resembled that pictured in a catalogue issued by the Society of Gardeners in 1730.*

The expansion which subsequently took place coincided with enthusiasm built up in England for the type of landscape garden being made all over the country for owners of great houses; Bridgeman, Kent and others revolutionized the art of gardening, in revolt against the stiff Dutch style of William III and the formality of Le Notre. These Pleasure Gardens were laid out, so far as their size and position allowed, in the likeness of royal palace gardens, and displays were contrived to give ordinary people an impression of luxurious surroundings for leisure hours. According to one modern writer, eighteenth-century summers *were* warmer and drier than ours of the twentieth century; but he does not produce much in the way of evidence. Most of the gardens had pavilions and supper booths, and between 1739 and 1749 Marylebone acquired a Great Room for balls and entertainments, wherein an organ was installed. Until 1763 this room was open for breakfasting, and for a concert which began at noon. Admission tickets cost 2/– and 1/– each.

In 1760 a cook named Trusler took charge of the catering, and his daughter's rich seed and plum cake and almond cheese cake took pride of place on the list of refreshments. One of her relatives became a clergyman and later a well-known bookseller. A picture of 1755 shows fashionably dressed promenaders in the Grand Walk. People of substance now had their 'country' houses in Marylebone High Street, and it was customary for such residents to take subscription tickets for balls and concerts held in the Pleasure Gardens.

* See Plate 45.

An old dominie, Dr John Fountayne, would sometimes stroll in from the Manor House School with his friend Mr Handel. The story goes that on one occasion the composer asked his companion what he thought of a piece the band was playing. They sat listening for a little while, and then the worthy doctor proposed that they should move on, saying 'It's not worth listening to—very poor stuff!' 'You are right,' growled Handel. 'It *is* very poor stuff. I thought so myself when I had finished it.' At this period Thomas Lowe, a tenor who had made a name at Vauxhall, rented Marylebone for £170 per annum and put on a series of concerts with the best singers in the town. In 1765 the programme included songs from Boyce's *Solomon*, and a Mrs Vincent sang Handel's *Let the Merry Bells go Round*, accompanied on a novel instrument called a tintinnabula.

It was seldom that a proprietor managed to make money out of these Pleasure Gardens. Lowe soon got into debt, and was followed by Dr Samuel Arnold. Between 1772 and 1774 there were tremendous displays of fireworks, put on by a pyrotechnician named Torre. His masterpiece was called 'The Forge of Vulcan', on which a curtain rose and 'discovered Vulcan and the Cyclops at the forge behind Mount Etna. Fire blazed, and Venus entered with Cupid, begging the others to make arrows for her son. On their assenting, the mountain erupted and a stream of lava poured down its sides'. These fireworks began to annoy neighbouring residents, for they sometimes erupted into private gardens, and protests were made to the authorities, who refused to prohibit the displays.

When all this is added to three evening concerts a week, with Dr Arne conducting catches and glees, Handel's *Acis and Galatea* performed, and much else, there seems to have been plenty of entertainment for every taste; but Arnold, like Lowe, failed to make the place pay. In 1774 a mineral spring was advertised here, as 'Marybone Spa', but even that failed to attract the public in sufficient numbers. Concerts came to an end in 1775, and in 1776 the gardens were closed. Although very well known for a period, Marylebone never achieved the popularity of Vauxhall or the prestige of Ranelagh. A few old trees survived into the nineteenth century at the northern end of Harley Street, and the Victorian Marylebone Music Hall, with a public bar attached, stood on the site of the old Rose of Normandy Tavern, from which there was once an entry to the gardens.

The Gardens of Ranelagh, which survive as a public park near the Royal Hospital in Chelsea, were originally private gardens belonging to the Earl of Ranelagh's house. Some time after the Earl's death in 1712 a Mr Lacy of Drury Lane Theatre drew up plans for turning it into a place of public entertainment, and by 1741 the great Rotunda (at first known as the Amphitheatre) was erected in the grounds. This was opened in 1742 with a grand breakfast, and soon became the vogue. Horace Walpole wrote: 'I have been breakfasting this morning at Ranelagh Garden: they have built an immense amphitheatre with balconies full of little ale-houses. It is in rivalry to Vauxhall and cost above £12,000.' A month later he quoted the cost as £16,000. He gives a detailed picture of the scene:

> 'A vast amphitheatre finely gilt, painted and illuminated; into which everybody that loves eating, drinking, staring or crowding is admitted for twelve pence.'

By 1744 he was going every night to Ranelagh.

> 'Nobody goes anywhere else; everybody goes there. My Lord Chesterfield is so fond of it, that he says he has ordered all his letters to be directed thither . . . The floor is all of beaten princes; you cannot set your foot without treading on a Prince or a Duke of Cumberland.'

Some writers have compared the Rotunda to the Pantheon in Rome. Londoners may rather think of the British Museum Reading Room, which it resembled in size and to some extent in appearance. Not that the Museum has ale-houses in the balcony; some students may wish it had. Nor is the Reading Room lit by 'numerous hanging chandeliers, each with a gilt crown, containing candles in crystal bells'. When all were lit, the effect at Ranelagh's Rotunda was 'very glorious'. There was a good orchestra, and by 1746 an organ, which, in later years, was played by the celebrated Dr Burney.

An ecstatic account of a visit to Ranelagh is put into the mouth of Lydia Milford in Smollett's novel *Humphry Clinker*. 'Ranelagh looks like the enchanted palace of a genie, adorned with the most exquisite performances of painting, carving and gilding . . . crowded with the great, the rich, the gay, the happy and the fair; glittering with cloth of gold and silver, lace, embroidery, and precious stones . . .' The usual charge for admission to all these delights was now half a crown, which included the 'regale' of tea, coffee, and bread and butter. On firework nights the price of entry went up to 3 shillings or more. Tickets costing from half a guinea to two guineas were issued for masquerades.

The evening concerts usually began at 6.30 or 7 pm, and between the acts

47. Vauxhall on a Gala Night. Early 19th-century engraving

48. Silver season ticket by Hogarth, Vauxhall

49. Westminster Abbey, the Little Cloister Garden
50. Roof-top cloister garden, Derry and Toms

51. London amateurs showing their garden to Queen Elizabeth The Queen Mother

52. Metropolitan Police Station garden near Sloane Square

53. All Hallows Wall, London Wall

the assembled company walked in the illuminated gardens to the sound of horns and clarinets. This place was laid out in gravel walks, with rows of elm and yew trees, a formal flower-garden, and a 'beautiful octagon grass-plat'. Lamps were attached to the trees, and at the far end of the main walk there was a Temple of Pan. But this garden was less secluded than Vauxhall, and not designed for the private meetings and flirtations which were carried on at the latter resort.

In 1749 a 'Grand Jubilee Masquerade' was advertised to celebrate the Peace of Aix-la-Chapelle. Horace Walpole said that it was by far the prettiest spectacle he ever saw; nothing in a fairy tale surpassed it.

> 'It began at 3 o'clock; at about 5 people of fashion began to go; when you entered, you found the whole garden filled with masks and spread with tents, which remained all night very commodely. In one quarter was a maypole dressed with garlands, and people danced round it to a tabor and pipe, with rustic music, all masked, as were all the bands of music that were disposed in different parts of the garden; some like huntsmen with French horns; some like peasants, and a troop of harlequins and scaramouches in the little open temple on the mount.
>
> 'On the canal was a sort of gondola adorned with flags and streamers, and filled with music, rowing about . . .
>
> 'The amphitheatre was illuminated, and in the middle was a circular bower, composed of all kinds of firs in tubs, from 20 to 30 feet high; under them, orange trees, with small lamps in each orange, and below them all sorts of the finest auriculas in pots; and festoons of natural flowers hanging from tree to tree. Between the arches, too were firs, and smaller ones in the balconies above. There were booths for tea and wine, gaming-tables, and dancing, and about 2,000 persons. In short, it pleased me more than the finest thing I ever saw.'

By the third quarter of the eighteenth century, garden concerts, firework displays, and the showing of 'transparent pictures' in the grounds had become regular features of the entertainment provided, and a great annual regatta and ball filled the Thames from London Bridge to Millbank with craft. The river banks resembled a vast fair-ground, and at sundown, the races over, a procession of boats moved to Ranelagh with bands playing and flags flying. The huge ball held in a 'Temple of Neptune', erected for the festivities in the gardens, concluded this gala occasion.

After a period of stagnation in the 1790s, the fortunes of Ranelagh had a revival; a spectacle called 'Mount Etna' (that mountain was in everyone's mind because of the great eruption) drew crowds for a little while, and after that some balloon ascents were a nine-days' wonder; but in general the public had suddenly grown weary of this Pleasure Garden, and it had to close in 1803. By 1805 the Rotunda had been demolished. The organ went to Tetbury Church in Gloucestershire, where it was in use until 1863, and the land, after serving as a playground and allotments, became a public park. A historian visiting the site in 1871 found one avenue of trees surviving, with a few of the old lamp-irons attached to their trunks—these had been the 'fire trees' of early advertisements.

The latest London Pleasure Garden is that in Battersea Park. Originally devised as part of the Festival of Britain in 1951, it has been continued as a permanent feature of the park. It is a kind of fair-ground, particularly attractive to children and young people.

SECTION SIX

Smaller Gardens, and the Horticultural Societies

Westminster Abbey, the College Garden

WESTMINSTER ABBEY has one of the oldest gardens in England. That part which is now known as the 'College Garden' was originally the herb garden attached to the monastic infirmary, and when Edward the Confessor finished the building of his great church (which he just lived to see consecrated in 1065,) it was no doubt already surrounded by the usual adjuncts of a monastery, including an enclosure where the Infirmarian gathered his simples for use in treating the sick. One of the most tranquil and secluded places within the precincts today is the Little Cloister, which used to be the infirmary. Approached by a narrow passage well named *The Dark Entry*, this small enclosure, green with ferns and damp mosses, centred upon its stone basin and fountain, suggests something lifted bodily from an ancient legend, so far removed is it in spirit from the traffic of modern London outside.

The monks cultivated more than one garden within the Abbey precincts, and on the far side of the Long Ditch forming the boundary were the Abbot's Garden and Abbey kitchen garden. For centuries the present Dean's Yard was known as 'The Elms', from a fine grove of those elegant trees which graced it. The story goes that when Elizabeth I came to the throne, she sent for Abbot Feckenham (who had been reinstated by Mary), and had to endure a slight delay while the prelate finished planting some elm trees. Among them stood a great oak, which was uprooted by a violent storm in 1791. Dean's Yard was the site of the monastic farm and granaries, as may be seen from a map of sixteenth-century Westminster in the Abbey exhibition. The Long Ditch flowed along what is now Great College Street, outside the wall of the infirmary garden, and so into the Thames. On the way it was used to turn a mill from which Millbank takes its name.

Abbey Orchard Street commemorates another section of the cultivated land, and Osier Street recalls a small island bed which grew osiers in the millstream. This crop, sold to basketmakers who worked in the vicinity, fetched the sum of ten shillings a year. The Infirmarian used to trade in fruit: one John de Mordon obtained nine shillings for his apples in 1362, and ten shillings for apples and pears the following year. Possibly he sold the celebrated 'Warden Pear', that variety being mentioned in Abbey documents as having been grown at Westminster in the fourteenth century. It was first raised in Bedfordshire, by the Cistercians of Warden Abbey, and 'Warden pies' became highly popular. I cannot find any record of that curious fruit the Melicoton, which was a peach grafted upon quince, in cultivation by the monks. Perhaps it came later.

The Cellarer receives mention as being custodian of another large garden, position unspecified. This may have been the *convent garden* familiar to us as 'Covent Garden', and used in our time only for the sale of orchard and garden produce. Another piece of land at Westminster, variously called 'Maudits' or 'Caley's', had been made over to the Abbey in exchange for ground elsewhere by Thomas Maudit, Earl of Warwick, in the thirteenth century. The second name derived from 'Calais', and was given to it at a time when wool staplers from that French port came to live there. Petty France, where Milton had a house, also took its name from French residents. Hereabouts was once a 'coney garth' or rabbit warren, similar to the enclosure at Lincoln's Inn which provided food for Londoners over many centuries. Gardening at Westminster in monastic times must have been greatly affected by frequent flooding of the Thames—an occurrence made less common by the construction of the Embankment.

The College Garden of Westminster Abbey has been for some years in charge of a woman, Mrs Couchman; one of the very few members of the female sex to hold such a responsible position in the horticultural world of London. I remarked to her on the rather impoverished appearance of the soil—sour city stuff—and inquired how often it was given loads of peat, compost, or new supplies of good loam, such as the gardens of Buckingham Palace enjoy. Renewal, it seems, is a serious difficulty here in the Abbey: not so much on account of the cost, although there are enormous demands on available funds, but for the very practical reason that the approaches are all too narrow to admit mechanical transport. There are no really convenient places outside to tip loads, and it is a long way to wheel material from Dean's Yard. Yet, remembering the manner in which other London gardeners have contrived to remove polluted soil and replace it with fresh clean earth, one must hope that a way will be found before long to improve that of the College Garden.

At the far end of the enclosure parts of the original wall may still be seen, with traces of archways in it. These apertures probably allowed access to the mill stream, which filled a fishpond inside the garden. Masses of oyster shells have been unearthed during digging operations in flower beds and when planting trees—a white mulberry is a fairly recent addition. It is well known that larks were classed as game birds in the Middle Ages, and indeed up to the Victorian era, and special little spits were made to roast the tiny carcasses on; but only recently have I discovered that the oyster was known as the 'sea-lark'—possibly because its flavour was thought to resemble the flesh of the bird.

In recent months the College Garden has been thrown open to the public on one afternoon each week. It must look its best when the mature trees of pink Japanese cherry are in full bloom. The gold-splashed *Elaeagnus pungens aureo-maculata* of the hideous name and beautiful foliage flourishes, rather surprisingly, here; also the good old purple spiderwort (*Tradescantia virginiana*), a plant tolerant of smoky conditions, which was first grown in England in the early seventeenth century, just across the river in Lambeth, by John Tradescant. Mrs Couchman pointed out a low wooden building over against the Houses of Parliament, put up for use as an air raid warden's post in the Second World War and now adapted for BBC broadcasts during sessions of Lords and Commons. When the announcer says that a programme will be heard coming from the Westminster studio, this is the place to which he refers. Soon after my visit, listeners to the ten o'clock news from London were told by a reporter on the spot that he could hear the clamour made by Members of Parliament after the vote had been taken which decided Britain's application to join the Common Market. On that night of 28 October 1971, I thought of the little hut alongside the old infirmary garden, and of all the historic occasions the garden had witnessed, heard, or lived through.

The Worshipful Company of Gardeners

IN AN address to the International Conference on Roses in 1958, Lord Nathan, a past Master of the Company, said he thought that the existence of a Gardeners' Company in the City of London might sound incongruous:

> 'Yet in the heart of the Bank of England—in the very centre of the City—is a garden. This is symbolic. The Bank of England has grown from small beginnings into the world's banking house, but commercial grandeur has not been allowed to smother this relic of its past. The garden remains as a treasured reminder to soften the harsher outlines of material success.
>
> 'The City itself also reflects these two aspects of past and present. To some the City represents finance, an international emporium of business. To others it recalls the City of ceremonial, ancient customs, and pageantry. These are two facets of a single organism, and both are essential characteristics which explain the uniqueness of that combination of romance and enterprise which still maintains the City as the chief financial centre of the world. This sense of history, implicit in the City's traditional ceremonial, which gives colour and depth to its day-to-day activities, is an acknowledgement, maybe unconscious, of what the present owes to the past. And among those influences which played their part in the building of the modern City, the guilds or companies occupy a foremost place.
>
> 'The 83 guilds extant today are traditional survivals of a medieval economy. Records show that they existed at least as early as the twelfth century, and there is reason to believe that they developed from religious organizations which had as their object the practical pursuit of religion and worship at a parish church. Within the walls of the ancient City, London was densely populated. To serve the needs of its citizens there were more than a hundred parish churches. The influence of religion in the Middle Ages is difficult for us to understand today. It was the mainspring of existence, and demanded from every man a devotion that pervaded his whole life. Accordingly there grew up around each of the City's churches

parish guilds, or neighbourhood associations, composed of those who worshipped there. In common with other ancient towns, those who followed the various crafts and trades of London tended for convenience to group themselves in particular localities, as the street names of the City still bear witness. (Take for example Wood Street and Bread Street and Ironmonger Lane.) It was natural therefore that the many parish guilds were largely identified with particular trades. In their beginnings, the craft element of the guilds may have been fortuitous, due to this habit of the members of each trade living together in its own quarter of the City.

The urge for mankind to combine in groups with others of similar interests is a natural instinct; but whereas in modern society associations of men have limited functions, the medieval guild embraced every aspect of life. Under the shadow and instruction of their parish church, their members accepted the fraternal responsibility which their religion demanded of them. Surviving ordinances of the early guilds make it clear that, in addition to regular and frequent worship in church, the care of needy members in sickness and poverty, decent burial and masses for the souls of departed brethren were the essence of guild life. A reminder of this powerful force in guild organization is seen today in the predominantly pious note of the companies' mottoes: for instance, the motto of the Gardeners' Company, *In the sweat of thy brows shalt thow eate thy bread.* Apart, however, from these directly religious activities, the association of men with like trade interests led naturally to a mutual organization of their trades. Thus the early guilds came to unite the functions of the modern trade unions, employers' associations, mutual benefit societies and the social club, while all was infused with the spirit of religion.'

Consideration of Lord Nathan's account of the early guilds brings the inescapable question: has the decline of religion, whose powerful influence in the Middle Ages is so 'difficult for us to understand today', resulted in the hiving-off of splinter groups—'employers', 'workers', 'white-collar employees' and so on, to the detriment of society as a whole?

The Gardeners' Company evolved from a guild, first mentioned in City Corporation records as far back as 1345, and it was incorporated by Royal Charter of James I in 1605. This incorporation extended to 'the gardeners of the City of London and within six miles thereof'. In 1607 ordinances for the government of the Company, including a grant of livery, were approved by the Lord Chancellor, and in 1616 a further Charter of James I gave the court powers of search for defective wares within the city and a radius of six miles.

The Company (see p. 191) controlled the 'trade, crafte or misterie of gardening; planting, grafting, setting, sowing, cutting, arboring, rocking, mounting, covering, fencing, and removing of plantes, herbes, seedes, fruites, trees, stocks, setts, and of contryving the conveyances of the same belonging'. It was empowered to search for and destroy any unwholesome or rotten goods in the markets, and nobody could set up as a gardener without its permission. There were special regulations for 'foreigners'—the French and Flemish refugee gardeners who were at times regarded with a certain amount of jealousy. The issue of a warrant by Sir Edward Littleton, Recorder of London, in 1632—a document which instructed the King's Officers in London, Middlesex, Surrey, Kent, and Essex to apprehend any person using the trade of gardening in contempt of the Company Charters—has been commemorated annually since 1908 by a presentation of flowers, fruit and vegetables to the Lord Mayor of London on the anniversary date.

In its early days the Company was preoccupied with the 'trade, craft or misterie of gardening' within a six-mile radius of the city, and with the provision and ordering of markets in London; but by the nineteenth century there was no scope for commercial gardening in the area it governed. It still survives, ranking as 66th in the list of City Livery Companies, its energies now directed into different channels. In late Victorian days several benevolent projects came into being; a scholarship, a pension fund for a retired gardener, and endowment for an orphan were founded, and these continue in augmented form today. In 1905 the Company received a warrant from King Edward VII enabling it to continue to bear its traditional armorial bearings and supporters, duly exemplified by the College of Heralds. It is doubtful whether the motto, *In the sweat of thy brows shalt thow eate thy bread*, applied to the celebration of the 300th anniversary of the first Royal Charter, which took place at the Albion Tavern in Aldersgate on 18 September that same year.

In 1911 Queen Mary was presented with her Coronation bouquet by the Company. Each subsequent year of her life she received a replica of this bouquet on the anniversary date. The Gardeners' Company extended this custom by presenting wedding bouquets to the Lady Elizabeth Bowes-Lyon (now The Queen Mother), to Princess Marina in 1934, to the Duchess of Gloucester in 1935, to Princess Elizabeth (now Queen Elizabeth II) in 1947, to Princess Margaret in 1960, and to the Duchess of Kent in 1961. Alone among modern royal brides, Princess Mary carried no flowers at her wedding. She preferred a prayer book. The Princess had conferred upon her in 1933 the Honorary

Freedom of the Company. This honour was given to her brother, the Prince of Wales (later King Edward VIII) in 1935. Both Queen Elizabeth The Queen Mother and our present Queen receive replicas of their Coronation bouquets each year.

After the First World War the Master and Clerk of the Company visited the stricken market gardens of Belgium, and as a result members raised the sum of £3,000 to assist the Belgian horticultural industry. In the past fifteen years the Court of the Company has paid four official visits to the Ghent *Floralies*, and one visit to France for the International *Floralies*. In 1949 the Company inaugurated a competition for the best City window-box and garden, which continues to attract a large entry. In 1951 two cups were donated to the National Association of Almshouses, for competition among almshouse gardens; and in 1954 the London Teaching Hospitals Gardens Competition was instituted, followed in 1955 by a similar contest to encourage gardens at non-teaching hospitals. The 'Flowers in the City', and competitions for Church gardens, are now being run in conjunction with the Metropolitan Public Gardens Association. It is interesting to see awards being won by representatives of other nations in the city. In 1969, for instance, the Mutual Life Assurance of Australasia won first prize for its window-boxes, and the Union Bank of Switzerland came second. When the City Corporation created the St Paul's Garden in 1951, a suggestion put forward by Lord Nathan (Past Master 1955–6), the Gardeners' Company gave three bronze heads for the fountains.

Window boxes came into fashion as far back as 1603, according to Thomas Fairchild (1667–1729), author of *The City Gardener*, who gardened in Hoxton. He wrote of many plants to be seen in the city: ilex, Spanish broom, guelder rose; syringa and lilac in Soho Square; pears 'about the Barbican'; a vine bearing good grapes in Leicester Fields; figs in Chancery Lane, and lily-of-the-valley 'in a close place at the back of the Guildhall'. This author dealt with the problem of smoke pollution long before it was taken seriously by most people. He left a bequest for a lecture to be delivered annually on Whit Tuesday in St Leonard's Church, Shoreditch. The subjects he set were 'The wonderful works of God in Creation', or 'The certainty of the Resurrection of the Dead, proved by certain changes of the animal and vegetable parts of the Creation'. The lecture nowadays is often delivered in St Giles's, Cripplegate. In 1970 it was given by the Very Reverend Martin Sullivan, Dean of St Paul's, a New Zealander. He took for his text the first subject, applying it to a number of urgent social and moral problems in modern life.

A laurel wreath is still laid by the Master and Clerk of the Gardeners' Company on Fairchild's tomb in Shoreditch. The Company maintains at its own expense an up-to-date library of reference books on all aspects of horticulture. This collection is housed in the Guildhall Library, and is freely available to the public.

Derry and Toms' Roof Garden

THE journey from Westminster to Kensington High Street was quickly made in a Circle train, but the change of mood needed to appreciate a modern roof garden after the ancient precincts of the Abbey seemed likely to take longer. This fear was groundless, for there was nothing brash to be seen, and much that looked far more mellow than could be expected. The reproduction 'Tudor Garden' on this Kensington roof suggests the sixteenth century rather better than the 'Knot Garden' in the shadow of that greatest of all Tudor piles, the Palace of Hampton Court; although the four-centred Tudor arches imported from some demolished stately home cannot be compared with the glories of the old palace as a background. Like the Knot Garden, the Tudor Garden contains many plants of which sixteenth-century gardeners had no knowledge; in regard to the plants used, both reproductions are open to criticism; but on balance I preferred the 'feel' of those courts and alleys in the hanging gardens of Kensington.

The Derry Gardens were projected when designs for a new store first took shape on the architect's drawing board. In 1930 Mr Bernard George, FRIBA, was commissioned to design the structure with the unusual feature of a large roof garden in mind. The soil to cover 1½ acres to a depth of over two feet, added to the weight of masonry required for walls, arches, pergolas, paving and roof restaurant, had all to be supported, and made a material addition to the normal requirements of a department store. There was also the question of waterproofing the floors beneath. This was achieved by having a bitumenized layer under the soil, which has proved highly efficient. It is thought that the soil and vegetation provide sufficient insulation to maintain an even temperature, in which no expansion and contraction occurs to cause cracking of the bitumen.

In his offices in Young Street—once the home of Thackeray—Mr George worked out the scheme in close contact with Mr Trevor Bowen, Director of Derry and Toms, in whose imagination this great garden first took shape. It is the largest in the world to be constructed at a height of over 100 feet above ground level: an achievement to be respected, and a record in which Londoners may take pride. The new store was finished in 1933, and two years later gardening began on the roof. This work took three years, and the cost of turning $1\frac{1}{2}$ acres of roof top into an oasis of trees, shrubs, grass and running water amounted to £25,000. Were such a grandiose scheme to be carried out today, the sum would almost certainly be ten times as great.

When in 1938 the Earl of Athlone opened this unique venture, it was found to comprise not one garden but three, cunningly interlocked to form a harmonious whole. The manner in which a visitor is led gently from one section to another, without awkward divisions or abrupt changes, is a triumph for the landscape architect, Mr Ralph Hancock, who deployed the 'art that conceals art' in his design. He introduced over five hundred varieties of trees and shrubs, and imported special stone from Pennsylvania to house the alpine plants, this material being in his view the best to withstand the atmosphere of London. At that time it had not been purified by any smoke abatement regulations.

The soil is on average about eighteen inches deep, above nearly twelve inches of drainage material. Water used in these gardens is pumped up from three artesian wells below the store. In addition to the ornamental use of water, large amounts are constantly required to offset heavy evaporation due to heat rising from the building, and it is not unusual to see hoses in action even during rainstorms. The Head Gardener, Mr Carter, has a staff of three assistants, and when these gardens close in October they are all kept extra busy with pruning, spraying, bringing tons of peat and compost up by lift, and devising new planting schemes in preparation for reopening in the spring.

Probably the best way to tour the roof gardens is to walk straight ahead from entrance to aviary, round the Spanish Garden with its Moorish pergolas, Court of Fountains, 'convent walls' and campanile, then through a secret arch and along a narrow shaded walk into the Woodland Garden. On a blazing June day the contrast of scene and temperature is unbelievably refreshing. From the hot glowing masses of flowers and a Southern glitter on light walls and paving, one takes a plunge into the greenest of English groves, with meandering stream, waterfall, and shadowed pool where fish glide to and fro, all so suggestive of an estate deep in Sussex or Somerset that momentarily it is hard to credit that the effect is entirely artificial.

There are ducks, which actually nest and bring off their broods, and a posse of flamingos recently imported from Chile. These expensive immigrants, valued at £75 each, have to be dosed with a carotin preparation to maintain their characteristic rosy flush, and their wings are regularly clipped to prevent absenteeism. A large sun pavilion restaurant and terrace overlook a lawn where these birds parade, together with pigeons and sparrows on the look-out for crumbs. It is a pleasant place for luncheons and teas during the summer season, the terrace adorned with such unusual plants as dwarf peach trees in tubs which bear, despite their miniature height, full-sized peaches to tempt the roving eye. The vines and fig trees of the adjacent garden also bear fruit, but neither grape nor fig has so far succeeded in ripening up here.

The remaining garden is the Tudor replica already mentioned, a place of soothing mellow charm, unfussy and solid, with an air of peace about it even when thronged with people. No wonder a local clergyman used to come here to write his weekly sermon, seated on one of the oak benches in a shady recess. One great attraction of these roof gardens is the way they combine the intimate charm of seclusion with vast prospects over London, to be seen from certain look-out points provided in the walls: loopholes on to the outer world. This is as good a place as any for taking a bird's eye view of the metropolis, from St Paul's to Sydenham, and the Houses of Parliament to Richmond Hill. After gazing at this panorama it is restful to drop back into the shade of silver birch, chestnut, oak and elm, willow and laburnum, some of them upwards of thirty feet high.

Millions of visitors come to see this extraordinary place, and all may be glad to think of the charities which benefit from the entrance fees. The present total is not known, but as long ago as 1960 more than £120,000 had been distributed to London hospitals. Members of the royal family have from the very beginning been interested visitors. Princess Alice, a granddaughter of Queen Victoria, accompanied her husband the Earl of Athlone; Princess Arthur of Connaught came; Princess Mary; the Duchesses of Kent and Gloucester; Princess Marie Louise and Lady Patricia Ramsay. Perhaps the most devoted royal visitor of all was the late Queen Mary, who came on several occasions and took the deepest interest in every detail of the garden's progress.

The London Gardens Society

AT THE beginning of the century the late Lord Noel-Buxton and a group of friends founded the London Gardens Guild, with the primary aim of encouraging people to grow flowers in window-boxes to cheer drab and crowded districts. This valuable innovation has been carried on and greatly extended by the London Gardens Society, which, from a small office in Buckingham Street off the Strand, carries out a large programme of activities, covering every sort of garden and window-box in the metropolis, and as far afield as Greenwich, Deptford, Isleworth and St Paul's Cray. Annual contests are organized over a wide range of horticultural effort; some of these are carried out jointly with the Worshipful Company of Gardeners. The Noel-Buxton Trust makes donations to the Society's funds, as do several of the great City Companies. The list of local Horticultural Societies now affiliated with the LGS has grown too long to be included in the annual reports of the latter body, and covers territory as far spread as Lewisham, Norbury and Wimbledon.

Trophies are competed for with zeal by both teaching and non-teaching hospitals, by Metropolitan Police Stations* and by the Horticultural Societies (points gained individually being aggregated to each group's credit), as well as by the owners of private gardens and window displays. The Noel-Buxton Cup, awarded to the garden 'cultivated under exceptional difficulties' is an imaginative conception which appeals to all who know what troubles the city gardener has to face and overcome. One of the worst hazards in our time is the erection of high blocks, which suddenly deprive cherished gardens of the sun they need. Many a devoted gardener in London has had to bear this kind of imposition on his home and plot of land. It is remarkable to see how doggedly the sufferers will set about rearranging their schemes, going without the sun-loving plants which used to fill the borders with bloom in summer, and substituting shade-tolerant subjects to give pleasure of another kind with their contrast of form and subtler shades in leaves and barks. You cannot keep a good

* The Gerald Road Police Station has the station code AL picked out in plants.

gardener down, however high you may raise cement and glass screen blocks around his land.

Membership of the Society is open to all, whether resident in London or not, and more annual subscriptions will be welcome to offset against the inevitable rise in expenses. Parties of members are taken in summer and autumn to visit famous gardens. In recent years the Directors of Kew and of Wisley have personally conducted these groups and given freely of their knowledge, to the immense pleasure of members. These activities deserve to be more widely known.

Queen Elizabeth The Queen Mother is Patron of the London Gardens Society, and by no means a figurehead. Every summer she spends a day touring selected gardens all over the London area, and in every kind of weather. In 1968 the day was hopelessly wet; but her Majesty was undeterred. Clad in a waterproof cape, and with a large umbrella in her hand, she was photographed for the annual report, looking as though the experience had been a genuine pleasure—as indeed it probably was. For this member of the royal family is herself a keen and well-informed maker of gardens. Spending much of her early life in the lovely gardens of St Paul's Walden Bury, with a beloved brother (later Sir David Bowes-Lyon) who became the President of the Royal Horticultural Society, 1953–61, and was awarded the Victoria Medal of Honour, The Queen Mother has done much to improve gardens at the various royal residences, and recently at her remote Castle of Mey in Caithness has made a 'garden fit for a queen'. In 1961 the RHS bestowed on her its highest honour, the Victoria Medal of Honour—not as the usual kind of honorary award so often accepted by royalty, but as a mark of appreciation for her knowledge and influence in the sphere of horticulture: an informed influence, all the more to be admired when the enormous amount of duties and demands made on the time of royalty in these islands is taken into account. All gardeners must obtain inspiration from this royal patron, even if their gardens are not suitable for the cultivation of her favourite magnolias.

Some City Gardens

THIS chronicle is supposed to go back no further than the reign of Elizabeth I, but London has chosen to perpetuate so many early memories by street names that strict adherence to dates would be tiresome. Vine Street, now famous for its police station, really is situated on ground that nourished a vineyard long ago, when it belonged to the Bishop of Ely. That prelate enjoyed forty acres of garden, orchard and vineyard on the banks of the Upper Fleet River, or Holbourne, a stream long since put underground because minor rivulets are not wanted in great modern cities. Plum Tree Court and Saffron Hill recall other plantings in the Bishop's garden. His wine is described as having been more like vinegar; thirty gallons of this 'verjuice' were produced in a year.

Extra hands would be brought in to weed and dress the vines, and for the grape harvest. When science permits us to view actual scenes from the past, not acted reproductions of it, I should like to see a warm day in early autumn in the Bishop's vineyard, with men and women carrying baskets of ripe fruit to be trodden in vats until the crimson juice is all squeezed out. Alicia Amherst* has imagined the scene:

> 'The mellow rays of the sinking sun light up the walls and many towers of the city, and the distant pile of Westminster is half hidden by mists rising from the river. There, too, the vintage is in full swing, and the song of the grape-gatherers breaks the stillness of the October evening.'

Alexander Neckham in his twelfth-century *De Naturis Rerum* refers to the song of the grape-gatherers, which seem to have been akin to other work-chants, such as the waulking songs of weavers, and sea-shanties. In a modern street index of London there are no fewer than seventeen names derived from the vine—Vine Street, Vinehill, Vineries; even the name 'Finsbury' was originally 'Vinesbury'.

The busy thoroughfare of Moorgate is named from a gate which really did open on to a moor. Mayor Thomas Falconer in 1415 'caused the wall of the citie

* *London Parks and Gardens* (1907).

as yield the most fragrant and odoriferous flowers, and are aptest to tinge the air upon every gentle emission at a great distance'. Borders were to be full of carnations, pinks, violets and other scented plants, so that the whole city would be 'sensible of the sweet and ravishing varieties of the perfumes'. In the rebuilding plans officially submitted by Sir Christopher Wren there was also some provision for a 'green belt'; but neither of these schemes was carried out. Charles had other demands on his royal purse, always depleted by wars and court extravagance.

Of the various small oases still left, the gardens of the City Companies are now for the most part only tokens of the semi-public places of recreation, containing arbours and bowling alleys, which used to be available for the enjoyment of such citizens as could pay for admission. The Merchant Taylors' garden stretched from Threadneedle Street to Cornhill, and an account dated 1572 makes mention of a 'Bowllynge Alley, Terras, Erbes for the garden and for furnishing of Knottes'. The remaining fragment still gives off a whiff or two of Tudor atmosphere. Right up to Victorian times the Drapers' Company had a large garden, a place loved by Macaulay when young. The mulberry orchard which once extended to London Wall is long forgotten by citizens, most of the land is solidly built over, and the remaining garden is just sufficient to whet an appetite for the past. A little further west, in Coleman Street, the Girdlers' Hall garden can still show one mulberry propagated from a tree planted there in 1750, and the Tallow Chandlers have a Catalpa. Among the trimmest of all City Companies' gardens is that of the Goldsmiths opposite their Hall in Gresham Street. It is essentially an 'architectural' garden, with contrasted types of paving, neat lawns, seats in shallow embrasures of the enclosing wall, and a few well-sited trees. The large garden of Stationers' Hall in Warwick Lane contains a fine plane tree flourishing on the spot where the Master and Wardens were accustomed to make bonfires from the heretical books which they were empowered to seize. Some of us would not be sorry to see bonfires made of the grimy stuff churned out by the sewer press today.

According to Mr F. E. Cleary* there are about 750 trees growing within the City of London. Although declared a smokeless zone as far back as October 1954, this very congested area still suffers heavily from the pollution of exhaust fumes, and it is one of the most difficult places in England in which to cultivate trees. It says much for the gardeners that 750 specimens are thriving. It is hard to find suitable sites to plant more on city pavements, because for years it has

* *The Flowering City* (1969).

been the Corporation's policy to remove public services from under roads to below pavements, so that necessary maintenance work does not impede the flow of traffic. Pedestrians, of course, can be made to 'walk the plank' or squeeze through narrow apertures. Often there are vaults and cellars below the pavements, to make matters worse for those who want more trees.

In 1969 Mr Cleary enumerated seventy-four small open spaces and flower beds in the city, where hazards of petrol fumes, wind, and pigeons had to be faced. A vast number of bedding plants for these is raised each year in the Corporation nursery at West Ham, and thousands of bulbs are put in for spring and early summer bloom. The redevelopment of the city after bomb and fire damage sustained in the Second World War gave opportunity for the creation of many little plots for shrubs, flowering plants and trees. One much grander project is the Festival Garden by St Paul's Cathedral, designed by Sir Albert Richardson, with wall fountains of the Gardeners' Company. The area adjoining the southern part of the Cathedral has been laid out to link up with a piazza at Ralli House, and the whole conception provides a spacious and popular place for crowds to move about or just to sit in the sun.

The large gardens in Finsbury Circus were acquired by the Corporation in 1900, as an open space to be maintained for the recreation and enjoyment of the public. A bowling green, originally made in 1925, was enlarged in 1968, with a new pavilion. A band plays at lunchtime throughout the summer. In recent years the planting here has undergone a face-lift as great in its way as that I have described in the garden of Buckingham Palace. Away have gone the stuffy old Victorian shrubberies, and in their place are groups of azaleas and magnolias, with such unexpected items as *Enkianthus campanulatus* and *Pieris japonica.* Mr Peter Stagg, the man responsible for the city's open spaces, finds that, as they seldom suffer from hard frost, more tender shrubs can be grown against walls; and he likes to introduce maples for the attraction of their bark; *Prunus thibetica; Parrotia persica* for autumn foliage, and *Hamamelis mollis* for winter flower.

The London County Council, familiarly known as the LCC, came into being in 1888 and ceased to exist in April 1965, when the Greater London Council, GLC, was formed. A year before its demise the LCC issued a booklet full of proposals for the future development of London's parks. A face-lift for the entrances, to make them more inviting; floodlighting of flower beds at night; greenhouse displays with advice available for amateurs; summer pavilions made into all-the-year heated meeting places; tennis courts flooded for skating in winter; even artificial ski-slopes and rock faces: these are some of the suggested innovations. It remains to be seen how many will be taken up; but so long as existing charms are not spoilt, it does seem as though the open spaces should be utilised more fully for every age-group and taste. The only point I am dubious about is the floodlighting, for the garish emerald greens, electric blues and ruby colours seen in Edinburgh at Festival time, and in Torquay at the other end of the kingdom, have made me feel that plants will soon need a society to protect them from such vulgarization.

That admirable organization, the British Standards Institute, in 1966 published a booklet *Recommendations for Tree Work*, which every local authority and amenity society should own. It was prepared at the request of the Institute of Landscape Architects, and covers such points as cuts, pruning, crowning, reducing and shaping, bracing, feeding, tree removal and safety measures. At a conference on 'Your Town in the Seventies' Mr Duncan Sandys, MP, President of the Civic Trust, had this to say on the subject of trees:

> 'It only takes a few minutes to cut down a tree with an axe or push it over with a bulldozer, but it may take a couple of generations to replace it. We must, therefore as far as possible hold on to all the trees we already possess, and I'm glad to say that this is now increasingly recognized by local authorities, architects, planners, and the owners of property.'

Lord Cockburn in 1849 could not say anything as hopeful of Edinburgh. He wrote a letter to the Lord Provost of that city, a document regarded as outrageous because the Judges were not supposed to interfere in the life and business of the market place:

> 'Our trees—where are they? I could name at least eight places, all within the city, that I remember being graced by very respectable groups of them, well placed and well growing. Not a twig of them lives. There seems to have been little perception of the peculiar beauty of street trees, or even of a single tree, in immediate connection with a building. The system has been to massacre, or so treat as certainly to kill, every outstanding stem. I cannot recollect any Edinburgh tree finding a public defender. I would as soon cut down a burgess without a fair trial and a verdict, as a burgh tree. And even with such a law, the tree, I fear, would require many peremptory challenges of the jurors!'

It was reprinted a few years ago under the heading of *Will we ever Learn?*

The best known tree of London is called (of course) the 'London Plane'. According to Mr Miles Hadfield this name is a modern invention, for he has not traced it further back than 1915. His description of the tree's origin is worth quoting. John Tradescant the Younger brought the Western Plane from America in 1631. Earlier than that, by 1590, we had the Oriental Plane—a European tree mentioned by classical writers as one of the most beautiful of trees, a shade-giving tree. People used to make offerings to it. The Reverend Anthony Watson described one at Nonsuch, a low, spreading tree with branches strutted for people to walk underneath. Most botanists think that our London Plane is a cross between the two.

The puzzle is, where and when did the cross occur?—for nobody has seen the Western Plane in flower in Britain, and to obtain a hybrid you must have flowers. Mr Hadfield believes that the Western Plane was taken to Spain and there crossed with the Oriental Plane, which is found in that country. So it may be that our London Plane should be called the Madrid, or Barcelona, or Cadiz Plane. The great period of its planting in London began with the town planning schemes of John Nash at the start of the nineteenth century. Some of the oldest and finest are those in Berkeley Square, planted in 1789. We should be badly off without this fine tree, although many others are able to live and thrive in London. In Webster's book *Trees of London* mention is made of upwards of 220 distinct species in Hyde Park and Kensington Gardens alone. Within the City of London, the safest choice is considered to be the seven 'old faithfuls'—London Plane, Norway Maple, Lime, Whitebeam, Catalpa, Cherry and Acacia.

The second largest garden within the city is known as Postman's Park, Aldersgate Street, second only to Finsbury Circus. This park, with which is incorporated the churchyard of St Botolph without Aldersgate, was purchased by public subscription in 1900. To celebrate Queen Victoria's Jubilee in 1887 G. F. Watts caused the installation of fifty tablets in memory of heroes who gave their lives to save others. There are many fine trees here, a statue of Sir Robert Peel—who gave his name to the London 'Bobby' or 'Peeler', and a goldfish pool and fountain. The churchyard of St Botolph, Bishopsgate is another large open space, a pleasant area of grass, trees, flower beds and one surprise—a hard tennis court. Under the Burial Act of 1855 the churchwardens were required to maintain it in good order; but the Corporation has now taken over this responsibility.

There are some forty churches in the City of London, as well as the great cathedral of St Paul, many of them surrounded by gardens. The Worshipful

Company of Gardeners, in association with the Metropolitan Public Gardens Association, organizes annually a competition for the best-kept church garden, a contest that grows in popularity each year. In 1969 this was split up into two sections according to size. A report of the judges in 1964 included suggestions for planting churchyards for attractive appearance with the minimum of labour and expense. Shrubs, such as deutzia, philadelphus, spiraea, hibiscus, *Buddleia davidii*, *Hypericum patulum*, tree paeony and hydrangea, with ground cover plants below them, were strongly advocated. Bedding-out, it was considered, should be reserved chiefly for in-filling while permanent plantings were being established. The list of 'absolutely hardy perennials, impervious to most handicaps' may be of interest: Yellow Loosestrife, Purple do.; *Campanula rapunculoides*, *C. lactiflora*, *C. glomerata; Macleaya cordata;* Galega (Goat's Rue); Hollyhock; Hemorocallis (Day Lily); *Geranium grandiflorum*, and London Pride. As a London child I thought of the latter and Japanese anemones as the two uncrushables, but the anemone does not appear in this list.

I have a fondness for little pieces of garden in the midst of traffic and noise, just a few steps from the busy pavement, where feet may be given a rest; somehow the narrow barrier of a hedge, the cheeping of sparrows, and smells of geranium and heliotrope, remove the mind ten times the distance from the city and its business that the legs have traversed. It is a hallucination, but a very pleasing and valuable one. One of those seats at All Hallows Wall, London Wall, fits my requirement admirably.

The Metropolitan Public Gardens Association

THIS Association, formed in 1882, had as its original title 'The Metropolitan Public Garden, Boulevard and Playground Association'—which soon proved too unwieldy for constant use, and was by 1890 reduced to its present form. The Chairman, Lord Brabazon, in his first Annual Report dated October 1883, set forth the aims of the new Body as follows:

> 'To endeavour to secure, for purposes of health and recreation, available vacant plots of ground, large or small, within the Metropolitan area; to obtain the right of laying out, and planting, and seating, all disused burial-grounds, waste places, and enclosed squares. These, according to the circumstances of the case and the requirements of the locality, will be laid out either as gardens, or as garden and playground combined, or as playgrounds pure and simple.
>
> 'The first will be merely resting-places, designed principally for adults, well provided with benches; as far as is consistent with strict economy they will be made attractive by means of grass and flowers, shrubs and trees.' [The second, garden and playground combined, were to have] 'broad stretches of concrete pavement, interspersed with shrubs, and trees, grass and seats.' [Playgrounds exclusively for the use of children would be] 'watched over by some intelligent man in charge of the ground, possibly an army pensioner, who during certain hours would be able to instruct the children in simple gymnastics.'

The objective was to meet

> 'one of the most pressing wants of the poorer districts within the Metropolitan area, namely breathing and resting-places for the old, and playgrounds for the young, in the midst of densely populated localities, especially in the East and South of London.'

A gloomy picture is painted of the lives led by poor inhabitants, the majority of whom seldom escaped from their dismal surroundings. On rare occasions some of them managed to get a glimpse of suburban country, but for the most part they had no refuge from 'noise, slavery and closeness'. The Chairman said that

> 'to these poor souls the hospital, with its quiet and method, is a haven much to be desired. It is a noteworthy fact that, after a brief sojourn in its wards, the hardness of expression, which many a patient wore on entrance, to a large extent disappeared.'
>
> 'Now, the provision of garden and playground, though of course no panacea for human suffering and misery, will largely help to brighten the lot of those who live as described. There will be a spot where, for a time at least during the summer months, there may be a retreat from the suffocating sickly smell of the dwelling, where the eye may be refreshed with a glimpse of nature, and where the ear may rest from the jangle of voices and the rush of traffic. There will be spots, too, exclusively for children, where they will be out of harm's way under the supervision of a judicious caretaker, who will prevent tyranny and misconduct, and where they may enjoy health-giving exercises . . . It will be found that these merciful retreats are in constant use, that they are thoroughly appreciated, and that under ordinary supervision no injury is done.'

This first Report ends with a list of subscribers, headed by the name of Her Royal Highness Princess Frederica of Hanover, Hampton Court Palace, who gave four guineas, followed by about fifty titled subscribers in order of precedence. After that some four pages of commoners are listed with their contributions, mostly of one or two guineas. A Mr Charrington of Anchor Brewery in Mile End gave £15, and Samuel Morley, Esq., MP, £20. It would be easy enough for some of us today to regard all this as the work of pampered rich people, trying to salve their consciences by handing out a few guineas for the relief of the exploited poor. But if the project is examined in greater depth, it soon becomes clear that not only alms but a vast amount of very hard work was put into it, and much achieved thereby in a surprisingly short time.

The Association stated in the beginning that there was no intention of superseding or overlapping the work of other amenity societies already engaged in similar enterprises, but only of uniting with and supplementing such efforts.

Octavia Hill, who in 1865 began her schemes for improving the housing of the London poor, had already paid attention to the need for open spaces. Her plans for the well-being of tenants always included a playground or garden, and some kind of hall or indoor meeting-place also—the term 'community centre' had not yet been invented. With the aid of John Ruskin's money, this amazing young woman soon managed some of the best-kept working class dwellings in London. She was in demand as a writer and speaker. George Eliot gave her support. A royal princess asked to be shown some of the houses, incognito. A lecture given by Octavia at Bristol in 1869 caused some disagreement with Ruskin, for it was called 'The Importance of Aiding the Poor without Almsgiving'. She believed in helping them to help themselves, while he thought in terms of State aid.

In spite of this argument they remained friends, and Octavia developed the work with the aid of keen helpers, among them Henrietta Barnett and Emma Cons. A disused stable behind the home of Octavia Hill's family was used for meetings and plays, and from this germ of an idea sprang the partnership of Emma Cons and her niece Lilian Baylis, which resulted in the transformation of a second-rate music hall near the Elephant and Castle into the 'Old Vic' theatre: a place designed to bring great acting within the reach of most people. Not only ideas, but bricks and mortar too were spreading like wildfire in the London of the 'seventies and 'eighties. Common lands were menaced by the new railway lines. It was taken for granted that, since railways and progress went hand in hand, all obstacles must be removed; just as our thinking now is inclined to put the motor road first.

Octavia Hill resisted this encroachment with all her powers, for she had the vision to see how vitally important open spaces were going to be. It is said that she invented the term. Her sister Miranda started a group (the Kyrle Society) with the aim of acquiring small green places as 'lungs' in built-up sectors. Olivia served as treasurer, and from this modest beginning the ideas of the Metropolitan Public Gardens Association evolved. In its first report two grants to the Kyrle Society are listed: £100 for the laying out of a disused burial-ground at St George's, Bloomsbury, and £100 for St Peter's, Bethnal Green. After the year 1883 there is no further mention of the Kyrle Society, which was presumably merged in its greater partner. Octavia Hill became a firm supporter of the Commons Preservation Society—formed in 1865, and later renamed the Commons, Open Spaces and Footpaths Preservation Society. She begged people to take their places with a few 'unknown heroes fighting an uphill fight for a great cause in its early stages'. One of those crusaders—a lakeland clergyman,

Canon Rawnsley, was to be associated with Octavia and Sir Robert Hunter in the foundation of the National Trust in 1893. But that work is nationwide, and we must remain in London.

In 1881 Parliament passed *The Metropolitan Open Spaces Act* which afforded facilities for utilizing closed burial grounds for public recreation, and enabled the Association to work out plans for opening a large number as public gardens. The first report lists no fewer than forty-two which had been or were about to be utilized as gardens 'in which the public may sit and walk about, but not for the playing of games'. This crusade had not begun a moment too soon, for already speculative builders were attempting to get hold of some of the ground for housing schemes; there were then no planning regulations to control the use of land.

From its inception the Association laid down a rule that, on completion of each piece of ground for its special purpose, the next care must be to convey it to some public body for permanent maintenance. It was 'not designed to relieve local Authorities of their obligations, but to assist and encourage them in their performance'. By adherence to this policy the Association was able, with limited funds, to accomplish far more than could have been attempted otherwise. The Chairman (now Lord Meath) reported in 1890 that it had been instrumental in passing an Act through Parliament, the *Open Spaces Act, 1890,* by which greater facilities were given to local bodies for the acquisition and maintenance of open spaces, and legal barriers which experience had shown to be detrimental to such work removed. He reminded the Association that the Authorities had not always the courage to initiate reforms, and that it was of paramount importance for this voluntary work to continue, and by 'example, encouragement and advice to push on the good work'. Although membership stood at the small figure of 776, a map of London issued with this report shows 218 projects completed between 1882 and 1890, and 100 acres of playing fields newly opened to children on Saturdays. Some of the idle rich were not so idle, after all.

It is interesting to compare a paragraph from *The London Gardener*, the Association's annual magazine-style report for 1969, with one culled from the report of 1890. The latter has a note on *Tree-planting*:

> 'The munificence of one member enabled the Association to offer £100 each to twenty of the London Vestries and District Boards for the planting of plane trees in thoroughfares, on condition that they should replace and maintain the trees. More than half have accepted the gift, and it is most

gratifying to know that so many hitherto dull and monotonous streets will be brightened in this way. The object of this offer was to induce these bodies to continue the work themselves.'

The special Tree Conference number of *The London Gardener*, issued at the end of 1969, looks forward to European Conservation Year, 1970, in the following words by the Association's Chairman, Mr F. E. Cleary:

'Surely one of the fundamental duties of a Local Authority, be it Parish Council, Rural District Council or County Council, is to maintain the physical features of its area to the highest possible standard by the provision of open spaces, large or small, the planting of trees, the provision of seats and playgrounds, and a constant attack on all who despoil the towns and countryside . . . European Conservation Year was promoted because all over Europe in the towns, cities and countryside there is a diminution of standards, a deterioration of environment, and a spoliation by mankind of his habitat. It is no good talking about environment and it is no use writing about conservation. What we want is action, and the lead must come from Central and Local Government, who can inspire the citizen and encourage civic societies and a host of other voluntary organizations to play their part . . . Of course it costs money, but money spent on open spaces or trees or seats is money invested for many years—and what better than an investment to keep England a green and pleasant land?'

Words were followed by deeds. In 1970, to commemorate European Conservation Year, the Association presented a tree to each of the London Boroughs. The Chairman wrote:

'It seems a far cry from 1882, when our Association was a pioneer of the *Disused Burial Grounds Act* to preserve such grounds as public open spaces. There is nothing new in conservation . . . The Corporation of the City of London, with whom our Association has worked closely for over seventy years, was responsible for saving Epping Forest, Burnham Beeches, Highgate Woods, Kilburn Park, West Ham Park, Coulsdon Common and Farthingale Common in the south of London from development nearly 100 years ago.

'Our Association is particularly concerned with the Metropolitan area, which today is the 600 square miles of Greater London. It is no easy task.

> It is true that we can concentrate much of our energy on Central London, and our association with The Worshipful Company of Gardeners and the City Corporation is something that has produced most gratifying results. Improving environmental conditions in an urban area is difficult, but it is a challenge. The "Flowers in the City" campaign has encouraged hundreds of firms in the City to have window boxes and floral displays around their premises, with the result that for four years in succession prizes have been won in the "Britain in Bloom" competition. The same can be accomplished in any city if there are sufficient people determined to promote and support such activities. Nothing is ever achieved without enthusiasm.'

The present secretary of the Association, Mr Michael Upward, is also secretary of the Alpine Garden Society and himself a skilled gardener. With these assignments he combines expeditions to remote Himalayan regions in search of plants—a mixture of administration, horticulture and plant-hunting reminiscent of Sir Joseph Hooker more than a century ago.

A Town Garden of the Cement and Concrete Association at Wexham Springs

THE next small garden on my list took me into Buckinghamshire, to the imposing headquarters of the Cement and Concrete Association at the combined estates of Fulmer Grange and Wexham. In these seventy acres the Association has carefully maintained the original gardens, with their fine sweeps of old turf, interesting specimen trees, formal sunken rose garden and natural lake; but there have also been some very modern innovations, both office buildings and outdoor landscaping work. In this pleasant setting the Association has planned exhibitions of concrete paving in a very wide range of styles; of block screen walls; raised flower beds; pools; fountains; pergolas; seats; plant containers—even litter bins, all made in some form of concrete.

It is a surprise to discover how many kinds of paving alone can be produced in this material. A series of display walls and frames shows recent advances in the use of concrete, with the numerous patterned and exposed-aggregate finishes now available for pre-cast products, and some of the possibilities of *in situ* concrete. All kinds of textures and patterns are now given to pre-cast goods, and the colours used here include grey-green, grey and black alternating, and four shades of brown and dark grey in a mixed paving for a garden path. There is even a large sculpture, carried out *in situ* with coloured cements and a variety of aggregates, grit-blasted and finished with applied mosaic in small areas. This concrete sculpture was made in 1964 by William Mitchell, and is a group entitled 'The Corn King and the Spring Queen'.

A practical invention is called 'grass concrete'. The units allow wheeled traffic to use the paving, but also permit grass to grow up through the interstices. Such slabs can be used on embankments, in the construction of steep batters. Most of the exhibits are chiefly designed for use in public gardens and those surrounding factories and power stations; but even the gardener with little space may find useful devices which can be adapted to his needs, such as the miniature retaining wall units known as 'Monowall'. These may be laid without concrete foundations, and are useful for terracing, constructing raised beds, flank walls for steps, or for children's sandpits.

The paved water garden, the one I had come to see, was designed by Sylvia Crowe—a past president of the Institute of Landscape Architects—and aims at providing an outdoor extension to the staff dining room; a place for taking the air, strolling or resting after a meal. It is in essence a town garden, one where people may walk without soiling their shoes, and with a small proportion of living plants to man-made structures. In this instance it is a tiny section of a large garden area, and leads down to an informal planted shrubbery and woodland beyond. But, as an urban garden in a restricted space, it would be charming, and acceptable as a self-contained unit.

In Miss Crowe's own words:

> 'The pattern of paving, planting, steps and fountains slides in the direction of the garden pool, to guide the eyes away from the vehicle standing and towards the water and trees. The informal pool is designed to lie naturally against the background of rhododendrons, and the ground has been shaped down to the water's edge. The arrangement of plant-boxes provides a firm stop, and some foliage. No planting could be done against the wall itself owing to the emission of hot air. The "pencil" fence will suggest trunks in a jungle of foliage when the creepers have grown, and it will provide a simple foil to the wall designed by Mitzi Cunliffe on the other side. The colouring, largely in tones of pink and grey, is designed to go with the colour of the building. The grey is echoed in the foliage of lavender, rosemary, *Iris dalmatica* and pinks.'

Here the designer has coped successfully with a difficult task, for the building from which it leads is faced with large-scale dark grey slabs, and the Mitzi Cunliffe screen wall with its bold interlocking patterned pre-cast units was already a permanent feature of the site. Both these could easily have overpowered the small paved garden; but the simple dignity of lay-out and planting more than hold their own. The upper level, against the building, is paved with random squares and rectangles interspersed with three strips of black concrete of different lengths. Between these are narrow beds of soil planted with creeping thyme, *Acaena buchanani* and gentian, and dwarf lavender. The 'pencil' fence is an ingenious device made from asbestos cement pipes, four inches in diameter,

54. Finsbury Circus

55. Ellen Willmott

56. Gertrude Jekyll, by W. Nicholson

57, 58. A town garden by Sylvia Crowe

59. The Great Herb Garden at Lullingstone Castle

filled with concrete and painted a matt grey. I particularly liked the three-tier fountain, consisting of shallow concrete trays on different levels, down which water trickles gently and descends to the pool below. Stone chippings in several colours cover the bottoms of the trays.

Big white plant containers have been built up from a number of two-foot-square pre-cast boxes, and are very effective. A darker, and still larger, one holds *Aralia chinensis* and a bold *Yucca gloriosa*. One of the benches in this corner is buttressed by fragrant rosemary. Hellebore and mullein, silver ivy, purple leaved bugle, acanthus and herbaceous geraniums provide quiet colour to offset the rhododendron plantation behind the pool. If I had doubts beforehand about a 'concrete garden', they were banished by this example.

Elizabeth Coxhead's Garden

THIS garden surrounds a detached brick-built house of medium size on a corner site in the prosperous suburb of Gerrards Cross in South Buckinghamshire. It measures 140 by 57 feet, and sounds commonplace. Does the garden merit inclusion here just because it is typical of thousands of gardens in London's commuter belt, or has something unusual been evolved from prosaic beginnings? Miss Coxhead's book, *One Woman's Garden*, published in 1971, suggested to me that on this modest suburban plot she had somehow managed to achieve a certain distinction, without straying far from the norm of neighbourhood setting and taste. I had to find out, and was soon invited to see for myself.

The physical reasons which caused this single-handed woman gardener to re-design her father's legacy and bring it within her scope to maintain are not of first importance. The garden stands firmly on its own roots as a creation, irrespective of the amount of labour being expended—or husbanded—by intelligent planning on the part of its owner; in truth it seems to have gained by her limitations. Those who wish to know exactly how this has been accomplished should study her book. I am here concerned mainly with results.

One of the first tasks to be carried out was the abolition of gigantic privet hedges. They enclosed this land on three sides, giving seclusion indeed, but at the cost of heavy and constant effort to keep them trimmed. Also, they took up a lot of space, and greedily leached the soil for yards on either side. Had I been present at the time of their up-rooting, I might have been dubious about the effect of baring the soul of the garden to every roving eye. For me, a garden must be above all a secluded place. Miss Coxhead, being more generously sociable and a less introverted character, took the opposite view. Perhaps she is also blessed with particularly well-mannered neighbours, for she says that no one stops to stare in. The gains were great, including the view of attractive trees on adjacent land. In her opinion the suburban plot should be disposed to reveal the benefits of neighbours' gardens as well as to plant out the sight of their houses; both objectives to be achieved by careful siting of trees and other screen material.

The next step was to substitute cement for gravel paths—another change which I might have feared to make, feeling that so much concrete all round the house and up to the garage would look harshly obtrusive. It is always an enlarging experience to be proved wrong. When these paths are seen now, a little earthy from use, their surface pleasantly textured by swirling grooved patterns and their edges clothed with ruffles of thyme, pink, lamb's ear, dwarf artemisias and acaena, the critic has to admit that concrete, even in a 'natural' type of garden such as this, can perfectly well be integrated if the gardener takes sufficient trouble.

Miss Coxhead decided that no part of her garden could be allowed to have an off-season. It was too small, too visible, and every square foot must supply interest all the year round. All, that is, except the month above all when most English people expect to enjoy their gardens—glorious June. Each summer this gardener used to leave England for France, where she spent four weeks at Cruzille, a holiday house shared with other members of the family. These regular absences induced her with splendid logic to discontinue the cultivation of midsummer bloomers such as lupin, delphinium, paeony and bearded iris. It must have taken strength of mind to banish all those old herbaceous friends. The delphinium and lupin, less at home in this dry chalky soil, were easier to part with than the happier iris and paeony; but away they went, except for one special iris, valuable for its decorative striped foliage, which was carefully preserved. Coming as it did from her old family garden in the foothills of the French Alps, its blossom season could be enjoyed in June on the other side of the Channel.

By the time our garden in Buckinghamshire had been denuded of privet hedges; of June flowerers; of a couple of Japanese cherries and a crab-apple—all grown over-large and greedy—it looked forlorn and bare. How long would it take to refurnish those gaps? Miss Coxhead drew comfort from the fact that she now possessed what she describes as the most exciting plant of all—'Scope'. She had scope for shrubs, 'a bit of the best of everything'. The best and most suitable for her purpose were winkled out with the utmost care from garden books, catalogues, shows and well-known gardens—the names of the plants, that is, for no sly snitched cuttings ever hid in her handbag. (Well, hardly ever.) Hidcote, she found, gave the most thrilling inspiration for a small garden like hers on dry, chalky soil, being itself divided into sections or 'rooms' and sited on similar terrain.

The shrubby veronica (now renamed hebe) became a theme-plant. The varieties with long flower spikes, bred from a wild native of the New Zealand cliffs, did not all survive frosts; but 'Autumn Glory', 'Great Orme', 'Marjorie' and 'Midsummer Beauty' proved satisfactory, together with some charming grey-leaved dwarfs, such as *H. pagei* and *H. albicans*, and the bronze-gold *H. armstrongii*. Too few people realize the variety of medium-sized and dwarf shrubs this family can provide. I am fond of *H. cupressoides*, which looks like a neat conifer and surprises the uninitiated by bursting into flower.

Roses are not particularly suited to this soil, and varieties subject to black spot get it badly, being too far out to benefit from the deposits of London soot which still, despite smoke abatement, help to control this ugly disease. Miss Coxhead feels almost as lukewarm as I about rose-beds and rose-gardens, with the exception of the 'old' roses—and these are banned because of their June flowering and failure, for the most part, to give a repeat performance. But roses she had to have; so she selected some modern hybrids of the most graceful habit available, and with at least a trace of fragrance, and interplanted them with foliage shrubs. The purple cotinus and weigela (both named *foliis purpureis*), and dark berberis (*atropurpurea*) were tried out and found to be attractive with her roses: deep red 'Europeana' and cherry-red 'Rosemary Rose', and the mauve-pink 'Africa Star'. Yellow roses were accompanied by the gold-variegated euonymus and hardy fuchsias and martagon lilies. To these were added metallic blue domes of rue, and grey senecio, and one bluish juniper, *J. squamata meyerii*, underplanted with white winter heath. The effect of this mixed planting has almost convinced me that modern roses can look good in a garden as well as in flower arrangements. But I wish the breeders would invent bushes a little less like stout-limbed hockey hoydens. (No disrespect to that game; but rose bushes were prettier in Victorian days, before ladies were seen red-legged on the field.)

Another section of this garden, a rock bank against part of the south-west frontage, has been named 'Chiltern Alp'. It might have been dubbed a rockery before such things went out of fashion. In her youth Miss Coxhead was an alpine climber, and her French holiday home was near enough to what she describes as 'strips of natural rock garden' to allow intimate acquaintance with its flora. From first crocus braving icy blasts to *Anemone pulsatilla* and *A. narcissiflora*, soldanella, columbine and gentians, to the late summer alpine aster, she knows them all. Had I been familiar with these plants in the wild, the sight of any of them or their relations on a tame garden bank would, I think, have seemed a depressing anti-climax. But although she seldom attempts to transfer alpine plants from France, Miss Coxhead enjoys her small English moraine and is not made homesick for the mountains by it. The usual dwarf conifers are here companioned by some of the smaller hebes already mentioned, by the lovely cream-flowered rock broom *Cytisus kewensis*, and by the miniature willows, *Salix lanata* and *S. boydii*—perfect foils to a deep maroon-coloured *Anemone pulsatilla* from Waterperry.

The small *Euphorbia myrsinites*, which makes a neat clump by rockery steps, is pleasing even in midwinter with its fleshy glaucous leaves. Plants that help to keep the Alp gay in late summer and autumn include the handsome pink dandelion, *Crepis incana*, the silver-leaved *Androsace languinosa*, *Polygonum vacciniifolium* and the clear blue stars of *Cyananthus integer*. This Alp scores from being so apparently casual in the disposition of both rocks and plants, as though all the components have been gently led rather than dragooned into their places. This approach frequently pays dividends in any part of a pleasure garden, but is of supreme value in the difficult task of rockery construction. We all know too well those regiments of tombstone rocks, those pallid almonds spattered over chocolate pudding, those limpets encrusting the sides of a mimic tidal basin, and the stiff array of alpine plants in their pockets. Unnatural contrivances such as these can never develop into pleasing pictures, however interesting and well-grown the plants may be. Arrangement is all-important—and difficult—but worth the expenditure of time and thought, whether one intends to cultivate rich and rare specimens or to make-do with a trayful of little pot plants from the nearest shop.

Miss Coxhead's garden has been made into something memorable because she has given as much care to the planning as to the physical preparation and planting of it. In the preface to her book she writes that a woman's garden is less a work of art than a man's, being more an imitation of, and improvement upon, Nature. I am inclined to reverse that opinion. The more a gardener watches, imitates and tries to improve upon Nature, the more likely he (or she) is to achieve a work of art. Men, I think, are often more concerned with the technical job of growing fine plants than with the observation of how Nature employs them to advantage. The great Gertrude Jekyll remarked that the size of a garden had very little to do with its merit. I believe she would have liked this one.

Like so many of us, Miss Coxhead is a member (Fellow is the correct word) of the Royal Horticultural Society. At the annual general meeting in February 1971 she seconded a vote of thanks to the President, Lord Aberconway, using these words:

> 'I speak as a totally undistinguished Fellow of the Society, but I am sure I speak for many when I say that my annual subscription to the R.H.S. is just about the best investment in pleasure that I make in the course of the year. I get not only Chelsea and Wisley and the monthly pleasure of the *Journal*, but also the very great association of Vincent Square. I never turn the corner into Elverton Street without a lift of the heart, knowing that I am going to see much of beauty, and also certainly something new to me—often many things. I have a particular affection for the coffee bar where I rub shoulders with the great ones of the gardening world, park superintendents and other Olympian figures, and I eavesdrop shamelessly on the most fascinating conversations. I am sure there must be many gardeners in my position, who come to London perhaps once or twice a month, and who, if they only realize it, can have at Vincent Square the amenities of a London club at a fraction of the cost . . .'*

It would be fun to know just how many plants used by Miss Coxhead were first seen, or heard of, at Vincent Square or in the *Journal*. Did that leading citizen of her mixed border, *Atriplex halimus*, gain admission through this door? Or the whipcord hebes, *H. hectori* and *H. lycopodioides*? Assuredly contact with the RHS will have taught her not to cringe at names like those. Familiarity here breeds, not contempt but confidence. That brightest star of her garden, the iris with handsome gold-striped foliage, came from Cruzille; so far the experts have disagreed about its name. It has appeared on Mr Alan Bloom's Bressingham Gardens stall at one of the Vincent Square shows, and in time Miss Coxhead hopes that this iris will be made available at a price the ordinary Fellow can afford.

> 'For plants with spiky leaves are an essential accent, but the yuccas and phormiums tend to be over-large for the small garden, while the leaves of the ordinary German iris, though stately, are a trifle dull. My lovely Cruzille iris is the answer: equally beautiful in shape and colouring, and perfectly to scale. And when in late May I saw the flower, a good, bold, blue-purple flower far superior to the general run of wild irises, it seemed to me that this was one of the great plants of the world.'

So writes Miss Coxhead. I am sorry now to leave her little garden, even though this parting is but a paper farewell.

* *Journal of the RHS*, April 1971.

The Royal Horticultural Society

THE Society which gives so much pleasure to Elizabeth Coxhead and to thousands of her fellow gardening enthusiasts all over the country, began, like most great enterprises, in a small way. On 7 March 1804 seven men met in Mr Hatchard's house, No. 187 Piccadilly, to discuss the formation of a Horticultural Society. Their names were: Sir Joseph Banks, Mr John Wedgwood, the Rt. Hon. Charles Greville, Mr William Forsyth, Mr William Townsend Aiton, Mr Richard Salisbury and Mr James Dickson of Traquhair, who was also one of the founders of the Linnean Society. The first meeting was adjourned; at the second, a friend of Wedgwood, Mr John Hawkins, was also present and thus had his name included in the list of founders of the Horticultural Society of London. The Lord Chamberlain, the Earl of Dartmouth, became its first president, and it was incorporated by Royal Charter in 1809. In 1932 the Hon. H. D. McLaren (later Lord Aberconway), as President of the Society, unveiled at the house, now Hatchard's bookshop, a tablet to commemorate the event of 1804.

That most coveted award, the Victoria Medal of Honour, was instituted in 1897 to mark the sixtieth year of Queen Victoria's reign. It was given to sixty British people resident in the United Kingdom who had made noteworthy contributions to the art and craft of horticulture. A luncheon was held on 26 October 1897 at the Hotel Windsor, Victoria Street, Westminster, and the medals were afterwards distributed in the Drill Hall. One speaker eloquently stressed the need for adequate premises to be owned by the Society. He had not many years to wait. The Vincent Square building, now so well known to all who care about horticulture, was opened in 1904.

The original Victoria medal was designed by a Miss Margaret Giles of Edinburgh. As the President, Sir Trevor Lawrence, remarked: 'Nothing could be more becoming, when we are celebrating the Jubilee of Her Gracious Majesty, than that some members of her own sex should become medallists.' He referred to Miss Gertrude Jekyll and Miss Ellen Willmott. They belonged to the largest group (apart from their sex), that of practical gardeners; others honoured were eight botanists, fourteen nurserymen and several collectors and hybridizers. For some reason Miss Willmott did not attend the ceremony, and so Miss Jekyll was the only woman present. Her old friend Dean Hole, the famous rose-grower, said in his speech that if they were doing honour to Her Majesty, their lady guest was certainly the *Queen of Spades*. It is a curious fact that the Society, whose feminine membership is believed to equal, if not outnumber, the male 'Fellows'—the exact figures being a carefully guarded secret —had no woman serving on its Council until in 1968 Mrs Frances Perry was elected. This novel appointment had taken a hundred and sixty four years to come about.

On the death of Queen Victoria it was decided to increase the number of medallists to sixty-three, in honour of the years of her reign. Holders have been limited to that total ever since. During this century it has been customary for the President's remarks when bestowing the medal to be printed in the *Journal*, but on the occasion of the first presentations no record was issued of services for which the award was given. By the end of the nineteen-sixties there had been nine women recipients, one of them (Miss L. Snelling) a botanical artist.* Miss Eleanor Ormerod, who received the medal in 1901, was eulogized by the President in these words:

> 'Miss Ormerod is known the world over for her most patient and painstaking investigations into the life-habits of all insects, friends or foes, affecting agricultural or horticultural products. It is impossible to cite one aspect of her work more than another, for she has observed and traced the life-history of all such insects, from the smallest to the greatest, from the currant-bud mite to the goat caterpillar and the stag beetle, and she has informed horticulturists what to cherish as friends of gardening, what to destroy, and how best to do it.'

There can be little doubt that the two women honoured by the Royal Horticultural Society in 1897, Gertrude Jekyll and Ellen Willmott, still stand at the top of the horticultural tree, so far as female gardeners are concerned. Both possessed a profound knowledge and understanding of plants, and skill in the design of gardens; but in their lives and characters they were utterly different. Ellen Willmott, enormously rich and (in youth) beautiful, had her English home and garden at Warley Place in Essex. She also possessed an Italian garden at Ventimiglia and a French one near Aix-les-Bains. Gertrude, who was what is modestly called 'comfortably provided for', had never been beautiful, but became

* Mrs Frances Perry was awarded the VMH in 1972.

a lovable and greatly loved person in her old age; while the proud and spoilt Ellen declined, with her fortunes, into a sour, lonely and pitiable recluse.

Gertrude Jekyll was a Londoner by birth, born in Grafton Street in 1843, and her love of plants began with the sight of daisies and dandelions growing in Berkeley Square. When she was five her family moved to Bramley House near Guildford, and there the foundations of her abiding interest in plants and trees were laid. But she was also keenly artistic, and at seventeen became a student at the Kensington School of Art—later the Royal College of Art. Under the combined influences of Ruskin and William Morris she became a highly skilled craftswoman in various media, which she practised assiduously and studied later on in Italy and other countries.

After her father's death in 1876, the Jekylls removed to a smaller home, where Gertrude in 1878 took the momentous step of planning her first garden. She was thirty-five and unmarried. In the woodland setting of Munstead House her 'natural' garden attracted attention. Two famous men, William Robinson of Gravetye and Dean Hole of Rochester, came to see it. Evidently they approved of the garden and of its maker. By 1881 we find Gertrude judging at the 'Botanic Show' in Regent's Park, the Botanic Society's precursor of Chelsea Flower Show: an assignment that brought her into contact with the principal horticulturists of the day, including G. F. Wilson—whose garden near Cobham formed the nucleus of what are now the Royal Horticultural Society's gardens at Wisley. He helped her to acquire knowledge of hardy shrubs and other plants, particularly the novelties then coming to the United Kingdom from China, such as azaleas, rhododendrons, lilies, cherries and maples. Her artistic talent and training enabled her to group these to advantage, and with William Robinson she founded a new school of gardening, outclassing the formal strip bedding of the Victorian style. She called it 'making living pictures with plants'.

By the time she was fifty, Gertrude Jekyll had achieved much; but her talents were spread over too many fields to bring her fame. Then her eyesight gave serious trouble, and all fine work was absolutely forbidden. Now, well into middle life, she perforce painted all her pictures on a large scale out-of-doors—and so, from disability came her great career as a gardener and garden planner. In 1892 she had the good luck to meet a rising young architect, Edwin Lutyens, who became attached to his older friend and sought her help in the laying out of ground to suit the houses he designed. A close partnership developed, and it became the rage for those who could afford it to have 'a Lutyens house with a Jekyll garden'.

After a few years Lutyens was commissioned to produce the perfect house for his friend. Here, at Munstead Wood, Gertrude Jekyll lived happily for the last thirty-four years of her long life. By the time it was ready her articles were appearing regularly in Robinson's paper *The Garden*, and in other publications, notably *The National Review*, *The Edinburgh Review*, and *The Guardian*. She had developed into an authority on gardening, and in 1899 published her first book, *Wood and Garden*. This had considerable success, and was followed a year later by *Home and Garden*. Both books were illustrated with her own photographs. There was no desire for grandeur in Miss Jekyll. The description of her new house, as one approached it, is of itself sufficient to reveal her simplicity and good taste.

> 'My house is approached by a footpath from a quiet, shady lane, entering by a close-paled hand-gate. There is no driving road to the front door. I like the approach to a house to be as quiet and modest as possible, and in this case I wanted it to tell its own story as the way into a small dwelling standing in "wooded ground".'*

The author was well supplied with the sort of friends who could help and inspire her work, including Canon Ellacombe—whom she visited in his famous garden at Bitton Vicarage near Bristol; and Ellen Willmott, owner of large grounds at Warley Place in Essex, where she is said to have employed eighty-five gardeners. A beautiful and rich young woman, fifteen years junior to Gertrude Jekyll, she painted well, sang in a Bach Choir with Beatrix Havergal (the founder of Waterperry Horticultural School), played the violin to professional standard, and is remembered for her immense knowledge of plants and for the great book *The Genus Rosa*, which was sumptuously illustrated in colour by Alfred Parsons, ARA.

She devoted much of her energy and financial resources to the improvement of her Essex garden and to other gardens acquired at Ventimiglia and Aix-les-Bains. It was her custom to attend meetings of the Royal Horticultural Society in London with puzzling specimens drawn from one of her gardens in her lapel, and watch to see how many members of the Floral Committee were unable to identify it. Sir William Lawrence, who was Treasurer of the RHS from 1924 to 1928, and first President of the Alpine Garden Society, used to mention in his articles for *Gardening Illustrated* what Miss Willmott had worn in her buttonhole at the last show.

* *Home and Garden* (1900).

Although senior in years and even better known, Gertrude Jekyll wrote of her with characteristic generosity as 'My friend Miss Willmott, the greatest of living women gardeners'. That friend published another book, *Warley Garden in Spring and Summer*, full of her own photographs. Gertrude Jekyll wrote in all over a dozen, some in collaboration with Edward Mawley, Christopher Hussey and Lawrence Weaver. All are still worth reading if you can get hold of them. She was never too grand to take an interest in small gardens owned by humble people, and by her writings and example she probably did more to develop ideas and improve standards of gardening by amateurs than any other single horticulturist of her time. My late friend, Margery Fish, followed to a great extent in the Jekyll tradition, helping to revive forgotten cottage garden flowers, set off by a great variety of foliage plants, which she constantly helped people in every walk of life to cultivate with success.

Gertrude Jekyll lived to be eighty-nine. She died peacefully at her Surrey home in 1932, enjoying her garden almost to the last, even when it had to be visited in a wheel-chair. Ellen Willmott's end, which occurred in 1934 in her seventy-seventh year,* was surrounded by tragedy. All that wildly extravagant expenditure of her young days came to a stop abruptly, for her investments had for the most part been made in Germany, and disappeared in the First World War. The gardens in Italy and France had to go, and most of the gardeners at Warley too. Greatly embittered, she lost her looks faster than Nature alone would have stolen them; she sold possessions secretly in order to live, and turned into a recluse amid the ruins of her once cherished garden. When in 1932 the compiler of *Curtis's Botanical Magazine Dedications* applied to her, she declined to state her age and produced a portrait made about fifty years earlier, at a period when, as Sir William Lawrence noted, she 'broke more hearts than lances'—which was scarcely a true description of her in later life. Eventually the house had to be demolished, and many years afterwards Dr W. T. Stearn wrote of the grounds:

> 'It is hard to believe today, in the present wild state of Warley Place, that so much care, labour, thought and money had been spent . . . although survivors among the trees, shrubs and bulbs indicate clearly enough the work long ago of a keen planter.'

It would be absurd to suggest that these women have been singled out for mention as being the greatest gardeners in the annals of the RHS; but, in what

* There are conflicting reports of her age.

is still very much a man's world, it is clear that they must have been outstanding to have reached such eminence in its counsels. To select a man, or men, from well over three hundred male recipients of the Victoria Medal of Honour would be impossible. A number of them have places in other sections of this book. Sir George Taylor, Sir Edward Salisbury, Sir David Prain, Sir A. Hill, Sir Joseph Dalton Hooker, were all Directors and Messrs W. J. Bean and W. M. Campbell Curators of the Royal Botanic Gardens, Kew; Mr W. G. MacKenzie has been since 1945 Curator of the Chelsea Physic Garden; Sir Eric Savill and Mr T. H. Findlay created and maintain the Savill and Valley Gardens at Windsor; Sir Thomas Hanbury gave the Wisley estate to the Society, and G. F. Wilson owned and made the original garden; Miss Jekyll's friends Dean Hole and Edward Mawley were great rosarians of the nineteenth century, and Canon Ellacombe was another great gardener of that period; in our own time Mr S. M. Gault was for years an outstanding Superintendent at Regent's Park, and Mr T. Hay (father of Roy) was Superintendent of the Central Royal Parks; Dr W. T. Stearn, eminent botanist, was for some time the Society's Librarian; the Earl of Morton is Chairman of the Picture Committee and active on several others; the present Lord Aberconway (like his father before him) is President of the RHS; others who have held that office (and received the VMH) are Sir Trevor Lawrence, Lord Lambourne, Lord Wakehurst, and the Hon. Sir David Bowes-Lyon. In the Nursery world no fewer than four members of the Rochford family have received the VMH; also Mr Amos Perry of Enfield, and, head of a firm renowned at Covent Garden market, Mr William Poupart. All are connected in some way with my text.

In the early part of the nineteenth century the Society carried out its aims, as defined by John Wedgwood, to the full: 'to collect every information respecting the culture and treatment of plants and trees, as well culinary as ornamental'. It led the way by sending out its own collectors to search the world for new species. Men like David Douglas and Robert Fortune devoted their lives to tracking down and bringing home to this country plants and trees hitherto unknown to us. It is difficult now to grasp what an enormous wealth of fresh material the work of explorer-collectors provided for gardeners.

Douglas came from Scone, near Perth, serving his apprenticeship in the gardens of the Earl of Mansfield, and later working at the Glasgow Botanic Garden, where he attracted the attention of Professor W. J. Hooker (later to become Director of the Royal Botanic Gardens at Kew). It was Hooker who suggested that the RHS should engage Douglas as a plant collector. He left

London in 1823 for New York, mainly to acquire plants and seeds in use by American gardeners, together with information on the subject of fruit growing on their side of the Atlantic. A year later he again travelled to America, this time on a far more arduous expedition to the wild north-west coast bordering Pacific and Arctic seas. In Columbia he first saw the giant fir known to us as the Douglas Fir. For two years he undertook dangerous and exhausting treks by canoe, horseback, rowboat and on snowshoes. He was often short of food, menaced by Indians, frozen, soaked, and lonely; but he never slackened in his pursuit of plants.

Among those garden and pot plants which we owe to Douglas are *Lupinus polyphyllus*, which, crossed with *L. arboreus*, gave us the popular strain of Russell Lupins; *Garrya elliptica*, of the long grey catkins; *Ribes sanguineum*, the 'Flowering Currant'; and *Mimulus moschatus*, the sweet-scented musk our grandmothers loved. Unfortunately it has lost its scent. David Douglas was killed in 1834 in a horrible manner, being gored in a pit containing a trapped bull. The tragedy occurred in Hawaii and the victim was buried in Honolulu. In 1841 his countrymen erected a monument to his memory in the churchyard at Scone.

In 1843 Robert Fortune, a native of the Berwickshire Border country, was sent to China on behalf of the RHS in search of plants. His instructions ran: 'in all cases you will bear in mind that hardy plants are of the first importance to the Society, and that the value of plants diminishes as the heat required to cultivate them is increased'. He was provided with firearms for his own protection, and with some living plants as presents for those who assisted him. The transport of these was a major test for the Wardian case, which Dr Nathaniel Ward had invented a few years earlier (see page 76).

Fortune found chrysanthemums, tree paeonies, *Cryptomeria japonica*, and *Anemone japonica* (now *Anemone hupehensis* var. *japonica*.) Other introductions made by Fortune were the winter jasmine, the Chinese snowball tree, bleeding heart, and the Chinese bell-flower, *Platycodon grandiflorus*. On his return Fortune became Curator of the Chelsea Physic Garden. He made two more expeditions to the Far East, employed by the East India Company, with the primary object of introducing China tea into India. Later he went to Japan.

Long before these men went overseas for the Society, William Kerr had been sent, in 1804, to China, where Sir Joseph Banks wished him to collect plants for the Royal Garden at Kew. Kerr remained in China for nearly a decade, then left to supervise the Colonial Botanical Gardens in Colombo, Ceylon—which preceded the wonderful Botanic Gardens in Kandy. Kerr sent home to Kew the lovely yellow 'Banksian' rose, named after his patron; *Kerria japonica*, named after himself; *Nandina domestica*, *Juniperus chinensis*, and *Lilium tigrinum*—a plant raised in China, Japan and Korea for over a thousand years, not for its beauty but as an article of food. While on that subject, I must refer to the very first exhibit ever to be shown at a meeting of the Horticultural Society (not yet 'Royal'). This great event took place on 8 April 1805, when 'a Potatoe was exhibited by Mr Charles Minier likely to prove a valuable variety, the peculiar property of which is, that its tubers form so late in the season and have so thin a skin that they may be used through the winter, like young Potatoes'. From that homely appearance grew all the great shows at Vincent Square and Kensington, Chiswick and Chelsea, through nine reigns.

It would be easy to continue with a whole list of 'firsts'—the first charter granted to the Horticultural Society of London in 1809, the acquisition of its first garden (in Kensington) in 1818, the first show held under canvas at Chiswick in 1833, and so on; but that would soon become a catalogue. I will end with the first financial difficulties, which brought the Society close to bankruptcy in the 1830s and continued to harass it for over twenty years—a first which all hope will prove to be the last also. Thanks in some measure to the patronage of Prince Albert, the lean years passed, and prosperity flourished for a century. The *Journal* of the Society, begun in 1846, was discontinued for some years after the Jubilee in 1854; financial stringency at this period led to the sale of the library in 1859. The *Journal* reappeared at intervals from 1866, until in 1889 regular issues were resumed, becoming monthly in 1935.

In 1861 the Society received a royal charter and became the Royal Horticultural Society. It is possible that some of the difficulties through which it had been passing were caused by the emergence in 1839 of a rival group, the Royal Botanical Society, with its headquarters in Regent's Park. However that may have been, the RHS seems to have turned the corner when the royal charter was granted, and in time the combined operations of Kew and the Society overshadowed the Regent's Park group, which was finally phased out in the twentieth century. The great John Lindley, who was secretary of the RHS from 1858–63, died in 1865. In the following year his splendid library was acquired for £600—an asset which more than compensated for the enforced sale of books in 1859. The Society's present library in Vincent Square, which has been added to by gifts, legacies and purchases for over a century, now constitutes an invaluable reference centre. It bears the name of Lindley, and is freely open to all Fellows.

The long period of consolidation of the Society's work during the latter half of the Victorian era included the holding of innumerable conferences—Daffodil, Primula, Orchid, Conifer, Rose, Chrysanthemum, Dahlia, Carnation, Lily—and congresses—Apple and Pear, Apricot, Grape and Plum; the establishment of committees, institution of awards, and, by 1893, the sponsoring of a General Examination in Horticulture. The twentieth century opened grandly, with a contract signed for the building of a new hall, and the offer by Sir Thomas Hanbury of G. F. Wilson's garden and land at Wisley. Sir Thomas, a famous horticulturist, had developed his olive grove at *La Mortola* near Ventimiglia into an experimental botanic garden of great interest and charm. By 1889 it contained nearly four thousand different plants.

His offer was extremely opportune, for the Society had reached a stage where its earlier garden had to be relinquished, and available resources were being stretched to build the essential new hall in Vincent Square. The sixty acres at Wisley—in part garden and the rest farm land—were given on terms which allowed the Society to lease the latter so long as it was not required for cultivation, leaving room for expansion in later years. The Centenary in 1904 could now be celebrated in a blaze of glory, and at the Council meeting on 4 August 1903, when Sir Thomas Hanbury made his magnificent gift, a burst of applause was heard—the first in ninety-nine years of the Society's history. Ellen Willmott was present on that momentous occasion, and gave the assembly further details of G. F. Wilson's creation at Wisley.

Here one might expect to find a description of Wisley today, and details of all that it has meant to plant lovers in Britain and to the Royal Horticultural Society in particular. But, as this important garden plays so many parts, including the training of young gardeners and scientific work in its laboratories, it requires far more space than is available. The glories of the garden are described in detail every month by Mr C. D. Brickell, formerly the Society's Senior Scientific Officer and now its Director, and those who want to know more should join the RHS, visit Wisley at different seasons of the year, and read the *Journal*. The former Director, Mr F. P. Knight, VMH, succeeded Dr H. R. Fletcher, VMH, from whose authoritative book *The Story of the Royal Horticultural Society 1804–1968* most of this information is taken.

The activity most familiar to members of the general public is known as 'The Chelsea Show'—or, to gardeners, simply 'Chelsea'. The first was held in 1913, following a series of smaller events in the Temple Gardens; the first of these, held in May 1888, occupied two tents. In that year the Award of Merit was instituted for first-class plants newly introduced. The Fellows now numbered 1,636. When the Prince of Wales (later King Edward VII) opened the Temple Show of 1890, the President mentioned in his address that 'a central metropolitan hall or home for horticulturists of the United Kingdom was urgently needed'. Fourteen years afterwards, in July 1904, the new Royal Horticultural Hall in Westminster was opened by the King, accompanied by Queen Alexandra, and the first fortnightly show was staged there four days later. By the end of the year subscribers numbered 8,360.

In May 1912 a great International Horticultural Exhibition was held in the grounds of the Royal Hospital at Chelsea. This was promoted by a small public company, with the RHS acting as 'a benevolent godparent, rather than as the responsible promoter'. The great exhibition tent covered an area of three and a half acres—the largest ever erected up to that time—and was lit by electricity. Observing that the public was willing to flock to Chelsea for such a show, the Society, realizing that the Temple Gardens were now too small for its requirements, decided in 1913 to hold the first of a long series of Flower Shows in the Royal Hospital grounds. It was confined to the area between Monument Road and Eastern Avenue. No part of the Ranelagh Gardens was occupied, and the marquee was less than half the size of that now used. Even so, it allowed more space than had been available hitherto, and the event was a marked success.

By 1924 the exhibition hall in Vincent Square was proving inadequate for all the exhibitors and visitors who frequented the shows, and a site in Elverton Street was examined with a view to erecting a new and larger hall. In 1925 a lease of the land for 999 years was signed. Membership in 1923 had reached the figure of 19,000, and the Society's finances were in excellent shape. The New Hall was formally opened by HRH Princess Mary, Viscountess Lascelles, on June 26 1928. The Society held a great autumn show here in September, followed by an International Exhibition of Garden Design and a Conference on Garden Planning. In 1930 an International Horticultural Congress was held, and the Society gave a banquet to three hundred guests in the New Hall.

During the First World War the Society's programme of meetings and shows had continued with very little disturbance, and the reduction in membership was comparatively small, being overtaken in 1919 and raised above the pre-war figure by 1920. The Second World War had far greater effect on the shows; lighting restrictions prevented the holding of many, and the Chelsea Show was discontinued until 1947. Valuable work was done by the Society in encouraging the increased production of vegetables in gardens and on allotments. The RHS publication *The Vegetable Garden Displayed* became a best-seller. Among the

Society's other war-time activities were the organization of sales of gardening books, bulbs, plants, seeds and sundries in aid of the Red Cross, and the dispatch of vegetable and flower seeds to British prisoners-of-war in Germany. The setback in membership amounted to 8,948.

In 1945 it was found that the expenditure on wages, salaries, printing, fuel, postage and the rest had risen, while the income from subscriptions, hall-lettings, etc., was below pre-war level. The President, Lord Aberconway, therefore announced an increase in the subscription rates. Although this steep increase from £1 1s. to £2 2s. (for a single ticket of admission) and from £2 2s. to £3 3s. (for two) had at first an adverse effect on membership, that was only temporary and by 1950 the number had reached 38,268—an increase of 1,691 on the pre-war figure. Unfortunately this country had entered a period of inflation, and in 1968 the present Lord Aberconway, who in 1961 succeeded the late the Hon Sir David Bowes-Lyon as President, announced a further increase to £3 and £5, the traditional guineas having been abolished because decimalization of the currency was pending.

At the time of writing these subscriptions remain unaltered, but galloping inflation of expenses has to be met by the Society and its members alike. It is hoped to make ends meet by cutting certain commitments, including the intake of student gardeners at Wisley, and by attempts to raise income. The opening to the public of the gardens at Wisley on Sunday afternoons is a new departure; henceforth Fellows will have it to themselves only in the morning on Sunday. A substantial gain in admission fees should result from this.*

Another method is to increase membership, and here one recalls what Miss Coxhead said at the Annual General Meeting of 1971. For her yearly subscription of £3—less than the price of ten packets of cigarettes or a few boxes of chocolates—she enjoys Chelsea Flower Show and a variety of smaller exhibitions and lectures, the opportunity to rub shoulders with experts in every field of horticulture, the monthly *Journal* with its wide variety of articles and pictures, free admission to Wisley, and the use of the Lindley Library. Here is a marvellous and friendly club, open to all who take an interest in gardens and plants of every sort, including the growing ranks of the flower-arrangers. Let no one imagine that the Royal Horticultural Society is a haunt of plant bores and cranks. It is for everybody; no qualifications are necessary for membership; and if one gathers some useful knowledge in the course of being interested and entertained by gardeners and their products, what is wrong with that?

* In 1973 a single-ticket subscription will be £4·50.

10

The Herb Garden at Lullingstone Castle

THIS is probably the largest herb garden in Britain, ideally situated in a sheltered valley near Eynsford in Kent, and only twenty miles from London. Designed by that great expert on herbs and their histories, Eleanour Sinclair Rohde in 1946, it was at first run in association with Messrs Heath and Heather as a nursery for the cultivation and sale of herb plants. Owing to the recent death of Sir Oliver Hart Dyke, the crushing effect of death duties, and labour shortage, it has not been possible of late to maintain this grand conception as fully as it deserves; but there are hopes of restoring it to its original standard in time. It suffered before from a partial eclipse, in the late 1950s, when Lady Hart Dyke herself reclaimed it, unearthing from under a blanket of weeds a profusion of the original herbs, all stoutly resisting invasion by unauthorized plants. The huge complex of paths, which may be clearly seen in the aerial photograph, was also smothered in weeds. These had to be eliminated by sustained hard labour over many weeks, for the use of weed-killers might have damaged cherished herbs in the borders. No artificial manures are used here—only good farmyard stuff. The enclosing walls are known to have been in existence in the eighteenth century, but whether this piece of ground was used as a herb garden for the original manor house has not so far been ascertained. The list of plants which used to be cultivated and sold here shows over sixty culinary herbs, thirty fragrant ones for sweet-bags and pot-pourri, and about twenty used in medicine. The whole area is enclosed within walls of mellow brick, pierced by a horseshoe-shaped arch, and in this sunny and peaceful corner of Kent, free from factory pollution and seldom troubled by petrol or diesel engine fumes, the fragrances of the herb plants have full sway.

The little church of St Botolph (mostly Queen Anne, on a Norman foundation), peers in above the wall, companioned by some enormous cedars. Gatehouse and castle stand spaciously apart on wide green lawns. Of other buildings there is no sign. Except for the occasional group of golfers on the Down, this landscape to be broken neere unto Coleman Street, and there builded a posterne now called *Mooregate*, upon the Mooreside, where was never gate before. This gate he made for the ease of the citizens, that way to passe upon cawseys into the Field for their recreation'.* These fields were marshy, and although later dikes and bridges were made, it was long before the whole moor was drained. It was used for displays, sports and fights; Pepys in 1664 wrote of a 'fray' in Moorfields between butchers and weavers. During the Great Fire hordes of terrified people took what goods they could salvage and camped out there. The Fields were the chief open space for the City until nineteenth-century expansion swallowed them up. A few patches—Finsbury Square, the Honourable Artillery Company's ground, and Bunhills Fields—are all that remain.

We imagine the idea of a green belt to be entirely modern, overlooking the fact that Queen Elizabeth I, alarmed by the rapid growth of her metropolis, prohibited any new dwelling house to be built within three thousand paces of the gates of London upon pain of imprisonment and forfeiture of the materials brought for the erecting of such an edifice. The Queen had it enacted in these words:

> 'For the avoydinge of the great inconveniences whiche are found by experience to growe by the erectinge and buildinge of great nombers and multitude of cottage which are daylie more and more increased in manye parts of this Realme, be it enacted . . . noe person shall make, buylde or erect any manner of cottage for habitacion or dwelling unless the same person doe assigne and laye to the same cotage or buyldinge *fower acres of ground at the least*, being his or her owne Freehold lienge near the said cottage.'

Unfortunately the labouring people were prevented by this law from moving out. Few of them could come by four acres of land, so they were forced to multiply within the already congested area of the city. The richer classes, who were in a position to move outwards, caused John Evelyn to exclaim testily that 'mad intemperance' of building had made London almost as large again within his memory. After the Great Fire, Evelyn showed Charles II his scheme for a garden city, even more ambitious than the much later suburban projects at Welwyn and Hampstead. He had a vision of a great garden city, surrounded by plots of open ground thirty or forty acres in extent, planted with 'such shrubs

* Stowe, *Survey of London.*

an oven with her own hands, and served the simple, dignified meal, I was aware that *noblesse oblige* is not a dead cliché, and that perhaps the present owners of such historic homes, fighting to maintain them against appalling odds, demonstrate the true value and strength of tradition as none of their more fortunate earlier compatriots succeeded in doing.

This is not snobbery, which is a temporary and trumpery affair. It is a deep-rooted instinct, telling me that standards are themselves like great roots, vital to the life and stature of our human family tree, and that the struggle to nourish and perpetuate them is what chiefly distinguishes men from apes. One of my best friends is an old stonemason, who left school at the age of twelve and has toiled at quarrying and walling for sixty years. I am no less at home with him and his wife in their little Cotswold cottage than with Lady Hart Dyke in her grand castle. In fact, they have far more in common than might be apparent to a superficial glance. Each is committed to the fostering of traditional standards, and both are craftsmen in differing fashion. And what has all that to do with gardening? Everything, I believe. Gardening is an art and an avocation, requiring long training, informed experience, and selfless dedication to the well-being of soil and plant. Our country has for centuries upheld this tradition of the good gardener. Does it appear to be slipping a little, are the rewards of modern technology—quicker returns, less effort, easy cash, soft living, achieving a successful take-over bid? We must not despair. Sooner or later the gaudy bubble will burst, and then we shall see a return to the old long-term ideals, perhaps pursued with renewed vigour after a temporary eclipse.

11

The Society of Herbalists

THIS organization exists to perpetuate ancient knowledge of the healing properties inherent in many plants, both indigenous and imported. Its President, the Hon. Lady Meade-Fetherstonhaugh, has devoted many years to one specialized field of work, using the plant commonly known as Soapwort (sometimes Bouncing Bet, or to the botanist as *Saponaria officinalis*), with the aid of which she performs miraculous feats of rejuvenation upon old tapestries, rugs, brocades and banners. The Soapwort, which may be seen growing at Lullingstone in the Herb Garden, is used with pure spring water, and operates only on fabrics of natural fibre (no synthetics) dyed with vegetable dyes. It is not geared to modern man-made textile fibres and aniline dyestuffs. The astonishing power of this plant, not only in removing dirt and discoloration, but in restoring life and colour to old fabrics, has to be seen to be credited. At her old home, Uppark in Sussex, Lady Meade used to show visitors a sample, before treatment, of Italian brocade from which the curtains of 1740 were made. The rest, treated with Saponaria, hang at the windows in fine condition, while the sample is dingy and limp, 'Fit only for the dustbin', as its owner said.

The Society of Herbalists, started in 1927 by Mrs C. F. Leyel, helps people to obtain skilled herbal treatment for skin troubles and every sort of ill that afflicts the human body. It also supplies, through the associated Culpeper shops, pure herbal soaps and cosmetics, and a diversity of herbs for cooking. Membership at a very modest fee is open to all who are interested in herbs and wish to know more about them. As Mrs Leyel wrote in her book *The Truth About Herbs* (1954).

> 'Herbalism is the oldest healing art in the world. It may be defined as the art of healing by the use of non-poisonous herbs, administered internally or externally in the form of tinctures, extracts, distillations, pills, ointments or plasters prepared from the whole herb or root. Its history can be traced back through the civilisations of Rome, Greece, Assyria and Babylon to Sumerian times and even beyond.'

This art has never been lost. Mixed though it was with ignorance and superstition, it has now made use of modern discoveries, and remains an integral and widely used branch of modern medicine. Though often scorned by orthodoxy, it is slowly coming back into its own. Two factors tend to make herbal treatment less popular in our hurried times than the quick symptom-reducing effect of drugs. First, they are generally slow to heal. It may take a year to rebuild a gravely poisoned organ. Second, as herbs cure causes by removing them, the initial results of treatment may be an increase in the severity of the symptoms. This is a temporary nuisance which must be borne. A rash may be due to an imbalance in the blood. As the blood is purified by the herbs, the poison is flung out—not less, but even more into the skin. When the blood is purified, the rash is gone for ever.

The Society of Herbalists possesses one of the most complete dispensaries for herbal medicine in the country, wherein one can find medicinal extracts, oils, seeds, flowers, barks and powders from many lands. It takes a pride in being able to supply whatever a consultant may prescribe. Here one may share the fellowship of all who have faith in herbs and who would like to see a revival of herbal healing to offset the increasing use of drugs, the misuse of which is producing a crop of diseases, both physical and mental. Drug addicts are now turning to the Society of Herbalists for help, for herbs treat the whole man on the physical, etheric, psychic and mental planes. They are at once food and medicine for the body and the mind. The use of composted vegetable material in place of artificial manures—a field in which many members of the Society have been pioneers—is another of its interests. From this it is but a short step to all forms of pure and fresh foods.

It seemed fitting to close with the subject of herbalism, for this amalgam of horticulture and medicine can be traced back through the civilizations of Rome, Greece, Assyria and Babylon to Sumerian culture of over two thousand years before Christ. Yet the ordinary gardener, who may take no interest whatsoever in herbs, is the most important person of all. For him—or her—the words of Stephen Switzer in 1715, though quaintly worded to modern ears, will never lack meaning:

> *Go on and prosper, ye illustrious Lovers of Gard'ning; Exercise there will be enough, till this and all other Arts shall be swallowed up in the Ruins of this tottering World, and Nature herself shall breathe out her last Gasp; till You, Happy Souls, shall every one have received the Reward of your Virtuous Labour. And this which has been the utmost of your Ambition Here, shall be fully compleated in the more durable and unbounded Felicities of a joyful Hereafter.*

Short Book List

ALLEN, Mea; *Tom's Weeds*; Faber 1970
ALLEN, Mea; *The Hookers of Kew*; Joseph 1967
AMHERST, Alicia; *A History of Gardening in England*; Quaritch 1896
AMHERST, Alicia; *London Parks and Gardens*; Constable 1907
BACON, Francis; *Of Gardens*; 1625
BEAN, W. J.; *The Royal Botanic Gardens, Kew*; 1908
BELLOT, H. H. L.; *The Inner and Middle Temple*; Methuen 1902
BOWLES, E. A.; *My Garden in Spring*; Nelson 1914
BOWLES, E. A.; *My Garden in Summer*; Nelson 1914
BOWLES, E. A.; *My Garden in Autumn and Winter*; Nelson 1915
CHURCH, Richard; *The Royal Parks of London*; Dept. of the Environment 1956
CLEARY, F. E.; *The Flowering City*; The City Press 1969
COATS, Alice M.; *Flowers and their Histories*; Hulton 1956
COATS, Alice M.; *Garden Shrubs and their Histories*; Vista 1963
COLE, Nathan; *Royal Parks and Gardens*; 1877
COLVILLE, F. L.; *The Worthies of Warwickshire*; 1869
COXHEAD, Elizabeth; *One Woman's Garden*; Dent 1971
DANE, Clemence; *London Has a Garden*; Joseph 1964
DARTREY DREWITT, F.; *The Romance of the Apothecaries' Garden at Chelsea*; Chapman & Hall 1922
DENT, John; *The Quest for Nonsuch*; Hutchinson 1962
DODGE, Bertha S.; *Plants that Changed the World*; Phoenix 1962
DUNN, W. H.; *R. D. Blackmore*; Hale 1956
EARLE, Theresa; *Pot-Pourri from a Surrey Garden*; Smith Elder 1896
EARLE, Theresa; *More Pot-Pourri from a Surrey Garden*; Smith Elder 1898
FAIRBROTHER, Nan; *Men and Gardens*; Hogarth 1956
FAIRCHILD, Thomas; *The City Gardener*; 1722
FARRER, Reginald; *On the Eaves of the World*; Arnold 1926
FARRER, Reginald; *The Rainbow Bridge*; Arnold 1926
FLETCHER, H. R.; *The Story of the R.H.S.*; O.U.P. 1969
GATTY, C. L.; *Mary Davies and the Manor of Ebury*; Cassell 1921
GREEN, David; *Gardener to Queen Anne*; O.U.P. 1956
HADFIELD, Miles; *Pioneers of Gardening*; Routledge 1955
HADFIELD, Miles; *Gardening in Britain*; Hutchinson 1960
HAZLITT, W. C.; *Gleanings in Old Garden Literature*; 1877
HILL, W. Thomson; *Octavia Hill*; Hutchinson 1956
HOWARD, Philip; *The Royal Palaces*; H. Hamilton 1970

HOWE, Bea; *Lady With Green Fingers*; Country Life 1961
JACOBS, Reginald; *Covent Garden*; Simpkin Marshall 1913
JEKYLL, Francis; *Gertrude Jekyll*; Cape 1934
JEKYLL, Gertrude; *Wood and Garden*; Longmans 1899
JEKYLL, Gertrude; *Home and Garden*; Longmans 1900
JOHNSON, Louisa; *Every Lady Her Own Flower Gardener*; Kent 1840
LAW, Ernest; *Hampton Court Gardens Old and New*; 1928
LOUDON, Jane; *Gardening for Ladies*; Murray 1840
LOUDON, J. C.; *Arboretum Britannicum*; 1838
LYSONS, Daniel; *Environs of London*; 1795
MACGREGOR, J.; *Gardens of Celebrities and Celebrated Gardens*; Hutchinson 1918
MASSINGHAM, Betty; *Miss Jekyll*; Country Life 1966
MAUGHAM, C.; *Markets of London*; 1931
NUSSEY, Helen; *London Gardens of the Past*; Lane 1939
PEEL, D. W.; *A Garden in the Sky*; W. H. Allen 1962
POPE, Alexander; *Rape of the Lock*; 1712
POPE-HENNESSY, J.; *London Fabric*; Batsford 1939
ROBINSON, W.; *The English Flower-Garden*; Murray 1897
ROHDE, E. S.; *The Scented Garden*; Medici 1931
ROHDE, E. S.; *The Story of the Garden*; Medici 1932
ROHDE, E. S.; *Herbs and Herb Gardening*; Medici 1936
ROPER, Lanning; *The Gardens in the Royal Parks at Windsor*; Chatto 1959
SACKVILLE-WEST, V.; *The Garden*; Joseph 1946
SACKVILLE-WEST, V.; *In Your Garden*; Joseph 1951
SACKVILLE-WEST, V.; *In Your Garden Again*; Joseph 1953
SACKVILLE-WEST, V.; *More for Your Garden*; Joseph 1955
SACKVILLE-WEST, V.; *Even More for Your Garden*; Joseph 1958
V. Sackville-West's Garden Book; edited P. Nicolson; Joseph 1968
SANDS, Mollie; *The Gardens of Hampton Court*; Evans 1950
SHEWELL-COOPER, W. E.; *The Royal Gardeners*; Cassell 1952
SITWELL, Sir George; *On the Making of Gardens*; Duckworth 1951
SOUTHWORTH, J. G.; *Vauxhall Gardens*; Columbia University Press 1941
STROUD, Dorothy; *Capability Brown*; Country Life 1950
TAYLOR, Geoffrey; *Some Nineteenth-century Gardeners*; Skeffington 1951
TAYLOR, Geoffrey; *The Victorian Flower-Gardener*; Skeffington 1952
TAYLOR, Gladys; *Old London Gardens*; Batsford 1953
TEMPLE, Sir William; *Upon the Gardens of Epicurus* 1685
TURRILL, W. B.; *Royal Botanic Gardens, Kew*; Jenkins 1959
WEBBER, Ronald; *Covent Garden*; Dent 1969
WEBBER, Ronald; *The Early Horticulturists*; David & Charles 1968
WELCH, Charles; *The History of the Gardeners' Company* 1900
WHITTLE, Tyler; *Some Ancient Gentlemen*; Heinemann 1965
WILKINS, Eithne; *The Rose-Garden Game*; Gollancz 1969
WILLMOTT, Ellen; *Warley Garden in Spring and Summer*; 1909
WILLMOTT, Ellen; *The Genus Rosa*; 1910–14
WILLSON, E. J.; *James Lee and the Vineyard Nursery*; 1962
WROTH, Warwick; *London Pleasure Gardens of the Eighteenth Century*; 1896

Index

Aberconway, Lord, V.M.H., 309, 311, 316, 321
Adam, The Brothers, 223, 227, 250
Addison, Joseph, 41, 106, 109, 129, 222
Agricultural Research Council, 78
Aiton, W., 81, 195
Aiton, W. T., 81–4, 246, 311
Albert, Prince, 47, 48, 83, 87, 141, 241, 242, 318; Memorial, 241, 249
Albury Park, 47, 262
Alchorne, Stanley, 75
Allen, Mea, *Tom's Weeds*, 213, 327
All Hallows Wall, 296
Alpine Garden Society, 150, 302, 314
American Museum in Britain, 192
Amherst, Alicia, 101, 241, 246–8, 256, 290; *London Parks and Gardens*, 247, 256, 290, 327
Anne Boleyn, 8, 257
Anne of Cleves, 9
Anne of Denmark, Queen, 13, 15, 36
Anne, Queen, xii, 23–5, 39–41, 44, 45, 101, 123, 130, 244, 259, 265
Apothecaries, The Worshipful Society of, xv, 65–70, 75–7, 79, 193
Arne, Thomas, 225, 271
Arnold Arboretum, 61
Ashmolean Museum, 201
Ashmole, Elias, 201
Athlone, The Earl of, 286, 287
Austen, Ralph, *The Spiritual Use of an Orchard*, 253

Bacon, Sir Francis, xii, 18, 105–7, 109, 110, 117–119, 181, 205; *Of Gardens*, 105, 117, 327
Balfour, Lady Eve, 137, 154; *The Living Soil*, 154
Banks, Sir Joseph, 74, 75, 81, 82, 93, 311, 317
Barton, Sir Dunbar Plunket, 104, 109
baskets, 222, 277; (duck-nesting), 243
Bean, W. J., V.M.H., 86, 316, 327
Beddingham, Philip, xv
Bedford, Duke of, 223, 224; Earl of, 217, 218, 220
Belfast, H.M.S., 260
Bellot, H. H. L., 110, 111, 327
Bentham, George, 92, 93
Bermondsey Spa, *see* Pleasure Gardens
Berwickshire, xii, xvi, 317
Bible, Authorized Version of, 13, 14

Blackmore, R. D., 205–12; epilepsy of, 206, 210; *Lorna Doone*, 205, 207, 210, 211
Blackwood's Magazine, 210
Bliss, Sir Arthur, C.H., 52; *As I Remember*, 52
Bond, John, 62
Boswell, James, *Life of Johnson*, 221
Botanic Gardens: Ceylon, 317; Glasgow, 316; Royal, *see* Royal, Edinburgh and Kew
Botanic Magazine, The (Curtis), 75, 315
Botanic Society of London, *see* Royal
botany, study of, 66, 74, 75, 77, 78, 80, 82, 83, 84, 86, 92, 95–8, 100, 101, 139
Bowen, Miss D., xvi; (Trevor), 285
Bowes-Lyon, The Hon. Sir David, V.M.H., 58, 165, 166, 289, 316, 321
Bowes-Lyon, Lady Elizabeth, 282
Bowles, E. A., 165–75; *My Garden in Spring*, 170–5, 327
box, 22–4, 39, 40
Bridgettine Order (nuns), 226, 227
Bridgeman, William, 38, 41, 42, 131, 246, 270
Brighton Pavilion, 46, 47
British Association, 93
British Broadcasting Corporation, 279
British Entomological and Natural History Society, xv (*see also* South London N.H. Society)
British Museum, 46, 71, 78, 253, 269, 272
British Standards Institute, *Recommendations for Tree Work*, 294
Brown, Lancelot ('Capability'), 28, 133, 228, 229, 245
Buckingham, Duke of, 45, 200, 244
Buckingham House, 42, 45, 46, 245
Buckingham Palace, xii, xv, 15, 29, 43, 45–53, 246, 247, 262, 265, 278, 293; cascade, 49; flamingos, 49; Head Gardener, *see* Nutbeam; lawns, 49; Waterloo vase, 49, 50
Burney, Dr, 272
Burney, Fanny, *Evelina*, 269
Burton, Decimus, 83, 84, 89
Busby, E., xv
Busby, James, 232
Butler, Samuel, 105, 225, 238

'Cabbage King, The', 202–4

Camden, *Britannia*, 30, 34
Canterbury, Archbishops of, 102, 103, 256
Caroline of Anspach, Queen, 25–7, 41, 42, 80, 245, 246
catalpa, 105, 113, 252, 292, 295
Catherine of Aragon, Queen, 4, 8, 257
Catharine of Braganza, Queen, 19
Catherine Howard, 10
Catherine Parr, 10
Cement and Concrete Association, 303–5
Chambers, Sir William, 80
Charles I, King, 13, 15–17, 22, 36, 102, 217, 238
Charles II, King, 17, 18, 20, 21, 26, 27, 36, 37, 68, 70, 120, 123, 220, 221, 241–6, 257–9, 264, 291
Charlotte, Queen, 45, 47
Chaucer, *Canterbury Tales*, 256
Charterhouse, 9, 255
Chelsea College of Science and Technology, 78
Chelsea Flower Show, 213, 313, 318–21
Chelsea Physic Garden, 65–79, 193, 195, 196, 316, 317
Chelsea, Royal Hospital, 65, (Road) 68, 271, 320
Chippendale, 223
Christ's Hospital, 71
Church, Richard, 4; *The Royal Parks of London*, 248, 327
Cinchona, 70, 90
Civic Trust, 294
Clarendon, Lord, 19, 102
Cleary, F. E., M.B.E., F.R.I.C.S., xvi, 292, 293, 301; *The Flowering City*, xi, xvi, 292, 327
Coats, Alice M., 55, 327
collectors, plant, 21, 61, 70, 83, 85, 86, 90, 91, 93, 101, 144–50, 302, 312, 316–18
Commissioners, Crown Estate, 56, 62
Commons, Open Spaces and Footpaths Preservation Society, 299
Commonwealth, The, xii, 238, 258, 263
Company of Gardeners of London, The, *see* Gardeners
companies, city, 282, 292 (*see also* Apothecaries)
competitions, 283, 296, 302
compost, 53, 137, 193, 278, 286
Congreve, William, 221, 222, 224
Constitution Hill, 48, 244
Cook, Captain, 74
cotton industry, 72
Couchman, Mrs, xvi, 278, 279
Country Life, 104, 132, 133, 157, 328
Covent Garden Market Authority, 224
Covent Garden Market, *see* Market
Cowley, A., 125
Cowper, F., xv
cows (in central parks), 243
Coxhead, Elizabeth, xvi, 154, 182, 306–10, 321; *One Woman's Garden*, xvi, 306, 327
Cranmer, Archbishop, 8, 10, 102
Crawford, J. H. G., A.L.A., F.S.A.Scot., xvi
Creevey, Thomas, 46
Cromwell, Oliver, 17, 27, 200, 238, 242, 250; Richard, 17
Cromwell, Thomas, 8, 9
Crowe, Sylvia, P.P.I.L.A., 304
Crowson, E. L., xv
Crystal Palace, 214, 224, 228, 241
Culpeper, Nicholas, 325
Cunliffe, Mitzi, 304
Curtis, William, *Flora Londiniensis*, 75; *see also Botanical Magazine*
Cutty Sark, 259, 261

Dane, Clemence, *London Has a Garden*, 225, 327
Darwin, Charles, 84, 88, 89
deer, 9, 11, 13, 26, 31, 32, 34, 40, 56, 58, 84, 86, 87, 237, 239, 250, 258, 263
Derry & Toms, Messrs, xvi; Roof Garden, 285–7
Dickens, Charles, 112, 141, 223
Dickson, James, 311
Discovery, H.M.S., 260
Dissolution of the Monasteries, 4, 9, 196, 219, 222, 226, 227, 237
Dog and Duck, *see* Pleasure Gardens
Doggett, Thomas, Coat and Badge, 68
Douglas, David, 316, 317
Drewitt, Dr Dartrey, 65, 69, 72; *Romance of the Apothecaries' Garden at Chelsea*, 65, 327
Dryden, John, 109, 222, 224
Duck Island, St James's Park, 49, 242
Dutch Gardens, *see* Gardens

Earle, Theresa, xv, 137, 151–6, 182; *Pot-Pourri from a Surrey Garden*, 151–6, 327
Edinburgh, Duke of, 58
Edinburgh Royal Botanic Garden, *see* Royal Botanic
Edward the Confessor, King, 255, 277
Edward I, King, 190
Edward III, King, 7
Edward VI, King, 10, 217
Edward VII, King, 44, 49, 282, 320
Elizabeth I, Queen, 4, 7, 8, 10–13, 15, 33–6, 69, 113, 191, 227, 237, 257–8, 277, 290, 291
Elizabeth II, Queen, *see* Queen, H.M., The
Elizabeth The Queen Mother, *see* Queen Mother, H.M., The
Ellacombe, Canon, 167, 314, 316
Ely, Bishop of, 218, 290
Embankment, Thames, 65, 68, 75–7, 102, 260, 278
Environment, Department of the, xvi
Erasmus, 69
European Conservation Year, 301
Evelyn, John, 17, 19, 36, 38, 39, 70, 101, 117, 120–5, 200, 201, 238, 242, 243, 246, 258, 291,

292; *Diary*, 101, 120–2, 200, 201, 238, 242, 243, 258
Exhibition, The Great, 214, 224, 241

Fairchild, Thomas, *The City Gardener*, 283, 284, 327
Fairfax, General, 238, 242
Falkner, Sir Keith, 323
Farrer, Reginald, 144–50; *The Rainbow Bridge*, 144, 145, 148, 149, 327; *On the Eaves of the World*, 146, 327
Field, The, 157, 162
Fiennes, Celia, 240
Findlay, T. H., M.V.O., V.M.H., 58, 62, 316
Finnis, Valerie (Lady Scott), xv
Finsbury Circus, 293, 295
Fire of London, The Great, 20, 67, 79, 291
Fisher, J. M., xv
Fish, Margery, 315
Fleming, J. G., xvi
Fletcher, Dr H. R., V.M.H., xvi, 165, 319; *The Story of the R.H.S.*, 165, 319, 327
Forsyth, William, 75, 311
Fortune, Robert, 75, 76, 316, 317
Fountayne, Dr John, 271
Fowler, Charles, 228
Fuchs, Leonard, 197
Fulham Palace, 21, 100, 101, 123
Fuller, *Market Gardening in Kent and Surrey*, 191
Fulmer Grange, 303
Franck, Miss N., M.A., xvi
Frederick, Prince of Wales, 27, 80, 269

Garden City, 291
gardeners, *see under individual names*
Gardeners, The Worshipful Company of, xvi, 15, 191, 219, 280–4, 288, 293, 295–6, 302
Gardener's Chronicle, 166
Garden History Society, 98
Gardening Centre (Syon Park), xv, 140, 195, 226–33
Gardening Illustrated, 314
gardening, market, *see* Market
gardening, nursery, *see* Nursery
Gardens:—Scented for the Blind (Greenwich) 262; Botanic Society, Regent's Park, 81; Bowles, E. A., Myddelton House, 166–75; Buckingham Palace gardens, *see* Buckingham Palace; Castle of Mey, 289; Cecil House, 11; Chatsworth, 228; Chelsea (Sir Thomas More's), xii, 68, 69; Chelsea Physic, 65–79, 193, 195, 196, 316, 317; Chiswick, *see* R.H.S.; Church, 295, 296; City companies', 292; Derry & Toms', (Roof) 285–7; Dutch, 5, 21, 39, 40, 107; Elizabeth Coxhead's, xvi, 306–10; English ('Capability' Brown), 133; Evelyn (Sayes Court), 121, 122, 258; Fulham Palace, 21, 100, 101, 123; Gerard, John, *see* Herb; Gray's Inn, xii, 104–10, 113, 114; Hampton Court, xii, 3–29, 40, 68, 87, 98, 101, 130, 207, 240, 285; Hatfield, 15, 199; Herb gardens, (Gerard's) 12, 66, 190, 192, (Kew) 81, 98, (Lullingstone) xvi, 322–4, (Rohde, E. S.) 159, 162–4, (Syon Park) 232–3, (Hidcote), 307; Jekyll, Gertrude, 313–15; Kensington, xii, 39–44, 47, 75, 101, 240, 241, 248, 249, 295; Kew, *see* Royal Botanic Garden; Knot, 'Knotte', 4, 5, 14, 16, 22, 29, 35, 98, 106, 108, 117, 285, 292; Lambeth Palace, 102–3; Lincoln, Earl of, 190; Lincoln's Inn, xii, 104, 106, 107, 113, 114; Market, *see* Market gardens; Newhall, 200; Nonsuch, 30–7; Nursery, *see* Nursery; Parkinson's, 16; Physic, 66, 84–5; Pleasure gardens, *see* Pleasure gardens; Police, 201, 288; Pope's (Twickenham), 129–32; Queen Mary's Rose, *see* Regent's Park; Royal Botanic, *see* Royal Botanic Gardens; St Paul's Cathedral, 283, 293, 295; Staple Inn, 104; Tea, *see* Pleasure gardens; Temple, The, 104, 105, 107, 110–12, 154, 260, 320; Theobalds, 11, 105, 190; Town, at Wexham Springs, 303–5; Tradescant's, 66, 200, 201; Westminister Abbey, xvi, 217, 277–279; Windsor Great Park (Savill and Valley), xii, xv, 54–62, 316; Willmott, Ellen, 312, 314, 315; Wisley, *see* R.H.S.; *Woman's Realm* at Syon Park, xv, 230, 231, 232
Garden, The, 162, 314
gas lighting, 246, 269
Gault, S. M., M.B.E., F.L.S., V.M.H., xv, 316
Gay, John, 129, 220
Gentleman's Magazine, The, 199
George, Bernard, F.R.I.B.A., 285
George I, King, 25, 26, 41, 68, 71, 244
George II, King, 26, 27, 41, 42, 71, 72, 80, 240, 244
George III, King, 27, 28, 42, 45, 47, 56, 81, 84, 245
George IV, King, 28, 46, 47, 54, 246, 251, 269
George V, King, 54, 56, 58
George VI, King, 54, 58, 59
Gerard, John, 11, 12, 66, 169, 190, 192; *Herball*, 11, 67, 74
Gibbons, Grinling, 123, 225
Glanville, Mrs P., xv
Gloucester, Duchess of, 282, 287
G.L.C. Parks Department, 248
Golden Hind, The, 261
Golsmith, Oliver, 105, 222, 224
Goodall, Sir Stanley, R.C.N.C., 51
Goodchild, Mrs Mary, 164
Good Gardeners' Association, 137
Gray's Inn, 104–10, 113, 114
greenhouses and conservatories, 19, 39, 41, 69–71, 73, 81, 83, 84, 89, 94, 102, 103, 123, 127, 128, 132, 193, 194, 202–4, 213, 214, 223, 224, 226, 228, 230, 231, 293

Greenwich: College, *see* Royal Naval; Mean Time, 257, 259; Park, *see* Parks
Grigg, Mrs Gladys, xv
grotto (Pope's), 129, 131, 132
Guildhall Library, horticultural books, 284
Guilds, City of London, 280, 281
Gwyn, Nell, 220, 221, 244
Gypsy Moth IV, 261
Guardian, The, 314

Hadfield, Miles, xvi, 98, 122, 144, 150, 241, 295; *Gardening in Britain*, 122, 144
Hales, *The Complete Treatise of Practical Husbandry*, 196
Hampden, John, 9, 16
Hampton Court, *see* Gardens
Hanbury, Sir Thomas, V.M.H., 316, 319
Hancock, Ralph, 286
Handel, G. F., 25, 245, 269, 271
Handicapped, Garden for (Syon Park), 230, 231
Hanmer, Sir Thomas, 111
Harrison, *Description of England*, 190
Harris, Richard, 8
Hart Dyke, Lady, xvi, 322–4
Hatfield, *see* Gardens
Hatton, Christopher, 112
Havergal, Beatrix, V.M.H., 314
Hawksmoor, Nicholas, 41, 259
Henderson, Arthur, 215
Henrietta Maria, Queen, 15, 16, 36, 258
Henry IV, King, 190
Henry V, King, 226
Henry VI, King, 112, 182, 190
Henry VIII, King, xii, 3–12, 30–3, 37, 178, 189, 190, 192, 200, 217, 226, 237, 257, 323
Hentzner, Paul, 34
Hepplewhite, 223
herbaceous border, 29, 47, 262
Herbalists, The Society of, xvi, 325, 326
herbals, 11, 66, 67, 74, 227
herbarium, 74, 80, 82, 85, 88, 89, 92, 95
herb gardens, *see* Gardens
Heslop-Harrison, Professor J., 99
Hill, Octavia, 299–300
Hogarth, William, 222, 269
Hogg, Dr Robert, 209, 212; *Fruit Manual*, 212
Holbein, Hans, 69
Hole, Dean, 312, 313, 316
Holmes, Oliver Wendell, 24
Holyrood Palace, 47
Hooker, Sir Joseph, V.M.H., 81–5, 87–9, 91–5, 302, 316; *Flora* (New Zealand), 92; *Himalayan Journals*, 88; *Index Kewensis*, 94
Hooker, J. and, Bentham, G., *Genera Plantarum*, 92
Hooker, Sir William, 81–9, 91, 92, 316; *Flora* (Commonwealth), 89; *Species Filicum*, 92; *Synopsis Filicum*, 92
Hope, Frances Jane, 231
horticultural societies, 288
Howe, Bea (Mrs Lubbock), *Lady with Green Fingers*, xv, 328
Howell, James, 109
Hoy, Thomas, 231
Hummums, 222
Hunsdon, Lord, 13
Hunter, Kathleen, 163, 164
Hutchinson, Col. John, 242
Hyde Park, *see* Parks

illuminations, 266, 268, 269, 272–4, 293, 294
Imperial College of Science and Technology, 78
Inns of Court, xv, 104–14
Institute of Landscape Architects, 304
Inverewe, 52, 57, 60, 85; Mairi Sawyer of, 52, 57
Islington Spa, Sadler's Wells, *see* Pleasure gardens

James, Edward Stuart, 25
James VI of Scotland, I of England, King, xii, 13–16, 36, 45, 50, 66, 67, 107, 243, 258, 265, 281
Japan, Emperor and Empress of, 99
Jekyll, Gertrude, V.M.H., 58, 141, 231, 233, 262, 309, 311–15; *Wood and Garden*, 314, 328; *Home and Garden*, 314, 328
Jesuit's Bark (Cinchona), 70, 90
Jodrell Laboratory, Kew, 93, 95–8
Johnson, Dr Samuel, 27, 46, 105, 221, 222, 224, 267
Johnson, Thomas, 67
Jones, Inigo, 13, 113, 217, 218, 220, 227, 258
Jonson, Ben, 13

Kalm, Peter, 73
Kennedy, Lewis, 194, 195
Kensington Gardens, *see* Gardens
Kensington Palace, xii, 23, 24, 37, 38–44, 75, 240
Kent, Duchess of, 43, 282, 287
Kent, Edward, Duke of, 43
Kent, William, 26, 28, 41–3, 131, 132, 245, 270
Kerr, William, 317, 318
Kew Gardens, *see* Royal Botanic
Kew Laboratory, *see* Jodrell
Kew Museum, 85, 91
Kew Palace, 98
King, R. W., D.F.C., xv
Kneller, Sir Godfrey, 222
Knights of St John, 107
'Knight of Ye Golden Tulip', 242
Knole, Sevenoaks, 178
Kyrle Society, The, 299

Lamb, Charles, 109–11
Lambert, Major-General John, 36, 242
Lambeth Palace, 102, 103, 201
Lansbury, George, 248

Laud, Archbishop, 102
Lawrence, Mr and Mrs William, 141, 142
Lee, James, 194–9, 328
Le Notre, André, 17, 18, 22, 241, 247, 258, 270
Leverhulme Trust, The, xvi
Leyel, Mrs C. F., *The Truth about Herbs*, 325
Lido (Hyde Park), 248
Lincoln Herald, The, 197, 198
Lincoln's Inn, xii, 104, 106, 107, 113, 114
Linnaeus, Carl, 71–4, 197
Linnean Classification, 66, 73, 197; Society, 73–75, 88, 311
litter, 248
London Gardener, The, 241, 300, 301
London, Bishops of, 100, 101, 217; bomb debris, 57; City of, xi, 280–3, 290–6, 301, 302; County Council (G.L.C.), 293; Gardens Society, The, xvi, 201, 288, 289; Museum, The, xv, 37, 43, 44; parochial charities, 65, 77; squares, xii, 134
London, George, 21–3, 39, 40, 122–4
Lorne, Marquis of, 210
Loudon, Jane and John, xii, 101, 113, 134–43, 195, 197, 328
Lucas, Alfred, 202, 203
Lullingstone Castle, xvi, 322–4
Lutyens, Sir Edwin, 313, 314
Lyell, Charles, 88, 95
Lytton, Earl of, 152

McLintock, David, xv, 51
mahogany, 223
Mall, The, 243–7, 249
manors: Byfleet, 9; Chelsea, 67, 68, 70, 71; Cuddington, 31, 34; Ditton, 9; Eia, 45; Esher, 9; Hyde, 237; Molesey, 9; Neyte, 219, 220, 237; Portpool, Purpool, 104; Walton, 9; Weybridge, 9; Wimbledon, 36, 242; Wiseley, Wisley, 9, 289, 316, 319, 321
manure, 192–4, 204, 322
Marble Arch, 47, 48
market gardeners and gardening, 73, 189–94, 202–16, 219, 222, 283
Market, Covent Garden, xii, 192, 202, 203, 205, 207, 209, 211, 215, 217–25, 278, 316
markets, other London, 189, 190, 192, 222, 282
Marvell, Andrew, 242, 254, 255
Marylebone Gardens, *see* Pleasure gardens
Mary, Princess, 8; Queen, 10, 11, 33, 227
Mary, Queen (William and Mary), 20–3, 38–9, 44, 101, 103, 107, 123, 126, 259
Mary, Queen (consort of George V), *see* Queen Mary
masques, 104, 108, 109
maze, 5, 16, 21, 23, 29, 31, 35
Meade-Fetherstonhaugh, The Hon. Lady, xvi, 325
Medical Research Council, 78
Melrose Abbey (inscription), 37
Metropolitan Police Gardens, 201, 288
Metropolitan Public Gardens Association, xi, xvi, 283, 296, 297–302
Mey, Castle of, 289
Miller, Miss J. L., xv
Miller, Philip, 71–3, 75, 195–7; *The Gardener's Dictionary*, 195
Milne, W. G., 86
Milton, John, 17, 183, 268, 278
Mollet, André, 18, (and Gabriel) 241, 258
Moore, Thomas, 77
Moore, Tom, 28
More, Sir Thomas, xii, 68, 69, 78
Morton, Lord, 78, 316
mount, mound, 6–8, 10, 16, 22, 31, 49, 98, 106, 108, 109, 129, 131
mulberry, xii, 15, 45, 47, 50, 107, 265, 292
Murray, J. L., xv, 256, 258, 262–4

Napier, Miss E., xvi
Nash, John, 46, 50, 250, 295
Nathan, Lord, 280, 281, 283
National Exhibition of Gardening (Syon Park), xv, 140, 195, 226–33
National Trust for Scotland, 57
National Trust, 300
Naval Constructors, Royal Corps of, 260
Neckham, Alexander, *De Naturis Rerum*, 290
Newton, Sir Isaac, 71, 121
New Zealand flora, *see* Hooker
Nicolson, Ben, 176
Nicolson, Nigel, xv, 176, 180
Nicolson, Sir Harold, 176, 177, 179, 180
Nicolson, Lady, *see* V. Sackville-West
Noailles, Vicomte de, 61
Noel-Buxton, Lord, 288; Trust, 288
Nonsuch, xii, 30–7, 295
North, Marianne, 94
Northumberland, Dukes and Earls of, 47, 140, 227, 228, 231, 232
Nottingham, Earl of, 38, 240
Nottingham House, 38
Noyes, Alfred, 80
nursery gardens and nurserymen: Bacon, 105; Brompton, 22, 39, 123, 124; Chelsea, 73; Furber, 101; Gray, 101; Henderson, 215; Kennedy, 194, 195; Kensington, 139; Kew, 89; Lee (vineyard), 194–9, 328; Loddige, 140; Perry, 316; Rochford, 213–16; Royal Exotic, 215; Shepherd's Bush, 139; Veitch, 215, 216; Wansdyke, 230; Wills and Segar, 215
Nutbeam, Fred, xv, 49, 52, 53

Observatory, The Old Royal, 257–9, 262, 263
Observer, The, 176, 181
Odling, Mrs, xv
Oldham, Richard, 86
Olympia Exhibition, 193, 195, 196
Orangery, 41, 43, 44, 50, 73, 80, 81
Ornithological Society, The, 242

Osborne House, 47, 49
Owen, Professor Richard, 207

paille-maille, 243, 244
Pall Mall, 243
Parkinson, John, *Paradisi in Sole*, 16
parks: Battersea, 89, 274; Bishop's, Fulham, 103; Bushey, 23, 25, 27, 28, 207, 209; Chelsea, 69; Green, The, 107, 245, 247, 249; Greenwich, xv, 18, 256–64; Hyde, xii, 40, 42, 89, 107, 214, 224, 237–49, 295; Kensington, *see* Gardens; Postman's, 295; Regent's, xii, xv, 81, 250–5, 313, 316, 318; Richmond, 58, 84, 86, 87; St James's, xii, 18, 45, 49, 55, 107, 237, 240, 242, 244–7, 249, 250; Victoria (G.L.C.), 248; Windsor Great, xv, 54–62
patron saints of gardening, 161, 162
Paxton, J., 214, 228, 240
Pepys, Samuel, 19, 20, 36, 39, 68, 106, 109, 121, 220, 222, 239, 246, 258, 265, 270, 291
Perry, Amos, V.M.H., 316
Perry, Mrs Frances, V.M.H., 169, 312
Philip of Spain, King, 10, 11
physic gardens, *see* Gardens
Physicians, Royal College of, 65, 67, 77
Piazza, Covent Garden, 217, 218, 220, 221, 224
pineapple (first in England), 18, 241
Placentia, Palace of, 256, 258, 260
Plague, the Great, 16, 20, 36, 68, 218, 239
Plantagenet, 112, 182
plant collectors, *see* Collectors
Platt, Sir Hugh, 14
Platter, Thomas, *Travels in England*, 12, 32, 34
Pleasure gardens, 265–74
Pole, Cardinal, 102
Pope, Alexander, 24, 26, 129–32, 207, 222
potato, 15, 19, 20, 318
Poupart, Jacques, 215; William, V.M.H., 316
Prain, Sir David, V.M.H., 77, 316
Princess Alice, 287; Princess Amelia, 267; Prince Arthur of Connaught, 287; Princess Augusta, 27, 80, 83; Princess Louise, 44, 210; Princess Margaret, 44, 282; Princess Marie Louise, 287; Princess Marina, 282; Princess Mary, 282, 283, 320; Princess Mary Adelaide, 90
Purdom, Bill, 145–8, 150

Queen, H.M. The (Elizabeth II), xv, 50–3, 58, 261, 282, 283
Queen Elizabeth The Queen Mother, V.M.H., H.M., 54, 58, 59, 228, 282, 283, 289
Queen Mary, H.M. (The late), 43, 54, 56, 58, 253, 255, 282, 287
Queen's House, The, 46
Queen's Garden (Kew), 98

Raleigh, Sir Walter, 15, 105, 205, 257
Ranelagh, *see* Pleasure gardens
rayon industry, 95
Reformation, The, 237, 255
Regent's Park, *see* Parks
Renaissance, The, 11, 21
Restoration, The, 36, 120, 238, 239, 250, 265
Richardson, Sir Albert, 293
Richmond Palace, 10, 13, 33
Richmond Park, *see* Parks
Robin, Jean, 199
Robinson, William, *The English Flower Garden*, 251, 313, 314, 328
Rochford family, 213–15, 316
rock gardening, 75, 94, 150, 308, 309 (*see also* Alpine Garden Society)
Rohde, Eleanour Sinclair, xv, 157–64; writings, 157–62, 328
Rohde, A., xv, 157
Roper, Lanning, 60, 328
Rose, John, 18, 21, 241
Rotten Row, 38, 240
Round Pond, The, 42, 44
Royal Botanic Society of London, 81, 251, 313, 318
Royal Botanic Gardens, Edinburgh, 61, 149
Royal Botanic Gardens, Kew, xv, 47, 50, 70, 80–99, 195, 207, 316–18
Royal College of Music, 323
Royal Horticultural Society, xvi, 53, 60, 61, 73, 75, 83, 112, 139, 141, 144, 150, 154, 165, 175, 209, 212, 251, 253, 289, 309, 310, 311–21; Gardens, (Chiswick) 81, 318, (Wisley) 61, 289, 310, 313, 316, 319, 321; *Journal*, 53, 62, 166–9, 179, 180, 212, 310, 312, 318, 319, 321; Victoria Medal of Honour, 141, 165, 289, 311, 312, 316
Royal Hospital, Chelsea, 65, 68, 320
Royal Meteorological Society, 266
Royal Naval College, Greenwich, 259–62
Royal Society, 18, 19, 71, 77, 93, 120,
Royal Toxophilite Society, 251
rubber, 90, 91

Sackville-West, V. (Lady Nicolson), xv, 176–85, 328
Sadler's Wells, *see* Pleasure gardens
St James's Palace, 38, 45, 47, 237, 245
St James's Park, *see* Parks
St Paul's Cathedral, 67, 253, 260, 283, 287, 293, 295
St Paul's Church, Covent Garden, 218, 220, 225
Sandys, The Rt Hon. Duncan, M.P., 294
Salisbury, Richard, 311
Salisbury, Sir Edward, V.M.H., 316
Savill Gardens, *see* Gardens, Windsor Great Park
Savill, Sir Eric, K.C.V.O., C.B.E., M.C., V.M.H., xv, 54–6, 58, 62, 316
seedsmen, 194
Serpentine, The, 42, 48, 246, 248

Shakespeare, William, 12, 13, 15, 50, 67, 112, 182, 205
Sheffield, John, 45
Sheraton, 223
Sheridan, R. B., 222, 224
Shewell-Cooper, Dr W. E., M.B.E., 137, 328
silk industry, 45, 265
Sissinghurst, 176–81
silviculture, 22, 23, 87, 89, 91, 93, 113, 122, 123, 125, 134, 140, 223, 229, 258, 262–4, 292–5, 300, 301; B.S.I. booklet, *see* British Standards
Skelton, John, 3
Sloane, Sir Hans, 67, 69–73, 76
Smith, Alfred William, 202–4
Smith, Sir James, 74, 75
Smoke Abatement Act, xii, 113, 264, 286, 308
smokeless zones, 53, 78, 121, 292
Smollett, Tobias, *Humphrey Clinker*, 272
Soil Association, The, 137
Somerset, 'Protector', 10, 217, 226, 227
Southey, Robert, 105
South London Natural History Society, 50
Sowerby, *English Botany*, 251
Spectator, The, 41, 129, 222
Sphere, The, 157
Stagg, Peter, 293
Stamp, Edward, 89, 90
Staple Inn, 104
Stearn, Dr W. T., V.M.H., 315, 316
Steele, Richard, 130, 222
Stephenson, R. A., xv
Stern, Sir, Frederick, V.M.H., 61
Stimpson Mrs J. M., xvi
'stoves', *see* Greenhouses
Stowe, John, 109, 291; *Survey of London*, 291
Sunday opening (Hampton Court), 3; (Kew), 87
Swan Walk, Chelsea, 65, 68, 72
Swift, Jonathan, 126, 127, 129, 222, 224
Switzer, Stephen, 39, 100, 101, 326; *Iconographia Rustica*, 100, 101
Syon Park, xv, 15, 87, 140, 195, 226–33

Tatler, The, 106
Taylor, Sir George, D.Sc., F.R.S., F.R.S.E., F.L.S., V.M.H., xv, 95, 98, 99, 316
tea, 6, 24, 263, 267, 272, 273
Tea gardens, *see* Pleasure gardens
Temple, Inner, 104, 105, 110; Middle, 104, 110, 112, 121, 206; Outer, 107
temple, shell (Pope's), 131
Temple, Sir William, 126–8; *Upon the Gardens of Epicurus*, 126, 328
tennis court, 6, 19, 35, 293, 295
Terry, Dame Ellen, 180, 225
Thackeray, W. M., *Vanity Fair*, 195; (Hotel) 222
Thames, River, 12, 48, 65, 68, 74, 75, 80, 82, 83, 87, 93, 100, 102, 129, 131, 190, 192, 194, 196, 217, 219, 222, 226, 237, 256, 259–61, 264, 273, 277, 278
theatres: Covent Garden, Drury Lane, 221; 'Old Vic', 299
Theobalds, *see* Gardens
Thistleton-Dyer, William, 93, 94
Thornton, Dr Robert, *The Temple of Flora*, 196
Tijou, Jean, 21, 24
Times, The, 157, 164, 209
tobacco, 15
Todd, H. M., *Vine Growing in England*, 196
Tower of London, The, 253, 260, 264
Tradescant, John (senior and junior), 66, 89, 199–201, 295
trees, *see* Silviculture
Turner, J. W. M., 222
Turner, Dr William, 227, 232, 233; *The Names of Herbes*, 227
Tusser, Thomas, *Five Hundred Points of Good Husbandry*, 7, 194
Tyburn, 48, 238, 250

Underwood, Mrs Desmond, 230
Upward, Michael, xvi, 302

Valley Gardens, The, *see* Gardens, Windsor Great Park
Vanbrugh, Sir John, 41, 259
Vauxhall, *see* Pleasure gardens
Vauxhall Gardens, J. G. Southworth, 268, 328
Veitch family, 215, 216
Victoria, Queen, 3, 27, 28, 43, 44, 46–9, 52, 80, 83–5, 87, 91, 94, 140, 141, 152, 246, 247, 287, 295, 311, 312
Villiers, A. E., xv
Villiers, Mrs, 152
vines, vineyards, 28, 29, 114, 132, 190, 194, 196, 200, 205, 208, 213, 231, 232, 283, 287, 290
vineyard nursery, *see* Nursery, Lee (vineyard)

Wakehurst Place, 99
Wallace, Alfred Russell, 88
Walpole, Horace, 18, 120, 121, 195, 207, 222, 240, 241, 272, 273
Walpole, Sir Robert, 26
Wansdyke Nursery, *see* Nursery
Ward, Nathaniel, 76, 317; *Growth of Plants in Closely-glazed Cases, The*, 76
Waterperry Horticultural School, 309, 314
Watson, Dr Anthony, 32–5, 295
Watts, G. F., 295
Watts, John, 69, 70
Webster, *Trees of London*, 295
Wedgwood, John, 92, 95, 311, 316
weeding women, xii, 11
Wellington, Duke of, 28
Wells—Bagnigge, St Chad's and St Pancras, Sadler's, *see* Pleasure Gardens
Westminster Abbey: Abbot, 45, 255, 277; Dean, xvi; Gardens, *see* Gardens; Lands, 45, 217, 222, 237

Westminster Pier, 260, 264
Whitehall Palace, 22, 68
wilderness: Hampton Court, 22, 23; Nonsuch, 31, 33–5; Bacon's, 117; Pope's, 131
Wilkins, Eithne, *The Rose-Garden Game*, 254, 255, 328
William Rufus, King, 254
William of Orange, King, xii, 5, 20–3, 38–40, 44, 101, 103, 107, 123, 126, 127, 240, 270
William IV, King, 28, 43, 46, 48, 50
Willmott, Ellen, V.M.H., 141, 311, 312, 314, 315, 319; *The Genus Rosa*, 314
Willson, E. J., *James Lee and the Vineyard Nursery*, xv, 328
Wilson, E. H., 59
Wilson, G. F., V.M.H., 313, 316, 319
window boxes, 283, 288, 302
Windsor Castle, 40, 54
Windsor, the late Duke of, 54, 283
Windsor Great Park, *see* Parks
Wise, Henry, 21, 23, 39, 40, 42, 123, 124
Wisley, R.H.S. Gardens, *see* Royal Horticultural Society
Wolsey, Cardinal Thomas, 3–5, 7, 8, 12
Woman's Realm Garden, *see* Gardens
Woods, Miss P., xvi
Worshipful Company of Gardeners, *see* Gardeners
Worshipful Society of Apothecaries, *see* Apothecaries
Wren, Sir Christopher, 20–2, 25, 38, 39, 68, 121–3, 257, 259, 292
Wright, Macer, 209
Wyatt, James, 43
Wyattville, Sir Geoffrey, 54
Wye, Harry, 55

York, Duke and Duchess of(later King George VI and Queen Elizabeth), 54

Zoological Society, The, 251
Zoo, The London, 251, 252

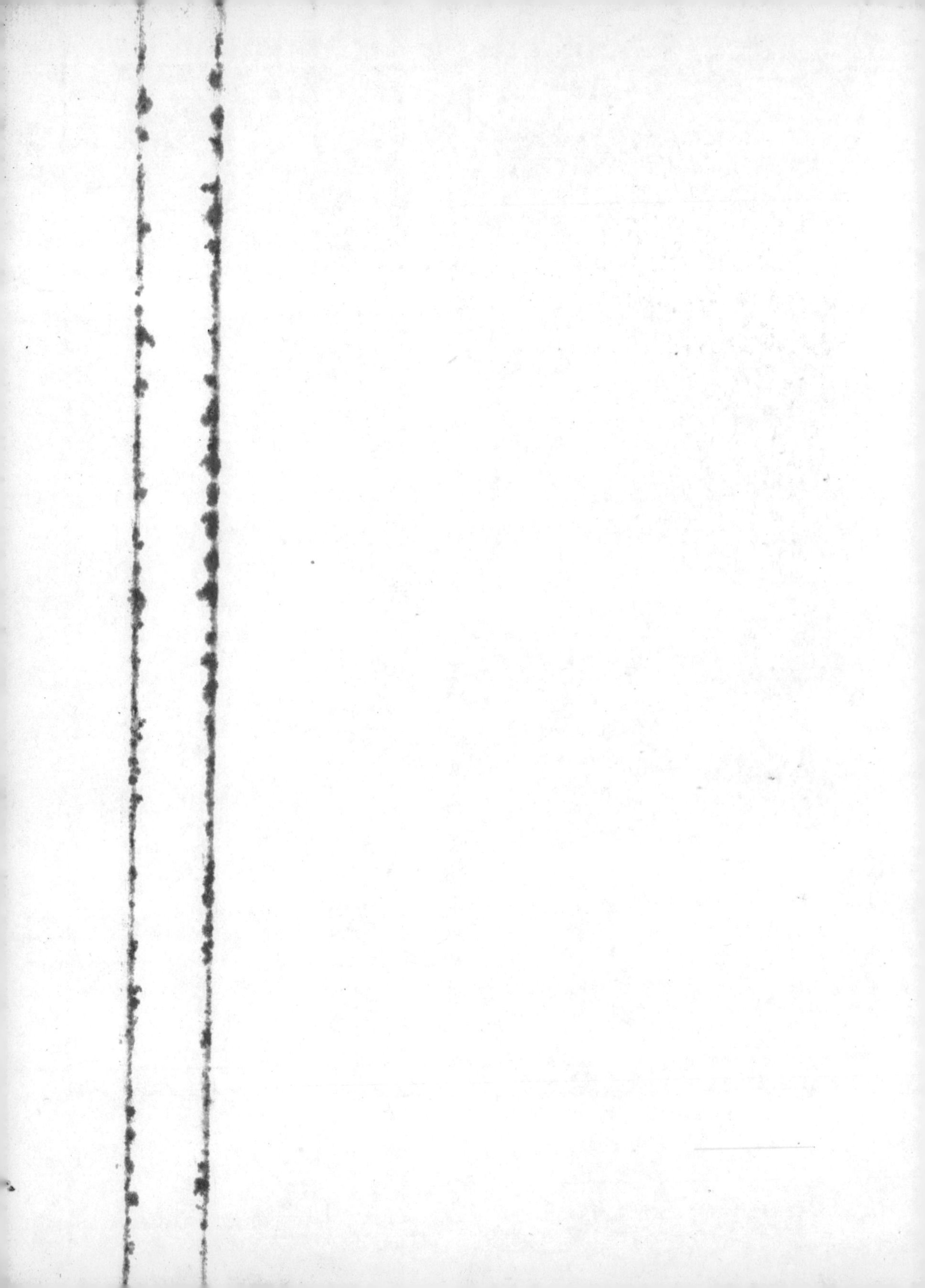

has looked much the same for centuries. It was never a monastic refuge from the world, yet there is about it an all-pervading contemplative hush. It is not hard to re-create in such an atmosphere the feeling of life as it was lived before the age of machinery, when the Manor of Lullingstone was visited by Henry VIII and royal jousts took place within the gates. In those days the Lady of the Manor would have been highly skilled in the use of herbs in kitchen and still-room, those plants succinctly described by the Pilgrim Fathers as being 'useful for Meate and Medicine'. Many a local resident must have been doctored with herbal remedies derived from the predecessor of this herb garden when illness or injury struck.

The original manor house forms the core of the greatly enlarged building we see today, which has now been divided up and partially let as separate apartments, including two in the Gatehouse. This, built about 1497, is one of the earliest in the country to have been constructed of brick. The late Sir Oliver Hart Dyke, with invaluable help from the Society for the Protection of Ancient Buildings, restored it with infinite care and skill. The Ministry of Works also provided some financial aid for the project.

In spite of greatly changed circumstances, this castle still lives an active and useful life, with no suggestion of the museum-piece about it. On occasion it acts as a centre of hospitality for the surrounding district—even for London. Sir Keith Falkner, Director of the Royal College of Music, sent me an account of a concert held at Lullingstone in June 1970 in aid of the New Building and Development Fund for the College. The performers were all students; it was a lovely summer evening; about two hundred guests came, and were able to wander through the charming grounds of the Castle. They heard two string quartets and a clarinet quintet, a talk by Sir Keith about the work of the Royal College and its needs, and then supper was served in the great rooms. This meal is described as having consisted of 'delicious food prepared by ladies of the Kent Committee, featuring as dessert great quantities of luscious fresh Kent strawberries with cream'. The effect was 'reminiscent of a night at Glyndebourne'.

When I lunched with Lady Hart Dyke on a warm September day in 1971, she had just finished clearing away traces of a week-end Harvest Festival Service, followed by tea, which had been served to a large congregation. Living-in servants may be scarce, or non-existent; gardeners either aged, or able to work here only at odd times after their ordinary jobs finish; but a house of this character has traditions and responsibilities which must be maintained at all costs. Watching my hostess as she brought floury potatoes and casserole from